Boys' Books, Boys' Dreams,

and the Mystique of Flight

Boys' Books, Boys' Dreams, and the Mystique of Flight

Fred Erisman

Texas Christian University Press • Fort Worth, Texas

Library of Congress Cataloging-in-Publication Data

Erisman, Fred, 1937-
Boys' books, boys' dreams, and the mystique of flight / Fred Erisman.
p. cm.
Includes bibliographical references and index.
ISBN-13: 978-0-87565-330-3 (alk. paper)
ISBN-10: 0-87565-330-8 (alk. paper)
1. American fiction—20th century—History and criticism. 2. Aeronautics in literature. 3. Flight in literature. 4. Children's stories, American—History and criticism. 5. Young adult fiction, American—History and criticism. 6. Children's literature in series—History and criticism. 7. Boys—Books and reading—United States. I. Title.
PS374.A37E75 2006
813'.5209356—dc22
2006000281

Cover and text design by Bill Maize; Duo Design Group
Printed in Canada

TCU Press
P. O. Box 298300
Fort Worth, TX 76129
817-257-7822
http://www.prs.tcu.edu
To order books: 1/800-826-8911

For

Patt and Wendy

per ardua ad astra

TABLE OF CONTENTS

ILLUSTRATIONS

PREFACE

They are the outcast orphans of serious literature and the starveling stepchildren of American technological history. Large-scale histories of literature normally make no mention of them, histories of children's literature fob them off as of little consequence, and only specialized popular-culture studies give them anything resembling attention. Histories of American technology ignore them outright, or give them only passing notice. Cecelia Tichi's *Shifting Gears* (1987) gives them barely two pages, Carroll Pursell's *The Machine in America* (1995) is wholly silent about them, and Ruth Schwartz Cowan's *A Social History of American Technology* (1997), citing Tichi, devotes a half-dozen lines of a single paragraph to them.[1] Yet, before the advent of television, before the coming of network radio, and even before the widespread presence of cinema, they were a principal source of entertainment and technical knowledge for American boys between the ages of ten and eighteen. "They" are boys' series books with a technological emphasis. For half a century they nurtured young Americans' interest in technology, the varieties of technology, and technological progress.

Between 1900 and 1950, adolescent American males had access to nearly seventy-five technologically oriented series embracing close to six hundred titles. The books covered most realms of technology, from automobiles and railroading to cinema and wireless, and, whatever their interests, young readers could find a series suited to the topic. Generalists had Richard Bonner's "Boy Inventors" (1912–1915; eight titles), the automobile-minded could turn to James A. Braden's "Auto Boys" (1908–1913; five titles), and wireless enthusiasts relished Roy J. Snell's "Radio-Phone Boys" (1922–1928; eight titles). Best-known of all, and the most inclusive in its range, was Victor Appleton's "Tom Swift" series (1910–1941; forty titles), whose versatile young inventor and his many creations remain an enduring part of American popular culture.[2]

Other technologies notwithstanding, aviation stories dominated the genre. Within the larger body of technically oriented series books, forty-six series comprising almost three hundred titles dealt exclusively with aircraft, aviation technology, and flying adventure. Like the technological series generally, they suffer from the same defects and the same neglect. Despite the books' numbers and their popularity, three major studies of the social impact of aviation, Joseph Corn's *The Winged Gospel* (1983), Robert Wohl's *A Passion for Wings* (1994), and Richard Hallion's *Taking Flight* (2003) make no mention of them. Roger Bilstein's *Flight in America* (rev. ed., 1994) takes only the slightest note of them, remarking that, from about 1910, "aeronautical themes became standard fare in juvenile literature," and citing Captain Wilbur Lawton's "Boy Aviators" books (1910–1915; eight titles) as representative. Nonetheless, the aviation series constituted a popular and far-reaching outlet for conveying aviation lore to American boys and for encouraging a consciousness of aviation that came to be known as "air-mindedness."[3]

In the larger realm of literature, series books are classed as ephemera at best. Libraries avoid them for largely practical reasons. Because the books appear in series, the library that buys one volume eventually must buy all; because they are cheaply printed and bound, they do not hold up in library use and must be rebound or replaced more often than mainstream works. Critics, in turn, dismiss them for aesthetic and intellectual reasons. The books' wooden dialogue, their trite descriptions, their frequently coarse ethnic stereotypes, and their cardboard characters offer little to satisfy cultivated readers' tastes, while their formulaic plots are dullingly repetitive and absurdly melodramatic. No one heeds them but the legions of their avid young readers.

George T. Dunlap, a founder of the Grosset & Dunlap publishing house, one of the major producers of the series books, reported aggregate sales of the most popular series as being in the millions. By the end of 1936, he said, the "Bobbsey Twins" series, begun in 1904, had sold 5,619,129 copies. The "Tom

One of the earliest (1912) of the boys' flying series. Erisman-Odom Collection, Mary Couts Burnett Library, Texas Christian University.

Swift" books, archetype of the technological series, begun in 1910, did even better, selling 6,566,646 copies overall.[4] The more specialized series, although at times shorter-lived, had comparably healthy sales. The science-fictional "Great Marvel" series (1907–1940; nine titles) sold nearly a quarter-million volumes during its lifetime, reaching a yearly high point of 14,325 copies in 1929. The "Ted Scott" flying stories (1927–1945; twenty titles), the longest-lived of the aviation series, sold over a million copies during their run, and attained a record of 205,747 copies sold in 1929.[5] Critical disdain notwithstanding, the books were in the hands of young readers, and the ideas they conveyed did not go unnoticed.

Viewed simply as a phenomenon responding to, and further stimulating, a continuing strain in American intellectual history, the aviation series books tell an intriguing story of the development and dissemination of one facet of popular culture in the United States. They pose, initially, questions of authorship. Some of the series writers were professionals in their fields, engineers or ex-military personnel, who had first-hand knowledge of their particular technical area. Others were simply enthusiasts, individuals eager to investigate a new and potentially profitable area of popular attention. A few didn't exist at all. These were the pseudonymous writers, whose pen names (e.g., "Captain Wilbur Lawton" or "John Prentice Langley") were intended to give an air of authenticity to the stories, or, as in the cases of "Gordon Stuart" or "Charles Amory Beach," were used by publishers to disguise the work of two or more authors within a single series.

The nature of series-book authorship is itself an area worth investigating. When an author publishes more than one series under his own name, how closely do the characters and story lines resemble each other, and what does the resemblance say of the author's own views? When an author chooses an air-related pseudonym, is it to hide potentially embarrassing revelation as a commercial writer, or is it to give the books added authority by evoking the resonance associated with a Langley or a Wright? And when the author is only a "house name," what are the contributions of the various writers, and how does the publisher maintain a modicum of consistency within the series?

A second matter worth investigating is that of merchandising, for the series books are undeniably products of the machine age. They were cheaply manufactured, widely distributed, and cheaply priced, making them available to the largest possible audience. Most of the series were published originally to be sold for twenty-five to fifty cents a volume. When their appeal began to fade, the plates were frequently subcontracted to reprint houses, to be republished at an even lower cover price. What was the audience toward which each iteration was directed? What appeals appeared in their advertising? What strategies were employed to win and maintain a readership? And what is their relationship to the mainstream industry publishing books for adults? These, too, are provocative questions.

Still more provocative is a third matter, the manner in which the books pick up on, and deal with, current events of widespread public interest. Most of the series, to some degree, originate in events attracting large-scale public attention; in the case of the aviation books, these are most often record-setting flights, highly publicized emergencies, or substantial commercial developments. Building upon these events, the authors reshape incident, chronology, and character to suit their particular interests or particular needs. The books become interpreters of the events, and, as such, contribute their part to the public dialogue surrounding such events. Since their audience is a young one, unlikely to be drawing knowledge from the same sources as the adult population, the books are a potent means of shaping youthful awareness of public figures and public events. How the books shape, abstract, and manipulate the historical record is a means of understanding what their originating culture considers valuable for its young.

Within the boys' aviation series, the public figure most often portrayed is that of "the pilot." Exclusively male, as befits the protagonist of a series directed toward adolescent boys, the pilot figures become potent role models, offering a model of manhood for a technological age. They are physically fit, mentally agile, technologically knowledgeable, and unflinchingly honest—persons whose attributes equip them to deal capably with the forces of nature, technology, and society. The air, for them, is at once a medium of adventure, exaltation, and commerce. As they reveal their mastery of all three realms, they give a practical demonstration of the qualities an individual will need if he is to function (and prosper) in the future. In the series books, young readers see this character evolving, from small-town boy to world-renowned celebrity, and the lesson of what has led to his success is clear.

What knowledge is considered valuable, how it is to be employed, and how it is conveyed leads to the final noteworthy characteristic of the books, for they are potent vehicles of information transfer. Whatever the technology featured, the tales impart substantive, often minutely detailed, information concerning its nature and its applications. Sometimes this information has an overtly occupational slant, as in addressing "What does a locomotive engineer/photographer/aviator do?" Sometimes it presents the technology as contributing to the accelerating pace of modern progress. And sometimes it serves to glorify and exalt the technology, presenting it as being not only the leading edge of progress but also a life-changing phenomenon. Nowhere is this vision more apparent than in the series books dealing with aviation, where the airplane itself, the evolving technology of aviation, and the intangible attributes accruing from flight are integral and essential parts of the adventure.

Their critical neglect notwithstanding, the aviation stories constitute a fascinating document of American intellectual history. Spanning fifty years of flight, from the Wright Brothers' first efforts to the coming of space exploration, they document the evolving course of American aviation. As they do, they tell the tale of three generations of young people who come of age in a culture increasingly conscious of the airplane and whose lives and outlooks become infused with the mystique of flight. In addition, they play their own part in contributing to that coming of age, teaching, leading, and influencing young Americans as they confront the wonders of the airplane. The books' story is a memorable one, one that in its idealism and vision is uniquely American.

NOTES TO PREFACE

1. Cecelia Tichi, *Shifting Gears: Technology, Literature, Culture in Modernist America* (Chapel Hill: University of North Carolina Press, 1987), 100–102; Ruth Schwartz Cowan, *A Social History of American Technology* (New York: Oxford University Press, 1997), 215. Deidre Johnson, *Edward Stratemeyer and the Stratemeyer Syndicate.* TUSAS 627 (New York: Twayne, 1993), is one of the better specialized studies of the larger series-book genre.
2. Harry K. Hudson, *A Bibliography of Hard-Cover Boys' Books.* Rev. ed. (Tampa, FL: Data Print, 1977); Philip H. Young, *Children's Fiction Series: A Bibliography, 1850–1950* (Jefferson, NC: McFarland, 1997); Deidre Johnson, *Stratemeyer Pseudonyms and Series Books* (Westport, CT: Greenwood Press, 1982).
3. Roger E. Bilstein, *Flight in America: From the Wrights to the Astronauts.* Rev. ed. (Baltimore: Johns Hopkins University Press, 1994), 19. Although the aviation series, like the other boys' series of the time, conventionally relegate women to the roles of mothers and sweethearts, the handful of contemporaneous girls' aviation books suggests that the benefits of aviation are as accessible to women as they are to men. David K. Vaughan, in "Girl Fliers in a World of Guys: Three 1930s Girls' Juvenile Aviation Series." *Dime Novel Roundup* 68 (February 1999), points out that these series show girl flyers who are "practical, capable, determined, hard-working, idealistic, and possessed of above-average amounts of resourcefulness and initiative," and make clear that "the field of aviation was open to girls who had the desire and determination to persevere" (pp. 17, 25). Thus, though the numerically dominant boys' series portray the utopia of the air as a generally male preserve, the girls' series, in a minority report, maintain that it can be an equal-opportunity society. A full listing of the girls' aviation series appears in *Girls Series Books: A Checklist of Hardback Books Published 1900–1975* (Minneapolis: University of Minnesota Libraries, Children's Literature Research Collections, 1978).
4. George T. Dunlap, *The Fleeting Years: A Memoir* (New York: Privately printed, 1937), 193.
5. Stratemeyer Syndicate Records. MSS. & Archives Section, N.Y.P.L., Box 82 "Cupples & Leon"; Box 85 "Grosset & Dunlap."

ACKNOWLEDGMENTS

Any person working on a long-term project accumulates numerous debts and obligations along the way, and I am no exception. Funding support for my basic research came from: three Faculty Research Grants from the Texas Christian University Research and Creative Activities Committee; a Hess Fellowship granted by the University of Minnesota Children's Literature Research Collections; and a Lindbergh Fellowship awarded by the National Air and Space Museum, Smithsonian Institution. The latter gave me a year's unencumbered work time at the Museum as the Charles A. Lindbergh Chair of Aerospace History, easily the most absorbing and exhilarating year of my professional career.

Principal research for this study was done in the Children's Literature Research Collections at the University of Minnesota, Minneapolis; the CLRC is one of the ranking children's literature archives in the world, and I could not have done this work without it.

Other research took place in the Archives and Manuscripts Division of the New York Public Library, which houses the Stratemeyer Syndicate Records, and at the Library of Congress, Washington, DC. My investigations into the technical side of aviation history were carried out in the National Air and Space Museum Library and Archives, Washington, DC, yet another extraordinary collection holding materials of unrivaled worth.

I am grateful to these organizations for allowing me to cite materials under their control:

—the New York Public Library, for permission to reprint excerpts from the Stratemeyer Syndicate Records, Archives and Manuscripts Division, New York Public Library, Astor, Lenox, and Tilden Foundations.

—Simon and Schuster, for permission to reprint passages from the Stratemeyer Syndicate's "Ted Scott," "Slim Tyler," and "Randy Starr" series.

As the project ripened, my colleagues Linda K. Hughes, Deidre Johnson, Judith D. Suther, and David K. Vaughan listened patiently and offered valuable suggestions. Sincere thanks to all. In addition, I'm especially grateful to:

—Karen Nelson Hoyle, Curator, and her staff at the Children's Literature Research Collections, world-class professionals one and all.

—Dominick A. Pisano, Curator, Aeronautics Division, National Air and Space Museum, for his friendship, his careful reading of the manuscript, his constructive suggestions, and his enthusiastic support throughout.

—Russell Lee, Peter Jakab, F. Robert van der Linden, Tom Crouch, Dorothy Cochrane, Tom Dietz, and Roger Connor of the Aeronautics Division, National Air and Space Museum; Valerie Neal, Michael Neufeld, and David Devorkin of the Division of Space History; and Phil Edwards, Dan Hagedorn, and William Baxter of the NASM Library and Archives. Their friendship, expertise, and collegiality made a research appointment into the experience of a lifetime.

—Judy Alter, Jim Lee, and Susan R. Petty of the TCU Press. Their enthusiasm for my project and their attentive editing made the transition from manuscript to final version a pleasure instead of a trial.

—my wife, Patricia L. Erisman, who's endured decades of being towed through one aeronautical site or another, but who puts up with me all the same. She's a wingman who's made all the difference.

Chapter One

Setting the Stage: Technology and the Series Book

By the middle of 1914, Franklin K. Mathiews knew that he had to take action. Mathiews, Chief Librarian of the fledgling Boy Scouts of America, saw his organization's image being tarnished by a steadily increasing body of inexpensive books. These books, which had begun to appear as early as 1911, featured Boy Scouts as protagonists and capitalized upon the growing popularity of Scouting. They offended Mathiews and his superiors, though, by the manner in which they portrayed Scouts and Scouting. The Boy Scouts of America, incorporated in 1910, was by 1914 attaining national prominence as a source of physical and moral guidance for American boys. Whereas the aim of the BSA was to produce young men schooled in woodcraft and responsibility, the Scouts of fiction appeared instead as early-day precursors of a chaste James Bond. They roamed the globe in search of adventure, triumphed over daunting odds with carefree ease, and, in the minds of Scouting authorities, did immeasurable harm to the organization's more modest goals.[1]

Mathiews took his concerns to the public in the fall, publishing in *The Outlook* of 11 November 1914 an essay, "Blowing Out the Boy's Brains," that spelled out his concerns in vivid language. In it he announced the existence of an "underground library" of sensational fiction of the most improbable sort:

> Boys move about in aeroplanes as easily as though on bicycles; criminals are captured by them with a facility that matches the ability of Sherlock Holmes; and when it comes to getting on in the world, the cleverness of the hustling boys is comparable only to those captains of industry and Napoleons of finance who have made millions in a minute. Insuperable difficulties and

> crushing circumstances are as easily overcome and conquered as in fairy tales.

Though he conceded the popularity of such books with youngsters and parents alike, he insisted "that the harm done is simply incalculable. I wish I could label each one of these books: 'Explosives! Guaranteed to Blow Your Boy's Brains Out.'"[2]

Over and above any distortion of Scouting's aims that might appear in these books, Mathiews identified two principal dangers. The first was that of a distorted reality, for the books presented the materials of adventure "with no moral purpose, with no real intelligence," and the young readers, their imaginations "literally 'blown out,'" would go into the world "as terribly crippled as though by some material explosion they had lost a hand or foot."[3] They would, he believed, go into adulthood expecting to encounter, on the one hand, rousing adventure, and, on the other, at every turning villains and schemers of all complexions. Reality would only be a disappointment, and the boys would become alienated misfits.

The second consequence of sensational reading, he continued, was even more far-reaching. The steady reader of these books, he contended, would soon be mentally and aesthetically burned out, besotted by qualities as destructive to the young reader as drugs and drink: "Story books of the right sort stimulate and conserve [imagination], while those of the viler and cheaper sort, by overstimulation, debauch and vitiate, as brain and body are debauched and destroyed by strong drink." Thus debauched, the young readers would go through life paralyzed aesthetically as well as vocationally:

> Not only will the boy be greatly handicapped in business, but the whole world of art in its every form almost is closed to him. Why are there so few men readers of the really good books, or even of the passing novels, sometimes of real worth? Largely, I think, because the imagination of so many men as boys received such brutal treatment at the hands of those authors and publishers who

> gave no concern as to what they write or publish so long as it returns constantly the expected financial gain.[4]

Numbed to beauty as much as to business and victimized by publishers and authors alike, the series-book reader would face only a shallow, flaccid, and colorless existence.

Despite the immediate concerns that Mathiews expressed, the series books that he so deplored were far better-established than he acknowledged. Called by some critics a "particularly American phenomenon" in their early days, the genre dated from at least 1835. In that year Jacob Abbott published the first of his twenty-eight "Rollo" books, a moralistic but generally realistic series recording the activities of a small-town boy. Other authors, seeing the opportunities that series provided, and building upon the precedent of the mid-century dime novel, soon followed suit. Their efforts were enhanced by technological developments of the time. The advent of the rotary press reduced manufacturing costs, and the spanning of the continent by the railroad eased problems of distribution; by the end of the 1860s over sixty series were in production for young readers, and the numbers continued to grow.[5]

All of these series shared certain qualities. Described by one authority as "three or more fictional works above picture book level that were advertised or marketed as a named group and that have a deliberate textual or thematic link among volumes," they were published in editions uniform among each series and identified by covers or other markers to make recognition on the shelf easy. (A twentieth-century analogue is the "Travis McGee" series of thrillers by John D. MacDonald; each volume has a color in its title, as in *The Scarlet Ruse* or *The Lonely Silver Rain*. Readers unable to recall individual plots are still likely to remember having read "Green," but not "Yellow.")

Some series had continuing characters while others did not, but each series was further unified by its larger theme or topic. Thus, the "Tom Swift" books emphasized the rapid development of modern-day inventions, fanciful and real; "The Boy Fortune Hunters," by Oz-books author L. Frank Baum

A typical series advertisement, showing its appeal to young readers. Erisman-Odom Collection, Mary Couts Burnett Library, Texas Christian University.

The AIR COMBAT STORIES FOR BOYS

The record of daredevil exploits of these army and navy fliers over the front makes breathless reading, and their adventures have the ring of truth in them for both author-flyers take them from their own rich experiences as wartime aviators.

DAREDEVILS OF THE AIR
by Thomson Burtis

Recounts Lieutenant Riley's adventures as leader of The Phantom Five against the enemy in the air.

FOUR ACES
by Thomson Burtis

As commanding officer of Special Flight A, Rud Riley and Jerry Lacey, the Manhattan Madmen, are thrown into the thickest and hottest of the air fighting.

WING FOR WING
by Thomson Burtis

Continues the record of the daredevil young airman's adventures as one of the leading aces in the war.

FLYING BLACK BIRDS
by Thomson Burtis

Stormy Lake leads a squadron of picked daredevils called the Black Birds against the famous German Red Devils led by Von Baer.

DOOMED DEMONS
by Eustace L. Adams

Ensign Jimmy Deal and his pals are reckless, carefree and fearless and their daredevil exploits make a story crowded with swift, thrilling action and racy humor.

WINGS OF THE NAVY
by Eustace L. Adams

Irrepressible Jimmy and his pal Pooch Mallory are assigned duty as observers on blimps, and get into all the scrapes their fertile minds can invent until the climax when they capture a German spy.

WAR WINGS
by Eustace L. Adams

Jimmy gets in as tight a spot as air combat can provide when he tries to land on his own field in a captured Boche plane. A fast-paced and exciting yarn.

GROSSET & DUNLAP
Publishers New York

(writing as "Floyd Akers"), followed a cluster of young entrepreneurs through exotic settings around the world as they progressed on their way to wealth; and Ralph Henry Barbour's "Football Eleven" series built each volume upon a different position in the football lineup, offering such titles as *Left End Edwards* and *Fullback Foster.*[6]

By the end of the nineteenth century, series books were a well-established genre, and, among them, two authors stood out: William Taylor Adams (writing as "Oliver Optic") and Horatio Alger, Jr. Each contributed important elements to the further development of the series book genre as the twentieth century neared. Optic injected the elements of exotic settings and sensational adventure. His "Young Americans Abroad" series took his youthful characters across the world, while his "Army and Navy Series" introduced the drama and romance of military life. Moving away from the moralistic stories embraced by Abbott and his followers, Optic used military scenes (notably of the Civil War) to enliven his tales and went on to incorporate his young protagonists into sea stories of "dash and vigor." To the dismay of literary purists, his works were enormously popular—so much so, in fact, that Louisa May Alcott, in *Eight Cousins* (1875) denounced them as "optical delusions."[7]

Even more influential was Horatio Alger, Jr., who, beginning with the "Ragged Dick Series" of 1867, gave his name to an entire sub-set of the series genre. This was the "rags to riches" story, and, as Russel B. Nye points out, it shaped series fiction for decades to come. According to Nye, Alger made four great contributions:

> [H]e explained and reemphasized the traditional American faith in self-reliance; he instructed his contemporaries in the complexities of a new kind of society; he reaffirmed the social values of middle-class virtues; and he, more than any other of his fellow-authors, recognized the changed nature of American urban life.

By adapting the series format to the urban, mercantile world, Alger showed readers and other authors the narrative potential of the contemporary scene. By reemphasizing self-reliance and conscientiousness as viable qualities within that contemporary scene, he prepared the way for the coming of scores of self-reliant, capable young protagonists, from Tom Swift and Ted Scott to Lucky Terrell and Rick Brant. And, by dramatizing the importance of seizing the fortunate moment when it chanced to appear, he set the scene for the "on-his-toes" and quick-to-act individual so central to series books in the twentieth century.[8]

Franklin Mathiews's criticisms of the boys' series, overheated though they may have been, were in great part valid. Many of the series were clumsily written, almost all were formulaic to the point of predictability, and very few escaped at least occasional improbabilities as their boys traveled about the globe with studied nonchalance. In his determination to make his point, however, he let pass two important issues. One was sensationalism. Although he faulted the series books for excessive sensationalism, he conceded that "the red-blooded boy, the boy in his early teens, must have his thrill; he craves excitement, has a passion for action, 'something must be doing' all the time; and in nothing is this more true than in his reading."[9] The young male reader was attracted to excitement, and, when he found it, he read it. Serious authors as much as series writers recognized the need for drama, incident, and suspense, and the difference in their utilizing the qualities was only a matter of degree.

George Dunlap, defending his publishing house's production of so many series, argued that reading was reading, and the series books served a useful purpose:

> There is no question, in my mind, that it is much better for a boy to read thrillers of the type that engaged our youthful attention than to fail to cultivate the habit of reading at all. . . . The taste for better things will come later on, once the habit of reading is established. In my later years, as a publisher, when chided by well-meaning critics for our activity in producing and

> selling juveniles of a more or less sensational character I have always taken the stand that 'you can't catch flies with vinegar.' You have got to give the boy books that make an appeal to his imagination rather than those that are supposed to teach him a highly moral lesson.[10]

Dunlap's point is a defensible one, and one that Mathiews sets aside in his concentration upon the pernicious stuff of the stories.

The other issue was that of imagination. This, for Mathiews, was of paramount importance, for

> One of the most valuable assets a boy has is his imagination. In proportion as this is nurtured a boy develops initiative and resourcefulness. The greatest possible service that education can render is to train the boy to grasp and master new situations as they constantly present themselves to him; and what helps more to make such adjustment than a lively imagination?

Clearly, only books "of the right sort [will] stimulate and conserve this noble faculty," and therein is a crucial matter he overlooks.[11] What of the book that deals with modern developments in the contemporary urban scene? Might not it be a better stimulus than another, albeit more "classical" one, that looks to the past or to some other realm for its story? What, in short, constitutes the "right sort" of book to appeal to the minds and hearts of the young contemporary reader? Mathiews never says, apparently assuming that kindred spirits among his readers would know the answer.

For Mathiews, however, one body of writing emphatically did *not* qualify for consideration. This was the work of Edward Stratemeyer (1862–1930), who, by the time of Mathiews's essay, had established himself as one of the principal producers (if not *the* principal producer) of American series books for the young. Never mentioned by name throughout the course of the essay, Stratemeyer and his products were undeniably the focus of Mathiews's scorn. "There is . . . one man who is as resourceful as a Balzac sofar as ideas and plots for stories are concerned," he wrote. "He cannot, though, develop them all, so he employs a number of men who write for him."[12] Stratemeyer and the Stratemeyer Syndicate embodied all of the elements to which he objected, as much for the manner of his production as for its content.

Born in Elizabeth, New Jersey, Stratemeyer was one of three children of German immigrants. After finishing his education in the Elizabeth public school system, he began working in his father's tobacco shop; leaving the shop in 1890, he opened a stationery store, which he ran until 1896. He married in 1891, becoming in time the father of two daughters, Harriet and Edna. Early on, he decided to make a career in writing, directing his efforts toward popular outlets. His first published story, "Walter Drumm's Heroism," appeared in *Young American* in late 1889, followed in the same year by a second story, "Victor Horton's Idea," published in *Golden Days.* Story followed story; Stratemeyer soon moved on to longer works, published as dime novels by the firm of Street & Smith, and graduated to hardcover fiction in 1894 when Merriam reprinted an *Argosy* serial, "Richard Dare's Venture; or, Striking out for Himself," as the first volume of the *Bound to Succeed* series.

In the same period, he was also gaining experience as an editor. From 1893 until 1895, he edited *Good News,* a boys' story paper published by Street & Smith. Here he became acquainted with other boys' writers, including St. George Rathborne, James Otis Kaler, and Gilbert Patten (the latter two better known as "James Otis," author of *Toby Tyler, or Ten Weeks With a Circus* and *The Silver Fox Farm Series,* and "Burt L. Standish," creator of the Frank Merriwell books, respectively). He gave up the position in 1895, briefly (until early 1896) took on the editorship of Frank J. Earll's story weekly, *Young People of America,* and moved at last to his own short-lived weekly, *Bright Days* (1896–1897).

Out of Stratemeyer's hectic writing and publishing endeavors came a secondary benefit—familiarity with working pseudonymously. The volume of his production demanded that he adopt one or more pen names, and he had no difficulty in adapting to the process. His earliest pseudonym, "Ned St. Meyer," saw print in his Street & Smith publications of 1890. He appeared as "Ralph Hamilton" in *Golden Days* in the fall of 1890, and in *Argosy* as "Arthur M. Winfield" in 1891. In addition, throughout the early 1890s, he was writing dime novels for Street & Smith as "Nick Carter," "Jim Bowie," and "Captain Lew James." His use of pseudonyms reached a peak of sorts when, in 1899, he completed William Taylor Adams's *An Undivided Union* as "Oliver Optic," and, in 1901, assumed Horatio Alger's name to write *Young Captain Jack,* the first of more than two dozen contributions (under his own name as well as other pseudonyms) in series capitalizing upon Alger's name and reputation.

Three names, however, marked Stratemeyer's debut as an author with whom to be reckoned. The first was "Roy Rockwood." Used initially by Stratemeyer in 1896, on the Beadle & Adams dime novel *Flying Fred, the Cyclist Ferret,* it was soon to reappear at the head of some of the most notable of the later series he produced. The second was "Captain Ralph Bonehill." Suitably macho in its implications of military valor and hunting skills, "Bonehill" first appeared as the author of "Gun and Sled; or, The Young Hunters of Snowtop Island," a *Young People of America* serial of 1895–96, and emerged in hard covers in 1900 with *For the Liberty of Texas,* first of the three-volume "Mexican War" series of 1900–1902.[13]

It was, though, as "Arthur M. Winfield" that Stratemeyer had his first true popular (and financial) success. The name, legend goes, he picked (or was prompted to pick by his mother) because "Arthur" was a homophone for "Author;" because "M." stood for "million," a worthy goal whether in volumes sold or dollars pocketed; and because "Winfield" compressed "win the field"—the desire to dominate the publishing scene as effectively as one might dominate a sporting event.[14] He had used the name before on a random assortment of short stories and individual volumes, but now he applied it to a series: "The Rover Boys."

With the Rovers, Stratemeyer at last had all the elements of the formula that was to make him wealthy. He had three appealing protagonists to whom he could give identifying traits: Dick, the serious-minded eldest; Tom, the prankish middle Rover; and Sam, the affable youngest. He had a reliable stock company of friends and antagonists to support or harass the trio as circumstances required. And he had a plausible milieu—upper-middle-class New York and the military-school environs of Putnam Hall. The initial volume, *The Rover Boys at School; or, The Cadets of Putnam Hall* (1899), set the stage for the twenty-nine volumes that followed, and Stratemeyer never looked back. As an advertisement for the first volume stated, Arthur M. Winfield "has penned nothing better than this story of life and adventure at an American military school, introducing as he does all sorts and conditions of boys, as well as several girls, and a plot that is bound to hold the reader's attention from start to finish."[15] Plots were not limited to the confines of Putnam Hall; subsequent volumes took the Rovers "On the Ocean," "In the Jungle," "Out West," "In Southern Waters," and "At College; or, The Right Road and the Wrong."

Along the way, the Rovers met adventure after adventure, all suitably thrilling yet singularly non-life-threatening. At school they dealt with studies and sports with equal enthusiasm; on vacation, they hunted lost mines, searched for a missing houseboat, pondered the puzzle of a deserted luxury yacht, and uncovered a cave used by thieves as a cache for loot. At every turning, they behaved as resourceful, proper American boys *ought* to act, confronting hazards with grit and backbone, accepting good fortune with modesty and good humor. Stratemeyer had indeed hit upon a formula that, if it exercised Franklin Mathiews beyond all reason, appealed to legions of American boys. By the time the series was shut down in 1930, it had sold more than five million copies.[16]

The success of the Rover series, Stratemeyer's own desire to "win the field" once and for all, and the recognition that he would never be able to write all the stories his imagination was generating led him to the creation, in early

1906, of the Stratemeyer Syndicate, a clearing-house for manuscripts written to order by contract writers.[17] While he himself continued to write, far more of his energy went to the managing of Syndicate operations and the creating of new stories. His publications soon came close to saturating the juvenile marketplace. When he died, in 1930, his organization was producing volumes published in more than fifty series. It continued well into the 1980s, operated by his daughters, Harriet Stratemeyer Adams and Edna C. Squier, and was ultimately sold to the publishing firm of Simon & Schuster.[18]

The Syndicate's organization was remarkably simple. Stratemeyer would write out a story outline of three to five typed, single-spaced pages, detailing the characters, plot, setting, principal events, resolution, and chapter divisions for the book at hand. This he assigned to a contract writer, who, for a flat fee (initially \$50 to \$100, depending upon the series and Stratemeyer's experience working with the writer), would expand the outline into a manuscript of two hundred pages and twenty-five chapters. The writing of the text normally consumed four to six weeks, and the writer waived all claim to any further payment or recognition.[19]

The completed manuscripts Stratemeyer would edit for length and consistency, then pass along to his own compositors for typesetting and plating. The plates, in turn, went to whatever publisher (principally Grosset & Dunlap, Cupples & Leon, and Lee & Shepard) had contracted for the series, and the book would be manufactured under the publisher's imprint with a Syndicate-assigned "house name" as the author. The initial books in a series were usually published as a cluster of two to three volumes (later expanded to five), with new titles following annually. "Captain Ralph Bonehill" and "Roy Rockwood," not surprisingly, were among the first of the house names used, but others, destined to become a lasting part of American popular culture, soon followed.

The first authors Stratemeyer used were associates from his days with Street & Smith, notably Howard and Lilian Garis and St. George Rathborne, all proven authors in their own right. Howard R. Garis (1873–1962), a New

Jersey neighbor of Stratemeyer and a reporter for the *Newark Evening News*, had published three novels and a range of short pieces; his first assignment with the Syndicate was the writing of "The Motor Boys" series (1906–1924; twenty-two titles) as "Clarence Young." Lilian (1873–1954), his wife, had written a women's page for the *Newark Evening News* from 1895 to 1900, but resigned her position shortly after her marriage. The author of several earlier children's books, she took on, with Howard's occasional assistance, "The Bobbsey Twins" series (1904-present; seventy-six+ titles and counting) as "Laura Lee Hope" and the "Dorothy Dale" series (1908–1924; thirteen titles) as "Margaret Penrose." St. George H. Rathborne (1854–1938), a writer with three decades' experience in the pulps, produced "The Outdoor Chums" books (1911–1916; eight titles) as "Captain Quincy Allen," and later wrote three of the "The Air Service Boys" books (1918–1920; six titles) as "Charles Amory Beach."[20] He contributed to other series as well. Other writers, attracted by advertisements in trade journals were added as the Syndicate's offerings grew, but the Garises, in particular, remained mainstays until long after Stratemeyer's death.[21]

In its early years, from 1905 through 1910, the Syndicate produced some fourteen series, with its principal offerings effectively establishing the practices, forms, and formulae that would characterize its productions throughout its existence. Among the early series, four stand out. The first is "Allen Chapman's" "Boys of Business" series (1906–1908; four titles) The author of the series is as yet unidentified; the books themselves, however, continued the motifs established by the Horatio Alger stories of the previous century. The books, each a free-standing volume without continuing characters, were directed toward "boys getting ready to enter business." The first volume, *The Young Express Agent; or, Bart Stirling's Road to Success* (1906), dealt with the operations of an express office in a small country town. The second, *Two Boy Publishers; or, From Typecase to Editor's Chair* (1906), involved small-town journalism and the job-printing business, and the two remaining volumes introduced concepts of the mail-order trade and general business practices. Each attempted to give some sense of the nature and flavor of the business emphasized, and each stressed the importance of sound business ethics as necessary for success.[22]

"The Boy Hunters" books, published as by "Captain Ralph Bonehill" but written by Stratemeyer himself (1906–1910; four titles), took up the outdoor scene. Four boys, members of a local gun club, set out to experience the joys of the out-of-doors life in a variety of ways. The first title, *Four Boy Hunters; or, The Outing of the Gun Club* (1906), included "full directions for camping out," while the second, *Guns and Snowshoes; or, The Winter Outing of the Young Hunters* (1907), was, the publishers said, permeated "with the odor of the pine forests and the glare of the welcome campfire in every chapter." The final volume, *Out With Gun and Camera; or, The Boy Hunters in the Mountains* (1910), "[took] up the new fad of photographing wild animals as well as shooting them." Its inclusion of the pastime of amateur photography illustrates, as Carol Billman points out, "Stratemeyer's quickness to incorporate the most recent social trends and pastimes into his work in the interest of salability."[23]

For all the popular appeal of the first two series, with their emphases on business success and out-of-doors recreation, the second two, "The Motor Boys" and the "Great Marvel Series," even more clearly indicated a major development in the future direction of the Syndicate—into the realm of technology and science. On the surface, "The Motor Boys" (1906–1924; twenty-two titles), written by Howard Garis as "Clarence Young," outwardly seemed no more than a domestic adventure series in the Rover Boys model. Three boys, Ned, Bob, and Jerry, acquire a touring car and go sightseeing throughout the United States and Mexico. In the first volume, *The Motor Boys; or, Chums Through Thick or Thin* (1906), the boys plan to "make a trip lasting through the summer;" in the second, *The Motor Boys Overland; or, a Long Trip for Fun and Fortune* (1906), they extend their travels to the Great West.[24] By the fourth volume, however, *The Motor Boys Afloat; or, The Stirring Cruise of the*

Dartaway (1908), they have added a motorboat to their stable, and, by the tenth, *The Motor Boys in the Clouds; or, A Trip for Fame and Fortune* (1910), an airship.[25] The books' emphasis upon "fame and fortune" is certainly important, but even more significant is their incorporation of the most up-to-date travel technology. Like the "Tom Swift" books to come, they proffered the picture of American youth as mechanically competent as well as adventuresome.

The final noteworthy series of the early period, "The Great Marvel Series" (1906–1935; nine titles), was easily the most intriguing. Published as by "Roy Rockwood," its first five and final two volumes were written by Howard Garis, with W. Bert Foster creating the sixth and John W. Duffield the seventh. In content it was unabashedly science fiction, constituting "the first series of hard-cover science fiction books printed in the United States, perhaps the world." While it extended the portrayal of technological competence developed by "The Motor Boys," it went well beyond automobiles and airships in its view of the technological world and its stories of speculative science. Teen-aged Mark Sampson and Jack Darrow, both orphans, fall in with Professor Amos Henderson, a prolific inventor, and with him have adventures terrestrial, subterranean, and interplanetary. The first book, *Through the Air to the North Pole; or, The Wonderful Cruise of the Electric Monarch* (1906), introduces the cast and takes them to the Pole via Henderson's electrically-powered airship; Stratemeyer's outline, a single page, cautioned Garis to "make [the story] bright and full of action, but not too sensational. Give it an air of probability."[26] The second and third volumes go equally far afield, taking Henderson and the boys to the South Pole in a jet-propelled submarine and, in an improved version of the same vessel, to the center of the Earth.

With the fourth title, however, *Through Space to Mars; or, The Most Wonderful Trip on Record* (1910), the series takes on a distinctiveness all its own. Mark and Jack, now students at the Universal Electrical and Chemical College, are recruited by Henderson to accompany him to Mars aboard his newly constructed spaceship. Dubbed *The Annihilator* "because it annihilates space," the

V-2-shaped ship takes them safely to Mars and back, producing "the most wonderful journey on record." From here on, there is no holding them back. Henderson and the boys travel to diamond fields of the Moon, the blue-water world Venus, and even a "counter-Earth" hidden in Earth's shadow. Along the way, they are flung into space in the sixth book, *On a Torn-Away World; or, Captives of the Great Earthquake* (1913), when they are caught in a volcanic eruption in Alaska.[27] With this series, Stratemeyer firmly staked out his claim to the creation of popular-science and pseudo-science stories for American youth.

The importance of the "Great Marvel" books lies in their combination of the commonplace and the scientific. If one omits the exotic settings and wonderful machines, the stories could just as easily be "The Rover Boys" or "The Motor Boys." Mark Sampson and Jack Darrow are characters directly out of a host of previous series, and their encounter with Professor Henderson is a fortunate happenstance worthy of Alger. Where Stratemeyer takes these materials, however, and how he directs "Rockwood" to do it, make them notable. Thus, Mark and Jack continue their education, and it is a technical education; by series' end, they are war veterans and distinguished professor-inventors in their own right. Moreover, their technical expertise is universally acknowledged and respected, making their success one of knowledge as well as business. Next, their adventures are presented with at least an "air of probability," linking the fanciful world with the actual. Finally, their world is portrayed as one in which technology is an accepted entity; machines are not limited to the laboratory, the descriptions of them are detailed, and the technology makes possible experiences more dramatic than any experienced by the Rovers or the Motor Boys. Whether or not it is the first true American science-fiction series, "The Great Marvel Series" prepared the way for some of the Stratemeyer Syndicate's greatest achievements.

By 1910, the Syndicate was on sound financial footing, and, despite the skirmish with Mathiews and the Boy Scouts after 1914, continued to grow. By the time of Stratemeyer's death in 1930, its fourteen series had grown to fifty-six, and many of its offerings and authors were household names. The patterns established in the early years proved their worth in shaping later series. The business- and career-oriented stories begun with "The Boys of Business" led to "Victor Appleton's" "The Motion Picture Chums" (1913–1916; seven titles), three boys' activities associated with the owning and operating of a film theater, and "Laura Lee Hope's" "The Blythe Girls" (1925–1932; twelve titles), the experiences of three sisters learning the world of merchandising in New York.[28]

Other realms did equally well. Outdoors stories continued their appeal. "Hope's" "Outdoor Girls" (1913–1933; twenty-three titles) opened the world of camping adventure to young women, while "James Cody Ferris's" "X Bar X Boys" (1926–1942; twenty-one titles) combined the attractions of the out-of-doors life with those of the classic Western. Technological tales flourished; "Allen Chapman's" "Radio Boys" (1922–1930; twenty-three titles) and "Margaret Penrose's" "Radio Girls" (1922–1924; four titles) offered details of the construction and operation of radio sets along with rousing adventure. New areas appeared, as well. "Appleton's" "Don Sturdy" series (1925–1935; fifteen titles) supplied readers with adventures of the sort associated in later generations with cinema's Indiana Jones, while "Roy Rockwood's" "Bomba the Jungle Boy" (1926–1938; twenty titles) followed the exploits of a teen-aged version of Edgar Rice Burroughs's Tarzan.

Three series published under two names in the years after 1910, however, established lines that were to be among the Syndicate's most long-lived offerings. The first, and arguably the most memorable, was an unprecedented combination of the technological and the business-career motifs, "Victor Appleton's" "Tom Swift" series (1910–1941; forty titles). Written principally by Howard R. Garis, the Swift stories blended the excitement of technical discovery with the satisfactions of financial success, capturing the spirit of the times in a way that few other books, serious or popular, have managed to do. Their appeal, as Russel B. Nye notes, was that

> it was not Rockefeller or Carnegie, Honus Wagner or Eddie Plank who were the implied heroes of the Swift books, but the Wright brothers, Steinmetz, Tesla, Edison, and the others who were pushing back the frontiers of knowledge and invention. Whereas Alger's boys faced the problems of an urbanized, acquisitive society, and the Merriwells the ethics of the competitive contest, Tom Swift grasped the technology of the machine age and brought it under control. He made scientific discovery exciting and technological advance adventurous, and most of all he made both seem useful and optimistic.[29]

Tom was a hero ready-made for the era of the back-yard experimenter, and those experimenters were rife.

When the Swift series began to appear, popular publications of the time already reflected the spirit and accessibility of do-it-yourself experimentation. *Popular Science Monthly* presented a diverse range of technical and scientific topics to its readers, and even the venerable *Scientific American* published regular features on metalworking, woodworking, astronomy, electrical matters, and aviation. The issue for 10 May 1910 carried Frederick K. Cord's "How to Build a Houseboat for $300;" "The Inventor's Department" for 24 December 1910 was devoted to critiques of perpetual motion machines; "The Home Laboratory" in the issue of 21 January 1911 offered instructions for the liquefying of nitrogen oxide and the construction of an improved spark gap for wireless work; and the issue of 6 May 1911 opened with an appreciation of Charles Proteus Steinmetz.[30]

At a still more popular level, Hugo Gernsback's *Modern Electrics* (1908–1913), succeeded by *The Electrical Experimenter* (1913–1920) and *Science and Invention* (1920–1929), combined accounts of new discoveries with how-to-do-it technical articles and a variety of technological fiction that Gernsback dubbed "scientifiction." (Indeed, several critics call *Science and Invention*'s all-scientifiction issue of August 1923 as "effectively Gernsback's first SF magazine.") *Science and Invention* in July 1926, for example, offered the first of a multi-part series on "How to Build Your Own Airplane," and, in April 1929, a fictional account of "Berlin to New York in Twenty-Six Minutes," a journey by rocket that included descriptions of acceleration forces and weightlessness. So widespread was the appeal of Gernsback's publications, in fact, that science-fiction author Robert A. Heinlein, writing in 1940, could have one of his characters, the elderly magnate D.D. Harriman, describe himself as a boy "who thought there was more romance in an issue of the *Electrical Experimenter* than in all the books Dumas ever wrote," confident that his readers would pick up on the allusion.[31] The times were ripe for a Tom Swift, and Stratemeyer supplied the need.

Tom, a home-trained inventor, lives with his father, inventor Barton Swift, at the family works in Shopton, New York. Here, as he matures, he progresses through a variety of technological achievements, starting in the earliest volumes by overhauling a motorcycle and a motorboat, then moving on to the creation of a motion-picture camera (1912), a giant cannon (1913), a photo telephone (1914), and a flying boat (1923). Each invention is described in some detail, each is threatened by mischief-minded evildoers whom Tom must vanquish, and each brings Tom generous profits in sales or royalties. One attraction of Tom's inventions is their timeliness; as Arthur Prager observes, they were "not only plausible but ahead of their time," with, for example, the "Photo Telephone" anticipating the Bell System's development by eleven years and Tom's "House on Wheels" (1929) closely following aeronautical pioneer Glenn Curtiss's "Aerocar" of 1928. Whether or not, as some suggest, Tom's activities were based upon those of Glenn Curtiss, the sales of the Swift stories, with their elevation of the inventor-entrepreneur to hero status, confirm Stratemeyer's consciousness of the power of contemporary trends. By the end of 1936, George T. Dunlap remarks, the series had sold "a total of 6,566,646 copies."[32]

The other two major series, both premiering in 1927, were so distinctive that they required a new house name. This was "Franklin W. Dixon," used only for (and forever associated with) the two series: "The Hardy Boys" (1927-present; seventy-one titles and counting) and "The Ted Scott Flying Series" (1927–1943; twenty titles). The "Hardy Boys" books, with their ever-young heroes, Frank and Joe Hardy, their comic, fat-boy sidekick, Chet Morton, and their myriad adventures extending to over seventy volumes, relied upon the long-term appeal of a basic formula. They took the basic model of "The Rover Boys," added the mobility of "The Motor Boys" (the Hardys, from the very first volume, are equipped with their own automobile and motorboat), and injected a mystery to be solved. It was an infinitely adaptable formula, as the longevity of the Hardys suggests. The series has survived extensive rewriting to remove dated language and ethnic stereotypes, it has adapted to new forms of transportation and communication as they have appeared, and it has generated television and comic-book adaptations, along with a generous stream of tie-in books and merchandise.[33]

The Hardys' adventures often verge upon the far-fetched. Like the young heroes Mathiews castigates, they encounter smugglers, counterfeiters, and spies, dispatching each with ease. Throughout these exploits, Frank and Joe are presented as typical teen-aged youths growing up in a small American town. They attend classes at the local high school, have a regular circle of friends (including girl friends, something of an innovation for Stratemeyer heroes), and keep disciplined hours under the supervision of their widowed father, detective Fenton Hardy, and their comically dictatorial Aunt Gertrude. The very normality of their lives accentuates the exoticism of their adventures, and allows Stratemeyer and his writers to make a quiet point: The most mundane of existences can hold adventure for the person equipped to discover it, and that equipping can come through a variety of means. The Hardys are ready for whatever life brings.

So, too, is Ted Scott. The Scott stories were prompted by the public sensation following Charles A. Lindbergh's Atlantic flight of 1927, and their creation is dramatic evidence of Stratemeyer's nose for timely topics. Lindbergh landed in Paris on 21 May. On 24 May Stratemeyer sent to Grosset & Dunlap a proposal for a flying series, and, on 27 May, he assigned the outline for the first volume, *Over the Ocean to Paris; or, Ted Scott's Daring Long Distance Flight,* to John M. Duffield. Duffield, a seasoned Syndicate writer (as "Appleton" he was contributing to the "Don Sturdy" series and, as "Rockwood," to "Bomba the Jungle Boy" and "The Great Marvel" books), proved his mettle; the manuscript was in Stratemeyer's hands by late June, and the Library of Congress logged its deposit copies on 12 August 1927.[34] The ocean flight successfully concluded, subsequent volumes echoed elements of Lindbergh's widely publicized activities as well as on-going developments in aeronautical history and technology.

The immediate significance of the "Ted Scott" stories, however, is the manner in which they, with the "Hardy Boys" books, blend the sensational and the mundane. Ted, like the Hardys, is an ordinary chap. Like numerous other Stratemeyer heroes, he makes his way by a combination of skill, perseverance, and luck. His upbringing is small-town, almost rural, and his education is largely self-attained. Like Tom Swift, he masters a complex and up-to-date technology, turning it to both personal and public benefit, and he confronts hazards with aplomb and success with modesty. He is, however, far more than either the Hardys or Tom Swift, a conscious advocate of the contemporary scene. His concerns are firmly grounded in the immediate present, and he is determined to improve the future. And, whereas Tom is a scientific polymath who can turn his skills to any endeavor, Ted is inseparably, even uniquely, identified with the world of flight. More than any other Stratemeyer protagonist up to the time of his appearance, he is the link between the world of reality and that of the seemingly attainable technological ideal.

Unifying all of the Stratemeyer series is a consistent and timely ethic—the pervasive sense of what a young person, especially a boy, *ought* to be and *can* be. As Peter A. Soderbergh points out, that ethic has four discernible elements, all of which recur uniformly (albeit in differing proportions) throughout the series; Stratemeyer, like *Star Trek* creator Gene Roddenberry, had a clear vision of how he wanted his literary universe to appear, and participating writers were not allowed to alter it.

The first element is "pluck," which might be defined as the quality of being "energetic, daring, and [determined]." Stratemeyer heroes, from the Rovers to Ted Scott, are ready to act and, once started, difficult to dissuade. They accept risks when they must, but their actions are considered ones. The characters are rarely if ever downright rash, but they are often at the cutting edge of prudence. Risks are a part of life, the books imply, and the up-and-coming young man must be ready to confront them judiciously as he proceeds on his road to success.[35]

Second-listed in the Stratemeyer ethic is a sense of patriotism. Stratemeyer's fictional world is overtly and unequivocally American, a society led by a democratic government striving by principle to act for right and moral purposes. His protagonists, one and all, seek to heighten the status of the United States in the eyes of the world, and build national pride in the hearts of American citizens. Their actions set the model, for they place the prestige and interests of their country ahead of all else, even their own personal profit. Tom Swift more than once donates his patents to the government, foregoing any royalties or licensing fees, and Ted Scott is always ready to answer his country's call. In addition, they seek to live by a fundamental American tenet: "equal rights for all, special privileges for none." They are ready and willing to respect the concerns of other persons, even other cultures, but those groups must play as honorably in their dealings as Tom, Ted, and the others play in theirs.

Although Stratemeyer's world is a vigorously competitive one, his insistence upon the American doctrine of honesty and fair play leads to a secondary point, a staunch belief that justice will prevail. "Justice," in this instance, generally means being "against an oppressor [and] for an underdog." In the world of Stratemeyer fiction, respect for the United States and respect for its most cherished beliefs go hand in hand, and the heroes strive to operate by sound democratic doctrine. Standards are to be set openly, rules are to be followed scrupulously, and a person's success or failure will be determined by the merits of his case rather than by limiting restraints imposed by, or upon, someone else.[36] It is a democratic world, but it is also a meritocratic world, and Stratemeyer wants his readers to understand both.

The third component grows directly from the second. The Stratemeyer hero passionately believes that "honesty is not only 'the best policy,' but that it should be the only policy considered." From this conviction, in turn, comes the hero's tacit sense that he must "control his temper, return good for evil, and set an example for others."[37] These traits are not new in series books, and, throughout the nineteenth century, contribute to the host of immaculately priggish do-gooders who pervade the juvenile canon. Stratemeyer, however, tempers the potential priggishness with a touch of reality. His heroes, for all their commitment to the Right Way, make mistakes—mistakes from which they, like their readers, can learn, without benefit of an authorial sermon.

Finally, returning to the belief in justice that marks his world-view, Stratemeyer maintains that right will prevail, that "bullies, criminals, [and] renegades . . . would 'lose out in the end.'" By sticking steadfastly to the path that he knows, in both heart and mind, to be the proper one, the hero will "see his adversaries get their deserved 'comeuppances.'"[38] The success that the hero enjoys will be a multi-faceted one, intellectual and ethical as well as social and financial. It's a success he will deserve, because he has stuck to his convictions and played the game, resisting the pitfalls that tempt the lesser spirits, and the merits of his principled actions will not be lost on young readers.

These are the traits that unify the Stratemeyer series overall. They are extended, however, in the technological series, from "The Great Marvel" books through the "Ted Scott" and "Randy Starr" series, to include qualities especially applicable to a technologically oriented world. Recognizing that technology's impact upon society is inevitable, inexorable, and profound, Stratemeyer poses the question, "How best can Americans deal with that impact?" The answers are more complex than those running through the domestic and adventure series, but Stratemeyer, like the characters he advocates, does not shrink from addressing them. He offers, in the technical series, a roadmap for dealing with an increasingly technical and complicated existence.

Francis J. Molson, examining technological series books from the Stratemeyer Syndicate and other sources, identifies four principal expressions of technology in the United States of the early twentieth century: "invention, radio, auto, and aviation."[39] Or, seen in another way, the books deal with the *creation* of technical devices, then demonstrate the *application* of these same devices. They present the process of invention as a commonplace, and focus upon the most visible and accessible of its developments. The message is that these are realms that the ordinary citizen can embrace and understand, and it is not a far-fetched message. Tinkering with automobiles continues to be a part of the American teen-ager's milieu; amateur radio operators have moved from basement experimenters to valuable parts of the national civil-defense and storm-warning systems; and the Experimental Aircraft Association (which recognizes "home-built" aircraft as a sub-specialty within its larger scope) annually draws thousands of enthusiasts to its "fly-in" in Oshkosh, Wisconsin. History has borne out the pertinence of accepting the technical world.

The initial message of the technical books is that science, technology, and the changes that result from them are facts of life. They exist, they are not going to disappear, they are going to have far-reaching consequences, and they must be accepted. An early advertisement for the "Tom Swift" stories proclaims their goal of describing the "wonderful advances" going on in the world in an effort to interest "the boy of the present in the hope that he may be a factor in aiding the marvelous development that is coming in the future."[40] The issues here are straightforward. First, technological change is also technological progress; it is a positive and "wonderful" process. Progressive change "is coming;" its arrival may be in the near future or the distant future, but its arrival is certain. Finally, the "boy of the present," if he so desires and is properly prepared, can "be a factor in aiding" what can only be a "marvelous development" for the United States and the world.

Second, the books establish that technology is something that *can* be, and *must* be, mastered. Only by understanding its nature can a citizen deal with its requirements; only by dealing with those requirements can that person productively apply it to life; and only by understanding and productively applying technological knowledge can a citizen become a fully contributing member of his or her society. Thus, as Nye makes clear, the "Tom Swift" books are filled "with the excitement of a conquest of matter and space, the thrill of accomplishing with one's own brain and hands what others had hoped to do." Other works and authors carry on this excitement: The "Great Marvel" books support both higher education and technical education as Mark Sampson and Jack Darrow prepare themselves for later life, while Randy Starr, in a series of the 1930s, willingly takes on a substantial academic curriculum because it offers knowledge "playing no small part in flying work."[41] The technical world must be mastered for the excitement and the benefits it can offer, and that mastery requires effort.

Third, technological mastery will open the door to a world of new careers. The advances creating the coming age will also create new opportunities for work and involvement in that age. What is more telling, those careers will be directed toward the young, for the young will be better equipped to engage the future than are their elders. The time to come will be one fraught with challenges physical and intellectual; not only must new technologies and new vocabularies be assimilated, but the youthful participant must also be prepared for new physical demands. This is particularly true of careers in aviation, which requires "men of sound physique with good eyesight, quick mental reactions, capable of coming to a decision without any hesitancy." With their combination of the special, the wondrous, the innovative, and the demanding, the careers suggested by the books will make it possible for young people to carry out "'wonder' deeds, including the devising and performing of technological marvels."[42]

The final message of the technological series is that only through the acceptance, mastery, and application of technology will a person become a truly up-to-date, truly progressive American citizen. Stratemeyer's belief in this message is of long standing. As early as 1912, he urged Weldon J. Cobb, preparing to write the "Dave Dashaway" flying series, to give the books "plenty of action and new situations, and enough real 'aviation' background to carry them." His 1927 proposal for the "Ted Scott" books noted that "aviation has evidently taken a new hold on the public mind, and from now on will undoubtedly increase in interest," and he assured Grossett & Dunlap that the "stories will all be thoroughly up to date and will contain accurate information regarding flying machines, instruments employed, and general equipment." The emphasis carried on into the 1930s, when an advertisement touted the "Slim Tyler Air Stories" as "realistically written and so up to the minute in all their implications as to win ready admiration from all readers."[43]

Series books, by their very nature, ride the crest of the waves of public interest. Their stock in trade is whatever topic or issue is foremost in the public eye, and they capitalize upon that notoriety by giving the public what it wants. Their formulas, moreover, contribute to their appeal, for the innate familiarity of the formula reassures readers even as it encourages them to seek the next thrilling volume. Within the series-book genre, the technological series offer a special and particular appeal. Even as they illustrate and explicate the complexities of the coming world, they reassure their young readers by showing how those complexities can be either overcome or turned to one's advantage. In the process they inculcate a sense of modernity and a conviction that, to prosper, one must be up-to-date—not in the latest consumer fad, but in the qualities that are defining and shaping the society. Whatever their flaws (and Mathiews is correct in this respect; the flaws are genuine and many), the technical series address societal concerns that no mainstream genre even recognizes, and foremost among those books are the aviation series. Building upon the airplane as *the* symbol of modernity, they lead their young readers into and through a time of awesome change.

Notes to Chapter One

1 Peter A. Soderbergh, "The Great Book War: Edward Stratemeyer and the Boy Scouts of America, 1910–1930," *New Jersey History* 91 (Winter 1973): 238–240. An authorized history of Scouting is William D. Murray, *The History of the Boy Scouts of America* (New York: Boy Scouts of America, 1937). Scouting as a social movement is considered in Jay Mechling, *On My Honor: Boy Scouts and the Making of American Youth* (Chicago: University of Chicago Press, 2001).

2 Franklin K. Mathiews, "Blowing Out the Boy's Brains," *The Outlook,* 108 (11 November 1914): 652–653.

3 Ibid., 653.

4 Ibid., 653.

5 Deidre Johnson, "From Abbott to Animorphs, from Godly Books to Goosebumps: The Nineteenth-Century Origins of Modern Series," *Scorned Literature: Essays on the History and Criticism of Popular Mass-Produced Fiction in America.* Ed. Lydia Cushman Schurman and Deidre Johnson (Westport, CT: Greenwood Press, 2002), 147–148, 150.

6 Ibid., "From Abbott to Animorphs," 159, n.1.

7 Ibid., "From Abbott to Animorphs," 155; Russel B. Nye, *The Unembarrassed Muse: The Popular Arts in America* (New York: Dial Press, 1970), 62; Selma G. Lanes, *Down the Rabbit Hole* (New York: Atheneum, 1971), 136–157.

8 Nye, *The Unembarrassed Muse*, 63, 65–66.

9 Mathiews, "Blowing Out the Boy's Brains," 653.

10 George T. Dunlap. *The Fleeting Years: A Memoir* (New York: Privately printed, 1937), 74–75.

11 Mathiews, "Blowing Out the Boy's Brains," 653.

12 Ibid., 652.

13 Deidre Johnson, ed., *Stratemeyer Pseudonyms and Series Books* (Westport, CT: Greenwood Press, 1982), xvi-xix, 197–198, 41, 54–55.

14 Johnson, *Stratemeyer Pseudonyms,* 268; "Funeral Tonight for E. Stratemeyer," *New York Times,* 12 May 1930, 16.

15 Quoted in Johnson, *Stratemeyer Pseudonyms,* 277.

16 Arthur Prager, "Edward Stratemeyer and His Book Machine," *Saturday Review* 54 (10 July 1971): 17. For a contemporaneous view of Stratemeyer and his organization, see [Josephine Lawrence], "The Newarker Whose Name is Best Known," *Newark Sunday Call,* 9 December 1917, 1.

17 Johnson, *Stratemeyer Pseudonyms,* xiv-xvii.

18 Ibid., *Stratemeyer Pseudonyms,* xiv-xvi; E.S.S. and R.W.B., "Edward Stratemeyer," *Dictionary of American Biography,* ed. Dumas Malone. 1935–36 (New York: Charles Scribner's Sons,

1964), 9:125; Peter A. Soderbergh, "Edward Stratemeyer and the Juvenile Ethic, 1894–1930," *International Review of History and Political Science* 11 (February 1974): 69.

19 Carol Billman, *The Secret of the Stratemeyer Syndicate* (New York: Ungar Publishing Co., 1986), 21–23.

20 Johnson, *Stratemeyer Pseudonyms,* xx-xxiii; Douglas Street, "Howard R. Garis," *American Writers for Children, 1900–1960,* ed. John Cech. (Detroit: Gale Research, 1983), 191–199; "Garis, Lilian C.," *Who Was Who in America* (Chicago: Marquis Who's Who, 1963), 3:313.; Stratemeyer Syndicate Records, MSS. & Archives Section, N.Y.P.L., Boxes 65, 66.

21 Leslie McFarlane, in *Ghost of the Hardy Boys* (New York: Two Continents, 1967), gives a lively account of his joining the Syndicate and his subsequent work as "Franklin W. Dixon" and other *personae.*

22 Johnson, *Stratemeyer Pseudonyms,* 81–82.

23 Ibid., *Stratemeyer Pseudonyms,* 44–45; Billman, *The Secret of the Stratemeyer Syndicate,* 142.

24 "Chum," as it is used here and throughout this study, implies a friendship of kindred spirits. It is an association infused with shared interests, common skills, and mutual loyalty. Recurring throughout the series of the 1920s and 1930s, it captures the innocence of an earlier time.

25 Johnson, *Stratemeyer Pseudonyms,* 287–90.

26 E.F. Bleiler, "From the Newark Steam Man to Tom Swift," *Extrapolation,* 30 (Summer 1989): 110; Great Marvel Outlines, Stratemeyer Syndicate Records, MSS. & Archives Section, N.Y.P.L., Box 302.

27 Great Marvel Outlines, Stratemeyer Syndicate Records, MSS. & Archives Section, N.Y.P.L., Box 302.

28 Deidre Johnson, *Edward Stratemeyer and the Stratemeyer Syndicate* TUSAS 627 (New York: Twayne, 1993), 51–53.

29 Nye, *The Unembarrassed Muse,* 83.

30 Frank Luther Mott, "Scientific American," *A History of American Magazines, 1850–1865* (Cambridge: Belknap Press of Harvard University Press, 1938), 316–324; Frank Luther Mott, "Popular Science Monthly," *A History of American Magazines, 1865–1885.* 1938 (Cambridge: Belknap Press of Harvard University Press, 1957), 495–499. See also individual issues of *Scientific American,* Vols. 102–104 (1910–1911).

31 Mike Ashley, "Science and Invention," *Science Fiction, Fantasy, and Weird Fiction Magazines,* ed. Marshall B. Tymn and Mike Ashley (Westport, CT: Greenwood Press, 1985), 500–504; Fred Erisman, "Stratemeyer Boys' Books and the Gernsback Milieu," *Extrapolation* 41 (Fall 2000): 272. See also individual copies of *Science and Invention,* Vols. 14–16 (1926–28).

32 Prager, "Edward Stratemeyer and His Book Machine," 52; Chiori Santiago, "House Trailers Have Come a Long Way, Baby." *Smithsonian* 29 (June 1998): 76–85; William R. Gowen, "The Real Tom Swift," *Newsboy* 33 (January-February 1995): 5; Dunlap, *The Fleeting Years,* 193.

33 Johnson, *Stratemeyer Pseudonyms,* 98–100.

34 Ted Scott #1, Stratemeyer Syndicate Records, MSS. & Archives Section, N.Y.P.L., Folder 1, Box 255; Suggested Titles, Box 256.

35 Soderbergh, "Stratemeyer Ethic," 63.

36 Ibid., "Stratemeyer Ethic," 65.

37 Ibid., "Stratemeyer Ethic," 66.

38 Ibid., "Stratemeyer Ethic," 67.

39 Francis J. Molson, "American Technological Fiction for Youth: 1900–1940," *Young Adult Science Fiction,* ed. C.W. Sullivan, III (Westport, CT: Greenwood Press, 1999), 9.

40 Quoted in Johnson, *Stratemeyer Pseudonyms,* 23.

[41] Erisman, "Stratemeyer Boys' Books and the Gernsback Milieu," 279.

[42] Major Henry H. Arnold, *Bill Bruce, the Flying Cadet* (New York: A.L. Burt, 1928), 27; Molson, "American Technological Fiction," 19; Johnson, *Edward Stratemeyer,* 54–61.

[43] Edward Stratemeyer to Weldon J. Cobb, 15 July 1912, Stratemeyer Syndicate Records, MSS. & Archives Division, N.Y.P.L., Box 22; Edward Stratemeyer to Grossett & Dunlap, Stratemeyer Syndicate Records, MSS. & Archives Division, N.Y.P.L., Box 256; quoted in Johnson, *Stratemeyer Pseudonyms,* 22.

Chapter Two

Birdmen and Boys, 1905–1915

It took only six years for an author to see the possibilities available in a series of boys' books addressing aeronautical topics. This was Harry Lincoln Sayler (1863–1913). Born in Ohio and educated at DePauw University, Sayler was a journalist associated with the City Press Association in Chicago. In two series, "The Airship Boys" (1909–1915; eight titles), written under his own name, and "The Aeroplane Boys" (1910–1913; eight titles), written as "Ashton Lamar," he effectively created the aviation series genre.[1] Although Stratemeyer's "Great Marvel" books began their run in 1906 and the "Tom Swift" books in 1910, the "Great Marvels" offered only a single lighter-than-air vessel, a balloon-supported airship, before moving on to submarines and rockets, while "Tom Swift" did not turn to a heavier-than-air vehicle, a Blériot-styled airplane supported by air moving across its wings, until 1911. Sayler's tales of specialized airship and airplane adventure had the field to themselves.

Sayler's timing was impeccable. By 1909 the United States was increasingly aware of advances in aviation, and popular interest in aircraft and aviation technology was on the rise. This was not always the case. When the Wright Brothers packed their equipment and returned to Dayton, Ohio, following their pioneering flights of December 1903, they had established the reality of the airplane and of powered, heavier-than-air flight. The practicality had yet to be proven. That practicality involved several elements. Some were inherent in the airplane itself—reliably maintaining stability and controlling direction among them. Others were more abstract, looking to applications and capabilities and determining the limits, if any, of altitude, speed, and distance. The airplane itself was as yet too new, too fragile, and too experimental to seem to the public anything more than a fascinating toy.

The Wrights themselves were of little help in developing public perceptions of the airplane and its possibilities. Although they were working steadily to advance their skills and their equipment between 1903 and 1905, they worked unobtrusively. They made no particular effort to conceal their experiments, for their test field at Huffman Prairie outside Dayton was bordered by a busy tram line, but neither did they seek publicity. Thus, while they were making notable advances on an almost daily basis (Wilbur achieved the first complete in-flight circle on 20 September 1904, and, by October 1905 had managed a sustained flight of thirty-eight minutes, covering more than twenty-four miles), their work went largely unpublicized.

What notice they did receive was either obscure or tinged with skepticism. The first eye-witness account to see print was apiarist Amos Root's brief notice in his self-published periodical, *Gleanings in Bee Culture*, for 1 January 1905, hardly a mass-circulation journal, while, a year later, the *Scientific American* raised a figurative eyebrow over reports starting to emanate from France. In the issue of 13 January 1906, the journal quoted distance and time claims cited by the Wrights in a letter to French aeronaut Captain Ferdinand Ferber and noted that the claims "certainly need some public substantiation."

"It seems," the notice continued, "that these alleged experiments were made at Dayton, Ohio, a fairly large town, and that the newspapers of the United States, alert as they are, allowed these sensational performances to escape their notice." The conclusion was inevitable: "if such sensational and tremendously important experiments are being conducted in a not very remote part of the country, on a subject in which almost everybody feels the most profound interest," yet have not drawn the attention of the energetic and inquisitive American press, they must be questioned. "We have the right to exact further information before we place reliance on these French reports . . . [and] certainly want mor e light on the subject."[2]

Aggravating the skepticism was a growing public perception that Europeans had usurped the initiative in advancing aviation. Ferber and Gabriel Voisin were conducting well-publicized glider flights in early 1904, while, later that year, Robert Esnault-Pelterie challenged the Wrights' wing-warping method of control by using free-standing ailerons (small movable panels attached to the wing to aid in turning). Ferber began experimenting with a tethered powered glider in 1905 and, in October 1906, the dapper Brazilian, Alberto Santos-Dumont, who had already won the Deutsch Prize by circling the Eiffel Tower in an airship, achieved the first powered heavier-than-air flight in Europe. His canard-configured airplane *No. 14 bis* carried him almost two hundred feet at an altitude of ten feet to give him the Archdeacon Prize of 3000 francs. The following year, Louis Blériot, who was to fly the English Channel in 1909, began experimenting with monoplanes, while Henry Farman, flying a Voisin biplane, accomplished the first public aerial turn in Europe. Though the Wrights had already equaled or surpassed many of the endurance and distance achievements of the French and British, their work was unreported and the public saw only that records were going abroad.[3]

Louis Blériot and the Blériot XI, the aircraft that first crossed the English Channel (1909). National Air and Space Museum, Smithsonian Institution (SI 78-15731).

Aviation progress, however, was far from dead in North America. The Wrights had responded to the *Scientific American*'s questioning with a letter, photographs, and a list of witnesses sent to the Aero Club of America. The journal polled the witnesses and, bowing to their reports, announced that "there is no doubt whatever that these able experimenters deserve the highest credit for having perfected the first flying machine of the heavier-than-air type which has ever flown successfully and at the same time carried a man." The following year, in April 1907, the magazine proposed the *Scientific American* Aeronautic Trophy, to be administered by the Aero Club of America and awarded in a progressively more difficult series of challenges to "the machine which accomplishes the required flight in the shortest time and with the best display of stability and ease of control."[4]

The *Scientific American* did not stop there. Early in 1908 its editorial page took aeronautical competition to a new level, making an overt appeal to American nationalism. In "Shall America Take the Lead in Aeronautics?," it posed the question: "Is the United States to take its proper place as the leading nation in this era of development, or are we to follow along, two or three years behind the rest of the world, and buy our dirigibles and aeroplanes from abroad?" The initial steps in aviation, the editorial continued, were made by Samuel Pierpont Langley and the Wrights, and the Congress had weighed in by funding Langley's work. But more recent developments had come from overseas, and the United States was in danger of falling behind.

The editorial concluded with an appeal to the national spirit and a call to intellectual arms:

> It is high time that America moved forward to its former commanding position in the field of great inventions. Despite our brilliant record in the last century, in producing the reaper, the sewing machine, the electric light, the trolley, the telegraph, the telephone, and the typewriter, it must be admitted that of late years we have been somewhat outstripped by Europe in the

> introduction or development of epoch-making inventions. We cannot but feel that the solving of the most difficult of all mechanical problems attacked by man, that of air navigation, presents a field that should be peculiarly attractive to the genius of the American inventor.[5]

National pride and national status demanded that the country regain its primacy as a technological innovator.

Meanwhile, in Nova Scotia, Alexander Graham Bell and a group of friends (including the army's Thomas Selfridge and American motor-manufacturer and motorcycle champion Glenn H. Curtiss) had in 1907 formed the Aerial Experiment Association. Basing their operations at the Curtiss factory in Hammondsport, New York, the Association began the construction and testing of a series of aircraft of their own designs. The first, the *Red Wing,* flew in March 1908, in what was widely hailed as the first public flight in America. The second, the *White Wing* (both craft named after the color of their covering fabric), flew in May, powered by a Curtiss engine and carrying the first ailerons used in the United States. The third, the *June Bug,* was developed with a single aim: to win the *Scientific American* Trophy.[6]

Curtiss officially filed for the trophy competition in late June. Flying before Aero Club and *Scientific American* representatives on 4 July 1908, he won the trophy for the first time with a flight of nearly six thousand feet and a flight time of 1 minute, 42 seconds. It was the fifteenth flight for the *June Bug.* Reporting on the event, the *Scientific American* gave it full-page coverage, congratulated Curtiss on his achievement, and ended its article with the hope "that progress in aviation will be so rapid, that he will stand an excellent chance of winning it again in the future and much more difficult contests to be held."[7]

The second competition for the trophy required the covering of a minimum of twenty-five kilometers with a return to the starting point, and Curtiss quickly determined to compete. His craft this time was a design of his own,

An early model Curtiss Pusher (1915-1916). National Air and Space Museum, Smithsonian Institution (SI 91-3939).

the *Curtiss Racer No. 1.* Confident about his prospects, he had already filed an entry for the international competition to be held in Rheims, France; when he easily captured the *Scientific American* cup on 17 July 1909 with a flight of nineteen laps covering nearly twenty-five miles, he was ready to confront the Europeans.[8]

The Rheims competition, the first international contest for heavier-than-air ships, convened in August of 1909. It brought together most of the "public names" of aviation: Henry Farman, Louis Bréguet, and Louis Blériot, conqueror of the English Channel, of France; George Cockburn from England; and Curtiss from the United States. Only the Wrights were absent. When it ended, the United States was established as a world player: Curtiss had defeated Blériot, the favorite, in the Gordon Bennett International Aviation Trophy race with a speed in excess of forty-seven miles per hour, and had gone on to capture the *Prix de la Vitesse,* covering the 30-kilometer course in just under twenty-six minutes.[9]

The Wrights, meanwhile, were doing their part in stirring public interest in aviation. In the September 1908 issue of *The Century,* they published the first popular, detailed account of their initial gliding experiments, the Kitty Hawk flight, and their subsequent work at Huffman Prairie. Wilbur, flying in France in August 1908, was lionized by the press and public alike, while Orville, flying the brothers' entry in the military aircraft trials at Fort Myer, Virginia, in September 1908, drew crowds of politicians, journalists, and the general public and soon set an endurance record of an hour and fourteen minutes. His achievements there ended in the crash of 17 September, which seriously injured him and killed his passenger, Army Lieutenant Thomas Selfridge, the earlier collaborator with Bell and Curtiss in the A.E.A. Selfridge was the first to die in an airplane accident.[10]

Not all the Wrights' publicity was positive. In August 1909, they filed suits against Curtiss and Louis Paulhan, alleging that their control systems using independently-moving ailerons and a linked vertical rudder infringed upon the Wrights' patented wing-warping system. They contended that the later systems were natural developments from the principles covered in their patent and argued that all other aircraft builders should pay them a licensing fee. Public reaction to the suits was mixed. Few reports denied the Wrights' claim to the original control methods, but many questioned their challenge to Curtiss's and Paulhan's modifications. V.L. Ochoa, for example, writing in *Aircraft* magazine, asked "Are the Wrights Pirates?" and scalded them for their efforts to build a monopoly: "the 'mysterious' Wright brothers have unveiled themselves and are attempting to appropriate all the glory attached to the building of flying machines, and all the money resulting from the manufacture of them."[11] The quarrel quickly moved from the technical papers to the popular press, focusing a publicity spotlight on all of the litigants.

Even as the Wrights were drawing public attention to their aircraft and accomplishments, other persons were doing their share. In mid-1910, the widely respected engineer and experimenter Octave Chanute published a four-part series on "Recent Progress in Aviation" in the *Scientific American Supplement* and, later in the year, engineer Grover Loening offered a seven-part series on "The Practice and Theory of Aviation." In November 1910, the International Aviation Meet at Belmont Park offered $74,800 in prizes distributed over twenty contests. The competition included vying for distance, altitude, cross-country passenger carrying, and the Gordon Bennett Cup, and drew entries from France and England as well as from the United States. Among those competing were Hubert Latham and Roland Garros of France, Claude Grahame-White of England, and John B. Moisant, Arch Hoxsey, and Eugene Ely of the United States. The exploits of all, including the prize money won by each, were detailed in the lengthy coverage of the meet published in *Aircraft;* Grahame-White pocketed $13,600, while Moisant was second with $13,550.[12]

Glenn Curtiss also continued to garner publicity and awards. He followed his victories at Rheims with flights elsewhere in France and in Italy, and returned to the United States with some $15,000 in prize monies. With two winnings of the *Scientific American* trophy behind him, and tempted by the *New York World*'s offer of a $10,000 prize for the first flight between New York and Albany, Curtiss decided to try to clinch permanent ownership of the trophy with a record-setting, long-distance flight. Departing Albany on 29 May 1910 in a craft embodying all that he had learned in his previous flights, he followed the 130 miles of the Hudson River to New York, making two brief stops along the way for a total flying time of 2 hours and 51 minutes. There were no other flights of comparable distance during the remainder of the year, and he took final possession of the *Scientific American* trophy in January 1911.[13]

If the first decade of powered flight began in relative obscurity, it ended in a blaze of publicity and public acclaim. The United States had reclaimed its leadership in aviation, as the *Scientific American* had called for, and the public mind was increasingly conscious of advances in flight and flight achievements. The nation was ready for accessible, popular interpretations of the technology, and Harry Lincoln Sayler was ready to oblige.[14]

Sayler's first effort, the "Airship Boys" series, follows the familiar series formula established earlier by Stratemeyer and other writers. *The Airship Boys;*

or, The Quest of the Aztec Treasure (1909) introduces chums Ned Napier and Alan Hope, boy aeronauts living in Chicago. Funded by wealthy ethnologist Major Baldwin Honeywell and Colorado rancher Colonel Pedro Oje, they make an extended balloon flight through the American West in search of a long-lost Aztec treasure. Like the Wrights, they operate with little publicity. Their desire for secrecy puts them at odds with young reporter Bob Russell, but he wins their confidence and is allowed to fly with them and observe their doings from a base camp. They locate the riches in Arizona, but leave their airship and most of the treasure behind when their gas supply for the balloon is exhausted and they are forced to pack out.

The story continues in the second volume, *The Airship Boys Adrift; or, Saved by an Aeroplane* (1909). Ned and Alan, now accompanied by Bob Russell, who's been fired from his newspaper because he protected the boys' story, and Major Honeywell, return to the mountain-top site of their find. After discovering a hidden shrine and still more riches, Bob and the Major return to civilization with the treasure and the story, while Ned and Alan set out to repair the airship. When the airship is swept out to sea in a sudden windstorm, the boys save themselves by snagging the rigging of a derelict ship. Then, using the remnants of the airship plus bits and pieces from the derelict, they convert the balloon to a heavier-than-air vehicle and successfully fly to Central Mexico. There they encounter a lost Aztec tribe, make their way back to the United States, reunite with Bob and Major Honeywell, and return to Chicago rich and famous.

With Bob Russell to publicize them and Major Honeywell to fund them (joined later by another wealthy patron, manufacturer James W. Osborne), the Airship Boys proceed to make their mark in the world. *The Airship Boys Due North; or by Balloon to the Pole* and *The Airship Boys in the Barren Lands; or, The Secret of the White Eskimos* (both 1910) make up another connected story as Ned and Alan head northward in search of a fabulous deposit of copper ore and a mysterious tribe of white Eskimos, an endeavor that nets each of them $25,000 plus shares in the copper mine. The next two volumes, published in 1911, take them into the world of business competition. *The Airship Boys in Finance; or, The Flight of the Flying Cow* relates their development of a gasoline-fueled rocket engine and their partnership with J.P. Morgan in using the engine to develop a transcontinental airmail route; the "flying cow" of the title is lofted over Niagara Falls in a demonstration of an early version of the rocket, surviving reentry with bovine aplomb. *The Airship Boys' Ocean Flyer; or, New York to London in Twelve Hours* nets them a fee of $60,000 when they take their new, high-speed airplane to England to allow a new reporter friend, Buck Stewart, to cover the coronation of King George V and return photographs for a journalistic scoop.

The final two volumes, unlike the preceding ones, are anticlimactic. *The Airship Boys as Detectives; or, Secret Service in Cloudland* (1913), the last volume written by Sayler, takes the boys from Seattle to the Mexican border as they collaborate with the Secret Service in breaking up a ring of smugglers illegally bringing Chinese into the United States. Sayler died in 1913, but his publishers continued the series with one more volume. Written by DeLysle F. Cass but published under Sayler's name, *The Airship Boys in the Great War; or, The Rescue of Bob Russell* (1915) returns Ned and Alan to Europe, where German authorities have arrested Bob as a spy. Their airplane is destroyed during the flight back, and the series comes to an end.

Sayler's second series, "The Aeroplane Boys," which he wrote as "Ashton Lamar," is more complex than "The Airship Boys." Its first two volumes are linked by the young flier, Morey Marshall; the next three offer flying adventures unified by the presence of young Bob Osborne, son of an airplane manufacturer (not to be confused with James W. Osborne, of the "Airship Boys" series), as a supporting character; and the final volumes are separate, free-standing stories. Why the series develops in this fashion is unclear. Since the same publisher, Reilly & Britton of Chicago, produced all of the series, Sayler very likely wanted to avoid competing with himself by creating a second, almost-identical series.

The initial books, *In the Clouds for Uncle Sam; or, Morey Marshall of the Signal Corps* and *The Stolen Aeroplane; or, How Bud Wilson Made Good,* both published in 1910, continue the nominal realism of the "Airship Boys" books. Air-mad teenager Morey Marshall, discovering his late father's plan to power aircraft with liquid hydrogen in time to prevent foreclosure on the family homestead, takes the invention to Fort Myer, crosses paths with Orville Wright, and joins the Signal Corps to further his flying passion. He reappears as a background character in *The Stolen Aeroplane,* watching teenager Bud Wilson's triumph at the Scott County Fair, as Bud substitutes for a missing aviator in the scheduled air show and then sells his self-designed airplane for $300.

The second cluster, *The Aeroplane Express; or, The Boy Aeronaut's Grit* (1910), *The Boy Aeronauts' Club; or, Flying for Fun* (1910), and *A Cruise in the Sky; or, The Legend of the Great Pink Pearl* (1911), follows the fortunes of three groups of teens as they experiment with craft from the American Aeroplane Company of Newark, New Jersey, where George Osborne and his son Roy head the engineering section. In the first, Roy accompanies mining executive R.C. Cook to Utah, where he plans to use an Osborne airplane to supply his far-flung prospectors. Aviation meets the Wild West, and Roy returns to Newark with a profitable load of cliff dwellers' artifacts. In the second, three Florida teenagers buy an airplane from the Newark works, prowl the Everglades by air, and uncover a chest of long-lost jewelry. The third, also set in Florida, relates sixteen-year-old Andy Leighton's efforts to build a flying machine following plans left by his uncle. Roy Osborne aids in the construction, paying Andy a handsome fee for rights to the machine's engine and control mechanism. With the machine completed, Andy flies to the Bahamas, joins an English adventurer in the search for a fabulous pearl, and returns to Florida with a reward of £1000 to add to Osborne's payment.

The final volumes, *Battling the Bighorn; or, The Aeroplane in the Rockies* (1911) and *On the Edge of the Arctic; or, An Aeroplane in Snowland* (1913) are set in Canada, and follow the exploits of two sets of teen-aged inventors.[15] In the first, Frank Graham and Phil Ewing accept an uncle's invitation to take their radically new airplane, the *Loon,* on a hunting trip into the Canadian Rockies. In the second, Norman Grant and Roy Moulton agree to use their Deperdussin-style monoplane to prospect for oil and gas in the Canadian wilds; along the way they take part in a moose hunt and experience the Calgary Stampede celebration, piercing cold, turbulent blizzards, and the fiery blow-in of a gas well. Essentially Canadian travelogues, the two books, like the final two of the "Airship Boys" series, are anticlimactic, with a minimal amount of aviation detail.

Throughout both series, Sayler draws upon well-established series devices. He offers teams of affluent, technically-minded teenagers whose talents, like those of the Rover Boys, are complementary; of Ned Napier and Alan Hope he remarks: "Alan was careful, precise, and adept in detail. Ned had the 'dreams' and inspirations of an inventor."[16] Their technical interests are far-ranging, and when the boys are employed, they are often described simply as "inventors." Drawing upon convenient happenstance, he puts them into contact with even more affluent, generous patrons. He throws challenges of all descriptions into their path, letting them use a combination of skill and timely opportunism to overcome the problems. Their melodramatic trials overcome, he brings them home to commercial success, fortune, and acclaim, ready to move on to the next adventure and its profitable outcome. To this extent, the series not surprisingly resemble the pluck-and-luck books produced by Alger, Stratemeyer, and others.

What sets Sayler's books apart is his practice of grafting aeronautical details onto otherwise conventional stories. Although largely secondary to the actual plots (lost treasures, exotic natives, and picturesque settings are commonplaces in all the adventure series, whatever their nature), these details color the series in a variety of ways. First, they give a sense of aviation progress. Its name notwithstanding, the "Airship Boys" series reflects the transition from airship to airplane experimentation; from the middle of the second book on, Ned and Alan concern themselves exclusively with heavier-than-air machines.

Second, the two series offer an uncommonly forward-looking sense of the possibilities of flight. One of the earliest serious experimenters in aviation, Octave Chanute, writing in the American aeronautical journal *Fly* in 1909, offered a list of "Twenty-Four Uses for Flying Machines," suggesting, among other applications, "Public exhibition in cities," "Prospecting for precious metals," "Sending reporters to points of interest," and "Exploring Alaska, Mexico, mountains, etc."[17] All of these, and other uses, appear in Sayler's books. From geographical exploration to mercantile exploitation, from the possible advantages for journalism to their applications in mining and the military, he presents airplanes as practical machines. They will have a role to play in the world to come, and, he implies, it will be a significant, formative role.

Most notably of all, Sayler injects into the books snippets of relatively accurate aeronautical detail, reflecting the extent to which such information was becoming available to the American public and communicating it to his young readers as something of interest and value. That this is deliberate is apparent from a 1909 advertisement for "The Airship Boys" series, which calls them "Up-to-date, thrilling and scientifically correct." The up-to-date quality of the books Sayler reinforces with specific references to the celebrities of flight. Morey Marshall visits Hammondsport and sees Alexander Graham Bell; Bud Wilson's design incorporates "a combination of the Curtiss planes and the Wright rudders, with some ideas of Bud's in the wing warping apparatus;" and Roy Osborne makes reference to the tailplane designs of nineteenth-century French experimenter Alphonse Penaud.[18] Even more to the point, Sayler draws upon timely, contemporaneous sources to make his books reflect the latest current thought in aeronautical advances. So closely does he draw upon his sources, in fact, that he frequently uses identical phrasing or little-altered paraphrase.

One ready source, to which Sayler often turned, is the *Scientific American*. His description of Ned Napier and Alan Hope's plans for a high-speed aircraft in *The Airship Boys in Finance,* an airplane equipped with metal wings and "the sweeping, rounded form that lessens eddies and contributes to strength," comes almost verbatim from J. Bernard Walker's article of 22 October 1910, "The Racing Aeroplane of the Future—A Study." He relies again upon the magazine in 1913, having Alan refer to the Deperdussin monoplane that "did one hundred and eight miles an hour for Vedrines" in the James Gordon Bennett competition of 1912. His description of the ship, "a few inches over nineteen feet and twenty-one feet long," with a monocoque fuselage of "thin spiral strips, laid right and left around a frame and glued," similarly parallels "Our Staff Correspondent's" account in "The James Gordon Bennett Aviation Contest of 1912: How Vedrines Won," in the issue of 21 September 1912.[19] The monocoque design, strong and lightweight and using the fuselage skin as a structural element, did away with the need for most internal and external struts and wires, lessening air resistance and making the craft more streamlined. Almost as soon as the public press reported an event or development, Sayler made fictional use of it.

Among other available sources, two stand out. One is Octave Chanute's *Progress in Flying Machines* (1894), a compilation of essays on aeronautics providing one of the earliest American studies of flight theory. Citing Chanute by name, Sayler has Ned remark that "a man could fly as easily as a bird if he only thought so. That is, if he had the courage, a man with a pair of gliders could jump out of a balloon a mile up in the air and float gracefully to the ground." The views are not Chanute's, but rather those of a French experimenter, De Sanderval, whom Chanute quotes as saying, "If one had an unlimited height to fall in, affording plenty of time to think and to act, he would probably succeed in guiding himself at will." The other is the French journal *l'Aérophile,* where, in a series of essays published between 1908 and 1911, engineer René Lorin outlined a gasoline-fueled rocket engine that closely resembles that of the Airship Boys.[20]

A still readier source is Victor Lougheed's *Vehicles of the Air* (1909). Lougheed, a half-brother of Alan and Malcolm Loughead, founders of the

Lockheed aircraft firm, was a disciple of glider advocate John J. Montgomery (1858–1911) and an early popularizer of aeronautical research. His book initially offers a substantial overview of aeronautical history and theory, and then goes on to talk in detail of the principal extant types of airplane designs. Not surprisingly, it gives considerable space to Montgomery's gliders, and provides scale drawings of these and other types to enable experimenters "readily to reproduce and operate at least the simpler machines, several of which are exceedingly easy and inexpensive to build."[21] Published, like Sayler's series, by Reilly & Britton, it would have been ready to hand when Sayler needed information, and there is ample evidence that he used it freely.

When Ned blithely reports that "the operators working the Montgomery gliders out in California have dropped four thousand feet, turned completely over and landed right side up, after traveling eight miles of slants and circles," the data, despite other coverage of Montgomery's flights, are uniquely Lougheed's. The telescoping wings that give the Airship Boys' *Ocean Flyer* its high-speed capability appear in Lougheed's book, as does Roy Osborne's use of aluminum varnish to reveal cracks in the wooden structure of his airplane.[22] Finally, the frequent allusions to Montgomery's distinctive wing and tail designs reinforce the attention Sayler paid to Lougheed's writings, confirming his determination to have his stories genuinely up-to-date. The plots of his stories are commonplace and their involvement with aviation often tenuous, but Sayler knew the worth of authenticity, and he did his best to supply it.

Other authors were quick to follow Sayler's lead, and the second wave of aviation series emerges in 1910. Like the earliest books, these works overlay aeronautical details on familiar plots; as they do, however, they extend Sayler's examples by incorporating still more specific, timely references to growing public interest in flight and the steady advance of aviation technology. Among the earliest in this cluster are the "Silver Fox Farm" stories (1910–1913; four titles) by James Otis Kaler (1848–1912). Kaler, as "James Otis," had been writing books for the young since 1877. Today best-known as the author of

Toby Tyler; or, Ten Weeks With a Circus (1877), Kaler established himself as an author with a diverse range of historical and adventure stories, all of which document his receptivity to new developments in the juvenile field as they appeared.[23]

The "Silver Fox Farm" books, set on Barren Island off the coast of Kaler's native Maine, constitute a single developing story, spread across four volumes. The first, *The Wireless Station at Silver Fox Farm* (1910), sets the scene. When Paul Simpson's father decides to start a fox-breeding farm on Barren Island, Paul and his chum Ned Bartlett set up a wireless station to maintain contact between the island and the mainland. They quickly run afoul of smuggler John Ed Bingham, who scents a profit in stealing the foxes, enlist the aid of local rustic Zenas Cushing, thwart Bingham, and fortuitously rescue a wealthy yachtsman, Chester Sawtelle. Sawtelle promptly buys a half-interest in the fox-breeding project and announces his intention to build an airship on the island. The "airship" proves to be an airplane, and the second volume, *The Aeroplane at Silver Fox Farm* (1911), traces its development and initial flights. John Ed Bingham destroys the prototype and flees the scene on a steamer, but later successful flights lead Sawtelle to plan an aircraft factory on the island.

The final two volumes, *Building an Airship at Silver Fox Farm* (1912) and *Airship Cruising from Silver Fox Farm* (1913), trace the construction of *The Smuggler,* a powered, non-rigid dirigible, the boys' continued skirmishes with John Ed Bingham, and the timely rescue of yet another wealthy benefactor. When Bingham appears on their doorstep, claiming to have reformed and begging for mercy, Paul and Ned persuade Sawtelle to go along. Bingham becomes the custodian of the fox farm, the aircraft factory is assured of trouble-free operation, and the series comes to an end.

The merits of the "Silver Fox Farm" books lie in their melding of multiple technologies. They begin as a story of wireless experimentation, as Paul and Ned take up "what had presented itself to them as a mystery" and quickly gain "so much knowledge on the subject as to be able to intercept messages sent from a distance of thirty of forty miles." Kaler pointedly avoids any detailed account of their experiments, saying "much space might be taken up with technical description of wave detectors, circuit condensers, inductive coils, and in fact all that goes to make up a wireless station." Nevertheless, he lets Paul read aloud at length from a book on wireless history, and his very mentioning of the terms implies an assumption that readers will recognize and respond to them. The book's ending, moreover, looks back to wireless and ahead to aeronautics and other wonderful fields, as Sawtelle proclaims his belief that the island will "become a perfect paradise for inventors and experimenters, and it will surprise me if from it does not spring that which will astonish the nations of the earth."[24]

Airplane technology joins wireless in the second volume, as Sawtelle and the boys begin work on their flying machine. Lecturing Paul, Ned, and Zenas on aeronautics, Sawtelle details the differences of balloon, airship, and airplane, and lays out a major debate over airplane experimentation. This, he says is between:

> the aeroplane which primarily depends for its successful flight upon the adroitness in manipulation of the operator, who . . . balances his machine to suit the immediate necessity of the case, [and] the type which endeavors, by a scientific arrangement of planes, tails, etc. to adjust itself automatically to the diverse conditions which arise, thus sparing the manipulator as much as possible.[25]

This debate, between the fundamentally unstable aircraft that is controlled by the pilot (as in the Wrights' design), and one that is inherently stable, freeing the pilot from constant attention to the controls (as in the Voisin and Farman designs) occupied experimenters throughout the early years of flight. It is discussed at length in Alphonse Berget's *The Conquest of the Air* (1909) as reflecting the difference between the "American" and "French" schools of thought.[26]

Kaler continues to draw upon *The Conquest of the Air* in the next two volumes, adding dirigible ballooning to the other technologies. His reliance, which he explicitly acknowledges in a prefatory note to *Airship Cruising from Silver Fox Farm,* at last becomes overt borrowing. Sawtelle's description of the *Smuggler*'s passenger car, control system, and power arrangement is taken, with only minimal changes, from Berget's history. Thus, for example, Sawtelle's airship uses a "'stabilizator,' or elevating rudder, fitted to the front of the car" while that described by Berget is guided by a "'stabilizator,' or elevating rudder, fitted to the front of the car." Sawtelle's passenger compartment is built of "platinum tubes of thirty and forty millimetres' diameter," and that in Berget's account is composed of "steel tubes of 30 and 40 millimetres diameter."[27] Though the "Silver Fox Farm" books are a small segment of the aviation series, they speak to a growing public hunger for information about flight, and in addition attest to public interest in a range of technologies. Combining wireless communication, heavier-than-air flight, and lighter-than-air flight, the books tacitly establish all three technologies as accessible realms that can be mastered by the laity as well as by specialists.

The second series of this cluster, the "Boy Aviator Series" (1910–1915; eight titles) by "Captain Wilbur Lawton," returns to the more conventional mode, taking its young protagonists across the world with carefree nonchalance. "Lawton," actually John Henry Goldfrap (1879–1917), was a seasoned series author, producing "The Dreadnought Boys" series ("Tales of the New Navy") and the "Ocean Wireless Series" for Hurst & Company along with the "Boy Aviator" volumes. Billed as "Absolutely Modern Stories for Boys" that speak to the "wonders of modern science" epoch, the books relate the adventures of the prize-winning boy aviators, Frank and Harry Chester, as they roam the world in search of fortune and adventure.[28]

Frank and Harry also come from a familiar series tradition, and "Lawton" wastes no time in establishing their nature. In the opening pages of the first volume, *The Boy Aviators in Nicaragua; or, In League With the Insurgents* (1910), readers learn that:

> Frank, the eldest, was sixteen. A well-grown, clean-lived-looking boy with clear blue eyes and a fearless expression. His brother, a year younger, was as wholesome appearing and almost as tall, but he had a more rollicking cast in his face than his graver brother Frank, whose equal he was, however, in skill, coolness and daring in the trying environment of the treacherous currents of the upper air.[29]

All-American types through and through, they traverse the world in their self-designed airplane, the *Golden Eagle* (supplanted in later volumes by the *Golden Eagle II* and, still later, the hydroplane *Sea Eagle*), and encounter adventure after adventure, ranging from the violent to the exotic, yet invariably come out on top.

Their earliest venture takes them to Nicaragua, where they meet reporter Billy Barnes, become embroiled in a revolution, and seek out the missing mines of the Toltecs. These exploits are followed by *The Boy Aviators on Secret Service or, Working with Wireless* (1910), foiling moonshiners and Japanese spies in the Everglades, and off to Africa in *The Boy Aviators in Africa or, An Aerial Ivory Trail* (1910), meeting natives out of the H. Rider Haggard tradition and a dying race of winged humans. *The Boy Aviators' Treasure Quest or, The Golden Galleon* (1910) leads them to a galleon-load of gold snarled in the Sargasso Sea, while *The Boy Aviators in Record Flight or, The Rival Aeroplane* (1910) takes them across the United States and ends in Wild West excitement in the desert. In *The Boy Aviators' Polar Dash or, Facing Death in the Antarctic* (1910) they join the expedition of explorer Robert Hazzard in search of the South Pole and the lost treasure of Viking Olaf the Rover, and later engage in *The Boy Aviators' Flight for a Fortune* (1912) to salvage a trove of black pearls and gold dust near the mouth of the Mississippi. Their last exploit, *The Boy Aviators with the Air Raiders, A Story of the Great World War* (1915) takes them to France, where they fend off German spies, fly reconnaissance over combat lines, and license their airplane patent to France, since American neutrality forbids their selling aircraft.

The adventures are far-fetched and the descriptions of the boys' airplanes fanciful, but the books create an air of authenticity in other ways. Photographic frontispieces, unlike the hasty drawings that illustrate other series, show real airplanes, and several, notably that of *The Boy Aviators in Record Flight; or, The Rival Aeroplane,* are credited to *Scientific American.*[30] Moreover, the stories unfold against the backdrop of sponsored competitions and international aviation meetings. The boys have made their initial fortune winning "the $10,000 prize for a sustained flight offered by J. Henry Gage, the millionaire aeronaut," and are spoken of as equals to any of the competitors in the Hudson-Fulton competition won by Glenn Curtiss. *The Boy Aviators' Treasure Quest* opens with them competing for the Hempstead Plains Cup at Mineola, New York, while the $50,000 prize established by the New York *Planet,* Billy Barnes's employer, in *The Boy Aviators in Record Flight* is spurred by Glenn Curtiss's winning the $10,000 *New York World* prize for his Albany-New York flight.[31]

Other details parallel real-life advances, as well. In *The Boy Aviators in Nicaragua* and later volumes, Frank and Harry routinely mount wireless sets in their aircraft, reflecting reports of French and American experiments with airborne wireless transmission in 1910. They use a magneto-powered "jump-spark" ignition system in preference to the "make-and-break" system for its simplicity and ease of repair, suggesting an awareness of Victor Lougheed's arguments for the former in *Vehicles of the Air.* They even address the issue of aerial stability when, in *The Boy Aviators in Record Flight,* they investigate inventor Eben Joyce's "adjustable gyroscopic appliance for attachment to aeroplanes which renders them stable in any shifting wind currents."[32]

Possibly the greatest contribution of the "Boy Aviators" books, though, is their capturing the excitement of the "birdman" era, when record flights could be made almost daily, setting new records by minutes and yards rather than by hours and miles, and when aviation was still feeling its way as a field of endeavor. Frank and Harry are prize-winning celebrities with a privileged upbringing, but their achievements appear in the most democratic of terms. They, like the Wrights, take the accomplishments of the workshop and convert them to prominence and wealth. The books' message, while never stated explicitly, is readily apparent: "Aviators" come from the ranks of the public, and the field of endeavor is open to all Americans.

The final series of the middle period is John Luther Langworthy's "Aeroplane Boys" series (1912–1914; 5 titles). Also published as "The Bird Boys" (such reissuing and renaming was commonplace among series publishers), the books trace the doings of cousins Frank and Andy Bird as they dabble in aeronautics, make a foray into the tropics, develop a hydroplane, and ultimately find themselves guests on a cattle ranch. Once again, the heroes are familiar types, embodying all that is good in upper-middle-class life. Both are "healthy looking boys." Frank is the son of "the leading doctor in the town of Bloomsbury," a lakeside hamlet in New York State, while Andy, for his part, is "an orphan. His father had been quite a well known man of science, and a professor in college." Already a widower, Professor Bird vanishes while trying to cross the Panamanian isthmus in a balloon, and Andy takes up residence with his cousin.[33]

Their exploits follow a straightforward, developmental sequence. In *The Aeroplane Boys; or, The Young Sky Pilot's First Air Voyage* (1912), they are building a Blériot-style monoplane to take part in a local competition, a prize for the first flight to the top of a nearby landmark, Old Thunder Mountain. *The Aeroplane Boys On the Wing; or, Aeroplane Chums in the Tropics* (1912) is spurred by news that Professor Bird is alive, somewhere in South America. The boys fly to Colombia, cross paths with insurrectionists, encounter tapirs, jaguars, and anacondas, rescue Professor Bird, and return home in triumph. The third volume, *The Aeroplane Boys Among the Clouds; or, Young Aviators in a Wreck* (1912) finds them back in Bloomsbury. They rescue a rival from atop Old Thunder, decline an invitation to become professional fliers, and plan to continue their studies.

When the Bloomsbury bank is robbed, the boys are drafted into pursuit; *The Aeroplane Boys' Flight; or, A Hydroplane Roundup* (1914) relates their trek over Lake Ontario and their capture of the criminals. The final volume, *The Aeroplane Boys' Aeroplane Wonder; or, Young Aviators on a Cattle Ranch* (1914) takes them to an uncle's ranch in Arizona. Seeing the western location as a prime site for flying experiments, they ship their airplane ahead, astonish the cowpokes with their flying endeavors, rescue the housekeeper's five-year-old

The airplane meets the West in a 1914 installment to the "Bird Boys" series. Erisman-Odom Collection, Mary Couts Burnett Library, Texas Christian University.

daughter when she's captured by Indians, and return at last to Bloomsbury and normality.

As with the "Boy Aviators" books, the airplane technology, when it is described, is often fanciful. Like the preceding series, moreover, much of the books' appeal comes from the competitions cited. These are local affairs sponsored by local bigwigs, establishing the presence of aviation and flight experimentation at even the small-town level. Indeed, the boys are incensed when they learn that one of their rivals "spent two days around the aviation field over on Long Island, watching the way they ran the aeroplanes. And it is said that he went up several times with Curtiss in one of his biplanes, so as to learn how to handle the wheel!"[34] "Langworthy" gives an intriguing double vision here. Their rival is seeking an unfair advantage through expert training, he implies, but he also suggests that, in the best democratic tradition, the notables of aviation are accessible to all.

At the same time, the books touch upon actual advances in flight and flight technology. Frank and Harry develop a hydroplane capable of taking off from and landing on water, soon after Glenn Curtiss achieves the same feat, and they, too, take up the problem of maintaining in-flight stability. They recognize the dangers posed by instability, and Frank warns a friend of the hazards involved. Nonetheless, he looks to an eventual technological solution: Flying "is certainly the most dangerous calling going at present; but after the Wrights have put their latest balancing idea into general use, the number of dead aviators will drop fast."[35]

What gives the books their real distinction, though, is their portrayal of the "aviator" and of the potential of flight. For the first time, there are glimpses of the flier as a person set apart, a person of exceptional skill and capability. In the initial volume, the narratorial voice remarks: "Aviators must necessarily be built on the order of athletes, for their very lives may depend on instantaneous action and speedy thought that springs from intuition. It is not the profession of a lazy or clumsy individual." Andy adds to this view somewhat later in the book, when he learns that a flier has turned to crime: "Here we're just breaking into the honored ranks of air navigators, when some scamp has to go and disgrace his calling."[36] In speaking of "the profession" and the "honored ranks," "Langworthy" suggests a new and evolving view of flight and the airman. The person who once was a "birdman," subject, perhaps, to skepticism and ridicule, is beginning to appear in a new and heroic way, while the concept of "the purity of the air" is beginning to emerge.

That purity is apparent as Frank and Harry find in the sensations of flying a new sense of themselves and their endeavors. Their first flight brings its own epiphany: "If they should live to the century mark neither of those lads would ever forget the strange sensation that nearly overwhelmed them upon feeling themselves moving through the air for the first time, with no solid earth to depend upon." Flying, "Langworthy" implies is a remarkable and hypnotic sensation that gives its enthusiasts a sense unattainable by any other means. Near the end of the series, Frank reinforces this vision, remarking: "What could be as fine as this, sailing over the earth? I don't wonder that when a fellow has once started in to be an aviator he can't ever break away. Peril and accidents he laughs at; not because he's reckless always, but just on account of the fascination of the sport."[37] A sport it may be, but flying has an appeal not found in any of the earth-bound endeavors.

The final cluster of stories, the last to appear before the onset of World War I, is a transitional group, continuing the principal lines of development established by the earlier works. One series, Frank Walton's "Flying Machine Boys" (1913–1915; six titles) is rollicking adventure in the familiar series-story pattern. The other, the "Dave Dashaway" series (1913–1915; five titles), a Stratemeyer Syndicate product by "Roy Rockwood," looks to the continuing development of aviation as a technological field and as a field of personal endeavor. Stratemeyer had already shown an awareness of developments in flight in the "Tom Swift" series, where Tom, in 1911, built a monoplane "modeled after the one in which Blériot made his first flight across the

English Channel," and later went on to take part in an international air meet, flying against designs by Wright, Santos-Dumont, Blériot, Curtiss, and Farman.[38] Here he turns his attention wholly to aviation, and the two series, taken together, mark the end of the fledgling era of aviation stories, and look ahead to those of the near future.

"The Flying Machine Boys" books combine Progressive-era social consciousness with generic, often fanciful, aviation elements. The first volume, *The Flying Machine Boys in Mexico; or, The Secret of the Crater* (1913), introduces the three sixteen-year-old protagonists: Ben Whitcomb, Jimmie Stuart, and Carl Nichols, who are New York street urchins earning their keep as newsboys. Stranded on a tidal island during a newsboys' holiday, the three are rescued by the famous flier Louis Havens. Havens, liking their looks, teaches them to fly in a single day, then takes them on an expedition to Mexico. There they encounter jungle hazards and volcanoes, discover a gold mine, and return to New York as wealthy young men.

Later books continue the fantasy. In *The Flying Machine Boys on Duty; or, The Clue Above the Clouds* (1913), Havens is revealed as wealthy in his own right: "The millions he possessed had been inherited from his father, and instead of spending them along the Great White Way, he was devoting his entire attention to aviation."[39] He sends the boys to California in pursuit of bank robbers, where they cross paths with smugglers and sinister Asians, capture the thieves, and return home after rescuing the kidnaped Havens. More travels follow in *The Flying Machine Boys in the Wilds; or, The Mystery of the Andes* (1913), when the boys set out in search of a haunted temple on the shores of Lake Titicaca. The search turns into the pursuit of an embezzler who has fled to South America with cash from one of Havens's companies, and the story morphs into a classic chase-and-capture tale.

The trio's success as thief-catchers attracts the notice of the government, which, in *The Flying Machine Boys on Secret Service; or, The Capture in the Air* (1913), sends them to Canada to track liquor smugglers. Their exploits continue in *The Flying Machine Boys in Deadly Peril; or, Lost in the Clouds* (1914) when the boys take a holiday in the wilds of Idaho. On their outing they run afoul of a miners' strike, a cinnamon bear, and a bizarrely eccentric professor obsessed with a plan to fly the Atlantic in an airship. The professor is brought to his senses by the crash of his vessel, and the boys return to New York to begin their schooling. Their final adventure, *The Flying Machine Boys in the Frozen North; or, The Trail in the Snow* (1915), takes them back to Canada, searching for a friend of Havens who has information concerning an Arizona gold mine. The flying elements are negligible, but encounters with bears, wolves, and assorted ne'er-do-wells keep the book moving until its happy ending.

For all their melodrama, the books make sporadic allusions to developments taking place in the real world of aviation, and at times manage to convey to a small degree the growing fascination of flight. Havens speaks of the quest for sustained flight in *The Flying Machine Boys on Duty,* calling the perfect flying machine "one which will fly for days and nights without breaking down."

Barnstorming advertisement featuring the Curtiss JN-4D "Jenny" (ca. 1919). National Air and Space Museum, Smithsonian Institution (SI 85-12327).

Jimmie later duplicates the air-show stunt of transferring from one craft to another in mid-air, and national rivalries surface in *The Flying Machine Boys in Deadly Peril.* Stressing the need for continued experimentation, the professor reminds Ben that "The European countries beat us last year in the progress made in aviation. One year ago there were 2,500 licensed aviators, France leading all with nearly a thousand, while the Americans had less than two hundred."[40] National pride and the advance of knowledge go together.

Also present is an emerging sense that the act of flying is something unique in the human experience. The boys get a taste of this sense in the opening volume as they fly to Mexico. Havens's skill enables them to fly at night (an undertaking first accomplished by Claude Grahame-White in 1910, just three years previously), and they find the experience like nothing they have ever before encountered: "The stars at night . . . seem clearer, larger, brighter, than when seen through the heavy atmosphere which surrounds the lower levels of the air. Besides, there is a sense of freedom, of being master of fate, which is experienced in no other situation yet reached by man."[41] From this uniqueness, moreover, comes a distinctive bonding of flier and machine that, at times, approaches actual love. As Havens watches a night-time take-off, his reaction is close to spiritual: "The planes glistened like silver in the moonlight, and the song of the motors came to his ears like sweet music. The millionaire loved a flying machine as track-men love a swift and beautiful horse." Even in works so conventional as the "Flying Machine Boys" books, the appeal of flight works its magic.

Magic melds with reality in the "Dave Dashaway" books. Edward Stratemeyer's first venture into aviation as the focus of a series, the "Dashaway" stories reflect his evident conclusion that popular interest in flight was real and that young persons' interest would endure. He sent outlines for the first two volumes to Weldon J. Cobb in May 1912, stressing the importance of the books' being timely and accurate: "We want bright, up to date stories, but free from sensationalism. I would like you to give some information about flying machines in general, monoplanes, biplanes, etc., but not mention any particular makes, no manufacturers nor aviators, as we do not care to advertise anybody." He also recommends that Cobb buy copies of *Aircraft* and *Fly* magazines, along with "some practical book on flying machines and flying," for the stories "must have a touch of the 'real thing.'" The letter sets the tone for not only the "Dashaway" books but also the aviation series to follow—a mix of verifiable fact with timely and largely plausible action and adventure—and Stratemeyer anticipates needing "quite a few in this series." His judgment, as usual, is not far off.[42]

The five books of the series trace air-minded young Dave's apprenticeship in the world of aviation, his assimilation of its culture, and his eventual success as an honored, professional flier. The rewards he earns are as substantial as those netted by the Airship Boys or the Flying Machine Boys, but they come to him not for lucky finds or profitable inventions, but for his achievements as a flier. His devotion to flight is real and his response to it as ecstatic as any felt by his predecessors, but he tempers both with the recognition that flying is a demanding and challenging profession. He is the first professional aviator of the series genre.

The orphaned son of a famous balloonist, Dave runs away from home and, in *Dave Dashaway the Young Aviator; or, In the Clouds for Fame and Fortune* (1913), finds work as an airport handyman. Here he befriends fellow youngster Hiram Dobbs, meets the noted aviator Robert King, and, with King's backing, studies flying. He begins to earn extra money with flying for a film company and doing occasional air stunting, and, when he wins an air race while substituting for an ailing flier, is offered full-time work as a pilot with the Interstate Aero Company. Hiram accompanies him, as mechanic and obligatory sidekick.[43] His engagement with flight continues in *Dave Dashaway and His Hydroplane; or, Daring Adventures Over the Great Lakes* (1913), as he and Hiram field-test a new hydroplane; when it is stolen, the two track it to Canada and retrieve it to great acclaim. He flies the Atlantic in *Dave Dashaway and His Giant Airship;*

or, A Marvellous Trip Across the Atlantic (1913), pausing in his preparations only to test a still more advanced hydroplane.

Dave's studies pay off still further in *Dave Dashaway Around the World; or, A Young Yankee Aviator Among Many Nations* (1913), when he and Hiram take the *Comet,* a heavier-than-air craft of radical design, on a global flight, and reaches the top of his profession in *Dave Dashaway, Air Champion; or, Wizard Work in the Clouds* (1915). Still basking in the acclaim from his round-the-world flight, Dave enrolls in an important public air competition, sweeping the competition with a display of aerobatics and skywriting that establishes his supremacy in controlling an aircraft.

Cobb takes Stratemeyer's urgings to heart, and gives the stories a solid underpinning of aviation lore and language. As Dave begins his work at the airfield, Robert King tells him that the first step to mastery is "working around the hangars and doing odd jobs till you know a monoplane from a biplane and a pylon from an aileron." Dave's flight lessons begin with the fundamentals, as he learns to glide in a home-built training craft and he extends his learning to "a practical study of aeronautics . . . ; from the first time the pioneer airman harnessed a gasoline engine to a kite and called it a flying machine, down to the loop-the-loop somersault trick in aviation."[44]

He begins to pick up the practical distinctions between aircraft; an "articulated biplane" is different from the "headless screw traction design" of the round-the-world flier, and neither is to be confused with a "parasol-type biplane." With this knowledge comes practical skill, until he is able to deal confidently and competently with that most feared of aerial hazards, the "hole in the air." "A dead void caused by two opposing air currents colliding," "Rockwood" tells his readers, this peril "to the sky traveler is what a yawning chasm is to a speeding automobile. . . . Every part of the machine suddenly goes useless. The heavy mechanism simply drops."[45]

These are, by the standards of 1912 and 1913, cutting-edge data. The "articulated biplane" (a monoplane in the actual source) appears in *Fly* magazine for February 1912—one of the journals Stratemeyer urges Cobb to consult. "Rockwood's" descriptions of Dave's flying boat designs closely parallel those published in *The Curtiss Aviation Book* of 1912, very likely the "practical book" that Stratemeyer suggested he consult. W.J. Humphreys of the United States Weather Bureau describes the confluence of air currents and the resulting loss of dynamic control in "Holes in the Air," published in *Popular Science Monthly* for July 1912, while Adolphe Pègoud accomplished both inverted flight and the aerial somersault in September 1913, an event reported in *Scientific American* on 27 September 1913.[46] The series books are becoming a conduit for transmitting aerial information to the young.

Even as they begin to transmit fact, though, the "Dashaway" books do more. They communicate as well a view of life, a vision of flight, that marks a notable development from the views found in the earlier series. The opening page of the series establishes Dave's "flying fever," and the remaining volumes only intensify it. His first flight puts him "in a transport of delight." The scheme to fly the Atlantic is "enough to fire the enthusiasm of any live, up-to-date boy . . . the hope and dream of every ambitious airman in the world." When he and Hiram take to the air in their final, triumphant competition, they realize yet one more time that there is "nothing in the world equal to that delightful sensation of skimming through the air like a bird. It was almost rapture to realize that the turn of a wrist, or the pressure of his foot sent the airy, graceful fabric of steel and wood far aloft, like a pinion-poised eagle, ascending safely through space as would a speeding swallow arrow-aimed for a long, deep dive."[47]

These are potent words, and they would not be lost on Stratemeyer's readers. Adventures in the air do not need the added stimuli of Asian smugglers or emboldened thieves. The air itself is challenge enough, and the aviator who rises to that challenge will find himself uplifted figuratively as well as literally. It is an important step forward for the aviation series book.

The early aviation series flourished for barely six years, extending from 1909 until 1915. Their banner year was 1910, when thirteen titles were published in four series, mirroring the level of public attention to aviation. The year opened with the Wrights' winning an injunction against Curtiss and others. Curtiss made his Albany-New York flight in May, the *Scientific American* published its first ever "Aeronautical Issue" in October, and the year ended with the international competition at Belmont Park. Though the books' numbers declined in following years, they had firmly established aviation as the stuff of popular literature. They also established fundamental elements of the aviation story that later series would expand and perfect.

First, they introduce readers to the factual details of aircraft construction and technology. While they make clear the range of materials necessary and the careful construction skills required, they also present airplane construction as something within the reach of any moderately skilled person. Andy Leighton puts the view into words in 1911 when, after comparing the simplicity of the airplane to that of the bicycle, he enthuses: "Why, every boy in the country'll be makin' 'em. You need only some light, strong wood and wires, and a few yards o' varnished cloth, and there you are."[48] His optimism is borne out in the popular press. The Aeroplane Blue Print Company, advertising in the *Scientific American* in October 1910, offered plans for Curtiss, Bleriot XI, and Farman airplanes, and added: "Any one can build an Aeroplane from our Blue Prints. . . . Improved machines are bound to come, and these improvements will be suggested by practical men who study and build their own machines from our Blue Prints." The magazine itself offered reprints of aeronautical articles that had appeared in the *Scientific American Supplement,* including a package of detailed drawings "which will enable anyone to make a glider for $15.00." For his part, Victor Lougheed published *Aeroplane Designing for Amateurs* in 1912, continuing his advocacy of John J. Montgomery's ideas, but also spelling out theoretical knowledge necessary for the amateur aircraft-builder.[49] In reality as in the books, the airplane is increasingly being presented as an accessible technology.

Second, they make explicit the challenges of early flight—those matters of stability, endurance, altitude, and speed. These are problems that must be overcome if the airplane is to become a practical addition to the emerging technological world. And they *will* be overcome; the books leave no doubt of that and look to the time when airplanes are incorporated into every part of American life. Quoting from one of his beloved aviation textbooks, Morey Marshall in 1910 proclaims: "In war and peace, in commerce and pleasure, from the Pole to the tropics, these human birds will darken the air on pinions swifter than the eagle's wing."[50] The technical problems will be overcome, and nothing will hold back the advance of aviation

Third, the challenges of flight notwithstanding, the books present flight and its requisite skills as within the reach of any determined person. The ease of building an airplane is paralleled by the relative ease of mastering it. A 1911 article on "Learning How to Fly" in *Scientific American* lists "common sense, mechanical ability, patience, good nerves and good eyesight as indispensable attributes of the man who wants to fly." The person who possesses these traits will have no difficulty in the air, especially if he also possesses "the faculty of concentration, so essential in most sports."[51] The series books bear this out. Privileged youngsters like the Airship Boys or the Bird Boys and determined ones like Dave Dashaway will obviously take to flying with the greatest of ease, but, significantly, even street boys like the Flying Machine Boys will find aviation within their command. What they may lack in formal education they can make up for with native intelligence, and settle into the pilot's seat with the same readiness seen in their more fortunate contemporaries. Flying is a skilled enterprise, but its skills are attainable.

Fourth, and finally, the books affirm a vision of the future in which powerful airplanes under the command of careful, conscientious fliers will crisscross the world, making the society of the future a truly aeronautical one. Ned Napier and Alan Hope outline their vision of an aviation-centered North America to J.P. Morgan in 1911, planning among other things twenty-four-hour weather service, wireless guidance for craft in the air, and established air routes and universal signals for day and night flying, Morgan, with his legendary business acumen, sees even more: "This may not mean only the transportation of men. The lack of this, in times past, has created different nations on the same continent. With quick, easy, sure, and cheap intercourse between different peoples, the artificial boundaries that separate men into nations may disappear." It is, indeed, no wonder that, the following year, Andy Bird can speak of the boys' being "pioneers of the great uplift movement."[52] Aviation has a great future, and its only limitations are those of the people who embrace it.

The "birdman" stories come to an end with the onset of World War I, when what once had been an intriguing plaything for the dedicated amateur becomes a weapon of undeniable efficacy. The mechanical problems of the past have been solved. Reliable engines, more efficient wing design, and greater ease of stable flight make the airplane into far more than a plaything; indeed, as flown by the English, French, and German forces, airplanes take on an entirely new complexion. Their combat encounters become romanticized confrontations. The popular press lionizes the pilots of all the nations, feeding the emergence of a "cult of the aviator." This cult quickly evolves into the "cult of the 'ace,'" praising the skills, the ruthlessness, and yet the chivalry of the flying combatant, and the series writers are not slow to follow.[53]

NOTES TO CHAPTER TWO

1 A useful overview of Sayler's career and work is David K. Vaughan, "Pioneer of Aviation Series Books: Harry L. Sayler and the Airship Boys," *Dime Novel Roundup,* 59 (March 1990): 74–79.

2 "The Wright Aeroplane and Its Fabled Performances," *Scientific American,* 94 (13 January 1906): 40.

3 Bill Gunston, ed., *Aviation Year By Year* (New York: DK Publishing, 2001).

4 "The Wright Aeroplane and Its Performances," *Scientific American,* 94 (7 April 1906): 291–22; "Rules Governing the Competition for the Scientific American Flying Machine Trophy," *Scientific American,* 96 (27 April 1907): 191.

5 "Shall America Take the Lead in Aeronautics?" *Scientific American,* 98 (29 February 1908): 138.

6 C.R. Roseberry, *Glenn Curtiss: Pioneer of Flight* (Syracuse: Syracuse UP, 1991), 75–82, 90–106.

[7] "The Winning Flight of the 'June Bug' Aeroplane for the Scientific American Trophy," *Scientific American,* 99 (18 July 1908): 45.

[8] Roseberry, *Glenn Curtiss*, 168–176.

[9] "Termination of the Rheims Aviation Meeting," *Scientific American,* 101 (11 September 1909): 180–181.

[10] Orville and Wilbur Wright, "The Wright Brothers' Aëroplane," *Century Magazine,* 76 (September 1908): 641–650; Robert Wohl, *A Passion for Wings: Aviation and the Western Imagination, 1908–1918* (New Haven: Yale University Press, 1994), 21–30; Roseberry, *Glenn Curtiss*, 126–130.

[11] V.L. Ochoa, "Are the Wrights Pirates?" *Aircraft,* 1 (April 1910): 55. George F. Campbell-Wood's article, "The Wright-Curtiss- Paulhan Conflict" in the same issue (50–55) gives a good overview of the suits and the issues involved. See also "The Wright Aeroplane Infringement Suit," *Scientific American,* 101 (28 August 1909): 138.

[12] "The International Aviation Meet," *Scientific American,* 103 (5 November 1910): 361–62, 370–71; G.F. Campbell Wood, "The International Aviation Meet," *Aircraft,* 1 (December 1910): 358.

[13] Roseberry, *Glenn Curtiss*, 200–203, 272–280.

[14] The evolving public view of the Wrights and their achievements is examined in Roger E. Bilstein, "The Airplane, the Wrights, and the American Public," in *The Wright Brothers: Heirs of Prometheus,* ed. Richard P. Hallion (Washington, DC: Smithsonian Institution Press, 1978): 39–51.

[15] An eighth volume, *When Scout Meets Scout; or, The Aeroplane Spy* (1912), has so far proven unobtainable.

[16] H.L. Sayler, *The Airship Boys or, The Quest of the Aztec Treasure* (Chicago: Reilly & Britton, 1909), 103.

[17] Octave Chanute, "Twenty-Four uses for Flying Machines," *Fly,* 2 (November 1909): 18.

[18] Back matter advertisement in H.L. Sayler, *The Airship Boys Adrift; or, Saved by an Aeroplane* (Chicago: Reilly & Britton, 1909); Ashton Lamar [H.L. Sayler], *In the Clouds for Uncle Sam; or, Morey Marshall of the Signal Corps* (Chicago: Reilly & Britton, 1910), 54–55; Ashton Lamar [H.L. Sayler], *The Stolen Aeroplane; or, How Bud Wilson Made Good* (Chicago: Reilly & Britton, 1910), 29–30; Ashton Lamar [H.L. Sayler], *A Cruise in the Sky; or, The Legend of the Great Pink Pearl* (Chicago: Reilly & Britton, 1911), 130. For further information on Penaud, see F. Alexander Magoun and Eric Hodgins, *A History of Aircraft* (New York: Whittlesey House, 1931), 294–295, and Captain Holden C. Richardson, "Prophecy in Retrospect," *Southern Flight,* 19 (February 1943): 28–29, 39–40, 44, 45.

[19] H.L. Sayler, *The Airship Boys in Finance; or, The Flight of the Flying Cow* (Chicago: Reilly & Britton, 1911), 66; J. Bernard Walker, "The Racing Aeroplane of the Future—A Study," *Scientific American,* 103 (22 October 1910): 318; H.L. Sayler, *The Airship Boys as Detectives; or, Secret Service in Cloudland* (Chicago: Reilly & Britton, 1913), 47, 51; "Our Staff Correspondent," "The James Gordon Bennett Aviation Contest of 1912: How Vedrines Won," *Scientific American,* 107 (21 September 1912): 245.

[20] H.L. Sayler, *The Airship Boys in the Barren Lands; or, The Secret of the White Eskimos* (Chicago: Reilly & Britton, 1910), 107–108; Octave Chanute, *Progress in Flying Machines* (New York: American Engineer and Railroad Journal, 1894) 158–160 (cf. De Sanderval, "Recherches sur le vol plane," *L'Aéronaute,* 19 [November 1886]: 203–206); René Lorin, "La propulsion a grande vitesse des véhicules aériens," *l'Aérophile,* 17 (15 October 1909): 463–465. Lorin's design, now called a pulse detonation engine (or PDE), has taken on new life as a possible powerplant for hypersonic jets. See Bill Sweetman, "Ba-da-boom," *Smithsonian/Air & Space,* 18 (October/November 2003): 13.

[21] Victor Lougheed, *Vehicles of the Air.* 3rd ed. (Chicago: Reilly & Britton, 1911), 394. For Lougheed's professional activity compared with that of his half-brothers, see René J. Francillon, *Lockheed Aircraft since 1913* (Annapolis: Naval Institute Press, 1987), 2–4. A contemporaneous report of Montgomery's experiments is "The Montgomery Airplane,"

Scientific American, 92 (20 May 1905): 404–406; Montgomery's own account appears in Prof. J.J. Montgomery, "Some Early Gliding Experiments in America," *Aeronautics,* 4 (January 1909): 47–50. His career and accomplishments are reviewed in Lieut. H.B. Miller, "A Forgotten Pioneer," *Model Airplane News,* 14 (June 1936): 6–7, 42–44, and Tom D. Crouch, "Local Hero: John Joseph Montgomery and the First Winged Flight in America," *Journal of the West,* 36 (July 1997): 21–28.

22 Sayler, *Airship Boys in the Barren Lands,* 108 (cf. Lougheed, *Vehicles of the Air,* 139); H.L. Sayler, *The Airship Boys' Ocean Flyer; or, New York to London in Twelve Hours* (Chicago: Reilly & Britton, 1911), 45–46 (cf. Lougheed, *Vehicles of the Air,* 218); Ashton Lamar, *The Aeroplane Express or, the Boy Aeronaut's Grit* (Chicago: Reilly & Britton, 1910), 70–71 (cf. Lougheed, *Vehicles of the Air,* 328).

23 "Juvenile Story Writer Dies," *New York Times,* 12 December 1912: 13. The "Silver Fox Farm" stories are discussed in David K. Vaughan, "James Otis Kaler's Silver Fox Farm Series: Aviation Reaches the New England Coast," *Dime Novel Roundup,* 64 (June, August 1995): 59–66, 94–101.

24 James Otis [James Otis Kaler], *The Wireless Station at Silver Fox Farm* (New York: Thomas Y. Crowell, 1910), 8, 15, 150–151, 377.

25 James Otis [James Otis Kaler], *The Aeroplane at Silver Fox Farm* (New York: Thomas Y. Crowell, 1911), 14.

26 "The Wright and Voisin (Farman) Flying Machines Compared," *Scientific American,* 100 (9 January 1909): 18; Alphonse Berget, *The Conquest of the Air* (New York: G.P. Putnam's Sons, 1909), 230–234; "The Maurice Farman Biplane," *Scientific American Supplement,* 71 (13 May 1911): 300–301.

27 James Otis [James Otis Kaler], *Airship Cruising at Silver Fox Farm* (New York: Thomas Y. Crowell, 1913), 6–8; cf. Berget, 21–22, 64–66.

28 Back matter advertisement in Captain Wilbur Lawton [John H. Goldfrap], *The Boy Aviators in Nicaragua; or, In League With the Insurgents* (New York: Hurst, 191, unpaged.

29 Lawton, *Boy Aviators in Nicaragua,* 7.

30 See, for example, the central photograph in "The International Aviation Meet," *Scientific American,* 103 (5 November 1910): 362–363, which serves as frontispiece to Captain Wilbur Lawton [John H. Goldfrap], *The Boy Aviators in Record Flight; or, The Rival Aeroplane* (New York: Hurst, 1910).

31 Lawton, *Boy Aviators in Nicaragua,* 7; Captain Wilbur Lawton [John H. Goldfrap], *The Boy Aviators' Treasure Quest; or, The Golden Galleon* (New York: Hurst, 1910), 6–7; Lawton, *Boy Aviators in Record Flight,* 7–8.

32 Lawton, *Boy Aviators in Nicaragua,* 90–91; F.H. McLean, "Wireless Signaling in Aeronautics," *Scientific American Supplement,* 69 (15 January 1910): 34; "Wireless on Aeroplane," *Scientific American Supplement,* 71 (20 May 1911): 307; "Wireless Telegraphy and the Aeroplane," *Scientific American Supplement,* 72 (9 September 1911): 176; Lougheed, *Vehicles of the Air,* 284–287; Lawton, *Boy Aviators in Record Flight,* 32 (cf. Lucien Fournier, "Gyroscopic Balancing of Aeroplanes," *Scientific American Supplement,* 67 [15 May 1909]: 309–310).

33 John Luther Langworthy, *The Aeroplane Boys; or, The Young Sky Pilot's First Air Voyage* (Chicago: M.A. Donohue, 1912), 13–14.

34 Ibid., *Aeroplane Boys,* 83–84.

35 John Luther Langworthy, *The Aeroplane Boys Among the Clouds; or, Young Aviators in a Wreck* (Chicago: M.A. Donohue, 1912), 19–20; John Fulton Greer, "First Flight of an American Aeroplane from the Water," *Scientific American,* 104 (11 February 1911): 132; "Curtiss's Experiments in Rising from the Water," *Scientific American Supplement,* 71 (4 March 1911): 132; "Automatic Stabilizing System of the Wright Brothers," *Scientific American Supplement,* 71 (14 January 1911): 20–21. Grover Cleveland Loening gives an overview of several other proposed devices in "Automatic Stability of Aeroplanes: Comments on Some American Patents," *Scientific American,* 104 (13 May 1911): 470–471, 488–489.

36 Langworthy, *Aeroplane Boys,* 90, 101.

[37] Ibid., 160; Langworthy, *Aeroplane Boys Among the Clouds,* 71.

[38] Victor Appleton [Howard R. Garis], *Tom Swift and His Wireless Message; or, The Castaways of Earthquake Island* (New York: Grosset & Dunlap, 1911), 40; Victor Appleton [Howard R. Garis], *Tom Swift and His Sky Racer; or, The Quickest Flight on Record* (New York: Grosset & Dunlap, 1911), 180.

[39] Frank Walton, *The Flying Machine Boys on Duty; or, The Clue Above the Clouds* (New York: A.L. Burt, 1913), 8–9.

[40] Ibid., 25; Frank Walton, *The Flying Machine Boys on Secret Service; or, The Capture in the Air* (New York: A.L. Burt, 1913), 26–29; Frank Walton, *The Flying Machine Boys in Deadly Peril; or, Lost in the Clouds* (New York: A.L. Burt, 1914), 25.

[41] Terry Gwynne-Jones, *Farther and Faster: Aviation's Adventuring Years, 1909–1939* (Washington, DC: Smithsonian Institution Press, 1991), 18–19; Frank Walton, *The Flying Machine Boys in Mexico; or, The Secret of the Crater* (New York: A.L. Burt, 1913), 100; Walton, *Flying Machine Boys on Duty,* 33.

[42] Edward Stratemeyer to Weldon J. Cobb, 16 May 1912, Stratemeyer Syndicate Records, MSS. & Archives Section, N.Y.P.L., Box 22.

[43] Israel Ludlow, "The Aeroplane and the Motion Picture Camera," *Aeronautics,* 10 (January 1912): 13–14, is an early article examining the airplane's role in cinema.

[44] Roy Rockwood [Weldon J. Cobb], *Dave Dashaway the Young Aviator; or, In the Clouds for Fame and Fortune* (New York: Cupples & Leon, 1913), 92, 134; Roy Rockwood [Weldon J. Cobb], *Dave Dashaway and His Giant Airship; or, A Marvellous Trip Across the Atlantic* (New York: Cupples & Leon, 1913), 21.

[45] Rockwood, *Dave Dashaway the Young Aviator,* 171; Roy Rockwood [Weldon J. Cobb], *Dave Dashaway Around the World; or, A Young Yankee Aviator Among Many Nations* (New York: Cupples & Leon, 1913), 26; Roy Rockwood [Weldon J. Cobb], *Dave Dashaway, Air Champion; or, Wizard Work in the Clouds* (New York: Cupples & Leon, 1916), 26; Rockwood, *Dave Dashaway and His Giant Airship,* 21.

[46] "An Articulated Monoplane," *Fly Magazine,* 4 (February 1912): 17; Glenn H. Curtiss and Augustus Post, *The Curtiss Aviation Book.* (New York: Frederick A. Stokes, 1912), 144; W.J Humphreys, "Holes in the Air," *Popular Science Monthly,* 81 (July 1912): 54; "Turning Somersaults With an Aeroplane," *Scientific American,* 109 (27 September 1913): 240. The first usage of "holes in the air," which occurred in reports of the Los Angeles Aviation Meet of January 1910, is related in *The Curtiss Aviation Book,* 87–89; the debate over the existence of such phenomena spread quickly through the popular and technical press.

[47] Rockwood, *Dave Dashaway the Young Aviator,* 2, 120; Rockwood, *Dave Dashaway and His Giant Airship,* 6–7; Rockwood, *Dave Dashaway, Air Champion,* 27.

[48] Lamar, *A Cruise in the Sky,* 48.

[49] Aeroplane Blue Print Company advertisement, *Scientific American,* 103 (29 October 1910): 352; Munn & Co. advertisement, *Scientific American,* 103 (10 December 1910): 468; Victor Lougheed, *Aeroplane Designing for Amateurs* (Chicago: Reilly & Britton, 1912).

[50] Lamar, *In the Clouds for Uncle Sam,* 49.

[51] Antony H. Jannus, "Learning How to Fly: Hints from a Professional Aviator," *Scientific American,* 104 (24 June 1911): 624. In 1914, Jannus made the first commercial airline flight in the United States, launching the St. Petersburg-Tampa [Florida] Airboat Line. See Richard P. Hallion, *Taking Flight: Inventing the Aerial Age from Antiquity through the First World War* (New York: Oxford University Press, 2003), 326.

[52] Sayler, *Airship Boys in Finance,* 203–204, 207; Langworthy, *Aeroplane Boys,* 27.

[53] Wohl, *A Passion for Wings,* 282.

CHAPTER THREE

Aces and Combat: World War One and After, 1915–1935

War came to the aviation series almost as reluctantly as it came to the American public. Hostilities in Europe broke out in August 1914, but flying stories incorporating warfare did not begin to appear until 1915. Even then, the war was almost an afterthought; the first mentions were grafted onto the seventh volume of an on-going series, Gordon Stuart's "Boy Scouts of the Air" books, which had begun publication in 1912, when its young protagonists found themselves stranded in Europe at the onset of fighting. For adults as well as youngsters, the war was covered by the popular press, but it was presented as "the European war," stressing Americans' detachment from the events abroad. Aviation, too, was mentioned in passing, more in the technical press than in the popular, but, until the United States actively became a combatant, it remained a subject for blissful speculation, with some suggestive overtones of attitudes to come.

As late as 1916, an advertisement for the Wright Flying School reminded the public that "The world has its eyes on the flying man. Flying is the greatest sport of red-blooded, virile manhood," while a somewhat later advertisement touted the benefits of flying for all. "The Era of Flying as a sport is at hand," it trumpeted.

> Red-blooded, sturdy manhood has become imbued with the spirit of flight. The World has its eye on the flying man—and woman. . . . A Fall or Winter vacation at a flying school will increase the red corpuscles and make you over into a new being—a superman in physique as well as fact. (Your business in

> **New York—you can fly morning and night and be at the office during the day.)[1]**

For adults as much as for adolescents, flying was increasingly an expression of manhood and improvement, with the flying person a "new being" whose every quality was enhanced by flight.

When military aircraft began to appear in the aviation series, their initial involvement was relatively modest. Airplanes flew principally scouting, ground support, and bombing missions, and, apart from the danger inherent in flying *per se,* these activities were not particularly perilous; tales of air-to-air combat held off until 1918, when the Stratemeyer-created "Air Service Boys" series began its run. Once introduced, however, the combat tales captured an audience, and the air war's appeal continued long past the immediate era of the Armistice in 1918. Fourteen years later, the "Air Combat" series of the 1930s looked back to the distant romance of the dogfights and wood-and-fabric aircraft of World War I to attract young readers.

The military possibilities of the airplane were not long lost on its developers and the public. Despite a pervasive hope that the craft would somehow elevate society to a new freedom and clarity of vision, speculation about the potential of aerial war came quickly. The most public was H.G. Wells's novel, *The War in the Air* (1908), postulating a war carried out by the aerial forces, principally dirigibles, of Germany and the United States. For all of its fancifulness, Wells's novel was singularly prescient. It anticipated aerial *Blitzkrieg* tactics, saturation bombing, the vulnerability of cities as well as warships to aerial attack, and total war involving the civilian populations of both countries. If it did not foresee the air-to-air combat that came to characterize World War I in the popular mind, it still laid the foundations for a vision of the wars to come.[2]

Those foundations gained solidity the following year, 1909, when Louis Blériot flew the English Channel. The relative ease with which Blériot crossed the twenty-mile stretch of water insulating England from the Continent made his achievement as rich in political symbolism as it was in technological. No longer could England count on the protective effect of the Channel; what had taken hours to cross in a ship was now crossed in minutes by an airplane. Moreover, no other country in the world could feel secure. National boundaries, protected by fences, gates, and surface troops, ceased to exist as far as the airplane was concerned.

The European powers took these revelations to heart. As early as 1910, England, France, and Italy began experimenting with aerial reconnaissance. The Italians, in 1911, became the first to use aircraft aggressively, dropping bombs from the relatively stable platform of an airship. The American Isaac N. Lewis demonstrated his lightweight machine gun in Europe in 1912, and its possibilities as an aerial weapon were widely acknowledged by 1913. The principal problem of an air-borne machine gun, how to fire straight ahead through the arc of the propeller, was overcome in improvised fashion by the French flier Roland Garros, who attached metal deflector plates to the propeller at the level of the gun. This practice became unnecessary by 1915, when Anthony Fokker perfected a synchronizing mechanism that allowed bullets to pass between the blades of a rotating propeller.[3] The fighter aircraft was a reality.

Despite the steady acceleration of military aviation across Europe, the United States showed little interest in following along. Not until 1909 did the United States Army buy its first airplane, the Wright Military Flyer designated Signal Corps No. 1. Two years later, in 1911, Congress included $125,000 in the Army Appropriation Act, providing for, among other items, the purchase of further airplanes and the creation of a military flying school in College Park, Maryland. Technical experimentation accompanied the basic training endeavor at College Park, with aircraft being used to explore artillery spotting, air-to-air and air-to-ground communication with wireless, aerial photography, and the aerial uses of the machine gun. Funding continued to be minimal, however; total appropriations for military aviation through 1914 totaled $435,000.[4]

The outbreak of war in Europe brought new pressure to bear upon the American military. At the outset of the war, in August 1914, Germany possessed 232 combat-ready aircraft, France had 162, and England somewhat fewer than one hundred. The United States had eight. These made up the 1st Aero Squadron, based in San Diego, California, where operations had been moved in late 1913 when the College Park base was shut down. Congressional neglect notwithstanding, some ranking officers within the military grasped the possibilities of the airplane. One of these was General George P. Scriven, Chief of the Signal Corps, who reported in 1914 that the airplane had permanently changed military tactics and went on to press for an air contingent made up of fifty airplanes distributed among four squadrons.[5] This contingent, initially the Aviation Section of the Signal Corps, coalesced as the U.S. Army Air Service and, in 1926, became the Army Air Corps.

On the scientific side, there was progress. Congress created the National Advisory Committee on Aeronautics (NACA) in 1915 to lead and oversee technical developments in aviation. Though it was later to achieve notable advances in airframe design and propulsion, one of its earliest efforts was the publication, in 1916, of a "Nomenclature for Aeronautics" list. This listing, widely distributed in the technical and popular press, provided standard terms for describing aeronautical matters; from "aerofoil" and "aileron" to "wing rib" and "yaw," it established for the American public a common vocabulary of flight.[6] Military development, however, continued to lag. Nowhere was this more dramatic than in the deploying of the 1st Aero Squadron in aid of General John J. Pershing's pursuit of Pancho Villa.

Sent to Columbus, New Mexico, in mid-1916, the squadron was flying eight obsolescent Curtiss JN-3 airplanes, and the machines' shortcomings soon became obvious. Desert conditions quickly weakened the laminated wood propellers and wooden frames of the aircraft, flying sand crept into engines despite all precautions, and poorly prepared landing strips made landing-gear damage a constant problem. The airplanes themselves added to the difficulties, for they were underpowered from the start and unsuited for the high altitudes (up to 12,000 feet) of the Mexican mountains. By the time the Squadron was recalled, in February 1917, only two of the eight were operational, and even those craft were in borderline condition.[7]

When the United States reluctantly entered the war, on 6 April 1917, the military lacked personnel and material, manufacturers were unprepared to shift to a war footing, and aircraft development itself lagged behind the levels achieved in Europe. Early on, two groups were formed to expedite manufacturing and development. One, the Aircraft Production Board, took on manufacturing issues, identifying five major problems. These were:

1) A lack of agreement on what types of aircraft were needed;
2) A lack of systematic training for mechanics and pilots;
3) A pressing need to expand aircraft manufacturing facilities;
4) A need to enlarge the force of aeronautical engineers; and
5) A need to coordinate acquisition and allocation of raw materials and the shipping of completed aircraft.[8]

The other group, the Bolling Commission, looked to the military side. Headed by Major Raynal C. Bolling and including a mix of military and civilian engineers, the Commission was charged with five tasks:

1) Buying manufacturing rights to various European airplanes and their parts;
2) Obtaining sample aircraft and parts to serve as models for American manufacturers;
3) Establishing guidelines for the outright buying of European aircraft;
4) Arranging for the training of American personnel at European bases; and
5) Making American raw materials available to the Allies.

The Committee's actions were to shape the course of American aviation, for they recommended the buying of French and British pursuit aircraft, which represented the cutting edge of aeronautical technology. For its part, the United States was to take on the building of bombing and observation aircraft, which were less vulnerable to rapid obsolescence, and the development of new training aircraft and their engines. American fliers soon cut their teeth on British De Havillands and French SPADs and Nieuports, while American factories began to produce the Liberty engine and the Curtiss JN-4—the legendary "Jenny."[9]

The nation's official neutrality notwithstanding, American involvement in the aerial war had already begun. Volunteer fliers started serving with the French Air Force in 1915, and, in 1916, were regularized into Escadrille N124, the group that, in December 1916, became the Lafayette Escadrille. Barely a year later, in January 1918, the Escadrille became the 103rd Squadron of the U.S. Army Air Service, the first American fighter squadron. Flying SPADs marked with the head of an Indian chief in full war regalia, the Escadrille became one of the legends of the war. Other squadrons moved into the limelight as the American presence overseas increased. The 94th Squadron (its insignia, the "Hat in the Ring," became a public icon) was the home of Eddie Rickenbacker, ultimately America's leading ace with a record of twenty-six enemy aircraft shot down. For its part, the 27th Squadron produced Frank Luke, the second-ranking American ace, whose famed disregard for military discipline brought him a simultaneous court-martial and a recommendation for the Distinguished Service Cross. Killed in action after only six months' service, Luke later received the Congressional Medal of Honor.[10]

The attention given the exploits of men like Rickenbacker and Luke only accelerated an already established movement: the adulation of the "ace," whatever side he might be flying for. In a war that increasingly was seen as one of massed machines and forces, the easy recognition of an individual flier gave him an extra cachet. Through the romanticizing of such figures as Rickenbacker, Luke, Roland Garros, Ernst Udet, Georges Guynemer, René Fonck, and Manfred von Richthofen, the fabled "Red Baron," the victorious flying man came to be "equated with that warrior of the pre-machine age, the knight. Then, too, there was something refreshing about having heroes who were not military professionals of high rank." It was an image that melded

Using the appeal of World War I to appeal to readers of 1932. Erisman-Odom Collection, Mary Couts Burnett Library, Texas Christian University.

handily with the emerging view of the flier as a superman. Rightly or wrongly, the aces came to embody an expression of manly chivalry and honor within an otherwise faceless and inexorable military undertaking, an elite fraternity democratically open to any person of ability, whatever his origins.[11]

The coming of war also brought new attention to military aviation in America. Aeronautical and other publications quickly began carrying news of European aircraft development; *Flying,* for example, offered Henry Woodhouse's "Aeronautics and the War" in its issue of September 1914. The *Scientific American* printed such pieces as John Jay Ide's "The Flying Machines of the Warring Powers" (6 March 1915), complete with silhouettes and comparative descriptions of French, German, and British aircraft, and, in the *Scientific American Supplement,* an examination of "Fighting in the Air: The Influence of Design on Tactics" (15 January 1916). With American involvement official, the topics expanded. The *Scientific American* for 6 October 1917 gave over almost an entire issue to a consideration of military aircraft. It sharpened its focus with Austin C. Lescarboura's "With the American Airmen of Tomorrow," recording a visit a New York training school. Lescarboura ended his article in an "I told you so" vein, noting that had there been earlier attention paid to military aviation, the nation would have been prepared for war.[12]

Six weeks later, with Colonel H.H. Arnold's "Building American Aviation," the *Scientific American* made the final connection between military aviation, progress, and the future. In explicit, concrete language, Arnold outlined the steps being taken to build the Air Service—the search for "men of cool-headedness and responsibility, well educated;" the coming of the Liberty Motor; and the building of aviation schools to provide pilots, observers, and radio operators. Were the war to end in an instant, he concluded, "it would leave America secure in aviation. . . . The solidity of its development not only is justified by the bitter exigencies of war, but is part of America's future progress."[13] Aviation is in and of itself an engine of progress, and attention given it for whatever reason, whether military or commercial, will benefit the nation at large.

Harry Lincoln Sayler, who had originated the aviation series stories, prepared the way for the tales of World War I aviation, although the deed was achieved posthumously. He had begun the "Boy Scouts of the Air" books (1912–1922; fourteen titles) as "Gordon Stuart," offering a series billed as "stirring stories of adventure in which real boys, clean-cut and wide-awake, do the things other wide-awake boys like to read about." When he died in 1913, after having completed only five titles in the series, his publishers, Reilly & Britton, continued the books with other authors under the Stuart name. The next six titles, the ones most actively involved with the war, were written by G.N. Madison, and the final three came from Henry Bedford-Jones.[14]

Although the "Boy Scouts of the Air" books were marketed as a series, most are free-standing volumes, unified only by their backgrounds in Scouting and flying. The earliest, *The Boy Scouts of the Air at Eagle Camp* (1912), is principally a story of woodcraft. A Chicago-based Scout patrol dubs itself the "Golden Eagle Patrol" and sets out for northern Michigan, where they cross paths with an air-struck youngster and break up a smuggling ring. The flying elements are minimal, but the troop returns to Chicago committed to the pursuit of aviation. The second, *The Boy Scouts of the Air at Greenwood School* (1912), moves to the milieu of the private school. When a Boy Scout troop is formed at Greenwood School, Don Collins assumes its leadership, discovers a nearby hidden workshop where helicopter research is going on, and thwarts a group of malcontents who want to destroy the secret craft.

Sayler's third volume, *The Boy Scouts of the Air in Northern Wilds* (1912), takes the Otter Patrol to the United States-Canada border, where they rescue an aviation experimenter, Jared Phillips, and survive a variety of adventures in the forests. In *The Boy Scouts of the Air in Indian Land* (1912), the setting moves to New Mexico, where a diverse group of boys forms the Thunder Bird Patrol and builds an airplane following plans developed by an ex-army flier, a man known only as Hawke. The final volume by Sayler, *The Boy Scouts of the Air on Flathead Mountain* (1913), tracks former newsboy Hal Kenyon, now a scholarship student at a manual-arts school in Colorado, as he rescues the downed flier, Johnson Miles, and helps him in perfecting a new airship design.

The Madison titles initially continue Sayler's pattern. *The Boy Scouts of the Air on the Great Lakes* (1914) returns to the Midwest. The remaining members of the Wolf Patrol of Chicago spend the summer at the vacation home of two of their number, sons of a senator, and discover an experimental airplane being developed for the government. Military matters enter with the next volume, however, and continue to color the series through 1919. In *The Boy Scouts of the Air in Belgium* (1915), four Scouts on a hiking trip in Belgium are stranded when war breaks out, tinker briefly with an airship combining dirigible and airplane elements, and make their way safely to behind the English lines. *The Boy Scouts of the Air in the Lone Star Patrol* (1916) involves the Lone Star Patrol of Chichua, Texas, in border skirmishes with Pancho Villa's forces, winning the respect of the nearby military squadron for their woodcraft and fortitude.

The remaining three Madison titles constitute a single, continued story of two teen-agers' participation in the war. *The Boy Scouts of the Air on Lost Island* (1917) tracks Tod Fulton and his inventor father as they try to market the senior Fulton's new airplane to the American military. The story then moves to *The Boy Scouts of the Air on the French Front* (1918). When Mr. Fulton is kidnapped by a German agent, Tod and his chum, Jerry Ring, follow him to France. They rescue Mr. Fulton, and, with the blessings of both their families, enlist in the Army Air Service. The final Madison title, *The Boy Scouts of the Air with Pershing* (1919), follows Tod and Jerry's adventures in the army, where they make observation flights, engage in dogfights with German forces, and assist in planting an Allied spy behind German lines.

The final titles in the series, by Henry Bedford-Jones, return events to the United States, but the war's presence lingers. In *The Boy Scouts of the Air in the Dismal Swamp* (1920), a Scout patrol, led by Scoutmaster Buck Walke, a former army flier now working for the government, practices woodcraft in the Dismal Swamp of Virginia and encounters a group of belligerent moonshiners. *The Boy Scouts of the Air at Cape Peril* (1921) takes a second group of Scouts to the Outer Banks of North Carolina, where they spend time with a pilot and his flier-photographer sidekick, treating storms and flying outings alike as a thorough-going lark. Finally, in *the Boy Scouts of the Air on Baldcrest* (1922), three Scouts study flying and woodcraft under the tutelage of a former army flier, Pelham Dodge. The three books are far more local color and adventure stories than flying stories, but the airplane is a prominent part of all three.

For the most part, the "Boy Scouts of the Air" books break little new ground. Although they tend to have larger casts than earlier series, the characters are familiar: intelligent, middle- to upper-middle-class boys with a knack for machinery and an interest in aviation. Zike Worden is a first-class Scout with an aviation merit badge and a model-airplane builder before getting his badge. The Scouts of the Lone Star Patrol have a laboratory-workroom in the basement of the town library, where "every available inch of space held tools, appliances, paraphernalia of one sort or another," from a wireless set to an electrical bench. Jerry Ring is "an eager student of one of the scientific magazines . . . [and had] listened to many a discussion of the latest wonders of invention."[15]

As in the earlier books, the boys encounter an adult mentor or patron, who endorses their enthusiasms and supports their interests with information and money. The amateur aviator Pelham Dodge, for example, "was not only well-off in this world's goods, but what is better, he was rich in good sense and good humor. . . . He took his patrol on hikes; he taught them to swim; he initiated them into woodcraft in all its branches, and now that aviation was his hobby, he proposed to perfect the three whose parents allowed them to indulge in it."[16] The boys come away from their experiences with a new respect for skill and determination. The Scouting ethic underlying the stories reinforces these qualities, making the books, as a series, worthwhile additions to the genre and, quite possibly, studied responses to Franklin Mathiews's attack on Stratemeyer and the Syndicate-produced titles.

New to the series, though, is the war. The books' first steps are tentative, addressing matters of mobilization rather than combat, making *The Boy Scouts of the Air on the French Front* a thumbnail history of the early days of the war effort. Tod Fulton's father has invented an airplane capable of hovering in mid-air, but his achievement is ignored by the authorities. "Mr. Fulton had first tried to interest the United States government in the airship, but we were at peace then, and the officials were slow to see the necessity of holding the invention for our own use. But the Great War had broken out, and Mr. Fulton, pro-English at heart, had offered it to agents of Great Britain." Although he gives the British an option to buy, they delay until Fulton is tempted to sell to a German envoy masked as a private businessman. When the envoy is uncovered, Fulton sells his craft to the Americans, and it proves to be "of inestimable value to the boys in khaki."[17]

Hints of the reality of war soon creep in, with glimpses of the strain of combat and its effects on the flier. By the time Tod and Jerry begin flying *With Pershing,* they have "looked upon many dreadful sights. . . . The life of an air pilot is full of deadly risks, and by degrees he becomes hardened to things that previously might have caused his cheeks to pale or started his heart to beating like a trip-hammer." Running parallel with this motif, moreover, is the boys' growing awareness of the military flier's distinctiveness: "Airmen are hardly subject to the rules concerning ordinary soldiers; something about the peril they continually face makes them entertain more genuine respect for each other's valor."[18] The fliers' mutual respect complements the image of the "ace," adding yet another level of romantic appeal.

"Stuart" reinforces the flier's uniqueness by stressing the liberating qualities of flight and the traits of the aviator. Civilian or military, the flier is raised to a new level of feeling and perception when he makes his way into the air, with the books advancing the same emotional and physical benefits found in the

Wright Flying School advertisements. Dave Hartley of the Wolf Patrol, at the controls of a biplane, has "the most wonderful moment of his life. . . . All things had merged into a wild thrill of exultation as the machine swept forward, bounced, and finally surged quietly into the air." Dave's flight is a civilian one, but the veteran Buck Walke waxes equally eloquent about his military days, remarking that "When you get up three or four thousand feet and travel with your compass and map, you feel as if you owned the vast heavens and that the earth was your plaything."[19] The evolution of the flier continues, as a sense of comprehensive unity blends with the already established physical and mental attributes of the type.

In addition, the books continue their quiet commentary on aviation progress with the introduction of timely, accurate details. Sayler himself continues to draw upon Lougheed's *Vehicles of the Air* and the *Scientific American*. When the ex-army flier Hawke tells the Thunder Bird Patrol that "swinging [wing tips] to the rear will be to increase the lifting power, while at the same time reducing the resistance of the air," he echoes the book explicitly. In a section on swinging wing tips, Lougheed writes: "the result of swinging them to the rear will be to increase the sustention and the tangential component forward." The helicopter that Don Collins, Scout leader at Greenwood Academy, stumbles upon, a dragonfly-like craft equipped with three wings fore and aft and chain-driven rotors amidships, is a close copy of the French-built Cornu helicopter, a craft widely publicized in mid-1908. "Stuart" presents Don as knowledgeable enough about aviation history to give full credit to the French researchers: "The aviation world—and Frenchmen particularly—have dreamed of a quick-ascending airship since man-flight began . . . ," and the helicopter is reflective of the most advanced aeronautical research.[20]

Sayler's successors move to still more timely sources. Bedford-Jones introduces a discussion of the high-lift "Alula fighting wing" in *On Baldcrest*. A cantilever wing of planked mahogany, with tapering wingtips and reverse curves, as Pelham Dodge points out, it produces an airplane with a ground speed of 180 M.P.H. and the capability of reaching an altitude of 3000 feet in seventy-two seconds. The Alula wing was prominent in both the British and American technical press throughout 1920 and 1921, but test data giving both the ground speed and the rate of climb appeared only in *Flight* for 20 October 1921 and *Aviation* for 5 December 1921.[21] Both reports were well-timed for Bedford-Jones's use in his 1922 offering.

The second war series to appear, Horace Porter's "Our Young Aeroplane Scouts," takes a more militaristic approach. Horace Porter DeHart, a journalist, produced twelve volumes between 1915 and 1919, a cluster of travelogue stories following the activities of Billy Barry and Henri Trouville as they trek through the war zones. Advertised as "stories of two American boy aviators in the great European war zone" in which "the fascinating life in midair is thrillingly described," the books are initially even-handed in their presentation of the opposing forces. They steadily become more pro-British, however, and, with America's entry into the war, turn intensely jingoistic as they talk of the Allies.

Not surprisingly, the boys are already adept at flying. Both are scientifically well-informed, and both have taken advantage of their individual circumstances to build their flying skills. Billy is part of an aircraft-building family and has grown up around airplanes and aeronautical discussions, while Henri, a French aristocrat living in the United States, "loved mechanics, trained right in the shops, and even aspired to radiotelegraphy, map-making aloft, and other fine arts of the flying profession." The two are known to be "fearless as air riders," and so are ready to deal with any exigency of the air they might encounter.[22]

The "Young Aeroplane Scouts" books open with the war as an acknowledged fact. *Our Young Aeroplane Scouts in France and Belgium* (1915) sends Billy and Henri to France in an effort to salvage the assets of the Trouville family, which were left behind at the outbreak of the war. Flying scouting missions for the British, the two enter France and retrieve the lost gold and jewels, are captured by the Germans, and spend the remainder of the book traveling with a German agent, the super-spy, Herr Roque. In *Our Young Aeroplane Scouts in Germany, or Winning the Iron Cross* (1915), the boys fly missions throughout eastern Europe as agents of Herr Roque, are commended by the German army, and end up in Petrograd in the hands of Russian forces. Their story continues in *Our Young Aeroplane Scouts in Russia* (1915), as they foil an anarchist plot, fly one of Igor Sikorsky's immense multi-engined bombers, and, reunited with British forces, move on to the Middle East.[23]

Our Young Aeroplane Scouts in Turkey, or Bringing the Light to Yusef (1915), finds Billy and Henri thwarting a tribal uprising against the western powers and trekking on to Cairo. From Cairo, they go to London, in *Our Young Aeroplane Scouts in England, or Twin Stars in the London Sky Patrol* (1916), join the Royal Flying Corps, are sent to a British squadron in France, and soon find themselves once more dealing with Herr Roque and his sleazy sidekick, Max. *Our Young Aeroplane Scouts in Italy, or Flying With the War Eagles of the Alps* (1916), lets them cross paths with Guglielmo Marconi, inventor of the wireless, and fly throughout the Mediterranean and Adriatic region. They rejoin the British for *Our Young Aeroplane Scouts at Verdun, or Driving Armored Meteors over Flaming Battle Fronts* (1917), flying an armored supership of their own design and joining an elite squadron in Romania.

Their adventures continue in *Our Young Aeroplane Scouts in the Balkans, or Wearing the Red Badge of Courage Among the Warring Legions* (1917), as they rescue missing fliers and steal a German mystery ship. When the United States enters the war, Billy and Henri transfer to the Lafayette Escadrille, and in *Our Young Aeroplane Scouts in the War Zone, or Serving Uncle Sam in the Great Cause of the Allies* (1918), take part in a variety of combat sorties. Billy returns to the States to stir support for the war effort in *Our Young Aeroplane Scouts Fighting to the Finish, or Striking Hard over the Sea for the Stars and Stripes* (1918), but, back in France, engages in scouting, bombing, and strafing missions. He and Henri take part in *Our Young Aeroplane Scouts at the*

Marne, or Harrying the Huns from Allied Battleplanes (1919), experimenting with high-altitude bombing, and, in *Our Young Aeroplane Scouts in at the Victory, or Speedy High Flyers Smashing the Hindenburg Line* (1919), retrieve a fortune in gold and art from behind the German lines and see the end of the war.

The "Young Aeroplane Scouts" books, unlike the "Boy Scouts of the Air" stories, mince few words in describing the ravages of modern war. The accounts are generalized, to be sure, but dwell on battle damage and casualties in a way that the earlier series does not. Flying an observation sortie in Italy, Billy and Henri are shocked to see the hand-to-hand fighting on the battlefield beneath, and later see the ground forces' endless retrieving and burying of the dead. That they themselves are not exempt becomes clear when a squadron leader tells them that "the life of the average aeroplane pilot at the front is thirty-one days."[24] Far-fetched and romanticized though their travels may be, Billy and Henri—and their readers—learn that war is a dangerous undertaking. In conducting that war, the airplane plays an ever-increasing role. Aerial reconnaissance figures in almost every story. New tactics emerge, including ground strafing and aerial bombing: "Bombs dropped from aeroplanes are probably the most deadly missiles now in use—more deadly even than big shells. . . . A machine gun from an aeroplane is bad enough, but a well-placed bomb is a massacre."[25] Readers openly see the emergence of the airplane as a weapon.

The military uses of airplanes bring about changes in the aircraft themselves, and Porter keeps his readers up to date. In Germany, Billy and Henri learn of the many types of warplanes, from dirigibles to scouting craft. Those craft are contemporaneous designs, and are mentioned by name and structure, including a "twin-engine Goth biplane of the 'pusher' type," the sixteen-passenger Sikorsky biplanes, and the German "flying whale"—the L.F.G. Roland C-II, so called because of its bulbous, semi-monocoque fuselage and eye-like windows to allow downward vision. Billy himself acknowledges the pace of change when, late in the series, he observes that "This war is changing and developing the aeroplane almost from hour to hour. . . . What we called marvels of the air two years ago, have no more relation to the machines of to-day than the clumsy attempts of a barnyard fowl to the flight of a swallow."[26] Porter strives to ensure that his readers are conscious of the evolution taking place, and of the possibilities it may offer.

To support his efforts, Porter, like his predecessors, draws freely upon contemporaneous sources. The boys' 1916 encounter with the French "invisible aeroplane," covered with "a transparent material looking like mica or celluloid, or a mixture of both," incorporates material from Neal A. Truslow's "The Transparent Airplane" in *Scientific American.* There Truslow describes the covering as "a transparent material which looks like a cross between mica and celluloid." Porter's words describing the bizarre camouflage patterns adopted by the Germans ("khaki-colored planes with greenish-gray wings, planes with red bodies, green wings and yellow stripes, [and] planes with red bodies of wings of green on top of blue") come explicitly from a 1917 *Scientific American* article on "Queer Camouflage of German Aeroplanes." Finally, when Billy details the components of a modern airplane ("Nails, 4,326; screws, 3,377; steel strappings, 921 [etc.]"), his figures repeat verbatim those in a components list published in *Scientific American* for 9 March 1918.[27]

Porter's efforts to make his books timely, modern, and accurate place the volumes squarely within the mainstream of technological transmission to the young. The "Young Aeroplane Scouts" books continue, even accelerate, the communicating of technical aviation knowledge to American youth. Readers learn of the most modern aircraft on both sides of the war, how these airplanes look, what goes into their construction, and how they perform in contrast to the performance of earlier designs. No detail is too small for Porter's stories, from the number of screws to the configuration and coloration of the wings. The books assimilate aviation-related details as quickly as they become public, pass them along to young readers, and bolster the readers' sense of being at the forefront of modernity.

Edward Stratemeyer, ever the cautious businessperson, held off producing books of the aerial war until eight months after America's declaration of war. In early 1918, he launched the "Air Service Boys" series (1918–1920; six titles). Once in the field, however, he moved quickly; three titles appeared in 1918, one in 1919, and the final two in 1920. Outlines for these books are not available, but manuscript releases establish that two well-regarded authors within the Syndicate, St. George Rathborne and Howard R. Garis, produced the stories for the "Charles Amory Beach" house name. Rathborne (1854–1938) had been an associate of Stratemeyer's since their days at Street & Smith, where he contributed to the Nick Carter and Frank Merriwell stories; over his career, he produced some seventy novels and 250 boys' books.[28] Garis, meanwhile, having proved his worth with the "Motor Boys" and "Great Marvel" books, was busily turning out "Baseball Joe" and "Tom Swift" titles for the Syndicate.

Regardless of authorship, the "Air Service Boys" stories hew closely to the Stratemeyer formula. Tom Raymond, the son of an inventor, who "had always been deeply interested in aeronautics," and his chum, Jack Parmly, enter military service and travel the front lines in a variety of craft.[29] They are introduced in *Air Service Boys Flying for France, or The Young Heroes of the Lafayette Escadrille* (1918), where in 1917 they pass through the Signal Corps flying school and join the Lafayette unit. They capture a German spy, survive an air raid in London and dogfights in France, and win the *Croix de Guerre*. Their exploits continue in *Air Service Boys Over the Enemy's Lines, or The German Spy's Secret* (1918), retrieving stolen documents and uncovering a German spy ring as the United States enters the war.

The third and fourth volumes, *Air Service Boys over the Rhine, or Fighting Above the Clouds* (1918) and *Air Service Boys in the Big Battle, or Silencing the Big Guns* (1919), both by Garis, relate the boys' first encounter with the German "Big Bertha" long-range cannon, their rescue of Tom's father from the Germans, and a series of bombing sorties, culminating in their transferring to an American squadron in France. *Air Service Boys Flying for Victory, or Bombing the Last German Stronghold* (1920), set in late 1918, finds them flying bombing raids and ground-support missions as Allied pressure on the Germans intensifies. The final volume, *Air Service Boys Over the Atlantic, or The Longest Flight on Record* (1920), introduces the wealthy Lieutenant Colin Beverly, who has commissioned a long-range Martin bomber at his own expense to fly a bombing mission to Berlin and back. He offers the craft to Tom and Jack, and the two promptly fly the Atlantic non-stop.

Perhaps because of the circumstances of their writing (Rathborne was an older writer with little interest in technological detail, while Garis was giving most of his attention to the "Tom Swift" books, with their diverse examples of technological advances), the "Air Service Boys" stories contain relatively little aviation detail. Some aircraft types, notably Caudrons and Nieuports, are mentioned by name, the Lafayette Escadrille insignia is cited, and readers get an occasional glimpse of tactics and conditions. In *Flying for France,* for example, "Beach" reports how Nieuports would fly cover for observation planes below. Readers also glimpse the trials of open-cockpit flying through the description of aviators' "fur-lined union suits, with fur overcoats, gloves, and caps . . . ; they would be soaring to great heights, where the atmosphere was almost Arctic in its intensity."[30] For the most part, though, aviation details are generalized, serving only as background for Tom and Jack's derring-do.

Military detail of another sort, however, crops up in Garis's contributions. Thanks to Garis's varied interests and access to sources, up-to-date information concerning other weaponry finds its way into the books from his pen. In *Over the Rhine,* Allied forces must deal with the eighty-mile range of the "Big Bertha" cannon, giving "Beach" an opportunity to introduce a lengthy discussion of ordnance and artillery possibilities. The book offers details of a "sub-calibre" shell (cognate with today's sabot rounds, which give a small-diameter projectile a higher velocity by encasing it in a large-caliber sleeve) and the possibility of a "double shell" driven by the sequential firing in flight of secondary propellant charges. Garis acknowledged payment for this manuscript on 7 May 1918. Less than a month earlier, in its issues of 6 April 1918 and 20 April 1918, *Scientific American* published two articles discussing both of the shell types and providing the same distance and altitude figures used by Garis.[31]

Although technical detail may be lacking in the "Air Service Boys" books, emotional detail is present in abundance. Throughout the books, fliers appear as special persons, for "to be an aviator places one, especially in England and France, in a special class." The hazards, moreover, give the aviator special qualities: If a flier is to "make a success of his calling he's got to have nerves of steel," and, should he "lose his grip and confidence because of any unusual danger, his usefulness is gone."[32] The flier may receive the praise and admiration of allies, but he earns it with his physical fitness and mental discipline.

Along with a regard for fitness and discipline comes a sense of aviation history and the ongoing pace of its technical progress. The narrator in the opening volume reports that "the desire to learn to fly was rapidly becoming a fever in the veins of a multitude of daring young Americans." As one of those forward-looking young men, Tom Raymond has long been a student of the Wright brothers' work, and "his brain was filled with the amazing possibilities that awaited a successful termination of their work and that of the French experimenters who were working along similar lines." After he and Jack successfully fly the Atlantic, they see their accomplishment in visionary terms: "The main thing is that we . . . proved that the dream of all real airmen could be made to come true."[33] Aviation is a progressive enterprise, and they have made a contribution to its progress.

So, too, have others, as "Beach" goes on to point out. By the time *Air Service Boys Over the Atlantic* appeared in 1920, trans-Atlantic flight was a reality. The first crossing of the ocean by a heavier-than-air ship was accomplished by the United States Navy's Curtiss NC-4 in May 1919; John Alcock and Arthur Whitten-Brown, both veterans of British military service, made the first nonstop crossing in a Vickers Vimy bomber in June 1919; and the British dirigible R-34 made the first east-to-west crossing in July 1919. "Beach" gives credit where credit is due. Though Tom's father predicts that the boys' record will stand, "he could not foresee how even before the peace treaty had been signed a number of ambitious aviators would actually cross the Atlantic, one crew in a huge heavier-than-air machine, another in an American seaplane, and still a third aboard a mighty dirigible, making the passages with but a day or so intervening between flights."[34] The comment is telling, for it reminds Stratemeyer's readers that reality can outstrip art when it is propelled by aviation.

War's end saw a dramatic falling-off of interest in the military. The army underwent a period of rapid shrinkage, reflected in a slowing of promotions, a thinning of the ranks, and the rapid selling-off of surplus military aircraft, engines, and supplies. Curtiss JN-4s could be had for $1,500 each, or less; unflown Curtiss "Speed Scouts," still in their crates and equipped with Gnome rotary engines, went for $2,000; and H-16 flying boats, with a 95-foot wingspan and twin Liberty engines, were available for $11,053. *Aerial Age Weekly* initially proclaimed the sell-off as an opportunity to stimulate national interest in commercial and general aviation. The numbers of former military fliers flooding the market, however, at last prompted the magazine to run on its humor page a joke remarking that the next war could not come along until the United States had "gotten rid" of its current army of 200,000, and advertisements from veterans seeking some kind of aviation job were commonplace.[35]

The ready availability of a variety of aircraft in the immediate post-war years quickly produced a class of individuals called "gypsy fliers," or, later, "barnstormers." Military-trained aviators or air-minded civilians, these fliers snapped up the inexpensive airplanes and strove to make a living providing aerial thrills for the general public. Some traveled the country from open field to open field, offering airplane rides to the residents for a few dollars a flight. Others formed impromptu airshow troupes, performing aerobatics, parachute drops, wing-walking, and other daredevil stunts before a paying audience. Some went on to establish small commercial airfields, providing hangarage, repairs, flying lessons and occasional charter service to the public. A few, capitalizing upon the Prohibition era, turned to aerial rum-running. Such fliers lived a perilous hand-to-mouth existence at best, but they acquainted the American public with the possibilities of flight, encouraged popular regard for the aviator as a person set apart, and fueled a growing public interest in what was to become general aviation.[36]

Commercial interest in uses of the airplane grew as well, most notably in the creation of an aerial mail service. Government-sponsored air mail flights had begun in May 1918, and, in April 1919, the Post Office Department published a specifications list as a call for ten specialized mail-carrying airplanes. The craft were ideally to have a cargo capacity of 1,500 to 3,000 pounds, with a nominal cruising speed averaging 100 M.P.H. at an altitude of 6,000 feet. The following year, the Department announced plans for transcontinental airmail service, and called for bids on a number of proposed routes. The Air Mail Service began investigations into night-flying techniques in early 1923, and, in April of that year, began construction on a series of beacons spanning the route between Chicago, Illinois, and Cheyenne, Wyoming. By 1926 the line of beacons extended from New York to Salt Lake City, Utah. Better instrumentation accompanied developments in lighting and aircraft, and reliable, coast-to-coast air mail service was a reality.[37]

Not surprisingly, interest in war stories fell off as new topics occupied the press. After reaching a high of 25,730 volumes sold in 1919, Stratemeyer's "Air Service Boys" series declined until 1925, its final year in print, when its sales totalled three volumes. In the years following the Armistice, only two series of note attempted to take up the transition from military to civilian flight. The first was the "Aeroplane Boys" series (1921–1927; three titles) by Captain Frank Cobb, reprinted in 1927 as the "Aviator Series," covering the era between the Armistice and 1923. In three unconnected stories, *Battling the Clouds, or For a Comrade's Honor* (1921), *An Aviator's Luck, or The Camp Knox Plot* (1921), and *Dangerous Deeds, or The Flight in the Dirigible* (1927),

Cobb sets out to tell the tale of "ordinary boys . . . upon whose courage and clear-thinking the forward march of aeronautics has depended."[38]

The first volume, *Battling the Clouds,* follows chums Bill Sherman and Ernest Breeze from Fort Sill to army flying school in Lawton, Oklahoma. Ernest's goal, "now that the war is over," is to "do postal work, or ferry or excursion lines instead of hanging around an army aviation camp. My aim is to be as perfect a flier as I possibly can." Bill, less mundane, finds flying a near-religious experience: "He was so exalted and so thrilled by the wonderful experience through which he was passing that he seemed to hear all sorts of celestial sounds. . . . He felt as uplifted in soul as he was in body. Somehow he longed more than ever to be a good boy; to harbor good thoughts; to do good deeds.[39] The transcendental spirit evident here becomes more significant later, but Cobb's linking of flight and transcendence is a notable example of the emerging moral benefits seen to be gained from flight. The boys respond in different ways to the occasion of flight (Ernest wants to be "as perfect a flier" as he can, while Bill longs to "be a good boy"), but the idealism of both is explicit. Physically, intellectually, spiritually, and, now, idealistically and morally, the flier is becoming a special person.

An Aviator's Luck, the second volume, picks up its four teen-aged heroes at the Camp Knox training site, which is soon to be closed because most of its students "were going into aviation for commercial service." The boys befriend Lt. Ernest Beezley, *de facto* commander of the site, and join him in occasional flights. Their response is also exalting, even liberating: "On and on they flew. They no longer knew the country. Nothing seemed to matter. They were masters of space; they felt as though they could fly into the face of the sun itself; they felt as though they owned that vast infinitude about, above, below them." The final volume, *Dangerous Deeds,* has former military aviator Lawrence Petit flying jewels, money, and business documents about the United States and Europe. He becomes embroiled in a plot to steal the crown jewels of Morania, successfully returns the jewels, and then goes on to

England, where he gets a glimpse of the flying clubs that attest to the widespread presence of civilian, general aviation.[40]

Minor though they are, the "Aeroplane Boys" books offer a tantalizing glimpse of things to come. They project a society in which flying is commonplace, and two of the volumes even hint at the participation of women in sport flying. They suggest the coming of commercial aviation, whether in postal service, fixed-base charter service, or business applications, and the growing public acceptance of flight as a necessary consequence. And, most notably, they inject into flying a new metaphysical component. The qualities that make the aviator physically and intellectually superior now extend to his moral makeup, and Cobb paves the way for the presenting of aviation as a force of moral improvement.

More substantial, and more noteworthy, is Thomson Burtis's "Russ Farrell" series (1924–1929; five titles). Burtis, an army-trained pilot, did not see combat during his five-year career in the military, but by 1920 had achieved the rank of second lieutenant. He resigned his commission in 1923, knocked about in a variety of jobs, and finally turned to writing. Throughout the 1920s and 1930s he was a regular contributor to *American Boy* magazine, publishing stories with aviation, sports, and circus backgrounds that reflected his own experiences. His first book, *Russ Farrell, Airman,* like several of his later works, was serialized in *American Boy,* and appeared in hard covers in 1924. Thanks to the "Russ Farrell" and other flying stories, by 1928 he was well-established enough as an aviation author to be featured as one of the notables greeting contestants at the national model airplane contest held in Detroit.[41]

The five "Russ Farrell" books make up a thumbnail history of the life of a flier in the post-war army. The first, *Russ Farrell, Airman* (1924), covering the 1919–1921 period, follows Massachusetts-born Russ's experiences in the military, from basic training to his participation in the sinking of the *Ostfriesland* in 1921; in the process, Russ develops a high regard for the ideas of Billy Mitchell and gains a glimpse of the future of aviation. The second, *Russ Farrell Test Pilot* (1926) takes him to "Cook" Field (actually McCook Field, home of the Air Service's Engineering Division, its principal research-and-development facility) in Dayton, where he further samples that future. He competes in the 1924 Pulitzer Race, flies a variety of up-to-date experimental aircraft, from the de Bothezat helicopter to the Barling Bomber, a six-engined behemoth that, at the time, was the largest airplane in the world. On the side, he tests an earth-inductor compass and techniques for aerial crop-dusting. In the third, *Russ Farrell Circus Flyer* (1927), he joins an army-sponsored flying circus intended to raise the public's consciousness of aviation and takes part in the making of a commercial film with an aviation background.

The fourth title, *Russ Farrell Border Patrolman* (1927) takes him to the Big Bend region of Texas, where he flies with the Border patrol and thwarts a plot to smuggle illegal aliens into the United States. *Russ Farrell Over Mexico* (1929), the final volume, traces his activities on leave from the army, as he serves as a commercial flier for a consortium seeking to develop oil resources in Mexico. Far more adventurous and exciting than the "Aeroplane Boys" books, the "Russ Farrell" stories are among the earliest to mesh the "flying ace" mystique of the war years with the "gypsy flier" aura of post-war days to create a "flying type."

Burtis's characterization of Russ brings together a number of elements already present in aviation mythology. Russ is a thoroughly manly sort, whom any boy might hope to emulate; a "lean and rangy" youth, his eyes glow with "a veritable flame of excited anticipation" and he radiates "an effect of tingling vitality and abounding health" that complements his "inborn, cool nerve and the hot, surging spirit of the pioneer." He has been "a 'nut' about flying since the fascination of it had overcome him years before," and all other elements of life are secondary to his devotion to flight.[42] He is an early embodiment of the "aviator" type that will become a fixture in the literature as aviation develops, and anticipates in singular ways the actual appearance and personality of Charles A. Lindbergh.

Whatever their other merits, the Russ Farrell books make two significant contributions to the literature of the era. The first is their extensive introduction of up-to-date aeronautical information; the airplanes Russ flies are unquestionably real, and they play central roles throughout the books. This is clearest in *Russ Farrell Test Pilot,* for which, according to the editor of *American Boy,* Burtis "went to McCook Field at Dayton, Ohio, the foremost experimental airplane laboratory in the world, and gathered fact material to use in a new series. . . . Practically all the tremendously interesting *new* things described in these forthcoming air stories are being perfected now."[43] The "newness" of aviation developments is central to the book's appeal, and the prospects of the developments' becoming practical reality speak to aviation as progress.

External evidence confirms both the timeliness of his information and the likelihood of his being at McCook Field. The de Bothezat Helicopter (tested in February 1923) and the earth inductor compass (tested March 1924) are described in *Air Services Newsletters* for 1923 and 1924, a publication that Burtis, as an ex-army flier, would be aware of, while *U.S. Air Service,* another service-oriented magazine, discusses the Barling Bomber and aerial crop-dusting for boll weevils in its issues of August and December 1923. In addition, Russ's high-altitude flight replicates an incident happening to John A. Macready (holder of the altitude record and in 1924 chief of the McCook Field Flight Test Branch) that was not aired in print until 1926. Russ, like Macready, is trapped in a pressurized cabin at high altitude when a relief valve fails and comes close to losing his life.[44] One can only infer that Burtis drew on his army connections to talk with Macready and incorporate the story into his book.

The books' second contribution is their overt linking of aviation with personal worth and national, even cultural, progress. Russ's own zest for life is tempered with "a certain steady sense of responsibility combined with a desire to contribute, in some way, to something worth while in living." He understands the need to educate the public that General Mallory (Burtis's version of Brigadier General William "Billy" Mitchell) advocates: "America must be stimulated into proper interest in the possibilities of the air and proper development of them." Mallory, like Mitchell, sees aviation as a means to stir national identity and national pride. The European nations had early on seized upon advances in aviation, especially military aviation, to stimulate national pride and national unity; if a similar linkage can be stimulated in the United States, patriotic zeal will combine with technological prowess to open a wealth of new possibilities for flight. He is, therefore, mounting "a tremendous publicity campaign . . . to keep the air game in front of the people and get them thinking about it, and educated to what can be done right now."[45] Russ shares Mallory's passion, and throws himself into the project with fervent zeal.

Russ's enthusiasm is driven by his understanding that old ways must give way to new, and that work in aviation necessarily requires one to look to the future. Although he can feel that "all there was in life was bound up in the roaring diapason of power that flowed from the motor ahead of him," he also knows that "ducking around on the wings of ships for the fun of it, just because he could, no longer [was] the end and object of existence," and is "not sorry that the end was near. He had higher ambitions now—wanted to be more than just a successful daredevil."[46] He is an attractive representative of the progressive spirit that aviation encourages, and his appeal for young readers is undeniable.

Civilian developments notwithstanding, military flying of the World War I era made a comeback in two series appearing in the late 1920s and early 1930s. The first was Major Henry H. Arnold's "Bill Bruce" series (1928; six titles), written while Arnold was stationed at Fort Riley, Kansas, as commander of the 16th Observation Squadron. His assignment there was not a voluntary one. As Chief of the Air Service Information Office, Arnold, like his mentor, "Billy" Mitchell, had been an outspoken advocate for continued aviation research and an air force wholly separate from the army. Following Mitchell's court-martial in 1925, Arnold's superiors learned that he had been using the Information Office to encourage support for Mitchell. Offered either a court-martial or assignment to a less-desirable post, Arnold made the pragmatic choice.[47]

Arnold made the most of his new position, working steadily to raise the profile of the squadron and its single airplane. He had, though, ample time to work on other projects, and returned to his interest (seen in his 1917 writings) in publicizing aviation to the public. With the "Bill Bruce" books he attempted to interpret the appeal of aviation for young readers. Here, as in earlier times, he saw himself as a missionary for aviation, working to inform and excite the public about the history and possibilities of flight. In a later letter to a friend, he remarked that he wanted "to give facts, interspersed by thrills and sensations, which would give the reader a comprehensive idea of the development of aviation. The thrills and sensations filled the boy's desire in that direction while he absorbed the facts."[48] The series he produced spans American aviation from its earliest days to the (then) present, touches upon military and civilian applications, and gives a broadly historical picture of a realm in transition. By directing the series toward a youthful audience, he reinforces the appeal of aviation to the young and instills in them a sense of all that aviation may offer.

Bill Bruce and the Pioneer Aviators (1928) places its young hero, Bill Bruce (named after Arnold's second son, William Bruce Arnold) at the very heart of early aviation: He talks with Wilbur Wright, sees Glenn Curtiss's flight from Albany to New York, and, in the last section of the book, is present at the International Aviation Meet at Belmont Park in 1910. From these experiences he comes away with a nagging curiosity about the future. All of the airplanes he has seen, he muses, are "different in construction and principle, but had been built for the same purpose—to fly through the air. Which was the proper type and after which would the airplane of the future pattern?"[49] What path will aviation take? Will aircraft be stable or unstable, monoplanes or biplanes, tractor- or pusher-powered? The books go on to trace the ensuing developments and continue Arnold's fictionalized history of aviation.

Bill Bruce, the Flying Cadet (1928) has Bill joining the Army Air Service on the day the United States enters World War I, and follows him through a detailed account of basic training. Kept on as a test pilot and instructor, he feeds his curiosity about aircraft by flying Jennies, Thomas-Morse Scouts, and two-seater Le Peres, in the process introducing his readers to three current types. From his training and his subsequent experiences, he gains more than simple knowledge. As he awaits reassignment at story's end, Bill muses that "nothing that he did gave the zest to life that the thrills of aviation had given him."[50] He gets still more of those thrills in *Bill Bruce Becomes An Ace* (1928), when he is sent to France and billeted with the 94th Aero Squadron; his roommate, conveniently, is Eddie Rickenbacker, and he ultimately becomes an ace in his own right. Returning to the United States following the Armistice, Bill works briefly as a test pilot flying captured German aircraft, then is transferred to the 9th Observation Squadron. His work there is covered in *Bill Bruce on Border Patrol* (1928), as he compares the tedium of routine patrol flying in rickety DH-4s with the thrills and uncertainty of combat. He gets his share of flying, however, taking part in an air show race involving three more current types, a SPAD, an SE-5, and a captured Fokker D-VII; the latter, which entered service with the German forces in April 1918, was a singularly advanced design that is still considered the outstanding fighter plane of the World War I era.[51]

Rescued from patrol duty in *Bill Bruce in the Trans-Continental Race* (1928), he and two comrades take part in the Trans-Continental Reliability Race of 1919. The race, a brainchild of "Billy" Mitchell, was intended to test the mechanical reliability of a range of current aircraft, explore possible routes for transcontinental commercial flights, and keep aviation in the public eye. Most of the entries were DH-4 craft, but eight SE-5s, two Martin bombers, and two Fokkers were also included. Nine fliers were killed in accidents during the race, and the DH-4 came under further criticism for its housing the pilot between the fuel tank and the engine. The design aggravated the danger to the pilot of fire following a crash, and contributed to the DH-4's nickname of "Flying Coffin."[52] The final volume, *Bill Bruce on Forest Patrol* (1928), is a tired piece of work, taking Bill to the West Coast where he flies spotting missions for artillery practice, then moves to Oregon to spot forest fires for civil defense officials.

Overall, the books carry out Arnold's purposes. They talk of the educational value of model-aircraft building and the aeronautical knowledge that the hobby imparts; they supply information about the steady development of aviation; and they make evident the individual and corporate efforts entailed.[53] They add to their readers' awareness of aircraft types and the vocabulary of flight. They talk dispassionately of combat flying's hazards and demands, and show the technological developments that wartime flying has generated. They take a look at current efforts to advance aircraft technology, and they give a memorable glimpse of the problems of a military flier during the immediate post-war period. Most of all, though, they show flying as something that at last is practical—an enterprise that offers enormous possibilities for the future as hardware, instrumentation, techniques, and applications slowly come together into an accessible, reliable adjunct to contemporary life.

If the "Bill Bruce" books attempt to give a reasonably accurate picture of military flying, the "Air Combat Series" (1932–1937; seven titles), written jointly by Thomson Burtis and Eustace L. Adams, is unabashed wish-fulfillment. Appearing fifteen years after the end of World War I and oblivious to the political and technological developments that have occurred in the interim, the books look backward to the era of the Red Baron and the classic flying aces. Dust-jacket copy is a blatant appeal to the legendary past: "Daredevil exploits of these army and navy flyers over the front [make] breathless reading, and their adventures have the ring of truth in them for both author-flyers take them from their own rich experiences as wartime aviators."[54] The books openly draw upon the diverse appeals of the mystique of the wartime ace, the manly, all-American image of the aviator, and the adrenaline-rich excitement of the open-cockpit dogfight. They reinforce a growing stereotype, and they do it well.

To their credit, Burtis and Adams knew their material. Burtis, as we've seen, was familiar with army flying and tactics, though he never flew combat. Adams, for his part, served in France as a member of the American Ambulance Service in 1916, transferred to the U.S. Naval Service around 1917, and flew coastal defense patrols along the Atlantic Coast until war's end. He then built

First of the "Air Combat" series (1932), introducing "Rud" Riley and the excitement of military flying. Erisman-Odom Collection, Mary Couts Burnett Library, Texas Christian University.

a career as an editor and writer, working for *Popular Science Monthly,* contributing to the *Saturday Evening Post, Cosmopolitan,* and other "slick" magazines, and writing novels, including his part of the "Air Combat" series and his earlier (1927–1932) series of "Andy Lane" books.[55] His "Air Combat" volumes are marginally less swashbuckling than Burtis's, but the series overall unstintingly offers a flier's life as one of brisk adventure and conscientious non-conformity.

Burtis's four titles track the career of Texas-born Rudford "Rud" Riley as he starts to fly for the Royal Canadian Air Force, transfers to the American Air Service, and flies combat in Europe. *Daredevils of the Air* (1932), spans the 1915–18 period, introducing Rud, acquainting him with several airplane types, and establishing him as a first-class pilot. *Four Aces* (1932) follows him as he flies Italian Caproni bombers and American LePeres, and becomes part of a hush-hush photo-reconnaissance unit used "to get mosaics of particular importance and under particularly hazardous circumstances."[56]

Wing for Wing (1932) pairs Rud with the notorious Lieutenant Colonel "Stormy" Lake, a flier known for his indifference to regulations and disregard for safety, as the two begin a long and deadly competition with the German ace, Baron von Baer—an obvious reference to Manfred von Richthofen, the "Red Baron" of legend. In Burtis's final volume, *Flying Blackbirds (1932),* Rud takes command of the elite "Blackbird" squadron, a unit equipped with state-of-the-art aircraft and intended for special combat duties. Aided by "Stormy" Lake, he at last defeats Baron von Baer and anticipates further adventures with his "aërial shock troops."[57]

The scene shifts to the navy with Adams's three volumes, following a Dartmouth sophomore, Ensign Jimmy Deal, through a series of adventures in France. *Doomed Demons* (1935) establishes Jimmy as the bane of Lieutenant Commander "Bull" Meehan's life, follows him as he steals a Halberstadt seaplane and blocks a German submarine base by bombing a canal lock in Ostend, and ends with his winning the grudging respect of the traditionalist

Meehan. In *Wings of the Navy* (1936), he is assigned to flying blimp patrols along the English Channel, captures a German submarine, and strengthens his friendship with "Bull" Meehan. The final volume, *War Wings* (1937), takes him to the front where he flies as a spotter for Allied naval cannon used to shell enemy fortifications.

Whether written by Burtis or Adams, the "Air Combat" stories share a number of compelling traits. One is their wide-eyed admiration for the hardware of flight; although the aircraft are, by the standards of the 1930s, obsolete, they nonetheless appear as modern marvels of military might. Rud's unit gets some of the earliest Allied Nieuports, "faster by twenty miles an hour than any other ship . . . on either side." They live up to their billing, and Rud finds that his craft "seemed like a high-powered rifle contrasted to a popgun. It answered every whim, as though it knew what his mind was thinking." Even more remarkable are the ships given the Blackbirds, which are "so incomparably the best he had ever handled." The new aircraft, "horribly beautiful as they swept through the air like five shining black projectiles," are superb machines that give "those master flyers a new lease on life."[58] Though they may be obsolescent in reality, the airplanes featured in the series still embody the best of technological progress. Their advanced status enhances their pilots' exceptional flying skill, and they bring about a significant melding of man and machine.

A second shared trait is the books' furthering of the camaraderie of the air. The experiences that airmen share, be they army, navy, or, by extension, civilian, develop a brotherhood that outstrips anything found in mundane life. For Rud, even in his earliest days, the men of his unit seem to him a single, cohesive organism. The experiences they have undergone in the air have forged a kinship "deeper and more intangible than friendship," and their shared respect and trust "transcended anything that Rud had ever known." Bull Meehan, for his part, despite his curmudgeonly dismay over Jimmy Deal's recklessness, still can feel a professional rapport with the junior officer.

Flying as a passenger with Jimmy, he feels an unaccustomed warmth "toward the silent, helmeted lad in front of him. There was an intangible feeling of companionship between the two of them sitting up there so alone in the skies."[59] These bonds, intangible though they appear, are closer and more permanent than any found in the non-flying world.

Finally, the books strengthen the portrayal of the pilot-ace as a person who tends to be carefree and happy-go-lucky in his outlook, but who balances such irreverence with high competence in the air. Marked by a mixture of seriousness and self-mockery, "Rud, except in moments of great stress, never forgot to laugh at himself." Jimmy, for his part, "carefree, happy-go-lucky, loving a fight as well as he loved a frolic . . . , was outstanding at Dartmouth only in the number of times he was reported for infractions of rules." These traits, however, are the very ones that make them distinctive. Rud's quizzical skepticism helps him to grow from a "headstrong, fiery young Southerner into a poised, competent, clear-thinking man," while Jimmy, who is drawn to flying because of its "spirit of romance," at last impresses even Bull Meehan as having a special quality: "Youth, perhaps, unhampered by iron-clad discipline and tradition. A carelessness, perhaps, of the future."[60] Both youngsters are exemplars of healthy American manhood. The headstrong, devil-may-care outlook they embrace complements their technical skill and responsibility, making them distinctive citizens for an up-and-coming time, and their appeal is one no boy could resist.

Despite lasting for barely two decades, the war-era books still contribute substantially to the development of the aviation genre. They demonstrate that aviation had met and surpassed goals for flight that a column in *Aerial Age Weekly* had announced in 1919.[61] The Atlantic had been flown, and the Pacific was soon to follow. Observation techniques pioneered during the war were being applied to peacetime mapping and aerial exploration. Commercial mail transportation was a *fait accompli,* and scheduled commercial service was only a matter of time. While the airplane as a weapon was now an accepted fact, it was not condemned; its very versatility, as proven in the war, raised the possibility of countless peacetime uses. These uses involved applications to civilian life as well, whether in barnstorming as an entertainment or sport flying as a recreation.

By the early 1920s, airplanes were very much within the public eye. They were visible in the air, they could be touched and felt at air shows and local airports, and they seemed within the reach of persons of even modest substance. The events of the war made obvious the many possibilities of the airplane, and the selling-off of aircraft following the war put ships into the hands of persons who had previously only dreamed of being able to fly. Manufacturers, recognizing the growing appeal of flight, began to explore the possibilities of marketing new aircraft directly to the public, and schools of aviation continued their spread throughout the country. Despite the complexities of their construction and operation, airplanes were increasingly seen as accessible. They offered the chance for a newer, faster, freer life, and the public responded.

A second contribution is the books' emphasis upon the skills of flight. Although flying may be an increasingly accessible activity, it remains a demanding one, and the aspiring aviator must of necessity master its special skills. Fliers may be carefree and happy-go-lucky in their personal lives, but they are unfailingly conscientious and capable in their professional lives. The Air Service Boys examine all their equipment with care, for "their very lives might depend on a little thing, and no one could afford to neglect even trifles." Pelham Dodge makes clear to the Boy Scouts of the Air that "if there was one lesson I had learned [in the Air Service] it was carefulness. Before every flight I'd spend no end of time looking over the machine to see that every wire, screw and turnbuckle was in perfect trim." Burtis's General Mallory agrees in principle, staffing the "Blackbirds" with men who combine "a high degree of skill, initiative, daring, and downright flying genius."[62] Whatever its other attributes, flying is a skilled undertaking, and the conscientiousness it imparts is easily transferred to other pursuits.

Finally, and most provocatively, the books speak eloquently of the exalting qualities of flight. In the air one can find inspiration, determination, and uplift. Their settings may be the front lines of combat or the grass strips of the gypsy flier, but over and over, the books return to the ways in which the physical act of flying can lift a person out of himself. Whether it's a simple resolution to "be a good boy," as Bill Sherman determines in *Battling the Clouds,* the "higher ambitions" that Russ Farrell feels in *Circus Flyer,* or the intangible kinships forged among the men of the "Air Combat" stories, the books imply that there is more to life than simple existence. A human being can live an entirely productive, humdrum life and neither know nor desire anything better. Through the agency of flight, however, he can glimpse greater possibilities, and those possibilities can lift him to a new, and potentially greater, plane of existence.

They were not alone in their vision of flight. C.A. Wragg, writing in *Aerial Age Weekly* for 10 October 1921, offered to the air-sensitive public a vision of a new era, the "Aerial Age." In this age, aircraft will become aesthetic objects as well as practical ones, subliminally communicating a "harmony of proportion" to the citizenry and stimulating a broader, more balanced sense of one's very existence. Those citizens, moreover, will themselves be changed as persons, for the harmony of the aerial instrument will communicate itself to the individual spirit, with beneficent results for all. In flight, he remarks, "The soul is elevated and rests in the assurance of a larger fellowship than has ever before existed on earth. Such conditions and viewpoint are perhaps the best that could be contrived for the germination of the ideas that lead to the unity of races and to individual and international peace."[63]

Wragg is in essence preaching to the choir, spinning his vision for persons already attuned to aviation. Transmitting those views to an as yet unpersuaded audience would require something more, but the means to do so were beginning to fall into place. Aircraft were accessible and increasingly reliable. The linkage of aviation and national pride was complete. The physical and mental traits expected of the flier were essentially established and increasingly familiar to readers young and old. And the exalting, transcendent qualities of flight, already familiar to the readers of series books, were becoming known even to the adult world. An aeronautical society is ready to be shaped, and all that is needed is the appropriate catalyst. That catalyst appeared in May 1927, and the world of American aviation changed forever.

NOTES TO CHAPTER THREE

1 "The Aviator—The Superman of Now" [Wright Flying School Advertisement], *Flying* 5 (August 1916): 273; "The Aviator—The Superman of Now" [Wright Flying School Advertisement], *Flying* 5 (November 1916): 403.

2 Robert Wohl, *A Passion for Wings: Aviation and the Western Imagination 1908–1918* (New Haven: Yale University Press, 1994), 70–76.

3 Lee Kennett, *The First Air War 1914–1918* (New York: Free Press, 1991), 16–19, 65–66, 69.

4 Arthur Sweetser, *The American Air Service* (New York: D. Appleton, 1919), 9–16.

5 Kennett, *First Air War,* 21; Sweetser, *American Air Service,* 15, 25; Gen. George Scriven, quoted in Sweetser, *American Air Service,* 23, 28–29.

6 National Advisory Committee for Aeronautics, "Nomenclature for Aeronautics," *Aviation* 1 (1 November 1919): 215–216.

7 James J. Cooke, *The U.S. Air Service in the Great War, 1917–1919* (Westport, CT: Praeger, 1996), 10; Sweetser, *American Air Service,* 33–35.

8 Tim Brady, "World War I," *The American Aviation Experience,* ed. Tim Brady (Carbondale: Southern Illinois University Press, 2000), 106.

9 Brady, "World War I," *American Aviation Experience,*106–107. SPAD is an acronym for *Societé Pour l'Aviation et ses Dérives,* the successor to the failed Deperdussin Company.

10 John H. Morrow, Jr., *The Great War in the Air: Military Aviation from 1909 to 1921* (Washington, DC: Smithsonian Institution Press, 1993), 133–136, 203; James J. Hudson, *Hostile Skies: A Combat History of the American Air Service in World War I* (Syracuse: Syracuse University Press, 1968), 309; Norman S. Hall, *The Balloon Buster: Frank Luke of Arizona* (Garden City: Doubleday, Doran, 1928).

11 Kennett, *First Air War,*159, 165, 172–174.

12 *Scientific American,* 117 (6 October 1917): cover copy; Austin C. Lescarboura, "With the American Airmen of Tomorrow," *Scientific American,* 117 (6 October 1917): 242–243.

13 Col. H.H. Arnold, "Building American Aviation," *Scientific American,* 117 (1 December 1917): 414, 430.

14 Gordon Stuart [H.L. Sayler], *The Boy Scouts of the Air at Eagle Camp* (Chicago: Reilly & Britton), 1912): jacket copy; Harry K. Hudson, *A Bibliography of Hard-Cover, Series Type Boys Books,* Revised ed. (Tampa, FL: Data Print, 1977), 44.

15 Stuart, *Boy Scouts of the Air at Eagle Camp,*19, 98; Gordon Stuart [G.N. Madison], *The Boy Scouts of the Air in the Lone Star Patrol* (Chicago: Reilly & Lee, 1916), 36–37; Gordon Stuart [G.N. Madison], *The Boy Scouts of the Air on Lost Island* (Chicago: Reilly & Britton, 1917), 142.

16 Gordon Stuart [Henry Bedford-Jones], *The Boy Scouts of the Air on Baldcrest* (Chicago: Reilly & Lee, 1922), 13.

17 Gordon Stuart [G.N. Madison], *The Boy Scouts of the Air on the French Front* (Chicago: Reilly & Lee, 1918), 13–14.

18 Gordon Stuart [G.N. Madison], *The Boy Scouts of the Air with Pershing* (Chicago: Reilly & Lee, 1919), 110, 57.

19 Gordon Stuart [G.N. Madison], *The Boy Scouts of the Air on the Great Lakes* (Chicago: Reilly & Britton, 1914), 139; Gordon Stuart [Henry Bedford-Jones], *The Boy Scouts of the Air in the Dismal Swamp* (Chicago: Reilly & Lee, 1920), 96.

20 Gordon Stuart [H.L. Sayler], *The Boy Scouts of the Air in Indian Land* (Chicago: Reilly & Britton, 1912), 163; Victor Lougheed, *Vehicles of the Air,* 3rd ed. (Chicago: Reilly & Britton, 1911), 219; Gordon Stuart [H.L. Sayler], *Boy Scouts of the Air at Greenwood School* (Chicago: Reilly & Britton, 1912), 122–125; "Successful Test of the Cornu Helicopter," *Scientific American,* 98 (18 April 1908): 276; "The Cornu Helicopter," *Scientific American Supplement,* 65 (16 May 1908): 316–318.

21 Stuart, *Boy Scouts of the Air on Baldcrest,*46–47; "The 'Alula' Wing Demonstrated," *Flight,* 13 (20 October 1921): 687; "First Demonstration of the Alula Wing," *Aviation,* 11 (5 December 1921): 662.

22 Horace Porter [Horace Porter DeHart], *Our Young Aeroplane Scouts in France and Belgium, or Saving the Fortunes of the Trouvilles* (New York: A.L. Burt, 1915), dust jacket copy, 7, 9–10.

23 Sikorsky attracted international attention with his 1914 flight from St. Petersburg (Russia) to Kiev in the *Il'ya Muromets* biplane, a behemoth with room for fifteen passengers and a wingspan of 121 feet. Military versions of the craft served as bombers during the war. See Richard Hallion, *Taking Flight: Inventing the Aerial Age from Antiquity through the First World War* (New York: Oxford University Press, 2003), 328–331; "Sikorsky's Stupendous Biplane," *Scientific American Supplement,* 77 (7 February 1914): 91; and Maj. H. Bannerman-Philips, "Russia's Giant War Flyers," *Scientific American,* 111 (22 August 1914): 135, 138–139.

24 Horace Porter [Horace Porter DeHart], *Our Young Aeroplane Scouts in Italy, or Flying With the War Eagles of the Alps* (New York: A.L. Burt, 1916), 15; Horace Porter [Horace Porter DeHart], *Our Young Aeroplane Scouts at Verdun, or Driving Armored Meteors over Flaming Battle Fronts* (New York: A.L. Burt, 1917), 154; Horace Porter [Horace Porter DeHart], *Our Young Aeroplane Scouts Fighting to the Finish, or Striking Hard over the Sea for the Stars and Stripes* (New York: A.L. Burt, 1918), 82.

25 Horace Porter [Horace Porter DeHart], *Our Young Aeroplane Scouts in the War Zone, or Serving Uncle Sam in the Great Cause of the Allies* (New York: A.L. Burt, 1918), 49; Porter, *Our Young Aeroplane Scouts Fighting to the Finish,* 217–218.

26 Horace Porter [Horace Porter DeHart], *Our Young Aeroplane Scouts in Germany, or Winning the Iron Cross* (New York: A.L. Burt, 1915), 39; Porter, *Our Young Aeroplane Scouts in the War Zone,* 16; Horace Porter [Horace Porter DeHart], *Our Young Aeroplane Scouts in the Balkans, or Wearing the Red Badge of Courage among the Warring Legions* (New York: A.L. Burt, 1917), 61, 205; "The Roland," *Aviation,* 2 (15 February 1917): 98.

27 Horace Porter [Horace Porter DeHart], *Our Young Aeroplane Scouts in England, or Twin Stars in the London Sky Patrol* (New York: A.L. Burt, 1916), 204; Neil A. Truslow, "The Transparent Airplane," *Scientific American,* 113 (18 December 1915): 539; Porter, *Our Young Aeroplane Scouts in the War Zone,*8–9; "Queer Camouflage of German Aeroplanes," *Scientific American,* 117 (11 August 1917): 95; Porter, *Our Young Aeroplane Scouts Fighting to the Finish,* 70; "Mass of Material to construct an Airplane," *Scientific American,* 118 (9 March 1918): 213.

28 Air Service Boys Releases, Stratemeyer Syndicate Records, MSS. & Archives Division, N.Y.P. L., Box 65; "St. G.H. Rathborne, Novelist, Dies at 83," *New York Times,* 18 December 1938, 48.

29 Charles Amory Beach [St. George Rathborne], *Air Service Boys Flying for France, or The Young Heroes of the Lafayette Escadrille* (1918; Akron: Saalfield Publishing, 1919), 3.

30 Beach, *Air Service Boys Flying for France,* 162; Charles Amory Beach [St. George Rathborne], *Air Service Boys Over the Enemy's Lines, or The German Spy's Secret* (1918; Cleveland: World Syndicate Publishing, 1919), 62.

31 Charles Amory Beach [Howard R. Garis], *Air Service Boys Over the Rhine, or Fighting Above the Clouds* (1918; New York: George Sully, 1919), 88–91; Air Service Boys Releases, Stratemeyer Syndicate Records, MSS. & Archives Division, N.Y.P.L., Box 65; "The German Long-Range Gun," *Scientific American,* 118 (6 April 1918): 309, 332–333; J. Bernard Walker, "Velocity and Range of Guns," *Scientific American,* 118 (20 April 1918): 360–361.

32 Beach, *Air Service Boys Over the Rhine,* 17; Charles Amory Beach [St. George Rathborne], *Air Service Boys Flying for Victory, or Bombing the Last German Stronghold* (Cleveland: Goldsmith Publishing, 1920), 1–2.

33 Beach, *Air Service Boys Flying for France,*9–10, 4; Charles Amory Beach [St. George Rathborne], *Air Service Boys over the Atlantic, or The Longest Flight on Record* (Cleveland: Goldsmith Publishing, 1920), 196.

34 Robeson S. Moise, "Balloons and Dirigibles," in *American Aviation Experience,* 326; Terry Gwynne-Jones, *Farther and Faster: Aviation's Adventuring Years, 1909–1939* (Washington, DC: Smithsonian Institution Press, 1991), 79–89; Porter, *Air Service Boys Over the Atlantic,*216–217.

35 Curtiss Eastern Airplane Co. advertisement, *Aerial Age Weekly,* 13 (22 August 1921): 577; United States Navy advertisement, *Aerial Age Weekly,* 11 (19 April 1920): 175; "The Large Demand for Aeroplanes," *Aerial Age Weekly,* 11 (28 June 1920): 539–540; "Aeronitis," *Aerial Age Weekly,* 13 (30 May 1921): 282.

36 Joseph J. Corn, *The Winged Gospel: America's Romance with Aviation, 1900–1950* (New York: Oxford University Press, 1983), 74–75; Roger E. Bilstein, *Flight in America: From the Wrights to the Astronauts,* rev. ed. (Baltimore: Johns Hopkins University Press, 1994), 59–62.

37 "Our Winged Postmen," *Scientific American,* 118 (25 May 1918): 476–477, 490–492; "Post Office Department Issues Specifications for 10 Mail Planes," *Aerial Age Weekly,* 9 (28 April 1919): 330; "Postoffice Department Issues Call for Proposals for Operation of Aerial Mail Routes," *Aerial Age Weekly,* 11 (19 July 1920): 644, 648; William M. Leary, *Aerial Pioneers: The U.S. Air Mail Service, 1918–1927* (Washington, DC: Smithsonian Institution Press, 1985), 178–180, 212–217.

38 Royalty statements, George Sully & Co., Stratemeyer Syndicate Records, MSS. & Archives Division, N.Y.P.L., Box 88; Captain Frank Cobb, *Battling the Clouds, or for a Comrade's Honor* (1921; Akron: Saalfield Publishing, 1927), front cover copy.

39 Cobb, *Battling the Clouds,*92, 134.

40 Captain Frank Cobb, *An Aviator's Luck, or The Camp Knox Plot* (1921: Akron: Saalfield Publishing, 1927), 59, 63; Captain Frank Cobb, *Dangerous Deeds, or The Flight in the Dirigible* (1921: Akron: Saalfield Publishing, 1927), 158.

41 David K. Vaughan, "Thomson Burtis' Rex Lee Aviation Stories," *Dime Novel Roundup,* 59 (February 1990): 2–7; "Entrants in Post Plane Test May Go with Winner," *Washington Post,* 25 June 1928, 14.

42 Thomson Burtis, *Russ Farrell, Airman* (Garden City: Doubleday, Page, 1924), 7, 14; Thomson Burtis, *Russ Farrell Circus Flyer* (Garden City: Doubleday, Doran, 1927), 15. See also "Aviators to Bomb Ex-German Warships in Tests," *Aerial Age Weekly,* 13 (14 March 1921): 8.

43 "Russ Farrell, Flyer Up-to-date" [Editorial note to Thomson Burtis, "Airman Again"], *American Boy,* 26 (October 1925): 4

44 "The DeBothezat Helicopter," *Air Service News Letter,* 7 (5 March 1923): 1–2; A.M. Jacobs, "Unusual Navigation Tests at McCook Field," *Air Service News Letter,* 8 (12 June 1924): 1–2; "Barling Bomber—Army's Super Airplane," *U.S. Air Service,* 8 (August 1922): 15–19; C. Moran, "War on the Boll Weevil," *U.S. Air Service,* 8 (December 1923): 54–55; Thomson

Burtis, *Russ Farrell, Test Pilot* (Garden City: Doubleday, Doran, 1926), 53–56; First Lieutenant John A. Macready, "Exploring the Earth's Stratosphere," *National Geographic,* 50 (December 1926): 768–779. For an overview of McCook Field activities, see "What McCook Field is Doing," *Air Service News,* 9 (August 1925): 4.

45 Thomson Burtis, *Russ Farrell Over Mexico* (Garden City: Doubleday, Doran, 1929), 68; Burtis, *Russ Farrell Circus Flyer,*12–13; David G. Herrmann, *The Arming of Europe and the Making of the First World War* (Princeton: Princeton University Press, 1996), 74–75. "Air circuses" of the sort proposed by General Mallory are described in "Dayton Celebrates Aviation Day," *Air Service News Letter* 7 (20 June 1923): 1–2, and "McCook Field's Air Carnival for Army Relief Fund," *Air Service News Letter* 7 (29 September 1923): 11–13.

46 Burtis, *Russ Farrell, Circus Flyer,*2, 196.

47 David K. Vaughan, "Hap Arnold's Bill Bruce Books: Promoting Air Service Awareness in America," *Air Power History,* 40 (1993): 43- 49. Arnold's role in the larger development of American military aviation is examined in Dik Alan Daso, *Hap Arnold and the Evolution of American Airpower* (Washington, DC: Smithsonian Institution Press, 2000).

48 Henry H. Arnold, quoted in Richard G. Davis, *Hap: Henry H. Arnold, Military Aviator* (Washington, DC: Air Force History and Museums Program, 1997), 14.

49 Major Henry H. Arnold, *Bill Bruce and the Pioneer Aviators* (New York: A.L. Burt, 1928): 231.

50 Major Henry H. Arnold, *Bill Bruce, the Flying Cadet* (New York: A.L. Burt, 1928), 239.

51 Morrow, *Great War in the Air,* 300–302.

52 "The Transcontinental Air Race," *Scientific American,* 121 (25 October 1919): 423, 434, 436.

53 Arnold, *Bill Bruce and the Pioneer Aviators,*140–150.

54 Thomson Burtis, *Daredevils of the Air* (New York: Grosset & Dunlap, 1932), front cover matter.

55 David K. Vaughan, "Eustace Adams' Andy Lane Series," *Dime Novel Roundup,* 57 (August 1988): 52–60; "Adams, Eustace Lane," *Who Was Who Among North American Authors, 1921–1939,* Vol. 1 (Detroit: Gale Research, 1976): 8.

56 Thomson Burtis, *Four Aces* (New York: Grosset & Dunlap, 1932), 143.

57 Thomson Burtis, *Flying Blackbirds* (New York: Grosset & Dunlap, 1932),55. With his hair-raising flying skills and disdain for regulations, "Stormy" Lake is clearly patterned upon the 27th Squadron's flamboyant Frank Luke.

58 Burtis, *Daredevils of the Air,*20, 37; Burtis, *Flying Blackbirds,* 73.

59 Burtis, *Daredevils of the Air,* 154; Eustace L. Adams, *Doomed Demons* (New York: Grosset & Dunlap, 1935), 137.

60 Burtis, *Daredevils of the Air,* 2; Burtis, *Four Aces,* 71; Adams, *Doomed Demons,*30–31, 155.

61 [Henry Woodhouse], "What Next?" *Aerial Age Weekly,* 9 (7 July 1919): 804.

62 Beach, *Air Service Boys Over the Enemy's Lines,* 62; Stuart, *Boy Scouts of the Air on Baldcrest,* 51; Burtis, *Flying Blackbirds,* 55.

63 C.A. Wragg, "The New Age," *Aerial Age Weekly,* 14 (10 October 1921): 107–08.

Chapter Four

Interlude: Charles A. Lindbergh and Atlantic Flight, 1927–1929

The Wright Brothers' flight of December 1903 changed the history of world aeronautics, but that of Charles A. Lindbergh in May 1927 changed the course of American aviation history. No other aviation-related event, from the Wrights' initial flight through the landing of Apollo 11 on the Moon, so captured the public eye or exerted so long-lasting an influence on public attitudes toward aviation. In less than a month, Lindbergh (1902–1974) passed from being a little-known mail and military flier to a national celebrity and an aviation authority. Politicians, business persons, and the military avidly solicited his opinion on aviation issues, while the press portrayed him as an

Charles A. Lindbergh and the Ryan NY-P "Spirit of St. Louis" (1927). National Air and Space Museum, Smithsonian Institution (SI 87-15484).

emblem of all that was good in America. His climb to fame was unprecedented and his influence far-reaching.[1]

Given the hoopla that followed the event, the facts of Lindbergh's New York—Paris flight are surprisingly straightforward. Raymond Orteig, a French hotelier living in the United States, in 1919 established the Orteig Prize, a $25,000 award for the first nonstop, heavier-than-air flight in either direction between New York and Paris. The prize went unclaimed and unchallenged until 1926, when French ace René Fonck mounted an attempt using a three-engined Sikorsky S-35. Fonck's flight ended in a flaming crash shortly beyond the end of the runway at Roosevelt Field, Long Island, but the associated publicity drew Lindbergh's attention and set him to thinking about the prize.[2]

Lindbergh, who learned to fly in 1922 after being dropped from the University of Wisconsin, had by 1926 acquired a $500 Jenny and built a varied career. After two years as a barnstormer and stunt-flier (billing himself "Daredevil Lindbergh"), he spent a year as a flying cadet in Army training, graduating first in his class and commissioned a second lieutenant in the Reserve Corps. After another brief period of barnstorming, he took a job as chief pilot for the Robertson Aircraft Corporation, which had received the Chicago-St. Louis airmail route (CAM-2), and began regular flying on the route. Settled in St. Louis, he joined the 110th Observation Squadron of the Missouri National Guard as a first lieutenant, rising to the rank of captain in late 1926. His experiences as a mail pilot convinced him of the practicality of a New York-Paris flight, and, late in 1926, he began his preparations.[3]

He decided early on that he would fly alone, in a single-engined monoplane, trading multi-engine redundancy and crew support for fuel capacity and simplicity. Backed by a group of St. Louis bankers and businessmen, he talked with several aircraft manufacturers (principally Fokker and the Wright Aeronautical Corporation) before deciding upon the Ryan Airlines Company of San Diego, California. He and Ryan officials agreed upon a design, a delivery date, and a price in February 1927, and, taking a leave of absence from

Robertson, Lindbergh went to San Diego to oversee construction. The airplane was a unique design derived from the Ryan M-2 and labeled the Model NYP ("New York-Paris"). With the Department of Commerce registration number NX-211, it made its maiden flight on 28 April 1927. In recognition of his backers, he named it *Spirit of St. Louis.*[4]

Only now did his preparations begin to attract national attention. The first notice, a wire-service item on his plans, appeared in the *New York Times* on 6 February 1927; a somewhat longer report followed in the *Times* for 1 March 1927, when he filed his formal entry in the Orteig competition with the National Aeronautic Association. A substantial feature story, published on 20 March 1927, dwelt upon the entries of Commander Richard E. Byrd (already a notable for having flown across the North Pole), Lieutenant Noel Davis, and Captain René Fonck, who was planning a second flight. Byrd intended to use a Fokker tri-motored monoplane, Davis a Keystone tri-motored biplane, and Fonck a newly designed twin-engined Sikorsky biplane. Lindbergh and two French contenders, Charles Nungesser and François Coli, were mentioned only as afterthoughts.[5]

The atmosphere changed dramatically as April rolled into May. Byrd's preparations were delayed on 16 April when his Fokker crashed on landing and he broke an arm. Davis and his co-pilot were killed on 26 April when their craft crashed on a test flight, and Nungesser and Coli, leaving France in the single-engined Levasseur biplane *L'Oiseau Blanc* on 8 May disappeared over the Atlantic. Lindbergh, meanwhile, began attracting attention of his own. Flying from San Diego to St. Louis on 10 May he set a distance record for a non-stop flight by a single pilot. His arrival in New York on 1 May, even with his overnight stop in St. Louis, completed a total coast-to-coast flight of 21 hours, 20 minutes, easily besting the 1923 record of 26 hours and 50 minutes made by lieutenants Oakland Kelly and John Macready in a Fokker T-2.[6]

Lindbergh's arrival in New York intensified the publicity focused on all the contenders. Mechanical and weather delays slowed any immediate departure, the search for Nungesser and Coli gave the press ample opportunity to highlight the dangers ahead, and Lindbergh's own reticence to talk with journalists generated ever more speculation about his life and nature. Reports of an expected change in weather conditions over the Atlantic prompted him to cancel a planned evening at the theater, and, on the morning of 20 May 1927, he lifted off in the *Spirit of St. Louis* and set out for France. Thirty-three hours and 30 minutes later, at 10:22 P.M. French time, he landed at Le Bourget. His log for the flight recorded "Fuselage fabric badly torn by souvenir hunters."[7]

Nothing leading up to his flight prepared Lindbergh for his reception. Mobbed at the airport by well-wishers, he made his way to the American Embassy under guard and woke in the morning to find himself a celebrity. In the days that followed he visited Madame Nungesser, mother of the lost French flier, received the Cross of the Legion of Honor from the president of France, met with Louis Blériot, and attended a succession of banquets. On 28 May he flew the *Spirit of St. Louis* to Belgium, where he was made a Chevalier of the Royal Order of Leopold by the King and Queen. The following day he flew on to London. Here he met with King George and Queen Mary, received the British Air Force Cross, and was guest of honor at a dinner sponsored by the Royal Aero Club. These celebrations, however, were only a beginning. Boarding the cruiser *Memphis,* sent by President Coolidge, he recrossed the Atlantic, arriving in Washington, DC, on 11 June to find that he had been transformed from celebrity to hero.[8]

The shaping of Lindbergh's public image over the next months took several tacks. The specialized aeronautical press dwelt extensively on the technical achievements of the flight, but did its own part in feeding the myth-making process. Newspapers and the popular press fueled public emotion and focused public acclaim, escalating in intensity day by day, while Lindbergh himself, through his outward demeanor and brief published statements, added to the perceptions of him as a responsible, articulate spokesperson for American aviation. Every move he made, from his initial visit with Madame Nungesser to his later decision to take the *Spirit of St. Louis* on a cross-country tour to visit all forty-eight states and make a good-will flight to Mexico, was seen as evidence of his concern and his genuineness. In all that he did, he dominated the public eye.

In its general reporting, the aeronautical press focused attention on the technological elements of the flight. A lengthy article in *Aviation* written on the eve of Lindbergh's departure compared Byrd's Fokker with the Ryan craft, detailing the construction, dimensions, and instrumentation of the two ships and printing photographs of each. The following week, the journal's "New York-Paris Flight a Reality" gave a detailed, largely dispassionate account of the flight, "the greatest single feat in aviation history," listing the stages of its progress and giving a thumbnail précis of his career, while an editorial in the same issue remarked that "the airplane is bringing with it a new field for discovery, exploration and achievement."[9]

Other journals followed suit. The June issue of *Aero Digest* continued these themes, publishing details of the Ryan NYP design, the elements giving the Wright Whirlwind J-5C engine its reliability, and the innovative earth inductor compass. *Aviation* added two articles, one examining the importance of the pilot's careful monitoring of fuel and oil consumption during the flight and the other describing the Ryan design team that produced the NYP. Still later, in October, *Aero Digest* published Michael Watter's graph-laden treatment of "Engineering Aspects of Lindbergh's Transatlantic Flight," looking into the relationship of airspeed, weight, and fuel consumption to performance at various altitudes.[10]

The common theme among all the technical reports was that the flight was a triumph of engineering complemented by prudence, courage, and flying skill. Again and again, the accounts remarked on Lindbergh's scrupulous attention to detail. B.F. Mahoney, manager of the Ryan plant, called him "a model aviator. He is a good navigator, and has studied weather conditions until he is an expert meteorologist. He knows what he can do in a plane and then does it perfectly." Even more tellingly, Watter's engineering analysis concluded with the blunt statement, "The success of the flight was due to the careful technical preparations made beforehand and the experience and capability of the pilot. To test the plane . . . and to take the utmost advantage of an airplane at all times during the flight is not luck but science."[11]

These accounts seem reticent compared to editorial remarks made in both journals, for there emphasis shifted from the technical to the human. The flight may well have been an engineering triumph, but it was carried out by a young American flier. *Aviation,* the more restrained in its comments, merged daring and science, announcing that Lindbergh "has triumphed over fate with a cool determination that has made his name synonomous [*sic*] with courage and daring in every country on the globe. He has raised the art which he so skilfully practices to the pinnacle of scientific achievement." *Aero Digest* found in his achievements something elemental. Proclaiming him "a doer, not a talker," the journal went on to assert that, "Without the blaze or flare of personal exploitation or press agentry, silent as the setting sun that hides its splendour and brilliancy in the evening shadows of the western sky, came this youthful conqueror of the elements, the ocean, yes and even time itself."[12]

In a subsequent issue, *Aviation* went on develop a theme begun in the World War I era, the democratizing quality of aviation and the ready potential for aviation achievement. Lindbergh, it announced, belonged to the "aristocracy of achievement," a class that in the realm of flying is as democratic as it is aristocratic. The class, the editorial continues, is defined by its "outstanding things performed to light the way for the advance of humanity," and embraces "the whole courageous brood that has piloted man's new found means of mechanical locomotion across the ocean to Paris, to Berlin and else where . . . [as] messengers of good will and inspirers of human progress." Aristocratic in their deeds though these young airmen may be, they are linked by the democratizing nature of aviation. "There is something leveling, as well as elevating, about aerial adventure. The substitution of the pilot's helmet for the diplomat's high hat . . . appears to breed a mass comaraderie [*sic*] that tramples down political barriers and official puntilios [*sic*] between nations." Lindbergh's democratic openness in the most exalted of circles was the consequence of his flying experiences, and other persons and nations might well learn from the example.[13] Youth, democracy, courage, activism, carefulness, and technical competence—even in the technical press, the basic elements of the Lindbergh mystique were beginning to coalesce.

The popular press was less concerned with the technology than with the person, holding him up as an exemplar of national virtue and technological mastery. The day following Lindbergh's arrival back in the United States, P.W. Wilson in the *New York Times* proclaimed that "Lindbergh Symbolizes the Genius of America." Calling him a "type" rather than an individual, Wilson hailed the countless American "men as modest as Lindbergh, as indifferent to money, as considerate of the susceptibilities of others as susceptible themselves to a mother's influence." Because "he left nothing to chance that could be safeguarded by thought and skill," he is an extension of "the mechanical genius [that] is in the very atmosphere of a country where boys, untaught in physics, can build the radio and detect, by ear, in which of a dozen spark plugs there has developed a hint of iniquity."

That mechanical genius, in its turn, gave rise to the airplane he flew. Calling him the "partner of a perfect plane," Wilson went on to assert that "the Arab himself was not more devoted to his steed than is Lindbergh to the 'Spirit of St. Louis.' He reveres his 'ship' as a noble expression of mechanical wisdom, a creation as inspired by truth and beauty as any art and any theology." And, out of this reverential partnership, there comes an essential expression of the American faith in movement and progress: "Our faith is locomotion. We believe with all our hearts in the happiness of going somewhere else. We are elevated upward. . . . To fly is thus a supreme mysticism. To fly across an ocean is the beatific vision. Charles A. Lindbergh is our Elijah."[14] In him the careful technologist merged with the evangelical prophet, and the result was a symbol of the American national character.

Charles Evans Hughes, speaking at a formal dinner sponsored by the City of New York, continued the linkage. America, he said, was "picturing to herself youth with the highest aims, with courage unsurpassed; science victorious." Yet the real consequence, he continued, lay in the manner in which the flight revealed the moral character of Lindbergh himself, for "good will for its beneficent effects depends upon the character of those who cherish it." His conclusion hailed the flight as a victory for morality and a lesson for the future, hinting at a time when science, morality, and humanity would work together to shape a progressive, dignified society: "We are all better men and women because of . . . this flight of our young friend. Our boys and girls have before them a stirring, inspiring vision of real manhood. What a wonderful thing it is to live in a time when science and character join hands to lift up humanity with a vision of its own dignity."[15]

Report followed report in the days following Lindbergh's return, and each of them added to the public perception of him as a youthful spokesperson for American values as much as for aviation. The *Literary Digest,* quoting an upstate-New York newspaper, presented him as the nation's "perfect gentle knight, its boyish brave figure who embodies the spirit of the United States." His national tour through the summer and autumn of 1927, sponsored by the Daniel Guggenheim Fund for the Promotion of Aeronautics, became a crusade "to strike the air consciousness of the American people and give added impetus to commercial flying as a practical, safe and useful means of transportation." A later story dwelt upon his belief "that the greatest good can be done for aviation if the youth of the land and the children can be interested in it. . . . The future of aviation is in the hands of America's children who are themselves developing along with the development of aeronautical science."[16]

By the end of 1927, public emphasis on Lindbergh's relative youth had taken on a life of its own. In its July account of "Colonel Lindbergh's

Homecoming," *Aero Digest* called him "symbol of the soul of America's youth, a shy boy, a man of great achievement." In November, in an editorial entitled "The Spirit of Youth," the journal quoted Clarence D. Chamberlin, whose non-stop flight to Germany in June 1927, had supplanted Lindbergh's distance record, as saying that American youth would adopt the airplane as readily as his own generation had adopted the automobile. It then went on to cement the bond between flying and youthful males: "Boys already are more air-minded than their elders. . . . Something about sky travel enthralls the spirit of youth. No one followed the transatlantic flight of Colonel Lindbergh . . . with more rapt attention than did the boys."[17] Lindbergh and aeronautical achievement, boys and the fascination with aviation; the lines of future development were beginning to emerge.

All of the themes—youth, skill, technical prowess, and American worth—came together at year's end in a prose passage worthy of the series books. In a *New York Times* report of Lindbergh's setting out for Mexico and Central America, the reporter spared no adjective: "Intent, cool, clear-eyed and clear-headed, under conditions requiring supreme moral and physical courage and consummate skill, America's young viking of the air lifted his gray plane from a hummocky, soggy, puddle-bespattered morass into an underhanging fringe of threatening mists . . . and was off . . . personifying again in the hearts of his people their unofficial ambassador of good-will. And, as always, he flew alone."[18] Barely six months after he returned to the United States, Lindbergh had become in the popular mind the embodiment of courage, clear-headedness, physical and moral cleanliness embodying in every respect the nation's image of itself. It was a potent and compelling vision.

Lindbergh himself did nothing to slow the pace of his developing image, though all evidence points to his absolute sincerity in his public statements about aviation. His first remarks appeared in a series of by-lined columns in the *New York Times,* published while he was still abroad. These grew out of interviews in Paris with *Times* correspondent Carlyle MacDonald.

MacDonald, who was to draft the first version of *We,* the book-length account of the flight, dealt accurately with Lindbergh's ideas, but presented them as first-person accounts purporting to be the flier's own words. The colloquial tone of the columns so appalled Lindbergh that he resolved never again to depend upon a ghost-writer; his determination was reinforced when he saw MacDonald's draft of *We,* which continued the unbuttoned tone and convinced him of the need to write the book himself.[19]

Colloquial or not, the six columns established the topics that Lindbergh was to dwell upon for the next several years. The first alluded to his meeting with Blériot and their discussion of the future of trans-Atlantic air service. The second established his perception of European supremacy in aviation, whether civil or military, thanks to the widespread application of government subsidies. Since the United States was not inclined to grant such subsidies, he continued, any development would have to come through private investment. He returned to thoughts on an Atlantic service in the third, calling for a means of reliable radio communication, the building of floating aerodromes, and the development of multi-engined land and seaplanes.

The fourth column spoke of the superiority of American flying conditions, and the nation's lack of accessible and well-maintained airports. The development of these, like the development of multi-engined passenger aircraft, would have military merit as well as civil. He spoke of the potential for American aviation in the fifth column, asserting his intention to speak for aviation and cementing his belief that the United States could, and should, become a world leader in flight. The final column, concerned principally with his reception in New York, ended with a call to work: "Please regard me as a medium for having concentrated attention upon the subject of . . . aviation in general and do all you can to encourage aeronautics. I am convinced that aviation will soon take its place among the big activities of the United States."[20] The authentic Lindbergh speaks through MacDonald's prose, outlining a vision of aviation and the nation for American readers.

He continued and expanded upon his vision in *We,* which he wrote during the frantic July of 1927. The book was based upon the outline that MacDonald had prepared, but was wholly Lindbergh's work—approximately forty thousand words of "serviceable prose" recounting his boyhood, his introduction to aviation, and his flight itself. An appendix written by an editor at Putnam's, Fitzhugh Green, detailed Lindbergh's reception at home as well as abroad; "I think," said Lindbergh, in remarks leading into the appendix, that Green "has caught the spirit of what I tried to do for aviation." An instant best-seller, the book sold two-thirds of a million copies in the United States alone, and did equally well in Europe, giving him an unequaled outlet for his ideas.[21]

Although he necessarily focused upon his training and the Atlantic flight, Lindbergh reiterated his earlier points with little change. The airplane is the most modern form of transportation extant, and offers possibilities achieved by no other means. Its development so far had been largely by the military because of the expenses involved; however, private investment leading to the establishing of organized airline service should stimulate manufacturers and lead to the widespread development of commercially feasible aircraft. To these matters he added a new one, presented in a speech quoted by Green in the appendix. His flight, he said, "was the culmination of twenty years of aeronautical research and the assembling together of all that was practicable and best in American aviation." Basic research and development, enhanced by the potential of American industry and supported by public awareness of what aviation might do, was at the heart of aeronautical progress.[22]

Returning to the United States after an extended good-will flight to Mexico and Central America (December 1927—February 1928), Lindbergh resumed his efforts to popularize flying. He was driven in part by a conviction that future progress lay in expanding the accessibility of aeronautical knowledge and aircraft hardware. As he wrote in December 1927, in one of several reports of his Latin-American flight, "The next generation will fly as naturally as the last drove automobiles. Aviation is just being born, and the time will undoubtedly come when airplanes will be flown by every one."[23] The coming availability of aircraft, the assimilation of aircraft into all aspects of public life, and hopes that both offer for the future came to dominate his next series of essays.

Between August 1928 and February 1929 he produced twenty-five short essays, most published under the heading "Lindbergh On Flying." Printed initially in the *New York Times,* the pieces were syndicated nationally, carrying his ideas to readers across the country. Overall, the articles are surprisingly technical. The second examined the dynamics of flight and the functions of the various parts of an airplane—wings, engine, and controls—and the third the safety offered by the "slotted" wing, a movable panel along the leading edge of the wing that improves the craft's handling at slow speeds. A later one described aircraft instrumentation and the hazards of ice and fog, and subsequent segments took up the various types of airplane (monoplane and biplane, cabin and open-cockpit) as a guide to prospective buyers and the airplane's adaptability to general needs and uses, including sport flying, commercial transport, military applications, and amphibian designs for over-water flight. Others considered the equipment required for "blind" flying at night or in foggy conditions, the commercial implications of high-altitude flight and in-flight refueling, and the relationship of streamlining, power and speed.[24] The technology of aviation, he implied throughout, was growing steadily, and would readily overcome whatever obstacles the future might hold.

Other chapters in the series looked to the practical applications and commercial possibilities of aviation. Early on he talked of various small-scale uses of aircraft, from sightseeing flights to newspaper deliveries. He went on to reflect on the implications of expanding international air service through Pan-American Airways and Canadian Colonial Airways, and considered the requirements—e.g., all-weather runways, service and storage facilities—for an up-to-date airport. Two essays discussed the importance of substantial, systematic training, on the ground and in the air, for both commercial and military pilots. He wrote of the emerging cross-country combination of air and rail travel that he had helped Transcontinental Air Transport (the "Lindbergh Line") to develop, and he concluded with reflections on how best to "Help Aviation Meet Its Business Destiny."[25] Here the theme is utility: The airplane is neither a toy nor only a weapon. Its practical applications are limited only by the imagination of the public, and the faster the applications are sought, the quicker there will be progress.

The third cluster of essays is perhaps the most evocative, for in it Lindbergh took up the popular implications of flight. His position here was clear from the outset. In the opening essay, he said, simply, "There is no greater romance than the development of the airplane, and . . . the airplane has now become a vital part of our life." He gave an admiring overview of the advances in aviation, and ended, bluntly, "America has found her wings, but she must yet learn to use them." As the series matured, he spoke of "the natural desire of youth to take to the air, [for] it is one of the few remaining fields of constant adventure," and he understands that safe equipment will be necessary "when more and more people with no special qualification for flying are buying airplanes." All such goals can be attained with proper equipment and proper education, he continued, and he called attention to the work of the Daniel Guggenheim Fund for the Promotion of Aeronautics in "attempting to make the younger generation 'air-minded.'"[26]

Above all, he recognized the changes in world view that flight brings, and proclaimed them as a forward step in mankind's vision of itself. The air mail, he said, had served to break down local and regional borders, leading its pilots to feel that "the whole country is their flying field" and becoming "the greatest force for homogeneity in the United States." Others will come to share this vision as commercial aviation grows. Transcontinental passengers will "feel bound together with ties of mutual interest," for each will "no longer be a citizen of Illinois, but of the United States. His country is closing in around him." What once was a curiosity will become as widespread and as familiar as the automobile, the United States will become more truly united, and the distinctive attributes of flight will have profound effects upon the public's sense of itself and its society.[27]

Whether these columns were ghost-written or produced by Lindbergh himself is irrelevant. What matters is their using the Lindbergh name and the Lindbergh aura to gain readership and authority. They confirm his stature as a personification of aviation itself and they traffic in his appeal to shape readers' opinions. That most of the points made in the columns are common-sensical and accurate is also irrelevant. The same ideas advanced by a nonentity would almost certainly pass unnoticed, but, because Lindbergh was now a celebrated public figure, they become through his advocacy a national agenda that must be taken seriously. He had become the voice of American aviation, and in his *persona* one can find the future of the undertaking.

Two months after Lindbergh's return to the United States, the first issue of a new magazine, *Popular Aviation,* hit the stands. Intended to describe and interpret aviation developments for the general reader, it overtly linked the social and technical possibilities of flight to Lindbergh's deed and the model he presented. An opening-page manifesto, headed "Popularizing Aviation," made the linkage explicit:

> This is a changing world. The toy of yesterday becomes the necessity of today. The miracle of today is the commonplace of tomorrow.
>
> When young Charles Lindbergh sailed over the blue Atlantic . . . he was more than a courageous, adventuring American boy defying fate and imagination. He became a standard bearer.
>
> A new and more intense civilization is rushing in on the world out of the great unknown. Just as the wildest dream of Jules Verne could not encompass the achievements of the past few decades, so no living man can surely visualize the commanding future!

> The entire complexion of civilization is changing.
>
> Aviation will be one of the largest factors in this change.
>
> . . . . . .
>
> Popular Aviation is issued secure in the knowledge that these things are not a dream.
>
> It means to place in the hands of the young men of the nation the facts of this great new human adventure. Its columns will be easy to read, but authoritative; instructive, but written so that all can understand. If it will help to speed the great day that is coming and bring incentive to wealth and power to these young men whose will to achieve is ushering in a new era, we will feel that we have also contributed something to the accomplishment.[28]

The manifesto strikes several telling chords in the themes it introduces. Aviation is changing the world. Its changes will be for the better, and they will largely be carried out by the young. It is essential that the public be equipped to take part in, and benefit from, these changes. The process of change will be adventurous, but it will produce tangible, practical gain. This process is being led by Charles Lindbergh. Aviation, in sum, is the driving force of progress, and Lindbergh is its prophet.

Almost simultaneously, John Erskine, writing in the upper-middle-brow *Century,* continued the exaltation of Lindbergh, dwelling upon his personal qualities as seen by the public. The flight, Erskine wrote, was "a human achievement, common to the race, though made individual in him. . . . We recognized this kind of perfection of which flight is the symbol. We saw in the swift and certain airship, solitary but controlled between water and sky, our own modern version of chivalry." The flight, moreover, was chivalrous "in the new sense. It is a victory of man, in harmony with himself, against those limitations by which nature seeks in vain to fetter him."[29] Erskine makes explicit what other writers only hinted at: Lindbergh's flight possessed a symbolic quality speaking to some inarticulate inner part of the human spirit. The pilot—*this* pilot—had become in the public soul a standard-bearer of purity and responsibility as much as the knights of legend; he had simply done so in modern times, through modern means.

And here, Erskine concluded, was the real contribution of the flight and its aftermath. Lindbergh became for the public "a metaphor. We felt that in him we too had conquered something and regained lost ground. . . . His achievement was not simply in the realm of mechanics against the part of nature science attacks, but also in every day conduct in that realm in which we all find it hard to behave well."[30] His achievement is a dual one: He has overcome forces of nature through the exercise of technology, and he has overcome human failings through the exercise of character. He incorporates in himself all of the attributes necessary to be a leading, productive citizen of the world to come, and the populace should heed his example.

The two published statements, *Popular Aviation*'s and Erskine's, bring together all of the diverse elements of the Lindbergh phenomenon. They join the potential of youth; the necessity of conscientiousness and responsibility; the imperative of technical competence and general "know-how;" the elemental foundation of clean living and clear thinking; and the exciting inevitability of progress. No single one of these qualities is particularly notable; they are, in one form or another, as much a part of the historic American character as they are a part of the pre-1927 series books. But now, in 1927 and on into 1928, they are brought together, crystallized, and dramatized in a manner that gives shape, substance, and direction to the American ideal.

A young American has demonstrated how these traits can be embodied (or, at least, *thought* to be embodied) in a single person. That person, moreover, is a real and ordinary one, who has made his way through individual effort and democratic opportunity. He is an ideal Everyman, good-natured, capable, determined, responsible, mannerly, and far-seeing. In his fame, he stimulates a public fascination with aviation, flight, and fliers unprecedented in both reality and literature. He is all that an American—and particularly an American boy—might hope to be, and the secondary message is clear. The boyish Lindbergh could do and be these things; why, then, should not other American boys?

NOTES TO CHAPTER FOUR

1 The literature discussing the Lindbergh phenomenon is enormous. One of the earliest examinations, John William Ward's "The Meaning of Lindbergh's Flight," appears in *American Quarterly,* 10 (1958): 3–16. Walter S. Ross, *The Last Hero: Charles A. Lindbergh* (New York: Harper & Row, 1976) is a balanced consideration of Lindbergh's entire career, from his early acclaim to his public rehabilitation following his perceived flirtation with Nazism in the months preceding World War II. A concise popular overview is Dominick A. Pisano and F. Robert van der Linden, *Charles Lindbergh and The Spirit of St. Louis* (Washington, DC: Smithsonian National Air and Space Museum; New York: Harry N. Abrams, 2000). An extensive bibliography of Lindberghiana, exhaustive up to its date of publication, appears in Perry D. Luckett, *Charles A. Lindbergh: A Bio-Bibliography* (Westport, CT: Greenwood Press, 1986).

2 A. Scott Berg, *Lindbergh* (New York: G.P. Putnam, 1998), 91–92.

3 Charles A. Lindbergh, *We* 1927 (Guildford, CT: Lyons Press, 2002), 25–35, 63–83, 104–152, 169–193.

4 Charles A. Lindbergh, *The Spirit of St. Louis* 1953 (St. Paul: Minnesota Historical Society Press, 1993), 26–30, 55–57, 69–123.

5 "May Try flight to Paris," *New York Times,* 6 February 1927, E9; "Mail Pilot Files Entry for Paris Flight," *New York Times,* 1 March 1927, 16; Russell Owen, "Flight to Paris Lures Noted Pilots," *New York Times,* 20 March 1927, 5.

6 Berg, *Lindbergh,* 104–105; "The New York-Paris Flight Projects," *Aviation,* 22 (25 April 1927): 823–825; "The Transatlantic Plane 'American Legion,'" *Aero Digest,* 10 (May 1927): 428; "Nungesser and Coli Missing in Atlantic Flight Attempt," *Aviation,* 22 (16 May 1927): 1041–1042; "1,550-Mile Flight Made By Lindbergh," *New York Times,* 12 May 1927, 1; "Lindbergh Arrives After Record Hops," *New York Times,* 13 May 1927, 1,3.

7 Lindbergh, *Spirit of St. Louis,* 160–178, 504.

8 "United States to Europe and Return," *Aviation,* 22 (20 June 1927): 1354–1355, 1398.

9 Robert R. Osborn, "On the Atlantic Flight Preparations," *Aviation,* 22 (23 May 1927): 1082–1084; "New York-Paris Flight a Reality," *Aviation,* 22 (30 May 1927): 1120–1122.

10 George F. McLaughlin, "The Ryan NY-P Monoplane," *Aero Digest,* 10 (June 1927): 536–537; "The Wright Whirlwind J-5C Engine," *Aero Digest,* 10 (June 1927): 540; Bruce Goldsborough, "The Earth Inductor Compass," *Aero Digest,* 10 (June 1927): 542, 544; R.V. Cautley, "Fuel and Oil Consumption Important Factors On Long Distance Flights," *Aviation,* 22 (6 June 1927): 1214–1215, 1243; Russell H. Miles, "How the New York to Paris Plane Was Built," *Aviation,* 22 (20 June 1927): 1352–1353; Dr. Michael Watter, "Engineering Aspects of Lindbergh's Transatlantic Flight," *Aero Digest,* 11 (October 1927): 396–397, 483–485.

11 B.F. Mahoney, quoted in Miles, "How the New York to Paris Plane Was Built," 1353; Watter, "Engineering Aspects," 485.

12 "Lindbergh," *Aviation,* 22 (30 May 1927): 1119; "'Ray for Lindy!" *Aero Digest,* 10 (June 1927): 560.

13 "Aristocracy of Achievement," *Aviation,* 22 (20 June 1927): 1349.

14 P.W. Wilson, "Lindbergh Symbolizes the Genius of America," *New York Times,* 12 June 1927, 4. The equating of the man-horse bond with the man-airplane bond recurs frequently in the post-1927 aviation series.

15 Charles Evans Hughes, quoted in Fitzhugh Green, "A Little of What the World Thought of Lindbergh," in Lindbergh, *We,* 311–312.

16 "Why the World Makes Lindbergh Its Hero," *Literary Digest,* 93 (25 June 1927): 8; "Lindbergh Will Tour in Cause of Aviation," *New York Times,* 29 June 1927, 4; "Lindbergh to Tell His Story to Youths," *New York Times,* 13 July 1927, 4.

17 "Colonel Lindbergh's Homecoming," *Aero Digest,* 11 (June 1927): 31; "The Spirit of Youth," *Aero Digest,* 11 (November 1927): 518.

18 Richard V. Oulahan, "Soars Away at 105 Miles an Hour," *New York Times,* 14 December 1927, 3.

19 Berg, *Lindbergh,* 141–142, 165–167.

20 Captain Charles A. Lindbergh, "He Has Made 7,190 Flights in Five Years," *New York Times.* 28 May 1927, 1; Captain Charles A. Lindbergh, "Behind Europe in Flying Matters, Lindbergh's View of Our Status," *New York Times,* 2 June 1927, 1; Captain Charles A. Lindbergh, "Lindbergh Says Flying Boats Will Come in 5 to 10 Years," *New York Times,* 9 June 1927, 1, 4; Capt. C.A. Lindbergh, "Memphis Makes Record," *New York Times,* 10 June 1927, 1–2 "Captain Charles A. Lindbergh, "Lindbergh 'Ready for Anything;' 'Feels Good to Be Back,' He Says," *New York Times,* 11 June 1927, 1–2; Colonel Charles A. Lindbergh, "Lindbergh Says His Mind Is Ablaze With Noise and an Ocean of Faces," *New York Times,* 14 June 1927, 1,3.

21 Berg, *Lindbergh,* 165–167; Lindbergh, *We,* 232.

22 Lindbergh, *We,* 193–197, 295.

23 Colonel Charles A. Lindbergh, "Lindbergh Calls for Airways to Link Capitals of Continent," *New York Times,* 16 December 1927, 1, 3.

24 Col. Charles A. Lindbergh, "The Second Article of His Series Tells What Makes Planes Fly," *New York Times,* 2 September 1928, 99; Col. Charles A. Lindbergh, "The Third Article of His Series Discusses the Safety Quest," *New York Times,* 9 September 1928, 133; Col. Charles A. Lindbergh, "Instruments That Guide Pilots Through Darkness or Fog," *New York Times,* 30 September 1928, 151; Col. Chas. A. Lindbergh, "Differing Types of Planes Now Built to Serve Special Uses," *New York Times,* 18 November 1928, 12; Col. Charles A. Lindbergh, "Aircraft for Private Owners And How to Chose One," *New York Times,* 25 November 1928, 10; Col. Charles A. Lindbergh, "Blind Landing in Fog Still Presents Many Problems," *New York Times,* 20 January 1929, 12; Col. Charles A. Lindbergh, "New Possibilities Opened by Question Mark's Flight," *New York Times,* 27 January 1929, 8; Col. Charles A. Lindbergh, "Air Speed Limited Only by Power and Streamline," *New York Times,* 3 February 1929, 144.

25 Charles A. Lindbergh, "How Air Transport in America Has Reached a Healthy Basis," *New York Times,* 16 September 1928, 10; Col. Charles A. Lindbergh, "Airplanes Are Now Linking Up The Two American Continents," *New York Times,* 21 October 1928, 152; Col. Charles A. Lindbergh, "Main Needs That Must Be Met In Selecting Airport Sites," *New York Times,* 11 November 1928, 168; Col. Charles A. Lindbergh, "Air Corps Reservist Training Hours Deemed Too Few," *New York Times,* 13 January 1929, 142; Col. Charles A. Lindbergh, "Specialized Aviation Leaves Ocean Flight to Seaplanes," *New York Times,* 10 February 1929, 146; Col. Charles A. Lindbergh, "The New Year Brings Transport By Air- Rail to a Reality," *New York Times,* 6 January 1929, 142; Col. Charles A. Lindbergh, "Ways to Help Aviation Meet Its Business Destiny," *New York Times,* 17 February 1929, 150.

26 Col. Charles A. Lindbergh, "Lindbergh Writes of Aviation's Advance," *New York Times,* 26 August 1928, 1; Col. Charles A. Lindbergh, "Growing Industry of Aviation Offers a Fine

Future to Youth," *New York Times,* 16 September 1928, 134; Col. Charles A. Lindbergh, "New Types and Speedier Planes Being Evolved in Air Progress," *New York Times,* 14 October 1928, 10; Col. Chas. A. Lindbergh, "Guggenheim Fund Does Work Others Might Neglect," *New York Times,* 23 December 1928, 12.

27 Col. Charles A. Lindbergh, "He Sees Air Mail as Unifying The People and the Nation," *New York Times,* 28 October 1928, 168.

28 "Popularizing Aviation," *Popular Aviation,* 1 (August 1927), unpaged. The magazine has been published continuously since 1927, appearing now as *Flying.*

29 John Erskine, "Flight: Some Thoughts on the Solitary Voyage of a Certain Young Aviator," *Century Magazine,* 114 (September 1927): 514–515.

30 Ibid., "Flight," 518.

Chapter Five

The Golden Age, One: The Lindbergh Progeny, 1927–1939

Charles Lindbergh might have stepped from the pages of one of the aviation series, and publishers did not take long to seize the opportunity presented them. His youth, clean-cut manliness, and modest dignity had been established attributes of the flying-series hero for a decade or more. When his barnstorming and military past, his technical competence, and his progressive determination to speak for aviation were factored in, adding the qualities of carefree adventure, flying skill, and technological idealism to the public's perception of him, he became the stuff of which legends are made, and the series publishers and others scrambled to capitalize upon him in fiction.

The months following Lindbergh's trans-Atlantic flight saw an explosion in aviation materials and activities directed toward the young. Retail sales of model airplane kits grew from a quarter-million dollars in the three months following the flight to wholesale sales of close to $2 million by the end of 1928. One writer remarked that "there is no one to whom the romance of aviation makes more of an appeal than it does to the boy between seven and fifteen years of age." These youths, the target audience of the series books, were also prime candidates for model-making. Model-making clubs, which had existed quietly since the era of World War I, suddenly took on new prominence, creating "a highly specialized aircraft education for boys [the results of which] are bound to be far-reaching in the extreme in their effects upon the aviation of tomorrow." Sponsored by city administrations and corporate organizations and supported by aviation notables including Lindbergh himself, they served to introduce increasing numbers of young persons, boys and girls alike, to the wonders of aviation.[1]

One such group was the American Sky Cadets, directed toward "the air-minded chap" who "already knows something about the intricate and interesting problems of airplane design and construction and is rapidly learning more . . . about the romantic business of flying." In-coming "cadets" were awarded silver wings, and could rise to gold wings and the rank of flight commander or squadron commander by recruiting other members. The organization sponsored local, state, and national model contests for its cadets, supplied them with a subscription to *Model Airplane News,* and offered plans and expert advice to help modelers along their way. Another group, the later "Junior Birdmen of America," had as its slogan, "Today pilots of models, Tomorrow model pilots," and all strove to instill in their members a vision of flight that was an idealized version of the one Lindbergh presented.[2]

As the model-making movement grew, it rapidly became a vehicle for moral improvement as much as self-improvement. Model-making, individual betterment, and flying became more and more linked until the three were almost inseparable, linking the nobility of the air with the possibility of nobility in mundane life. Silas Weatherby's "Modelin' Planes," a poem appearing in a 1933 issue of *Model Airplane News,* states the conviction explicitly:

A feller isn't thinkin' mean,
Modelin' planes;
His thot's are mostly good an' clean,
Modelin' planes . . . ;
A feller's at his finest when
He's modelin' planes.
. . . . . .
This brotherhood of 'prop' and line,
And struts and wing is simply fine;
Boys come real close to God's design,
Modelin' planes.
A feller isn't plottin' schemes,

Modelin' planes;
He's only busy with his dreams,
Modelin' planes;
His livery is a lacquer pan
His creed—to do the best he can;
A feller's always mostly man,
Modelin' planes.[3]

The realm of model aviation (and, by implication, that of actual aviation) offers youngsters a chance to express the best that is in them, and that best will make them leaders of the society to come.

The aviation series picked up on these idealized views, and, trafficking shamelessly in the Lindbergh *persona,* gave them shape, identity, and personality. Eight series, which eventually totaled seventy-seven volumes in all, sprang into existence, introducing a host of manly young airmen. Some, like Henry Arnold's "Bill Bruce" books, were serious efforts to supply a historical context for the events of the day and inform the public of aviation's potential. Others, such as Levi P. Wyman's "Hunniwell Boys Series" (1928–1931; eight titles) were fanciful attempts to capitalize upon the new public interest in aviation with little regard for technical fact. Bill and Gordon Hunniwell, boy inventors from Skowhegan, Maine, toss together an electrically powered airplane and blithely travel to Australia, the Gobi Desert, and, after a flight around the world, to Cuba. Far-fetched though the stories were, Wyman, an educator and college dean, still managed to link them to Lindbergh. When the boys tell a shipwreck survivor that they are headed for Australia by air, the sailor's remark is: "Well, I'll be blowed. Your name Lindbergh?"[4] Here, as in the "Bill Bruce" books, young American men are the active agents in aviation, carrying the torch of aeronautical progress.

The best of the series—and, coincidentally, the longest-lived—were those that drew more or less directly upon Lindbergh to characterize their protagonists and story lines. Populated by characters with names like Amos Green,

Andy Lane, Rex Lee, or Ted Scott, the books in a variety of ways melded conventional series adventures with wholly new elements taken from the emerging world of aviation. They drew heavily on Lindbergh's publicized qualities and his published words to offer a substantially different kind of series story. While this new form did not stint on incident and excitement, it based its events on the outlook and values of the professional and technically trained flier, and an invigorated sense of what aircraft and aviation might mean for the contemporary world.

Among the first to climb aboard the Lindbergh bandwagon was Thomson Burtis, whose "Russ Farrell" books had already established him as an author in tune with the aviation world. His contribution to the post-Lindbergh era was the "Rex Lee" series (1928–1932; eleven titles), retelling much of his own career and the stuff of the "Russ Farrell" stories to take advantage of new public interest in aviation.[5] Rex, like Lindbergh, is tall, slender, and taciturn; he comes from an educated and affluent family, but turns his back on formal education to make his way as a barnstormer, military flier, and air-mail pilot. The first volume of his adventures, *Rex Lee, Gypsy Flyer* (1928), ties him explicitly to the Lindbergh mystique; it opens with Rex raptly reading a magazine article, "The Boy in the Silver Ship," an account of "'Slim' Lindley's" triumph over polar explorer "Commander Fowler" as he wins the Orteig Prize by flying the Atlantic in a silver-painted, "Bryan"-built monoplane.[6]

For all his links to the real-life character, Rex's later exploits are more flamboyant than any of Lindbergh's. In the next two volumes (both 1928), he follows a stint flying border patrol with the army by turning to detective work as a flying undercover agent investigating a seedy circus. *Rex Lee, Sky Trailer* (1929) finds him helping an old friend establish an air-taxi service, while, in *Rex Lee, Ace of the Air Mail* (1929), he becomes chief pilot for Coast Air Express and flies mail and goods throughout the American West. He stays in the West for *Rex Lee, Night Flyer* (1929), cleaning up a corrupt oil-boom town in Texas, then returns to the army for *Rex Lee's Mysterious Flight* (1930), doing flight tests and recruiting work. The final volumes become increasingly melodramatic, as he rejoins the circus as an *Aerial Acrobat* (1930), trails air bandits (1931), and becomes "the Sherlock Holmes of the air" as a *Flying Detective* (1932).[7] Throughout the works, however, whatever their nature might be, Rex's piloting skills, his aeronautical knowledge, and his commitment to aviation function as prominent elements in the stories.

The melodrama that accompanies his later doings notwithstanding, Rex himself evinces the traits commonly attributed to Lindbergh. He has "a great confidence in himself that was the result of experience and self-knowledge, minus conceit." He has "the eyes of a dreamer [and] the dreams he had dreamed in the past were coming true because he always had his mental feet on the ground." And he is, finally, a person whose passion for flight blends practicality and idealism into a single determination. "The air seemed to hold all the ingredients of paradise within itself for him. Added to his enjoyment . . . was a fundamental enthusiasm for it and a belief in its future. It was business and pleasure and adventure and almost life itself to him."[8] He is the Lindbergh spirit in a series-book adventurer's body, his modernity complemented by his progressive vision of the air-based world to come, and the combination is ready-made for the series.

A second series, the "Aviation" books (1927–1931; nine titles) by "John Prentice Langley," deals less with Lindbergh's military and barnstorming past than with his role as a record-setting flier trying to increase public awareness of aviation. The books proceed from the assumption, as their advertising spells out, that "There is no other topic of such world-wide interest as aviation," and so are intended "to further the interest in flying and to tell 'Young America,' in its own words, the fun, hardships, triumphs and thrills connected with this sport." The series, from the outset, is one deliberately designed to create, and capitalize upon, air-mindedness among its young readers. Although written by St. George Rathborne, a contributor to the "Air Service Boys" series, the books are not a Stratemeyer product, allowing "Langley" to develop his own background for the tales.[9]

That background is a bizarre one, even for the series genre. When injuries suffered in the Lafayette Escadrille prevent his taking any further active involvement in flying, a reclusive millionaire known only as "Mr. Carstairs" sets out to indulge his "absorbing passion" in "aviation in the scientific sense." He seeks out "a clever young representative, *à la* Lindbergh, who would play the game without the slightest desire for fame or fortune; being entirely satisfied with the inward knowledge that he was . . . winning fresh laurels in the cause of scientific aviation," and finances a succession of record-setting flights.[10]

The chosen representative is airmail pilot Amos Green, who, with his navigator and comic sidekick Danny Cooper, accepts Carstairs's challenge. Amos, a person "exceedingly modest and averse to the plaudits of the multitude," is also a dreamer, willing to take "every risk in the endeavor to advance the cause so dear to his heart, and help to make flying safe and sane, as well as opening up new air lanes for commercial purposes." Referred to throughout the books as "Cool Amos" or "Cool Green" for his calmness in the air, he and Danny proceed to replicate Lindbergh's flight and, later, other international record-setting flights in deepest secrecy. The aim, at Carstairs's insistence, is to "advance the cause of mastering the boundless regions of space beneath the ceiling of the sky," rather than to detract in any way from the acclaim being accorded Lindbergh, Byrd, and a host of other valiant souls.[11] While he encounters adventure aplenty during his flights, Amos never misses a chance to speculate upon the future of practical aviation.

With Danny by his side, Amos proceeds to carry out Carstairs's wishes. The first volume, *Trail Blazers of the Skies or Across to Paris, and Back* (1927), takes the two across the Atlantic and back in the days immediately following Lindbergh's flight; the second, *Spanning the Pacific or A Non-stop Hop to Japan* (1927), sees them trek from San Francisco to Yokohama using in-flight refueling, though they studiously avoid stealing any luster from the contemporaneous flight of Lester Maitland and Albert Hegenberger from Oakland to Honolulu.[12] Leaving Tokyo behind, they set out in *Masters of the Air-Lanes or Round the World in Fourteen Days* (1928); the flight is explicitly dated as taking place in July 1927, and they cross Russia, Europe, and England as they work their way back home.

Their next venture, *The "Pathfinder's" Great Flight or Cloud Chasers Over Amazon Jungles* (1928), takes them on a tour of South America, and is a story notable principally for its reflections on the continent's anger over American economic imperialism. Later journeys involve a trans-Arctic flight from Alaska to Europe (1929) dated as occurring in May and June of 1928, and a long-distance flight to Africa, whence they return by steamer (1929). The last books are essentially travelogues, beginning with a venture from California to Australia, via Hawaii and Fiji (1930, but internally dated as 1928). In Australia they collect a new airplane, a twin-engined Fokker amphibian, and, in *Bridging the Seven Seas or On the Air-Lane to Singapore* (1930), set out for Singapore via Java and Borneo. The final volume, *The Staircase of the Wind or Over the Himalayas to Calcutta* (1931), takes them through Thailand, China, and Tibet, where they reunite with Carstairs and are last seen planning new travels.

Amos's Lindbergh-like qualities, already established with his modesty and aversion to publicity, permeate the stories, with "Langley" frequently emphasizing them by specific reference to Lindbergh and other fliers of the day. At the outset, a test pilot tells Carstairs that "I know full well a lot more than mere *luck* took that sterling lad [Lindbergh] across to Paris," and goes on to remark on Amos's careful attention to his instruments and aircraft. Amos himself, arrived in Paris, tells his hosts of the "trip in as simple and unassuming language as possible, and with not an atom of the usual bluster and boast ascribed by foreign critics to the American character." *Spanning the Pacific* opens with a recapitulation of recent flights: Lindbergh to France, Chamberlin and Levin to Germany, Byrd to the coast of France, and Maitland and Hegenberger to Hawaii. Lindbergh's efforts to avoid publicity (especially following his marriage, in May 1929) are echoed in Amos and Danny's skill "at 'pulling the wool' over the eyes of would-be seekers after thrilling stories," while his prudent approach to preparation and flying is mentioned repeatedly. Indeed, it appears as late as the final volume, when Carstairs calls attention to "the safety-first principle with which wise chaps like Lindbergh . . . have always governed their actions in all their ventures."[13]

The "Aviation" books lack the high degree of up-to-the-minute information found in other series of the time. After the first volumes, events mentioned or sources implied tend to have occurred from eighteen months to two years prior to the date of publication. The stories are internally dated as taking

"Cool Amos" Green and sidekick Danny Cooper set out for flying adventures in the Far East (1930). Erisman-Odom Collection, Mary Couts Burnett Library, Texas Christian University.

place in 1927 through 1929, and a safety award to James Dyer mentioned as contemporaneous in *Bridging the Seven Seas* (1930) was actually awarded in December 1928.[14] Nonetheless, the books do their part in establishing the Lindbergh model as a vital part of the new series story; Amos and Danny parallel his career with their airmail past, and the books themselves invoke his name as a guide to responsible, successful flying.

Whereas the "Rex Lee" and "Aviation" series emphasize the attractions of barnstorming, flying for the military, or setting new aviation records, the two remaining Lindberghian series, "Andy Lane" and the Stratemeyer-generated "Ted Scott," emphasize the commercial and the technical. Their concerns are with the long-term socio-economic implications of flight. Though they are as filled with adventure and excitement as the lesser series, they also draw upon Lindbergh's interest in advancing commercial aviation and aircraft technology to inform their stories. The books that result are singularly rich in their dramatizations of flying's potential, and, despite their occasional implausibilities of event, make a substantial case for aviation as a practical, even necessary, adjunct to progressive American life. It is a lesson not likely to be lost upon avid young readers.

Eustace L. Adams's "Andy Lane" books (1928–1932; twelve titles) gain much of their appeal from Adams's use of his experiences as a Navy flier. Nautical imagery permeates them, the aircraft described are often seaplanes or amphibians, and the internal organization of Andy's flight arrangements proceeds with military precision.[15] At the same time, they also draw upon a range of Lindbergh-related traits: the flier's physical appearance and relative youth, his close relationship with his mother, his devotion to the technology of flight, and the spontaneous public excitement that his appearances and other activities engender. Andy Lane is significantly younger than Lindbergh, doubtless a change necessitated by the pre- and early-teen audience to whom Adams intended to appeal. His own traits, however, derive directly from Lindbergh's, as the books' advertising spells out: "Every boy who has thrilled to the daring exploits of Lindbergh, Byrd, Chamberlin and others will find in Andy Lane a splendid prototype of those intrepid heroes of the skies."[16]

After his family's finances collapse, teen-aged Andy Lane, son of a struggling inventor and a loving, domestic mother, gives up his dreams of flying and enrolls in an engineering course at Newton College. When his father perfects a fuel-saving carburetor, Andy persuades the Apex Aircraft Corporation to mount an endurance flight to demonstrate the device's worth. In *Fifteen Days in the Air* (1928), Andy, with the help of mechanic Sam Allen and radio buff Sonny Collins (son of a rival aircraft manufacturer), completes more than two weeks in the air in an Apex-built ship and lands to find himself famous and wealthy. He accepts appointment as consulting engineer with the booming Apex factory, and returns to his studies, though with new flights in mind.

Those flights follow in quick succession. *Over the Polar Ice* (1928) relates Andy's non-stop journey from New York to the South Pole and back. *Racing Around the World* (1928) follows Andy, Sam, and Sonny on an east-to-west global flight, ending with a merger of the Apex and Collins firms and Andy's becoming vice-president of the new company with a leave of absence to finish his studies. He then heads to England in pursuit of *The Runaway Airship* (1929) and, in *Pirates of the Air* (1929) assists in the start of regular transatlantic air service using Apex amphibians and mid-ocean landing platforms. The routes established, he persuades the Apex Corporation to undertake manufacture of a rocket-powered stratosphere airplane (*On the Wings of Flame*,1929), defends the commercial service against the predations of a disgruntled engineer in *The Mysterious Monoplane* (1929), and, in *The Flying Windmill* (1930), tests a multi-engined autogiro.

Andy's later activities have an even more commercial flavor. *The Plane Without a Pilot* (1930) involves his testing of an automatic pilot and establishing its applications for commercial aviation. *Wings of Adventure* (1931) follows the inauguration of London to Capetown air service, using the Apex Corporation's latest development, an all-metal flying wing. *Across the Top of the*

World (1931) begins with the sale of an Apex diesel-powered amphibian to the Chinese government, and ends with Andy, Sam, and Sonny stranded for three months on the polar icecap. The final volume, *Prisoners of the Clouds* (1932), takes Andy and his friends to Central America as they test an Apex-designed all-metal dirigible, and ends with a hint of romance for Andy after they rescue level-headed, golden-haired Sally Curtis from the jungle. (Another facet of Andy's devotion to aircraft is evident when Adams remarks that, although Andy "liked boys far better than he did girls," he quickly decided that "as long as a girl had to be carried away in this drifting balloon, he and Sonny were lucky that it was Sally."[17])

Three qualities characterize the "Andy Lane" books. The first is the presentation of Andy himself. In the course of the twelve books he ages from seventeen to just under twenty, but is consistently described in Lindbergh-like fashion. Tall, slender, and fit, he has "keen blue eyes, a little wrinkled at the corners from too much squinting into wind and sun, [that] were set beneath a bronzed forehead and a tousled shock of sun-bleached hair." As his deeds increasingly capture the public eye, he becomes an idolized celebrity; "the most talked of boy of eighteen in the world today . . . , the public worships [him] just as much now as it did when [he] smashed the world's endurance record." Lindbergh's publicized regard for his mother comes into play, as well, for though Andy is "a hero known in every country in the world," he accepts his mother's treating him as "just her beloved nineteen year old boy who simply would persist in taking chances when there seemed to be no need of it."[18] Crowds follow his every move, yet he retains a quiet humanity. He is every boy's Everyman, a young person with whom other boys can easily identify, and one who offers them a guide to the future.

Second is Adams's frequent incorporation of up-to-date technology in the books. Although the majority of Apex-built aircraft are conventional, even conservative in design (they resemble contemporaneous Sikorsky craft, tending to be amphibians, both mono- and biplane designs, with pylon-mounted or under-wing engines), the books by and large reflect the latest developments of the times. The mid-ocean floating landing fields described in *Pirates of the Air,* a "surface large enough to permit the landing and taking off of the largest airplanes," were brainchildren of engineer E.R. Armstrong, and were intended to make commercial, transoceanic flights feasible using the equipment of the day. Though they were made unnecessary by advances in engine technology and airliner fuel capacity, they were given serious consideration at the time and had the endorsement of Lindbergh, Byrd, and other experts.[19]

The Flying Windmill gives an accurate description of the "flapping hinge" perfected by Juan de la Cierva (1895–1936), inventor of the autogiro. The autogiro resembles the helicopter in having a large, overhead rotor that adds to its lift and permits near-vertical takeoffs and landings. This is, however, an unpowered rotor, and gains its lift from the forward progress of the craft, created by a single, conventionally mounted propeller engine in the front; multi-engined autogiros of the sort described by Adams remained only designs. The autogiro's ability to take off and land in short distances gained it considerable attention in the 1930s, and there was widespread enthusiasm for it as an aircraft that might be adapted to popular use. Amelia Earhart set an altitude record of nearly 20,000 feet in one, another landed on the lawn of the White House, and advertisements for the craft showed its owners flying to golf clubs or hunting lodges for a day's recreation. It never lived up to its publicity, and was ultimately supplanted by the helicopter.[20]

The Plane Without a Pilot reflects the development of the Sperry "automatic pilot," a device originally created in 1912 to address the problem of in-flight stability. More advanced models (like the one described by Adams) permitted essentially "hands off" flying under normal conditions, and still later versions made possible many of the solo long-distance flights of the era, such as Wiley Post's round-the-world flight of 1933. The "flying wing" of *Wings of Adventure* is a clone of the massive Junkers G-38 launched in 1930, from its corrugated-metal wing to its four embedded diesel engines and box-kite tail,

The Junkers G-38 (1930), model for the flagship of Andy Lane's Apex Corporation in Eustace Adams' *Wings of Adventure* (1931). National Air and Space Museum, Smithsonian Institution (SI 72-17667).

differing primarily from the G-38 in having retractable landing gear. While not a true flying wing (i.e., a tailless aircraft consisting only of a wing, as in the modern warplane, the B-2 stealth bomber), it echoes the Junkers design by having only a rudimentary fuselage and housing its passengers and cargo within the wing structure proper.[21]

Even the seemingly fanciful all-metal dirigible of *Prisoners of the Clouds* is grounded in reality. Although airship development had been dominated by the Germans, who gained enormous publicity when the *Graf Zeppelin* completed its round-the-world trip in 1929, some research, encouraged by the Navy, continued in the United States. The semi-rigid, metal-clad airship ZMC-2, built by the Aircraft Development Corporation of Detroit to naval specifications, was launched in 1929 and performed successfully for the next decade. Its last flight was in 1939, and it was scrapped two years later.[22] Keeping up with current civil and military developments, Adams was doing his homework, and presented his young readers with a steady flow of intriguing contemporaneous designs and details.

Third, and finally, the books convey a well-developed portrait of the development of aviation as a business. Whether in design and manufacturing or in the creation of commercial air service, flight offers many opportunities for financial success. The initial volume ends with the head of the Apex firm telling Andy that "orders for airplanes and motors have poured into this office by mail, telegraph, cable and even radio. We shall have to put up a new factory to take care of the business." The second opens with Andy's being guaranteed unlimited fuel by the Superior Oil and Gas Company, for his endurance flight "accomplished as much for [the] oil company as it did for the Apex Company." Later books expand this commercial consciousness, as when the head of Apex prophesies that there will be "two paths through the skies, one for the ships heading toward New York, the other for those heading for Europe," or Andy sees the potential of the automatic pilot. "People will be ordering the Diesels and the gyroscope controls from all over the world," he says. "That will mean that the factory will make a lot more money and we, being stockholders, will get richer."[23] What only a few years earlier had been just a curiosity now opens the way to a practical enterprise with tangible benefits, and Adams prepares his young readers for their entry into the world to come.

Rex Lee flies for the excitement, Amos Green for the records, and Andy Lane for the good of the corporation, all dramatizing elements of the Lindbergh *persona*. Ted Scott, in contrast, flies for the sake of aviation. The longest-lived and most technologically sophisticated of the post-Lindbergh series, the Stratemeyer Syndicate's "Ted Scott Flying Stories" (1927–1943; twenty titles), by "Franklin W. Dixon," embraces the aims of the other series and adds to them a still greater concern: the degree to which aviation may, and should, become an assimilated part of everyday life. The books have, to be sure, their share and more of melodrama, trite events, and cardboard characters, yet from the outset they are grounded in the development of aviation, and they retain that foundation until late in the series.

That this grounding is intentional is clear from the proposal Stratemeyer submitted to Grossett & Dunlap on 24 May 1927. "Aviation," he wrote, "has evidently taken a new hold on the public mind, and from now on will undoubtedly increase in interest. . . . These stories will all be thoroughly up to date and will contain accurate information regarding flying machines, instruments employed, and general equipment." He reinforces his intention in the plot outline for the first volume, *Over the Ocean to Paris,* sent to writer John W. Duffield on 27 May 1927. After specifying that Ted is to work in the Devally-Hipson Aeroplane Corporation, he tells Duffield to "give some real aeroplane construction stuff;" when Ted at last sets out for France, Stratemeyer instructs him to include "some of the real stuff from the Lindbergh exploit—compass, propellers, engines, etc."[24]

The real-world frame of reference continues in the physical makeup of the initial volume, which is dedicated "To the Heroes of the Air." Listing the Wrights, Blériot, Byrd, Lindbergh, Chamberlin, and Maitland and Hegenberger, the dedication salutes them as those "who, by their daring exploits, have made aviation the wonderful achievement it is to-day."[25] Each succeeding title carries the same dedication, with new names and accomplishments—e.g., Hermann Koehl and James Fitzmaurice, who flew the Atlantic east-to-west (1928)—being added on occasion. The key phrase here is "wonderful achievement;" the dedication establishes that the Ted Scott stories are intended to sing the praises of aviation, and the books maintain that intention throughout the series.

In many respects, the initial books are vintage Stratemeyer. As in the "Tom Swift" and "Motor Boys" books, homespun melodrama accompanies Ted's more technical exploits, and *Over the Ocean to Paris, or Ted Scott's Daring Long-Distance Flight* (1927), incorporates both. Ted Scott, the air-struck foster son of two struggling hotel owners, impresses a pair of wealthy patrons with his courage and aeronautical knowledge, and the two magnates fund flying lessons for him. He enters the airmail service, flying for one of the civilian contract carriers, and, with further backing from his friends, successfully flies the Atlantic. *Rescued in the Clouds, or Ted Scott, Hero of the Air* (1927), the second tale, records Ted's gala reception back in the United States, spells out his plans for his own career and for aviation, and reports his gallant rescue missions to a flood-stricken region of the American South. The third volume, *Over the Rockies with the Air Mail, or Ted Scott Lost in the Wilderness* (1927), finds Ted once again flying the mail, surviving a crash in the mountains and becoming chief pilot for the line. The fourth, *First Stop Honolulu, or Ted Scott Over the Pacific* (1927), opens with Ted's setting a new altitude record of 47,000 feet, then follows his participation in a race to cross the Pacific.

Subsequent volumes continue the mix of melodrama and aviation advocacy, along with allusions to Lindbergh's 1927–1928 good-will flight to Mexico

The Curtiss-Bleeker Helicopter (1930), praised by Ted Scott in "Franklin W. Dixon's" *Flying to the Rescue* (1930). National Air and Space Museum, Smithsonian Institution (SI 91-1832).

and Central America. The three titles issued in 1928 take Ted to the Caribbean, to Mexico (where he becomes involved with revolutionaries), and, after thwarting a series of airmail robberies, to Australia. Those of 1929, including *The Lone Eagle of the Border, or Ted Scott and the Diamond Smugglers* and *Flying Against Time, or Ted Scott Breaking the Ocean to Ocean Record,* find him working to break the German-held endurance record, flying from Boston to Los Angeles in less than twenty hours, and scouring Brazil in search of a missing exploration party. Two polar flights occupy the stories of 1930, as Ted heads the aviation section of an Antarctic expedition, then treks through Alaska seeking a lost gold mine. The third volume of the year, *Flying to the Rescue, or Ted Scott and the Big Dirigible,* relates Ted's work with a new helicopter design, then his efforts to locate a luxury dirigible missing on its trans-Atlantic flight.

After Stratemeyer's death in May 1930, the frequency of the Scott books dropped to a book a year, a pattern continued until 1935, when the series was briefly suspended. Following a six-year hiatus, the books resumed in 1941, adding two more volumes before the series was finally terminated. Books of this period took on a more overtly scientific flavor, as Stratemeyer's daughters began to put their mark on the Syndicate's offerings. *Following the Sun Shadow, or Ted Scott and the Great Eclipse* (1932) is rich in astronomical lore, while *Castaways of the Stratosphere, or Hunting the Vanished Balloonists* (1935) draws upon the high-altitude balloon flights of Auguste Piccard in 1931 and 1932, and the National Geographic Society's ascent in 1934 (the outline for the latter volume directs Duffield to specific issues of *National Geographic Magazine* of 1933 and 1934 for details).[26] The final volumes of the series, *Hunting the Sky Spies, or Testing the Invisible Plane* (1941) and *The Pursuit Patrol, or Chasing the Platinum Pirates* (1943), attempt with little success to bring Ted into the era of World War II, ending the series.

Like the "Andy Lane" books, the "Ted Scott" stories are characterized by three consistent elements that run throughout the books. The first is Ted's obvious resemblance to Lindbergh; indeed, in the initial proposal, his name was "Ray Berg," and Stratemeyer's instructions point directly to the Lindbergh flight. Other traits are less blatant but no less imitative. Ted is, in his own right, a "lone eagle" figure of quiet competence, as the very title, *Lone Eagle of the Border,* makes explicit. He carries out his early exploits in solo flights, and, even when he later flies with a co-pilot, it is *his* skill and not that of his companion that invariably saves the day. When he returns from Europe, he responds to plaudits with Lindbergh-like modesty, and gives "the greater share of credit . . . to his plane." Moreover, like Lindbergh, he resents being called "Lucky," preferring to attribute his success to care. This care Ted extends, as did Lindbergh, to every aspect of a flight: "That 'luck,' if analyzed, would have been shown to consist in the great care and attention to detail that marked the beginning of all his trips."[27] He is the most Lindbergh-like of the series heroes, and he maintains this *persona* until well past Stratemeyer's death.

Second, Ted, more so than any other contemporaneous series hero, is a person with a deep and abiding personal identification with flight and aviation. He sees himself as a spokesperson for aviation in general, and American aviation in particular, intending to devote his subsequent career to the advancement of both. When he returns from France, he announces his plans to write a book, for he wants "to tell America what she ought to know, and to advance the cause of flying." Other concerns reflect those voiced by Lindbergh in his published statements. Like Lindbergh, Ted intends to campaign for "the establishment of air ports, [and] the development of commercial aviation, in which Europe lays all over us." When his book appears, it, like *We,* is acclaimed as being full of "force and interest because his heart was in the work and he knew just what he wanted to say to advance the cause of aviation."[28]

Later episodes accentuate his commitment to his profession and broaden his commitment to his country. He competes in a dangerous effort to set a new altitude record not to enhance his own reputation but to return the record to the United States: "The country of which he was so proud had snatched from overseas the record that it coveted, and he rejoiced that he had been the instrument in achieving this triumph for his people." He recognizes that aviation progress is an on-going process, and that no person can wholly anticipate the developments that will occur. "Aviation has made wonderful strides," he says in *Brushing the Mountain Top,* "but it's still in its infancy. There's room for all sorts of discoveries and improvements." His determination leads him to still greater achievements until, late in the series, even a British diplomat has to concede that "Young, virile, energetic America is the hope of the world, a sort of twentieth-century paradise."[29] In his devotion to flight and in his quiet patriotism, Ted is an attractive guide for the young folk who followed his adventures, and he speaks clearly for the appeal of aviation and aeronautical knowledge.

Finally, the books are exceptionally rich in aeronautical detail, information that is taken, in most cases, with little change from the most authoritative sources of the day. There is precedent for such borrowing: Other writers, beginning with H.L. Sayler in 1910, rely upon aeronautical texts to flesh out their stories, and every generation of writers afterward follows suit. Duffield, however, goes much further, regularly appropriating themes and details in lengthy passages excerpted from both the popular and the technical press. The details and dimensions of Ted's trans-Atlantic plane, the *Hapworth* (named after one of his benefactors, it appeared as the *St. Louis* in the original manuscript, but was renamed in copy-editing), match those of *The Spirit of St. Louis,* and come unacknowledged with little or no change from an article in the 20 June 1927 issue of *Aviation.* Ted's idea (in *Rescued in the Clouds*) for developing an "airplane station in mid-ocean" contains depth and distance figures along with entire passages taken directly from a July *New York Times* feature on "An Airplane Station in the Midocean." Anticipating the E.R. Armstrong designs that Eustace Adams employs two years later, the volume quotes engineering data and ocean-bottom descriptions appearing in the *Times,* and even reiterates the article's speculation that such a floating station would be valuable as a site for oceanographic and meteorological research.[30]

This pattern of detailed but unacknowledged borrowing continues throughout the Duffield-written volumes. In *First Stop Honolulu,* Ted comments on the construction of his engine valves and their remarkable service during his trans-Atlantic flight: "filled with a salt solution to promote more rapid dissipation of heat," they undergo "the equivalent of a laborer striking fifty two-hundred-pound blows a minute with a sixteen-pound sledge hammer." The details and images come verbatim from a note in *Aero Digest,* which makes the same points about those in the engine of *The Spirit of St. Louis.* The salt-cooled valve invented by Samuel D. Heron and developed at McCook Field in Ohio contributed to the reliability of the Wright Whirlwind engines that powered the *Spirit of St. Louis* and other record-setting aircraft of the times, and marked a notable advance in engine technology.[31]

The muffler that enables easy in-flight conversation in the cockpit during Ted's flight *Across the Pacific,* "a tube with the back portion perforated with small holes or gills," is described in the same words that Ted uses in the 18 June 1928 issue of *Aviation.* Similarly, the magneto compass ("a magnetron or rotating coil of wire . . . in a cavity within the bar") and radio altimeter Ted employs in *Flying Against Time* are detailed in two adjacent articles in *Science* for 14 December 1928, and are described in the language of the scientific journal; the articles' proximity to one another suggests that Duffield's use of both was a classic bit of serendipity.[32]

Still more extensive is the description of the experimental helicopter in *Flying to the Rescue.* A fantastic-sounding craft using four individually-driven propellers to power its main rotor and balancing them with "stabovators," it has specifications identical to those of the Curtiss-Bleeker helicopter discussed and pictured in *Aero Digest* for July 1930, and is described in passages taken without change from the article. The same aircraft, described in the same words, goes on to figure in the next volume, *Danger Trails of the Sky, or Ted*

Scott's Great Mountain Climb (1931). Duffield continues his practice of generous borrowing even into the final volume of the series, *The Pursuit Patrol*. Here he takes data on ethylene glycol as an engine coolant from an article in *Liberty* for 14 February 1942, and goes on to echo the article's mention of an air-borne cannon that fires through the propeller hub.[33]

Duffield's apparent plagiarism raises several literary and legal issues. In his defense, he was a contract writer producing four to eight books a year for Stratemeyer while holding down a regular job as a journalist. As "Roy Rockwood" and "Victor Appleton," respectively, he was principal writer for the "Bomba the Jungle Boy" and "Don Sturdy" series. As "Richard H. Stone" he launched the short-lived "Slim Tyler Air Stories" [1930–1932; six titles], probably writing later titles in the series, and he contributed to other series, as well. His livelihood required him to produce copy at a frantic rate. His use of materials from wherever and whenever he found them is understandable if not forgivable, and he obviously felt no qualms about discovery or censure.

Second, and more to the point, Duffield obviously was a careful, enthusiastic student of the accelerating pace of aviation technology. His ready familiarity with a wide range of such technical sources as *Aviation* and *Aero Digest*, evidenced throughout the run of the "Ted Scott" books, is surpassed only by his obvious delight in playing with technical details. The passages in which Ted describes the latest developments, even allowing for the obvious boost that Duffield gets from the language of his sources, are invariably among the liveliest of the text, and his enthusiasm is infectious. In aircraft technology, he and Ted say to their audience, one finds fascinating materials that are opening the way to the future; the person who can understand the milieu and speak the language will be the person who prevails. His attention to aeronautical development extends throughout his association with the "Ted Scott" books. As late as 1941, he assured Harriet Stratemeyer Adams (who had offered him *Hunting the Sky Spies*) that he had "kept pretty well in touch with aviation developments and there will be no trouble as regards the technical features of the work."[34]

Third, and most intriguing, although Edward Stratemeyer limited himself to generalized suggestions about the kind of information to be included, the Stratemeyer daughters seem to have openly encouraged Duffield's borrowings. The outlines they produced after their father's death give, if anything, more elaborate plot details than did the earlier ones, and go on to suggest specific sources from which Duffield might draw details. Most of the works suggested are periodicals (as in the frequent mention of the *National Geographic*), but others are as varied as Erna Fergusson's novel, *Dancing Gods,* or a 1941 address by Juan Trippe, president of Pan American Airways, before the Royal Aeronautical Society of London, and Duffield dutifully includes extracts from most of the sources recommended.[35] That the Stratemeyer daughters were unaware of his borrowing seems highly unlikely, and their continued supplying of sources is at least tacit approval of his technique.

Given the specific moral ethic that runs throughout the Stratemeyer books, and the larger moral ethic coming to be associated with aviation and flight, Duffield's actions are hugely ironic. He uses plagiarized (albeit scrupulously accurate) materials to bolster his accounts of a character whose life and activities are devoted to the most forthright candor and honesty. Morally and legally questionable though his borrowings are, there is some comfort in believing that he hoped his readers would recognize and respond to the authority with which he spoke and not think to consider the sources from which it was derived. Plagiarist or not, he took seriously Stratemeyer's order to include "the real stuff." His melodrama may have come from Stratemeyer's outlines, but his aviation lore comes from unimpeachable sources. His meticulous research makes Duffield an authoritative spokesperson for aeronautical knowledge, and the "Ted Scott" books are singularly reliable conduits of accurate aviation data for the readers toward which they were aimed.

Varied though the several series are in the ways in which they use the elements of Lindbergh's career, they are remarkably uniform in other respects.

All of them acknowledge that the airplane is a complex assembly of mechanical systems, each of which is necessary for the successful operation of the craft. These systems are in a constant state of evolutionary development, and, to be safe and of practical use, they must be mastered and controlled by a knowledgeable, responsible, and well-prepared person. All recognize that preparing for, and engaging in, the activity of flying necessarily requires the aviator to possess special skills and perspectives. Operating, as he does, in the three-dimensional realm of the air, freed from the constraints of earth-bound activities, the successful flier must develop a unique, distinctive outlook upon life in the larger sense.

That outlook, in turn, will enable the air-minded, air-competent individual to be a powerful influence in shaping the world to come. All of the Lindbergh-based series reflect their creators' grasp of the socio-economic potential and (to a degree) limitations of the airplane. With its speed, its ability to span distances quickly, and its freedom from the restraints of roadway or rails, the airplane will necessarily effect social change. Certain to become an integral part of daily life, the airplane will shape the way Americans conduct even the most mundane activities, and the air-centered society that results will be a testament to the progressive power of flight. The public enthusiasm for aviation that Joseph Corn notes building throughout the post-Lindbergh era pales beside the enthusiasm being communicated to American youth.[36]

Like Lindbergh himself, the aviation books make little effort to sugar-coat the technical side of aviation, offering it instead as one more part of the variety and wonder of flying in general. Aviation is a new and special realm, they imply, and the person who is to be a knowledgeable member of the society to come must understand its nature and its elements. One finds, therefore, the books implicitly and consistently offering instruction in the principles and vocabulary of flight. Characters talk of the basic needs for flight: airspeed, camber, dihedral, angle of incidence, lift, and drag. They discuss the requirements of three-axis control, considering roll, pitch, and yaw. They speak glibly and accurately of the means necessary to achieve that control—ailerons, rudders, and stabilizers (often called "flippers")—and the consequences of the loss of control, whether a stall, a spin, or a perilous dive.

Even the construction of the airplane comes in for detailed comment. The characters speak familiarly of struts, bracing, shock absorbers, and the benefits of streamlining, and, as new materials and techniques are introduced, they quickly appear in the books. Thomson Burtis devotes two pages to the mechanics of "rigging" a craft's fuselage, adjusting internal bracing and wires with turnbuckles and bubble levels until the entire structure is perfectly aligned and free of distortion. Eustace Adams makes a point of explaining the all-metal construction of the Apex flying wing, while "Franklin W. Dixon" gives Ted Scott, already a master of control systems and engine elements, comfortable familiarity with the properties of duralumin (a light, corrosion-resistant aluminum-copper-manganese alloy that came to be used throughout the industry for both internal and external construction). Knowing duralumin as he does, Ted can speak knowledgeably of its applications to save weight while maintaining structural rigidity.[37]

Like Lindbergh in his own writings, the books emphasize the varied instruments that are becoming so much a part of flight. Some are gauges familiar from the automobile—those monitoring fuel level, oil pressure, electrical status, engine temperature, and overall speed. Others, however, are new and unique to aviation: the altimeter, measuring the distance to the ground; the turn-and-bank indicator, indicating whether the craft is in level, straight-line flight; the tachometer, measuring engine and propeller revolutions, enabling a check on fuel consumption and forward progress; the drift gauge, revealing the effects of side winds; and the compass (frequently an earth-inductor model, like that used by Lindbergh, as well as the more familiar magnetic compass), to indicate direction of flight. Also new is a necessary duplication of instrumentation, for a multi-engined craft must have a full set of instruments for each engine, and multiple fuel tanks require a gauge for each tank.

The number and variety of aircraft instruments makes the cockpit daunting to the lay person. The aviator, however, understands the value of those instruments, for they are his guide to the aircraft's condition. The success of his mission and his very life depend upon them. He takes their complexity in stride, checking the instrument panel as almost second nature, trusts their data unquestioningly, and comes to depend upon them as essential adjuncts to a successful flight. "John Prentice Langley" remarks that "upon the ability of Amos and Danny to read and comprehend and properly utilize these complicated mechanisms depended the very lives of both pilot and navigator," but it remains for Eustace Adams to establish the instruments' worth most vividly. Cruising through the night in the "flying windmill," Andy Lane sees the lighted dials on the instrument panel before him as "the faces of friends who were helping him to guide his ship and to keep her safe in her steady course through the skies." The flier's increasing dependence upon the technology of his instruments is a central attribute of aviation, and the books establish its importance.[38]

Paralleling the importance of an airplane's instruments is the increasing reliability of other aircraft systems, especially the basic structure and the engine. This, too, is a part of the books' messages. Early craft were fragile things, built of wood, covered with cloth, and exposing their pilots to the open air. More modern craft have enclosed cabins and fuselages, metal frames, and, increasingly, metal coverings. Their durability and reliability increase accordingly, and they can withstand external conditions and carry out flight maneuvers that earlier models could not. Engine technology has made its own advances; the unreliable power plants of the early days and the oil-spewing rotary engine of World War I have been supplanted by engines like the Wright Whirlwind, which seem almost flawless in their endurance and reliability. More and more fliers take engine performance for granted, but Amos Green, recognizing what an advance has occurred, explicitly compares the Whirlwind's reliability to that of the human heart.[39]

Such reliability makes new uses for the airplane not only possible, but also practicable. Regularly scheduled commercial aviation, providing reliable service and an unprecedented degree of comfort, is now within reach. Regional and national airlines, like Transcontinental Air Transport, capitalizing upon Lindbergh's name, and Boeing Air Transport, precursor of United Airlines, became realities, and the books echo the progress. Rex Lee helps to make the Coast Air Express a going concern, "built on absolute reliability," for instance, and Andy Lane marvels over the duralumin furniture, carpeted deck, and curtained portholes that make the flying wing's passenger cabins islands of luxury.[40] Volume after volume, incident after incident, the aviation series feed the growing momentum of air-mindedness by extolling aviation's new security.

The aviator's familiarity with the details of flight, reliance upon instruments, and new confidence in the machine's reliability lead to a final innovation. This is the merging of man and machine—not one that leads to the creation of the cyborg so beloved of science-fiction writers, but one that creates persons who possess a spiritual affinity with the craft they fly. The process began with the publication of Lindbergh's *We*. Though the pronoun was intended to refer to the collaboration of Lindbergh and his St. Louis backers, the public saw it as embracing the pilot and his airplane. What resulted was a mental linking of man and machine that elevated the image of flight out of the ordinary. Instead of a simple exploitation of laws of nature and fluid mechanics made possible by an advanced technology, flight was transformed into an intimate cooperation of man and machine.

The aviation stories, not surprisingly, seize upon this intimacy. Recognizing the power of its appeal to the increasingly air-minded members of the younger generation, they make it a central part of their message. For them, the true flier, the best flier, is the one who relates to his aircraft not as a possession or a tool, but as a friend and ally. "John Prentice Langley" speaks of Lindbergh's book as revealing the *Spirit of St. Louis* to be "a veritable part of his own life," then extends the identification to all fliers, whose "faithful companions of their lonely voyages through space they grow to love." From love to worship is but a step, and Amos Green soon takes it. His regard for his airplane, and its Whirlwind engine in particular, grows until he is almost to "the point of worshipping it like a Hottentot does a fetish."[41]

For Rex Lee, there is no doubt. His response to the airplane combines emotion, affection, and spiritual affinity: "Somehow to him a motor was a thing alive, and a thing of marvelous beauty. His affection for his profession went further than the mere love of flying. An airplane was like a Sweetheart to him, and the dreams he dreamed of a sky filled with them were like a religion." In fact, Rex's religious response to flight implies a kind of monastic celibacy surpassing even that of Andy Lane. Considering the course of his relationship with a lady friend, he muses comfortably that "somehow girls didn't interest him as girls. It was as though his first and only love was the air, and he knew that for a long time to come it would have first place in his heart." Ted Scott also thinks of his craft as a sweetheart, but gives it qualities that the books seem to deny lesser beings, such as women: "It seemed to him a living, breathing pulsing entity. At times he found himself talking to it as though it were a sentient being that could respond."[42] The romance of flight offers a relationship that easily transcends anything offered by mundane or fleshly love.

Gilbert Seldes, writing in *The New Republic* on the eve of Lindbergh's flight, captures for his adult audience what the series books capture for youngsters. "Airplanes," he says, "are a triumph of applied science and a triumph of the human spirit at the same time. . . . Here is something better than machinery and better than man. Your eyes turn again to Lindbergh, the man who seems to pilot his plane as a rider his horse, identifying himself with its movements, in a sort of good-humored ecstasy."[43] What once was an exercise in mechanical skill, technical competence, and mental discipline becomes an organic process that is an extension of life itself. The joy of flight is no longer restricted to the intellectual satisfaction of mastering a complex mechanical process and temporarily defeating the law of gravity. Instead, it takes on qualities of the emotional, and even the spiritual. As the books seek to convey the excitement of flight, they present something far greater than a simple thrill. They offer instead a sense of flying as involving a total engagement with the craft and the activity, and issue a call to a whole new way of experiencing life.

In dealing with the experience of life, the books pose a challenging question. What, they ask, is the impact of aviation upon those who engage in it? What does it require of the person? What, in return, does it offer? And, most important, what are the larger consequences of committing one's self to a life of flying? Harking back to the stories of the "birdman era," the books acknowledge that flying requires particular talents and attitudes. Minimizing the physical demands of flying (technological advances make the simple activity of flying easier and more comfortable), they stress instead the mental and spiritual attributes of the aviator, and the qualities that emerge from the activity of flying. They offer their young readers, in fact, the vision of the aviator as a being special, separate, and superior, a person who by nature and profession stands apart from, and above, the mundane world.

The production of an aviator begins with the individual. To be successful, the books argue, one must be, to be sure, physically fit, possessed of good health and good eyesight. Those traits, however, are only the beginning, for they must be accompanied by deft physical coordination, acuity of mind, and careful training in the fundamentals of aviation. One of Ted Scott's mentors readily acknowledges that Ted has an appropriately athletic build, but points out there is more to becoming an aviator than just physical fitness. Clarity of thought, decisiveness of action, and the knowledge upon which to base those decisions are also among the earmarks of a good aviator, and "You won't know whether you have them all till they put you through a course of sprouts."[44] Many of aviation's skills can be learned, but they will be of little value unless the individual has the essential qualities to make the most of them.

When a person has those qualities, and when they are augmented by the acquired skills of the aviator, the results are apparent to almost all. In his stance, in his reactions, and in his larger outlook, the aviator is distinctive, standing out in any group. Even to a casual observer, for example, Rex Lee is no ordinary person. Having assimilated the skills of flight and made them his own, he is more at home in the air than on the ground or in polite society: He may have "the face of a man who was at once the eternal boy and yet a man," but "thousands of hours in the air had given his eyes the look which was in them. His body seemed to coördinate better, his brain to work faster, and his spirit to be more at rest when he was in the air."[45] The personal qualities He has are notable at all times, but they become most pronounced in the skies.

After the individual comes the society. As more and more persons begin to acquire the traits of the aviator, they will build a body of shared experience that will draw them into an elite subculture of those who know flight first-hand. This group, like any subculture, quickly develops its own rituals, symbols, mores, and conventions. These elements, in turn, overshadow more conventional traits, until aviators' engagement with flying, the books suggest, is able to supplant political and national concerns. Recognizing their common concerns and shared interests, pilots accept one another at face value, sharing information and experiences in the name of the common good in ways that less fortunate persons do not.[46]

The distinctiveness and intimacy of the piloting culture pervade the series books of the post-Lindbergh era. Andy Lane, acknowledging the in-flight greeting of another pilot, reflects on the camaraderie of his class: "The comradeship of the air is a friendly thing. Those who ride the wings of the storm . . . meet each other with something more than idle curiosity." Later he comes to see the society of aviators as a world unto itself, a "world of spruce, fabric, lighted cabins, and friendly men to which Andy belonged." Amos Green echoes the belief, remarking that whatever their politics may be, the fliers he meets in the Soviet Union are no different from those he knows at home: "Air pilots are about the same wherever you strike them—big-hearted chaps every one, and with a feeling of comradeship toward others of the same calling." And the origins of this comradeship, "Langley" goes on to observe, lie in the combination of shared skill, shared experience, and shared feeling: "The love of aviation, with its amazing victories and dangers, draws men into a close comradeship, such as nothing else on earth may."[47] Individual experiences lead to class experiences, and the class of airmen is one set apart by its appreciation of the common challenges and delights that its members experience.

The class is, however, set still further apart by its response to the qualities of flight. Just as flying creates persons who are more comfortable in the air than on the ground, or individuals who are able to interact most freely with other fliers whatever their national origin, it also creates persons who find in flight a liberation unlike anything that can be found on earth. Joseph Corn, writing of what he calls "the prophetic creed of flight," notes the views of several writers who argue that flying may well bring about a new kind of "species reborn in the heavens."[48] The juvenile aviation books endorse and advance this belief unhesitatingly. To their young readers they present a vision of personal experience that makes the individual into an enlightened being greater, more perceptive, and more liberal in outlook than any earth-bound creature. In their pages, the books suggest that aviation offers a chance to slip the surly bonds of earth and become something higher, greater, and finer than is possible through life's conventional range of activity.

All of the principal characters in these books experience the rush of exaltation to some degree. It may occur as the simple calming of spirit that Rex Lee experiences when he's in flight or the exaltation of Andy Lane as he once more strikes out "for distant horizons, for unknown adventures and for many, many hours in the air. . . . What greater thrill could there be than that?"[49] Whatever its manifestation, though, the feeling makes the person experiencing it aware of his unique place in the world. Through flight he is blessed with a vision of life and the world that sets him apart from his peers. There is no other term for the sensation but "religious experience," and the books mince no words in communicating its ecstasies.

Among the several flying heroes, it is Ted Scott who most frequently and most vividly undergoes this transformation. As early as *First Stop Honolulu,* his fourth adventure, the simple act of a take-off makes him feel "like an eagle released from its cage. All artificial barriers had dropped away. He was alone in illimitable space, and his spirit expanded in sympathy." His spiritual expansion leads to the first of several out-of-body experiences: "Emancipated from the trammels of the flesh . . . , Earth had slipped away from him. It seemed to be something dim and alien." Later adventures, if anything, only intensify the feeling. In *Across the Pacific* he undergoes another episode of spiritual detachment, but this leads to a humanitarian epiphany, "as though he were a disembodied spirit . . . pervaded with a compassionate pity for the great mass of humanity doomed to walk the earth." The following year, in *Over the Jungle Trails,* he achieves a near-Emersonian identification with the cosmos. His soul expands, and "he felt that he was brother to the sun and moon and stars." The process continues until in *Lost at the South Pole,* he is purged of the contaminants of corporeal life and becomes, at last, a free entity in its purest state: "The air seemed more his natural element than the earth. . . . All the soil and stain of earth seemed stripped away in that clean, cool upper air."[50]

The language and the passion, of course, are Duffield's contribution; no mention of these feelings occurs in any of the plot outlines that Stratemeyer furnished, and the outlines themselves deal only with the plot trajectory and the obstacles Ted must overcome. Yet these same qualities—transcendence, purity, compassion, a distancing from the common herd—occur to one degree or another throughout the various series, not just in the Stratemeyer products. Whatever the books' origin, they convey to their young readers an idealistic, even utopian vision of what flight can accomplish, and they make of aviation something far greater than a simple profession. It is an enterprise that can—

and will—change the individual. That change, if the person is prepared for it, will only be for the better, and the individual that results will be one who has the potential to change the world.

In the years following Lindbergh's flight, social change prompted and shaped by the airplane seemed a credible possibility. Earlier writers had speculated about how the airplane might become the catalyst for a dramatically improved world, but, whereas those writings had seemed only speculative, the means for change now appeared to be at hand. Technological advances made aircraft safer and more comfortable, increasing their appeal to the public. The widely publicized Safe Aircraft Competition of 1927—1929, sponsored by the Daniel Guggenheim Fund for the Promotion of Aeronautics, sought developments in the reliability and safety to "hasten the inevitable day when the airplane will be operated even in inexpert hands with at least the ease and safety of the motor car." Lindbergh himself spoke enthusiastically of developments in safety, and acknowledged the Guggenheim competition's role in encouraging designers to develop aircraft for "the average person who wants to fly." From the Fund's challenge came the Curtiss Tanager, a light plane equipped with a "floating" aileron, automatic leading-edge wing slats, and pilot-adjustable flaps that made it capable of short takeoffs, slow-speed landings, and unprecedented freedom from stalls.[51]

Safety advances were paralleled by manufacturing advances. Although the airplane was recognized as likely never to be as inexpensive as the automobile, its costs were being reduced to a point that at least put aircraft within the reach of a larger segment of the population. Henry Ford began the development of a single-engined, single-seat "flying flivver" that would be the airborne equivalent of the Model T. The craft drew extensive public attention, especially after Lindbergh flew one variant, but never lived up to expectations and the project was eventually scrapped. Other proposals followed, including autogiros and airplanes that could be converted from flying machines to roadworthy automobiles, but none proved practical. Nevertheless, the idea of an airplane that would be as accessible as the automobile persisted, and visions of the future invariably included such a machine.[52]

With these visions came new concepts for airfields. Recognizing that increased numbers of airplanes would require increased landing sites, and recognizing further that the needs of general aviation were different from those of commercial aviation, designers began to generate plans for airfields ranging from the streamlined to the futuristic. The pace picked up in 1929, when the Lehigh Portland Cement Company launched a nationwide design competition to develop fields "for the accommodation of each class of flying operations, scheduled air transport, private flying, and miscellaneous air services." Plans submitted ranged from elegant Art Deco edifices with underground boarding tunnels to utilitarian downtown strips stretching from the top of one skyscraper to another. Their vision of the modern city assumed the presence of aircraft, and all tacitly conveyed the message that aviation would leave its mark on daily life.[53]

That mark extended even to recreation. The initial number of *The Sportsman Pilot,* a periodical created to stimulate the creation of "aviation country clubs," featured an article describing a clubhouse shaped like an airplane. Golfers from throughout the region would fly to the facility and leave their aircraft at an adjacent hangar for shelter and service. Entering the clubhouse, they would find the transverse section (the "wings") housing locker, grill, and dining rooms on the first story, and, on the second, open-air decks for *al fresco* dining and observation of airfield operations. The longitudinal section ("fuselage") would hold staff and utility rooms on the first level, and, above them, guest rooms for fliers who were making longer stays. This structure, the author announces, captures handily the "similarities between the spirit of modernity as exemplified in our most conspicuous and brilliant facility, the airplane, and the spirit of our newest building." Both airplanes and buildings proclaim "what [their makers'] world is headed for; what his world wants; what the people he builds for are like underneath."[54]

The direction and sense of the public that buildings and aircraft proclaim for modern America involve several elements, the article maintains. First, the new American possesses a singular acuity of insight and a "pitiless honesty." From that honesty comes "the sharpness, the wit, and the sincerity of our new style; it must be as sharp and honest as the airplane." Second is a new degree of emotional engagement, prompted by an aesthetic reaction to the structures. "We have passed on to a new aesthetic love for our aircraft, and this aesthetic love will influence . . . our builders. This aesthetic love of flying is connected with its special and striking features of daring and breathtaking heroism." And out of those "special and striking features" comes the final element, the recognition, by individual and culture alike, that the dominant individual of the modern, aeronautical society is one with "the poise and the simplicity of the man who . . . may sit poised . . . in the calm of tremendous responsibility, a responsibility which he is equal to; and realize himself as potential master of motion and space."[55] The airplane, modern style, and the modern attitude toward the world are fused into a single, unified vision, with the human individual master of all.

The aviation series books wholeheartedly embraced this outlook. Committed as they were to singing the praises of flight, they did not take long to endorse the idea that aviation and daily life were soon to be inseparably wedded. When that wedding was complete, the citizens of the future would be living in a technologically integrated world enhanced and advanced by flight. Airplanes will supplant the automobile for even the most ordinary of errands ("Why should people creep along the earth when they can fly through the air?" Ted Scott asks at one point), and the very fabric of society will be shaped to accommodate to the airplane's qualities. "The fantastic things of today are the realities of tomorrow," the Secretary of Government Aviation tells Ted, and the books make it their aim to see those realities come to be.[56]

The first realm to be affected will be that of business. The increased speed of air travel and the emergence of reliable trans-continental service had already attracted the attention of the business community, and the books have no difficulty in postulating a world of air-borne business. Andy Lane sees the emergence of regular trans-Atlantic passenger and freight service to London, trans-Caribbean service to Havana, and airmail service linking North America, England, Europe, and Africa. Rex Lee thinks with equanimity of a world in which "huge, stately craft would sweep the sky, and a proportion of the business of the world go on in the limitless heavens," and Ted Scott foresees the building of airstrips atop urban stores, hotels, and office buildings for the benefit of their patrons.[57]

Ted has ample precedent for his speculation. In addition to the designs emerging from the Lehigh Competition of 1929, the Gibbons Company, a building firm located in Brooklyn, New York, in April 1928 published a two-page advertisement in *Aero Digest,* announcing its designs for "landing planes of every description in restricted areas, such as on top of buildings." The company is motivated, the advertisement continues, by its "pride in promoting international aviation with the same spirit as that of Colonel Lindbergh, with no mercenary purpose." Going on to cite Lindbergh and Chamberlin as evidence that "force of character and indomitable persistence are the things that win," the advertisement closes with a call for action: "AVIATION IS KNOCKING AT OUR DOORS NOW."[58] Ted, the Lehigh Competition entrants, the Gibbons Company, and numerous others agree that businessmen will take flying for granted as they carry out their activities, and soon come to depend upon airplanes, personal as well as commercial, as they in the past have depended upon the railroad and the automobile.

The realm of ordinary daily life will not be far behind. Household practices and routines will assimilate the airplane as readily as will business, and soon family members will think as little of a flying junket as they do of an auto ride. Short takeoff or vertical ascent craft will stimulate suburban flying by doing away with the need for an extended runway. Homeowners will be able to keep one or more airplanes in the garage, roll them out on a moment's notice, and speed off on errands. Sunday-afternoon picnic flights will replace the afternoon drive, and, whereas an automobile outing might involve fifteen or twenty miles, the airborne outing will cover several states and hundreds of miles. When this at last comes about, as Ted Scott happily predicts, "The skies will be fairly black with machines, the same as the roads now are full of automobiles on Sunday or a holiday."[59]

Just as Ted most keenly feels the transcendent influences of flight, so, too, does he understand its commercial possibilities and its social implications. He is devoted to bringing about the air-minded society of the future, and he wastes no opportunity to tout its virtues. In his view of the future, "It will be thought a disgrace, or at least a sign of poverty, not to own an airplane. And there will be enough fool-proof devices invented to make it as safe to drive an airplane as it is now to drive a car." That future, moreover, is near at hand: "I'm not talking of a hundred years from now. I'll give ten years, twenty years at most, before this becomes a reality."[60]

The time span Ted cites is significant, for it puts the aerial future well within the lifetime and working years of the youngsters to whom he speaks. Brought up to be air-minded, steeped in the lore of flight and proficient in its technology, assured of the heights—literal and figurative, worldly and spiritual—to which they can aspire, the American youths of the 1920s and 1930s are a receptive audience for the allure of the series books. Whether they incline toward Rex Lee, Andy Lane, and the commercial side of aviation, or whether they, like Ted Scott, embrace a larger, all-encompassing view of flight and the world, they are the individuals who will shape the future. Soon to be the businesspeople, homeowners, and family members who move through the backgrounds of the series stories, they are being encouraged to think of a cleaner, better time, when the attributes of flight meld with those of daily existence, and the world truly will have become a society driven by a zeal to live up to the exalting challenges of aviation.

NOTES TO CHAPTER FIVE

1 G. Anderson Orb, "The Juvenile Aircraft Industry," *Scientific American,* 143 (October 1930): 294–295.

2 "Wings for You!" [American Sky Cadets advertisement], *Model Airplane News,* 4 (February 1931): inside front cover; Joseph J. Corn, *The Winged Gospel: America's Romance with Aviation, 1900–1950* (New York: Oxford University Press, 1983), 113–120. *Model Airplane News* began publication in mid-1929 and, in 2006, is still a major journal for aircraft modelers.

3 Silas Weatherby, "Modelin' Planes," *Universal Model Airplane News,* 9 (September 1933): 8.

4 L.P. Wyman, Ph.D., *The Hunniwell Boys' Longest Flight* (New York: A.L. Burt, 1928), 22–23. See also "Dr. Levi P. Wyman, Author, Educator," *New York Times,* 18 April 1950, 31.

5 The fullest study of Burtis's career and works to date is David K. Vaughan, "Thomson Burtis' Rex Lee Aviation Stories," *Dime Novel Roundup,* 59 (February 1990): 2–7.

6 This story appeared, under the same title and over Burtis's byline, as a free-standing work in *American Boy* for August1927. A prefatory editorial note hailed it as "deviating only slightly from the actual details of Colonel Lindbergh's great adventure" and bringing the flight "home to you with all the vividness of a tense, personal experience."

7 Thomson Burtis, *Rex Lee, Flying Detective* (New York: Grosset & Dunlap, 1932), 146.

8 Thomson Burtis, *Rex Lee on the Border Patrol* (New York: Grosset & Dunlap, 1928), 16; Thomson Burtis, *Rex Lee, Ace of the Air Mail* (Grosset & Dunlap, 1929), 6; Thomson Burtis, *Rex Lee, Night Flyer* (New York: Grosset & Dunlap, 1929), 62.

9 John Prentice Langley [St. George Rathborne], *Chasing the Setting Sun or a Hop, Skip, and Jump to Australia* (New York: Barse & Co., 1930), 213; "Rathborne, St. George H.," *Who Was Who Among North American Authors, 1921–1939,* Vol. 2 (Detroit: Gale Research, 1976), 1195.

10 John Prentice Langley [St. George Rathborne], *Desert Hawks on the Wing, or Headed South, Algiers to Cape Town* (New York: Barse & Co., 1929), 14–16.

11 Langley, *Desert Hawks on the Wing,* 14–15; John Prentice Langley [St. George Rathborne], *Trail Blazers of the Skies, or Across to Paris, and Back* (New York: New York: Barse & Co., 1927), 22.

12 "The Army Flight to Hawaii," *Aero Digest,* 11 (July 1927): 16–18.

13 Langley, *Trail Blazers of the Skies,* 9, 154; John Prentice Langley [St. George Rathborne], *Spanning the Pacific, or A Non-stop Hop to Japan* (New York: Barse & Co., 1927): 12–13; John Prentice Langley [St. George Rathborne], *The Staircase of the Wind, or Over the Himalayas to Calcutta* (New York: Barse & Co., 1931): 214–215, 36.

14 John Prentice Langley [St. George Rathborne], *Bridging the Seven Seas, or On the Air-Lane to Singapore* (New York: Barse & Co., 1930), 200. See also "Wins Schiff Trophy for Safe Flights," *New York Times,* 15 December 1928, 13, and "Schiff Trophy Award," *Aero Digest,* 14 (January 1929): 10.

15 David K. Vaughan, "Eustace Adams' Andy Lane Series," *Dime Novel Roundup,* 57 (August, October 1988): 52–60, 68–73. See also Reginald Wright Arthur, "Eustace Lane Adams," *Contact! Careers of U.S. Naval Aviators,* Vol. 1 (Washington, DC: Naval Aviator Register, 1967), 147.

16 Back cover advertisement, Eustace L. Adams, *Racing Around the World* (New York: Grosset & Dunlap, 1928).

17 Eustace L. Adams, *Prisoners of the Clouds* (Grosset & Dunlap, 1932), 161–62. The girl-boy-airplane triangle appears frequently in the post-Lindbergh series stories (see the discussion of Rex Lee and Ted Scott, below), although there is no real debate as to its outcome. What wholesome American boy would choose to mess about with a girl when he had an airplane at his disposal?

18 Eustace L. Adams, *On the Wings of Flame* (New York: Grosset & Dunlap, 1929), 2; Eustace L. Adams, *Over the Polar Ice* (New York: Grosset & Dunlap, 1928), 2; Adams, *Racing Around the World,* 3.

19 Eustace L. Adams, *Pirates of the Air* (New York: Grosset & Dunlap, 1929), 49. E.R. Armstrong discusses his plans in "Seadromes and Ocean Flying," *Aviation,* 23 (28 November 1927): 1288–1290; a more popular treatment is Paul W. White, "Bridging the Ocean with Man-Made Islands," *American Magazine,* 108 (November 1929): 46–49, 165–170.

20 Eustace L. Adams, *The Flying Windmill* (New York: Grosset & Dunlap, 1930), 26; Richard Aellen, "The Autogiro and Its Legacy," *Air & Space/Smithsonian,* 4 (December 1989/January 1990): 52–59. A convenient study of autogiro history is Peter W. Brooks, *Cierva Autogiros: The Development of Rotary-Wing Flight* (Washington, DC: Smithsonian Institution Press, 1988).

21 Terry Gwynn-Jones, *Farther and Faster: Aviation's Adventuring Years, 1909–1939* (Washington, DC: Smithsonian Institution Press, 1991), 247–250; Marion Huggins, "Gyropilot Goes Cross-Country," *Aero Digest,* 17 (July 1930): 51–52, 208; Eustace L. Adams, *Wings of Adventure* (New York: Grosset & Dunlap, 1931), 6–7; Richard M. Mock, "The Junkers G-38," *Aviation,* 28 (18 January 1930): 113–117. A reliable historical overview of flying wing development prior to the advent of the B-2 is E.T. Wooldridge, *Winged Wonders: The Story of the Flying Wings* (Washington, DC: Smithsonian Institution Press, 1985).

22 Alexander Klemin, "A Successful Metal-Clad Airship," *Scientific American,* 140 (November 1929): 436–437, 454. See also Gordon Swanborough and Peter M. Bowers, *United States Navy Aircraft since 1911* (New York: Funk & Wagnalls, 1968), 493–494.

23 Eustace L. Adams, *Fifteen Days in the Air* (New York: Grosset & Dunlap, 1928), 191; Adams, *Over the Polar Ice,* 17; Adams, *Pirates of the Air,* 200; Adams, *On the Wings of Flame,* 214.

24 Suggestions for a new series, Stratemeyer Syndicate Records, MSS & Archives Section, N.Y.P.L., Box 256; Outline for *Over the Ocean to Paris,* Stratemeyer Syndicate Records, MSS & Archives Section, N.Y.P.L., Box 255, Folder 1.

25 Franklin W. Dixon [John W. Duffield], *Over the Ocean to Paris, or Ted Scott's Daring Long-Distance Flight* (New York: Grosset & Dunlap, 1927), unpaged dedication. "Dixon" was used for only one other Stratemeyer production, the immortal "Hardy Boys" series.

26 Outline for *Castaways of the Stratosphere,* Stratemeyer Syndicate Records, MSS & Archives Section, N.Y.P.L., Box 18, Folder Ted Scott #18.

27 Suggestions for a New Series, Stratemeyer Syndicate Records, MSS & Archives Section, N.Y.P.L., Box 256; Franklin W. Dixon [John W. Duffield], *Rescued in the Clouds, or Ted Scott, Hero of the Air* (New York: Grosset & Dunlap, 1927), 7; Franklin W. Dixon [John W. Duffield], *Through the Air to Alaska, or Ted Scott's Search in Nugget Valley* (New York: Grosset & Dunlap, 1930), 116.

28 Dixon, *Rescued in the Clouds,* 72, 85.

29 Franklin W. Dixon [John W. Duffield], *First Stop Honolulu, or Ted Scott Over the Pacific* (New York: Grosset & Dunlap, 1927), 2–3, 30; Franklin W. Dixon [John W. Duffield], *Brushing the Mountain Top, or Aiding the Lost Traveler* (New York: Grosset & Dunlap, 1934), 8; Franklin W. Dixon [John W. Duffield], *Hunting the Sky Spies, or Testing the Invisible Plane* (New York: Grosset & Dunlap, 1941), 144.

30 Dixon, *Over the Ocean to Paris,* 166–67; "Ryan NY-P a Development of the Ryan M-2," *Aviation,* 22 (20 June 1927): 1364–1368; Dixon, *Rescued in the Clouds,* 118–122; William Hovgaard, "An Airplane Station in the Midocean," *New York Times,* 3 July 1927, 8:1. The copyright deposit volume of *Over the Ocean to Paris* is logged by the Library of Congress as being received on 12 August 1927; that of *Rescued in the Clouds* is dated 12 September 1927.

31 Dixon, *First Stop Honolulu,* 120–21; "The Valves Used in Lindbergh's Plane," *Aero Digest,* 11 (August 1927): 175. For the salt-cooled valve, see Robert Jardine, "Technical Description of the Salt-Cooled Valve," *Aviation Engineering,* 5 (July 1931): 31–32. The copyright deposit volume of *First Stop Honolulu* is unobtainable.

32 Franklin W. Dixon [John W. Duffield]. *Across the Pacific, or Ted Scott's Hop to Australia* (New York: Grosset & Dunlap, 1928), 2–3; Richard M. Mock, "Engine Exhaust Silencers," *Aviation,* 24 (18 June 1928): 1794–1795; Franklin W. Dixon [John W. Duffield], *Flying Against Time, or Ted Scott Breaking the Ocean to Ocean Record* (New York: Grosset & Dunlap, 1929), 42–44; J.D. Tear, "Electromagnetic compass systems for aircraft," *Science,* 68 (14 December 1928): 597; E.F.W. Alexanderson, "Height of airplane above ground by radio echo," *Science,* 68 (14 December 1928): 597–598. The copyright deposit volume of *Across the Pacific* is dated 24 September 1928, and that of *Flying Against Time* 13 May 1929.

33 Franklin W. Dixon [John W. Duffield], *Flying to the Rescue, or Ted Scott and the Big Dirigible* (New York: Grosset & Dunlap, 1930), 4, 46–50; "Curtiss-Bleecker Helicopter," *Aero Digest,* 17 (July 1930): 110–112; Franklin W. Dixon [John W. Duffield], *The Pursuit Patrol, or Chasing the Platinum Pirates* (New York: Grosset & Dunlap, 1943), 22; Frederick L. Collins, "The Battle of Detroit: 1,000 Horses in the Sky," *Liberty,* 19 (14 February 1942): 34. *Flying to the Rescue* was logged by the Copyright Office on 15 October 1930, and *Pursuit Patrol* on 14 January 1943,

34 John W. Duffield to Harriet Stratemeyer Adams, 16 May 1941, Stratemeyer Syndicate Records, MSS & Archives Section, N.Y.P.L., Box 18–19 (Microfilm Reel 11).

35 Edna C. Squier to John W. Duffield, 29 July 1933, Stratemeyer Syndicate Records, MSS & Archives Section, N.Y.P.L., Box 16 (Microfilm Reel 28); Outline and manuscript, *The Pursuit Patrol,* Stratemeyer Syndicate Records, MSS & Archives Section, N.Y.P.L., Box 256, Ted Scott #20 folder.

36 Corn, *Winged Gospel,* 51–70.

37 Burtis, *Rex Lee on the Border Patrol,* 169–70; Adams, *Wings of Adventure,* 6, 19–21; Franklin W. Dixon [John W. Duffield], *The Lone Eagle of the Border, or Ted Scott and the Diamond Smugglers* (New York: Grosset & Dunlap, 1929), 8–9; Franklin W. Dixon [John W. Duffield], *Over the Jungle Trails, or Ted Scott and the Missing Explorers* (New York: Grosset & Dunlap, 1929), 86.

38 Thomson Burtis, *Rex Lee's Mysterious Flight* (New York: Grosset & Dunlap, 1930), 45; Langley, *Trail Blazers of the Skies,* 124; Adams, *The Flying Windmill,* 71–72.

39 Burtis, *Rex Lee, Flying Detective,* 100–101; Langley, *Spanning the Pacific,* 75.

40 R.E.G. Davies, *Airlines of the United States since 1914* (Washington, DC: Smithsonian Institution Press, 1998), 70–79; Burtis, *Rex Lee, Ace of the Air Mail,* 96; Adams, *Wings of Adventure,* 477–478.

41 Langley, *Spanning the Pacific,* 45–46, 135.

42 Burtis, *Rex Lee, Ace of the Air Mail,* 74, 211–212; Dixon, *The Lone Eagle of the Border,* 9.

43 Gilbert Seldes, "Transatlantic," *The New Republic,* 1 June 1927, 47.

44 Dixon, *Over the Ocean to Paris,* 35–36.

45 Thomson Burtis, *Rex Lee, Ranger of the Sky* (New York: Grosset & Dunlap, 1928), 2; Burtis, *Rex Lee, Ace of the Air Mail,* 85.

46 Langley, *Spanning the Pacific,* 153–154.

47 Adams, *Pirates of the Air,* 67; Adams, *The Flying Windmill,* 157; John Prentice Langley [St. George Rathborne], *Masters of the Air-Lanes, or Round the World in Fourteen Days* (New York: Barse & Co., 1928), 105; John Prentice Langley [St. George Rathborne], *The "Pathfinder's" Great Flight, or Cloud Chasers Over Amazon Jungles* (New York: Barse & Co., 1928), 70.

48 Corn, *Winged Gospel,* 39–42.

49 Eustace L. Adams, *The Mysterious Monoplane* (New York: Grosset & Dunlap, 1930), 30.

50 Dixon, *First Stop Honolulu,* 5, 8–9; Dixon, *Across the Pacific,* 54; Dixon, *Over the Jungle Trails,* 43; Franklin W. Dixon [John W. Duffield], *Lost at the South Pole, or Ted Scott in Blizzard Land* (New York: Grosset & Dunlap, 1930), 10.

51 Col. Charles A. Lindbergh, "The Third Article of His Series Discusses the Safety Quest," *New York Times,* 9 September 1928, 133; Col. Charles A. Lindbergh, "New Types and Speedier Planes Being Evolved in Air Progress," *New York Times,* 14 October 1928, 11:10; Harry F. Guggenheim, *The Seven Skies* (New York: G.P. Putnam's Sons, 1930), 101, 126–131; "Curtiss Tanager," *Aero Digest,* 16 (February 1930), 120–121.

52 Corn, *Winged Gospel,* 94–95, 96–104; "The Ford 'Flivver' Airplane," *Aviation,* 22 (17 January 1927): 138–39; George F. McLaughlin, "Ford's Latest Monoplane," *Aero Digest,* 10 (February 1927), 95.

53 Clarence M. Young, "Introduction," *American Airport Designs.* 1930 (Washington, DC: American Institute of Architects Press, 1990), 5; Corn, *Winged Gospel,* 104–106.

54 Elva de Pue, "Why a Modernistic Clubhouse," *Sportsman Pilot,* 1 (March 1929): 10.

55 de Pue, "Why a Modernistic Clubhouse," 44.

56 Dixon, *Lone Eagle of the Border,* 94; Dixon, *Rescued in the Clouds,* 115.

57 Adams, *Prisoners of the Clouds,* 11; Burtis, *Rex Lee, Ranger of the Sky,* 165; Dixon, *Flying to the Rescue,* 3–4.

58 "A Solution to Landing Planes of Every Description" [Gibbons Company Advertisement], *Aero Digest,* 12 (April 1928): 536–537. The capitalized text appears in the original. An even earlier proposal for an urban, elevated airport, to be built above steamship docks or railroad yards, is "The Metropolitan Flying Field," *Scientific American,* 135 (August 1926): 146.

59 Dixon, *Flying to the Rescue,* 3; Franklin W. Dixon [John W. Duffield], *The Search for the Lost Flyers, or Ted Scott Over the West Indies* (New York: Grosset & Dunlap, 1928), 44.

60 Dixon, *Search for the Lost Flyers,* 45.

Chapter Six

The Golden Age, Two: The Air-Minded Society, 1930–1939

Like so many other fabled eras in American life, the "Golden Age of Aviation" is a composite of many elements. Generally considered as running from 1925 to 1940, its coming was stimulated, without question, by the national enthusiasm for things aeronautical stirred by the Lindbergh flight. Other elements fed the enthusiasm, however, for the era embraced the emergence of modern civil and military aviation and the technologies that made both possible. Its attractions are varied and substantial: highly publicized technological advances that contributed to viable commercial flight, colorful personalities whose deeds and events captured the public eye and gave a human dimension to the technological marvels, and the stunning appeal of the steadily evolving aircraft. Even in the age of the Great Depression, flight and its practitioners continued to seem the forerunners of an air-borne society and an increasingly democratic public participation in the wonders of flight.

These elements made events of the Golden Age ready fodder for the series books writers. The technology offered an opportunity to praise mankind's mastery over nature. The personalities made attractive models for the series protagonists as they claimed headline after headline, proclaiming their prowess in the exciting new realm of flight. The aircraft themselves added no little romance. Open cockpits were giving way to comfortable cabins. Lumbering tri-motors were being surpassed by sleek, dual-engined models. Struts and wires were disappearing, replaced by internally braced structures with nothing interrupting their streamlining. Reliable, speedy passenger service was a reality, and increasingly affordable for all travelers. And overseeing all of these advances were the aviators, tangible personifications of all that aviation might do. It *was* an age of giants, technological as well as human, and series writers reveled in what it had to offer.

Once past the initial excitement of the first Lindbergh years, the series books of the Golden Age began to assimilate other aeronautical developments, becoming deeply engaged with aviation in the largest sense. They continued to rely upon adventure-laden plots, to be sure, and their young heroes took part in flying activities as remarkable as any of those executed by Ted Scott or Rex Lee. Nonetheless, the picture of the aviation world that they offered was more complex and more considered than the one found in the overtly Lindberghian series. Flying to their authors was more than simple record-setting and technical achievement. It was at last an enterprise with practical, real-world applications. In their volumes, the writers strove to convey an awareness of those applications, and used that awareness to spread the mystique of flight.

All of the series share certain characteristics. All, for example, feature one or more teen-aged (or slightly older), air-minded protagonists. Intelligent, well-educated, resourceful, and athletic, these boys become involved with flying in a variety of ways. Their professional involvement with flying is an inherent element of the story. The airplane is no longer merely an adjunct to other undertakings; now it is a central, necessary part of the events, and an element crucial to the unfolding of the plot. Finally, the aircraft, their construction, and their capabilities are described in accurate, detailed fashion. Even when the craft mentioned are fictional or disguised, the qualities they possess are those of the most modern airplanes of the times. The combination of attractive heroes and accurately described, totally integrated aircraft is a compelling one, and the series made the most of it.

The Golden Age had its origins earlier in the 1920s, even before Lindbergh's flight, stimulated by the government-sponsored airmail service. From the service came a perception of the aviator as a dashing, fearless individual equipped to deal with perils natural and mechanical. From it as well came more mundane developments, notably the completion in 1925 of the cross-country lighted airway, which made night flying of the mail practicable. The federal Air Mail Act of 1925, the "Kelly Act," also contributed; it established eight regional air routes that were offered for bids from independent contractors, and shifted the carriage of airmail from the government agency to the successful bidders. The winners became the first truly commercial air carriers. Close on the heels of the Kelly Act came the Air Commerce Act of 1926, giving the federal government authority to establish standards for licensing of pilots and aircraft and otherwise regulate aviation development.[1] The pieces were in place, needing only a catalyst to bring them together; when the nation was electrified by Charles Lindbergh's trans-Atlantic flight of 1927, the Golden Age began to take form.

The coming of commercial aviation was the most visible evidence of the growing era. The carriers stimulated by the Kelly Act quickly embarked upon a frenzy of mergers and takeovers that weeded out numerous small-scale companies and led to the first genuinely national carriers. Most of the carriers flew passengers on occasion, but Transcontinental Air Transport (TAT), launched in 1929 with the assistance of Charles Lindbergh and, carrying the cachet, "The Lindbergh Line," became the first line planned from the outset to carry passengers. Flying Ford 5-AT tri-motors for the daytime segments and connecting with the Pennsylvania and Santa Fe Railroads for night travel, it reduced coast-to-coast travel to forty-eight hours. For all its acclaim, TAT never proved profitable and, in 1930, merged with Western Air Express to create Transcontinental and Western Air (TWA). Other mergers were going on as well, variously involving a network of carriers linking New York and Miami, a second network of allied carriers in the southern and middle United States, and the Boeing Company and its associated routes with the result that, by mid-1931, national air transport was dominated by four companies. These were, respectively, TWA, Eastern Air Transport (formed 1930), American Airways (1930), and United Air Lines (1931).[2] Barely four years after Lindbergh's flight, a national air-commerce system was in place.

Making this system possible were technological developments that, if less visible and less dramatic than the formation of an airline, were no less essential to its success. In 1928, the Daniel Guggenheim Fund for the Promotion of Aeronautics provided for an Experimental Meteorological Service along the California coast. From this first venture emerged a national aeronautical weather service equipped to supply timely weather reports for all fliers, whether civil or commercial. The same year, the National Advisory Committee for Aeronautics (NACA) announced the development of a streamlined cowling for air-cooled radial engines. By cutting down on the drag created by a radial's exposed cylinders, the NACA cowling increased operating efficiency by 20 to 30 percent, and increased speed anywhere from 5 to 20 miles per hour.[3]

The following year, another Guggenheim-funded project bore fruit when Lieutenant James H. Doolittle, flying a navy NY-2 trainer with its cockpit wholly sealed to prevent any outside vision, took off, flew a 20-mile circuit, and successfully landed, using only his cockpit instruments. Four newly-developed and reliable instruments contributed to the mastering of blind flying. First was the Sperry artificial horizon, which provided constant data on the relationship of the aircraft to the true horizon, enabling the pilot to know whether the craft was level or banking, climbing or diving. Next was the Sperry directional gyroscope, indicating whether the aircraft was holding to its intended course. Third was the Kollsman altimeter, a device for measuring altitude in units as small as ten feet. And fourth was a directional indicator responding to radio signals, giving the pilot visual cues as to whether the aircraft was to the left or the right of the radio "beam."[4]

While all four of these instruments made major contributions to cross-country flying, the radio "beam" had the greatest national implications. The first three were self-contained, operating with specific reference to the aircraft, its altitude, and its attitude; they needed no outside connection. The radio directional guide, however, required an external source for its radio signal if it was to be effective, and the Department of Commerce Airways Division quickly responded. By mid-1930 a network of eight radio range stations covered the northeastern United States, with other stations projected to create northern and southern airways across the continent.[5] The signal was received visually (a vibrating-reed display on the instrument panel) or aurally (a "dot-dash" or "dash-dot" signal heard in headphones), giving pilots a dependable guide through even the worst conditions.

A final contribution came in the form of the all-metal, adjustable-pitch propeller. Whether of wood or of metal, propellers until the late 1920s had been of fixed pitch—i.e., the angle at which their blades cut the air was built into their configuration and could not be changed. Thus, a propeller giving high efficiency at the critical times of take-off and landing would be less efficient at cruising speeds, slowing the aircraft's speed and increasing fuel consumption. Small, slower aircraft like those of the World War I era had been able to manage with propellers of a compromise design. Larger aircraft, more powerful engines, and higher altitudes made the need for some means of adjusting propeller pitch urgent if the equipment was to be used to best advantage. Although some earlier experiments had been conducted by British researchers with varying results, such a device was impracticable until 1932, when the American Frank W. Caldwell developed a reliable, hydraulically powered two-pitch propeller that could be shifted in flight.[6] Coupled with the NACA cowling, the Whirlwind engine, and new developments in airframe construction, Caldwell's propeller helped to usher in the modern airplane.

Public excitement over aviation was heightened by the increasing visibility of aircraft in the skies and in the press. A major component of the excitement was the series of National Air Races, held annually between 1925 and 1940. Begun as the Pulitzer Races in 1920, the races drew substantial crowds from the outset; some 150,000 spectators attended the 1923 races in St. Louis, Missouri. Public interest grew even more intense, however, after the establishment of two further prizes. The Thompson Trophy Race, begun in 1930, was an out-and-out speed race with competitors circling pylons along a closed course, while the Bendix Trophy Race of 1931 set craft against each other in a point-to-point speed race over long distance. These events, while providing a testing ground for increasingly powerful engines and advances in aircraft streamlining, drew even greater public attention with their intensely fought competition, ever-present danger, and the larger-than-life personalities of the leading contenders.[7]

Not all aviation celebrities were racers, to be sure. Charles Lindbergh continued as a public idol. A *Washington Post* headline of 1928 dubbed him the "World's Greatest Aviator" in reporting his flying antipneumonia serum to the stricken Floyd Bennett, and newspapers in 1929 followed his taking part in the search for a downed TAT airliner. He gained further attention when, accompanied by his wife, Anne Morrow Lindbergh, he made extended flights to survey potential commercial air routes to Asia (1931), and across the Atlantic (1933). Even the model-making press took notice of the latter flight, and Anne's books giving her perceptions of both expeditions, *North to the Orient* (1935) and *Listen! the Wind* (1938), were best-sellers.[8]

Women, too, were beginning to make a mark in aviation. Persons such as Ruth Elder, Laura Ingalls, and the glamorous Jacqueline Cochrane won notice in the press with various distance and speed records, but the most prominent woman flier was undeniably Amelia Earhart. Earhart, the first woman to cross the Atlantic by air (she flew as a passenger on a 1928 venture), was determined to establish herself as a pilot in her own right. She worked in middle management for TAT, accompanying Lindbergh and other dignitaries on the company's inaugural flight; wrote on aviation topics for *Cosmopolitan* and *Sportsman Pilot* magazines; gave career counseling to women students at Purdue University; and, in 1932, successfully flew her Lockheed Vega solo across the Atlantic, the first woman and second person to do so. Her celebrity was real but hard-won. Her tousled hair and slender figure made her a favorite of photographers, and by 1935 she and First Lady Eleanor Roosevelt were considered the best-known women in America. Her prominence was only

Amelia Earhart and the Lockheed Vega 5A she used in her attempt on the women's speed record (1929), showing the NACA cowling. National Air and Space Museum, Smithsonian Institution (SI 74-9259).

increased by her disappearance over the Pacific in 1937, during the course of a round-the-world flight.[9]

It was, however, the record-setters and racers who achieved the most visibility. Some were able to combine records with real contributions to aviation progress. The one-eyed Oklahoman, Wiley Post, flying with navigator Harold Gatty in his Lockheed Vega, *Winnie Mae,* set a round-the-world record of 8 days and 15 hours in 1931; he duplicated the feat as a solo flight in 1933, beating his own record with a flight time of 7 days and 18 hours. His most substantial contribution, however, came in 1935, after he became interested in high-altitude flight. Wearing a pressure suit designed for him by the Goodyear Rubber Company and flying the *Winnie Mae,* he established the presence of the west-to-east "jet stream" and demonstrated its practicality for transcontinental flight.[10]

James H. Doolittle and the Gee Bee R-1 Racer at the Thompson Trophy Races (1932). National Air and Space Museum, Smithsonian Institution (SI77-11856).

The contributions of James H. "Jimmy" Doolittle were even more substantial. Doolittle, an army flier with a doctorate in aeronautical engineering from MIT, set a transcontinental speed record of 22 hours and 30 minutes in 1922, and won the Schneider Trophy in 1925, flying a Curtiss R3C-2 Racer at an average of 232 M.P.H. He proved the practicality of blind flying for the Guggenheim Foundation in 1929, and, after resigning from the army in 1930, joined the Shell Oil Corporation as an engineering consultant and company-sponsored air racer. As a racer he won the Bendix Trophy in 1931, flying from Burbank, California to Cleveland, Ohio, in a Laird Super Solution at an average speed of 223.03 M.P.H., and the Thompson Trophy in 1932, flying the lethal Gee Bee R-1 at an average of 252.6 M.P.H. His experiences with the Gee Bee ("the most unforgiving aeroplane I ever flew") and its reputation for killing pilots persuaded him to retire from air racing after the 1932 Thompson race, but he remained a legendary figure in the public mind.[11]

The air-racer universally recognized as the most colorful was "Colonel" Roscoe Turner. Turner, a one-time barnstormer and cinema stunt flier (he took part in Howard Hughes's *Hell's Angels*), turned to racing in 1929 and won the Bendix Trophy in 1933. Between 1930 and 1934 he set a succession of transcontinental speed records and, in 1935, flying a Boeing 247-D leased from United Air Lines, placed third in the England-to-Australia MacRobertson Race. By the time he retired from racing in 1939, calling it "a young man's game," he had won the Thompson Trophy three times and the Bendix Trophy twice. He was the only flier ever to win the Thompson three times, and shared with Doolittle the prestige of being the only other person to win both the Thompson and Bendix prizes.[12]

For all the publicity he gained from his achievements in the racing circuit, Turner became even better known for his antics on the ground. Although his

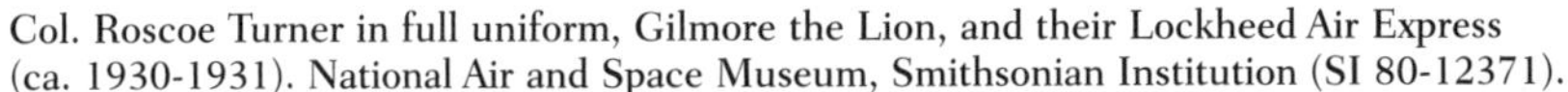
Col. Roscoe Turner in full uniform, Gilmore the Lion, and their Lockheed Air Express (ca. 1930-1931). National Air and Space Museum, Smithsonian Institution (SI 80-12371).

military rank was an honorary one, bestowed by the governors of Nevada and California, he never failed to bill himself as "Colonel" Turner. He complemented the title with a quasi-military uniform of his own design, including a light blue tunic, tan trousers, gleaming riding boots, and jeweled wings blazoned "RT." The uniform, combined with his dandified waxed mustache and ebullient personality, made him fair game for photographers and reporters, and he happily agreed to any and all opportunities to meet the press.

His master stroke of self-publicizing, however, came after he gained the sponsorship of the Gilmore Oil Company of California. Noting that the Gilmore trademark was a leaping red lion, Turner obtained a lion cub (obligingly named "Gilmore") for a mascot, and the two became regular features of air shows and other events. Until he grew too large for the cockpit, Gilmore often flew with Turner, wearing a parachute specially designed for him by the Irvin Air Chute Company. The two were as inseparably linked privately as they were in the public mind; when Gilmore died in 1952, Turner had him mounted and kept him as a part of the household. The lion's stuffed remains are now a part of the collection of the Smithsonian's National Air and Space Museum.[13]

Underneath Turner's studied flamboyance, though, was a careful, conscientious pilot deeply concerned with improving the public image of aviation. He recognized that publicity, so long as it was positive, would only benefit aviation, and so missed no opportunity to gain headlines for the enterprise. He lent his name to the Roscoe Turner Flying Corps, a children's group sponsored by the Heinz foodstuffs company "for the purpose of stimulating Young America's interest in Aviation." As he told Beirne Lay, himself a flier and writer, "Publicity helps. That's why I wear this monkey suit [his uniform]. . . . Nobody will ever know how much guts it takes for me to wear this circus outfit." More to the point, however, was Turner's recognition of the psychological impact of a uniform. Such garb, he wrote, "shows [customers] you mean business and can command respect. It is then your duty to uphold the dignity of the uniform and calling. . . . If you look like a tramp or a blacksmith, how can you expect to meet the people that are able to support your business?"[14] His gaudiness disguised a deep-seated professionalism and a recognition that advertising such professionalism would benefit aviation. In his way, Turner was a devoted and effective advocate for the cause of flying, making his case to adults and children alike.

For all the prominence and acclaim accorded the fliers of the time, however, the real stars of the Golden Age were the airplanes themselves. Their evolution was an aesthetic one as much as a technological one. New developments in metallurgy, powerplant technology, and construction techniques made the sleek, streamlined craft of the era possible, but the designers themselves, capitalizing upon these advances, contributed to the dazzling fame of the period's airplanes. The pace of the evolution is apparent in the two major aircraft that bracket the age. In 1926, the tri-motored Ford 5-AT dominated American airways. Outwardly similar to the Fokker F-10, it substituted all-metal construction and a corrugated aluminum-alloy skin for the Fokker's metal-and-plywood components. It was boxy, noisy, and uncomfortable, but it ushered in

The "City of Columbus," a Ford 5-AT Tri-Motor, in Transcontinental Air Transport livery (1929). National Air and Space Museum, Smithsonian Institution (SI 75-15206).

commercial air transport. Ten years later, by 1936, the dominant commercial airplane was the Douglas DC-3, a craft superior in every way. A singularly efficient airplane, comfortable, quiet, and reliable, its integration of streamlined elements gave it a distinctive beauty that was new to the aviation world.[15]

The technical and aesthetic evolution of the modern airplane begins with two brothers, Allan and Malcolm Loughead, and their chief engineer, John K. Northrop. Taking advantage of the Lougheads' development of a technique for molding plywood fuselages, Northrop in 1927 designed a sleek, streamlined, high-winged, single-engined monoplane, its cantilevered wing free of external wires and struts. The Vega, as the type was dubbed, was powered by a Wright Whirlwind radial engine and quickly showed its merits as a speed ship. Later modifications, including using more powerful Pratt & Whitney engines and adding an NACA cowling, made the Vega into a pilot's airplane. A Vega made the first trans-Arctic flight (1928), was the first to fly non-stop from coast to coast (1928), the first for a woman to fly solo across the Atlantic (1932), and the first to be flown solo around the world (1933). Over one hundred of the model were built, and no small part of its success was due to Northrop's design, which "obviously belonged off the ground" and set "a new standard for what flying machines should be."[16]

The Vega was only the first of a succession of notable Lockheed (the company name came from the pronunciation of "Loughead") craft. It was followed by the Air Express of 1928, which set a coast-to-coast record in 1929, and the cabin-model Orion of 1931, which saw service with American Airlines and TWA. The model best-known to the public, however, was the Sirius of 1930, for it was in one of these that Lindbergh flew his survey flights to Asia and Europe. A burly, low-winged, two-seat craft designed in great part by Gerard Vultee, the Lindberghs' Sirius set a transcontinental speed record in 1930, and served them reliably until they retired it in 1934.[17]

Rivaling and at times surpassing the Lockheed aircraft were the designs manufactured by John Northrop under his own name. After leaving Lockheed in 1928, he formed Northrop Aviation Corporation and began developing his own designs. In these airplanes, technology and aesthetics worked hand-in-hand. Northrop had long been a believer in all-metal construction and did pioneering work in the use of a honey-combed internal structure for wings. To this he added his ideas for an all-metal monocoque fuselage, in which the metal skin became an integral part of the load-bearing structure, doing away with the need for internal bracing. The outcome was the Northrop Alpha. A six-passenger, single-engined, low-winged monoplane, the Alpha was a triumph of aesthetics as well as engineering. Its streamlining, extending even to the enclosure of its fixed landing gear in sleek housings, gave it a sculptured look, and the overall impression it created was one of "a metallically feathered hawk." Seventeen Alphas were built, all ultimately going to TWA.[18]

Northrop followed the Alpha with a two-seat sport design, the Beta (1931), but only two of these were built; the deepening Depression had effectively

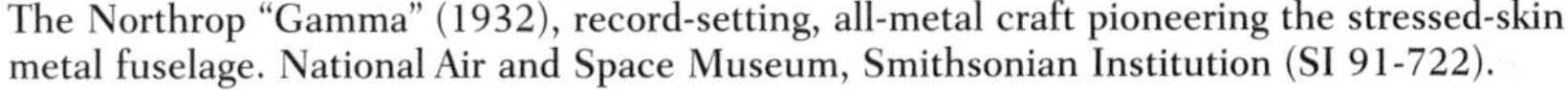
The Northrop "Gamma" (1932), record-setting, all-metal craft pioneering the stressed-skin metal fuselage. National Air and Space Museum, Smithsonian Institution (SI 91-722).

destroyed the market for sporting aircraft. Its successor, however, the Gamma (1932), was another story. Using all of the engineering experience he had gained with the Alpha, Northrop designed the Gamma as a high-speed mail express. The result was another elegantly sleek, unusually strong, and remarkably speedy aircraft. Flying the first production ship, Frank Hawks set a series of speed and distance records in 1933; later craft competed respectably in Bendix Trophy races, and one, flown by Howard Hughes, set a 1936 coast-to-coast speed record of 9 hours, 26 minutes. An additional demonstration of the Gamma's capability came through its service with explorer Lincoln Ellsworth's Antarctic expeditions of 1933–1936.[19] Proving yet again the merits of Northrop's all-metal, cellular design, the Gamma pointed the way to still further developments.

These came in two designs from the Boeing Company. The first was the Boeing Model 200, the "Monomail," a low-winged, single-engined, all-metal monoplane intended for mail and passenger service. Outwardly resembling the Alpha and Gamma designs, the Monomail differed from them principally in having retractable landing gear, adding to its aerodynamic "cleanliness." While only two Monomails were built (both flew briefly with United Air Lines), they gave Boeing valuable information about high-speed, stressed-skin design. These data paid off with the company's Model 247, the ship generally acknowledged as the world's first modern airliner. The 247 first took to the air in 1933, and, for a bit more than a year, was the most advanced commercial aircraft flying in the United States.[20]

Several qualities gave the 247 its distinctiveness. A twin-engined, all-metal, low-winged monoplane, the 247 offered unprecedented comfort for its passengers. It was heavily soundproofed, and provided individually controllable ventilation and heating for each seat. Its engineering was just as advanced: Retractable landing gear, external streamlining, and modular construction gave it a cruising speed of 165 M.P.H. and a cruising range of 660 miles without refueling. Overall, it offered high speed, notable strength, and the prospect of

Embodiments of modernity: a United Air Lines Boeing 247 and a Chrysler Airflow Coupe (1935). National Air and Space Museum, Smithsonian Institution (SI 82-5412).

profits coming primarily from passenger service. Its flaws, such as they were, were two: a capacity of only ten passengers and the interruption of the passenger aisle by the main wing spar, which crossed the cabin at mid-point and necessitated passengers' clambering over it to reach seats at the rear of the ship. These were, however, minor quibbles, and the 247 entered commercial service, billed by United Air Lines as "the world's first 3-mile-a-minute multimotored transports."[21]

The 247's very success was its undoing, for it led to the development of the airplanes that symbolize the Golden Age, the Douglas DC-1/DC-2/DC-3 series. Boeing, recognizing the advance the 247 represented, and as the parent company of United Air Lines, not surprisingly reserved the first cluster of production craft for United. When TWA, seeking a replacement for its Fokker F-10s, approached Boeing with an order for 247s, they were told the line would have to wait until United's needs were satisfied. TWA then queried other manufacturers, asking for a three-engined, all-metal design that would equal, or surpass, the performance and load-carrying ability of the 247. Only the Douglas Aircraft Company responded.[22]

The Douglas Company, headed by Donald W. Douglas, had since 1920 acquired the reputation of building reliable, substantial military craft. Douglas World Cruisers were the first airplanes to circumnavigate the world, M–1 and M–2 mail ships had done yeoman duty in the airmail service, and Douglas torpedo planes were workhorses of the navy. The move to production of commercial aircraft was logical, and Douglas engineers soon produced a design that, if anything, improved upon TWA's requested specifications. Using a combination of elements, including a cellular wing similar to that of the Northrop Alphas and Gammas (Northrop, by this time, had joined the Douglas firm), adjustable flaps to allow a relatively slow landing speed, two engines rather than three, equipped with NACA cowlings and adjustable-pitch propellers, and an all-metal fuselage capable of carrying twelve passengers without the obstructing wing spar, they created the DC-1.[23]

The rest of the story is legend. From the single DC-1 came the DC-2, an enlarged version capable of carrying fourteen passengers and cruising in excess of 200 M.P.H. Put into service with TWA in 1934, the DC-2 broke the New York to Chicago speed record four times in just over a week. Other lines, recognizing the DC-2's superiority, placed their own orders, and, later in 1934, a commercial-issue DC-2 flown by the Dutch airline KLM placed second in the MacRobertson Race, beating out Roscoe Turner's Boeing 247. American Airlines then entered the scene, asking Douglas to develop a berth-equipped "sleeper" version of the ship. This craft, the Douglas Sleeper Transport (DST) took to the air in 1935, a "stretched" version of the DC-2 seating twenty-one passengers and sleeping sixteen. In a very slightly modified form carrying twenty-four seats, the DST morphed into the DC-3—an aircraft called "the greatest airliner ever built," and one that eventually saw service, military as well as civil, throughout the world. The DC-3's reliability, speed, and economy

The airplane that changed the world: the Douglas DC-3 in American Airlines livery (1936). National Air and Space Museum, Smithsonian Institution (SI75-15206).

of operation made it an airplane that shaped developments following it as much as the Wright Flyer had shaped those following it.[24] With personalities and technology in place, the Golden Age needed only the myth-makers to cement its place in aeronautical history, and series writers were eager to oblige.

Two series of the period involve the coming of a viable general aviation for aviation hobbyists. These are Irving Crump's "Cloud Patrol" books (1929–1931; three titles) and Van Powell's "Sky Scout" series (1932; four titles). Crump, a journalist, writer for the young, and long-time editor of the Boy Scout magazine, *Boy's Life* (1918–1923, 1935–1952), made a practice of interpreting modern occupations for young readers. Using the running title of *The Boys' Book of* [topic], he produced volumes dealing with, among other subjects, railroading, flying, film-making, engineering, fire and police service, and the United States Coast Guard. Later works, given the running title of

Our [topic], examined *Our G-Men* (1937), airline flying, the Secret Service, the merchant marine, and the military.[25]

The "Cloud Patrol" books readily fit in with Crump's occupational interests. Don Craig, assistant Scoutmaster of a Boy Scout troop in the American West, leads a varied crew of boys through activities related to both Scouting and flying. When adult authorities realize the boys' genuine interest in flying, they arrange work for them at an aircraft factory, and, by series' end, the troop has a thorough grounding in practical aviation. *The Cloud Patrol* (1929) introduces Don Craig and his closest friends, Babe Crawford and Dan England. Working with the troop on a conservation project along the Snake River, they befriend a forest ranger and a military officer at nearby Fairbanks Field. They make numerous flights, principally with the ranger, learn the techniques of flying, and participate in the rescue of a nearby flooded community.

Subsequent volumes take Don, Babe, and Dan to New Jersey, where they have summer work as apprentice mechanics at the Fullerton Airplane Factory. In *The Pilot of the Cloud Patrol* (1929), they learn of dubious flying schools, become aware of the importance of educating the public about aviation and aircraft safety, and take part in a long-distance race sponsored by the International Air Craft Association. The final volume, *Craig of the Cloud Patrol* (1931), continues their work at the Fullerton plant, acquainting them with new techniques in streamlining and engine development, and giving them a glimpse of the developing market, international as well as domestic, for advanced commercial ships.

All three books preach the inherent appeal of flying and airplanes, and the joys of flying as an individual pastime. Although Crump rarely makes reference to actual aircraft, he obviously is aware of current events and developments, and builds them into his stories. *The Cloud Patrol* opens in 1927, as the boys await Charles Lindbergh's arrival during his cross-country tour in *The Spirit of St. Louis,* and speaks of his desire to spark interest in commercial flying and airport development. *The Pilot of the Cloud Patrol* talks of the dangers inherent in amateur fliers' using obsolete military craft, especially poorly refurbished Jennies, and gives a detailed picture of a working general airport. Ovington Field, adjacent to the Fullerton plant, has service hangars for the Fullerton aircraft and those of other airplane companies, public hangars and service facilities for private fliers, a weather station, and the latest safety features, including night-landing facilities. Though *Craig of the Cloud Patrol* never mentions the NACA cowling by name, its description of Fullerton's "hammered aluminum hood . . . which would break up the wind resistance of the ship, thus increasing its speed, and at the same time provide a more efficacious air-cooling system for the motor," echoes point-by-point the advantages of the NACA development.[26]

Just as current is the books' emphasis on the need for public education about flight. G.K. Fullerton, owner of the Fullerton Aircraft company, has become "a leader in the movement to educate the public to the use of airplanes for transportation purposes, and one of his first efforts . . . was to emphasize the safety of flying." Don reinforces this message, speaking of the damage done to aviation's image by crashes at fly-by-night training schools. Public familiarity with flying and its possibilities is essential, yet is constantly being threatened by irresponsible fliers and slipshod techniques. Thus, he says, the time and effort devoted by Fullerton and others to public education goes for nothing when "an outfit like that Graham Flying School is allowed to operate. They do more harm to the cause of aviation with one crack-up than can be undone through months of effort by Mr. Fullerton and his friends."[27]

For all their emphasis on its practicality and real-world applications, though, the books also convey the excitement of flight. Flying at night with his army friend, Don feels as though "they had floated off into another world; a spirit world, perhaps, where they drifted around through space." Later, now a licensed pilot flying in one of the Fullerton Company's latest ships, Don is even more overcome by the mystique of flight. Looking at the shrunken world beneath him, with its insect-like automobiles and barely visible people, he feels "strangely far off and disassociated. . . . Don had a feeling of being a mortal apart from the rest of the world, one freed of the restrictions of earth-bound beings." Even though aviation is increasingly a commonplace enterprise, its power to exalt is unchanged.[28]

The four volumes of the "Sky Scout" series, by "Van Powell" (pseudonym of A. Van Buren Powell) deviate slightly from the classic series format. Rather than following the doings of a single hero and his chums, the books are free-standing adventures, with a new cast for each volume. Those casts, however, are unimpeachable series characters: Three boys, their ages ranging from thirteen to seventeen, figure in each. Air-minded and technically skilled one and all, the lads find themselves drawn into air-related mysteries. Their aeronautical knowledge helps them to work their way through the puzzles, and they come away well-informed about the working of airplanes and the operations of aircraft factories and general-aviation airports.

Were the "Sky Scout" books Stratemeyer products, they might well be called "The Hardy Boys in the Air." In fact, the first three volumes were later reprinted as the "Air Mystery Series." The first, *The Mystery Crash,* follows Al and Bob Wright, like the Hardys sons of a private detective, and chum Curt Brown as they investigate industrial espionage at the local aircraft factory. Joining the factory as apprentices, they learn the theory and practice of aircraft construction, learn to fly, and handily solve the case. *The Haunted Hangar* shows Larry Turner, Dick Summers, and Sandy Maclaren learning to fly, acquiring airport etiquette, and helping solve the disappearance of the Everdail Emeralds. *The Vanishing Air Liner,* set in Southern California, draws Rodney Ellis and brothers Pat and Tim Kelly into the disappearance of the Ellis Aircraft Corporation's newest ship, and they help uncover a scheme to ruin the company. The final volume, *The Ghost of Mystery Airport,* puts Don McLeod, Garry Duncan, and Chick Brown at a struggling public airport operated by Don's uncle. The airport's business is being ruined by random crashes and rumors of a spectral airplane, but the boys trace the latter to night-time film projections generated by a business rival.

For all their melodrama, the books are rich in aeronautical lore and ambiance. Like the "Cloud Patrol" books, they rarely mention actual aircraft by name, but their plots and action draw freely upon current events and developments in the flying field. Al and Bob Wright work with radial engines and learn of recent experiments using diesel engines. As their education continues, they learn the importance of calculating lift, drag, and weight distribution at the design stage, and become proficient in the details of the five structural groups of an airplane—the fuselage, the supporting surfaces, the control group, the power group, and the landing group. Rod Ellis, meanwhile, learns the workings of the radio direction "beam" ("a pilot, flying a course toward the beacon . . . , would pick up the strong dot-dash, or dash-dot, if he happened to be to the left or right of his proper course"), and later sees off an acquaintance going to New York "on the two-day hop and train trip combined."[29]

Several advances appear in *The Ghost of Mystery Airport*. Don, Garry, and Chick witness the arrival of a mail plane launched from a ship several hundred miles at sea, an experiment to speed the delivery of sea-borne mail, and knowledgeably discuss the differences between an autogiro and a helicopter. Their knowledge of current developments extends even to design features, enabling them to unmask an industrial spy because he knows too much about the Handley-Page slot and its effects on airflow across the wing. Such slots figured in the success of the Curtiss Tanager in the Guggenheim Safety Airplane Competition, and soon became fixtures in military aircraft of the period.[30]

One of the most cryptic references to current events, however, occurs in *The Vanishing Air Liner,* where the Ellis works, readers learn, has been brought to the point of closure because of the loss of business created by the Depression. The firm is saved when an acquaintance, "standing high in aviation circles," persuades an airline company's directors "to place one order for a big air liner with the nearly bankrupt builder."[31] If one makes allowance for a certain amount of artistic license (the Douglas firm, thanks to its military contracts, was in no danger of failure), this is a thumbnail account of the events leading to the design of the DC-1 and its subsequent runaway success. In the world of the boys' aviation books, even manufacturing ploys are seen as providing useful insights.

Book for book, the "Sky Scout" stories are notably more worldly than the "Cloud Patrol" volumes. While they acknowledge "the sense of elation" that accompanies "the first solo flight of a youthful pilot who combines confidence in himself with knowledge of his 'plane,'" they lack the more spiritual, ecstatic mood that affects Don Craig and his chums. They go on, however, to spell out other personal qualities that also contribute to the distinctiveness of the aviator. They preach the gospel of preparedness, saying that "Lindbergh had the right idea" in thinking through in advance the exigencies he might meet. They teach airport etiquette, talking of "that most unpopular of airport nuisances, a 'dusting pilot,' whose carelessness flung damaging clouds on airplanes in hangars and people on the fields." And, throughout, they attest to the existence of "the most manly, most steady, best educated general class of men in industry—pilots!"[32] For Powell, the airman is conscientious, knowledgeable, and considerate, a member of a distinctive class of soundly prepared, eminently reliable individuals. It is an unforgettable evocation of the Golden Age's sense of the flier.

A second category of Golden Age series unabashedly offers itself as featuring stories of flying adventure. Two of the category, the "Great Ace" series (1928–1934; five titles) and the "Bill Bolton, Navy Aviator" books (1933; four titles), draw upon the military flying background of the author, Noel E. Sainsbury, Jr., to augment their heroes' adventures. Another two, the "Slim Tyler Air Stories" (1930–1932; six titles) by "Richard Stone" and the "Randy Starr Series" (1931–1932; three titles), by "Eugene Martin," are Stratemeyer products. Although they repeat the usual Stratemeyer formula combining a rags-to-riches story with various domestic trials (in the case of Slim Tyler, a swindle that has impoverished his family), they also continue the practice of drawing heavily upon contemporaneous sources. Their plots and characters may be cardboard, but their aviation lore is authentic.

Noel Sainsbury's "Great Ace" series, advertised as "rattling good flying stories told by an expert," builds upon its author's naval experience. The New York-born Sainsbury gained his basic flight preparation as a naval aviator, and retained active connections with the naval reserve, serving in the navy during the Second World War and retiring with the rank of lieutenant commander. Although he was trained as an engineer, he turned to fiction-writing in 1930, producing the "Great Ace" and "Bill Bolton" books under his own name and contributing to the "Dorothy Dixon" and "Malay Jungle" books under various pseudonyms.[33] Both of his protagonists have naval backgrounds, and his fondness for seaplanes and amphibians becomes clear throughout both series.

The first "Great Ace" book, *Billy Smith Exploring Ace, or By Airplane to New Guinea* (1928), introduces fourteen-year-old Billy Smith, who is living with his uncle at a naval air station while his explorer father is away. At the station, he learns to fly, then accompanies his uncle to New Guinea in search of his missing father. He returns in triumph, and wins an appointment to the United States Naval Academy. In the second, *Billy Smith Secret Service Ace, or Airplane Adventures in Arabia* (1932), Billy, now an Annapolis midshipman, is assigned to detached duty by special order of the president. He accompanies his father to Arabia, where, working in secrecy, he helps to guarantee American control of a vast oil discovery.

Billy Smith Mystery Ace, or Airplane Discoveries in South America (1932) finds Billy, still on leave from the Naval Academy, en route to South America, searching for an ornithologist from the American Museum of Natural History. He rescues his father and the ornithologist from the clutches of the lost tribe of Chibcha Indians, westernizes the Chibcha chief, and prepares the way for enlightened rule of the Indian kingdom. When *Billy Smith Trail Eater Ace, or Into the Wilds of Northern Alaska by Airplane* (1933) opens, Billy has resigned from Annapolis and is on his way to Alaska, seeking a colony of Neanderthals rumored to be living there. He locates the colony, runs afoul of a band of air-borne bootleggers, and mobilizes army troops to wipe out the law-breakers. In the final volume, *Billy Smith Shanghaied Ace, or Malay Pirates and Solomon Island Cannibals* (1934), Billy, searching for a missing heiress, is shanghaied by Australian toughs. Freed by Jan White, an English-speaking youth, he recovers his seaplane, returns with Jan to civilization, and, to his amazement, finds that "Jan" is really Janet White Clafflin, the object of his search. Though in close quarters with her for weeks, he has never twigged that she's female.[34]

The adventuresome, globe-trotting elements of the "Great Ace" books obviously form the nucleus of each story, but aviation plays its important part. None of the adventures could have taken place without aircraft, and Billy's reliance upon airplanes helps to dramatize their utility as tools of exploration and long-distance travel. These are, quite literally, "flying" adventures, and, though Sainsbury gives over a great deal of space to exotic adventure, he devotes equal attention and care to the aircraft. These are, moreover, undeniably *real* and up-to-date aircraft. Billy at various times flies a Fokker Universal, a single-engined craft built in the United States by the Fokker Aircraft Company of America, a Loening Amphibian, and a PN-7 seaplane from the Naval Aircraft Factory.[35]

Billy's fondness for the Loening Amphibian appears in his Alaskan venture, where he talks knowledgeably of the Loening's maneuverability, its roomy hull-fuselage unit, and its metal-framed wings. The Loening, he says, "will out-climb, out-manoeuvre and out-speed" its DeHavilland counterpart in every respect, and he has "looped and spun and stunted" the type as easily as he has land craft of similar weights. There's no denying the validity of his judgment, for his comments are taken almost verbatim from a 1927 *Aviation* article, W.L. LePage's "The Development of the Amphibian Airplane."[36]

Equally accurate is the books' portrayal of the special skills of sea-plane flying. On take-off, Billy knows to push "the stick all the way forward so as to raise the tail," thereby forcing the hull "out of the stream until they were skimming along on the step." The "step," Sainsbury later specifies, is "a break in the form of the bottom of the hull, designed to reduce resistance when under way." Sainsbury's cadet training bears fruit here. The skills and knowledge he gives Billy come unchanged from Lieutenant Barrett Studley's *Practical Flight Training* (1928), an adaptation of the *Flight School Manual* used at the Naval Air Station in Pensacola, Florida, that the author intended for use at civilian flying schools.[37]

Sainsbury's gift for melding melodramatic adventure with aeronautical fact emerges even more strongly in the "Bill Bolton" books, for which he bills himself as "Lieutenant Noel Sainsbury, Jr." *Bill Bolton Flying Midshipman* (1933) introduces Bill, an Annapolis cadet. When he and his millionaire father are forced down in their private plane off the coast of Florida, they are captured by a renegade miner and pushed into slave labor. Rescued by Osceola, a Carlisle-educated Seminole chief, they rally his people, storm the mine, and turn its crew over to the navy. The second book, *Bill Bolton and the Flying Fish* (1933), opens with Bill and Osceola en route to New York. When they stop to investigate a deserted yacht, they are dragooned into the pirate crew of Baron von Hiemskirk, who is terrorizing shipping with his flying submarine. They pretend to go along with the baron's plans, but secretly alert the navy and engineer his capture.

The third adventure, *Bill Bolton and Hidden Danger* (1933), opening two weeks after Bill and Osceola return from their submarine captivity, takes them to Maine. There they rescue a prominent businessman from gangsters, and help out the owner of a general-aviation airfield, whose business has been slowed by the Depression, making the book one of the few that mention the national economic crisis. The final volume, *Bill Bolton and the Winged Cartwheels* (1933), is almost wholly devoid of aviation materials. Having resigned from Annapolis with presidential approval, Bill takes up secret service work, trying to thwart the scheme of a crazed professor to create a nation of drug addicts by distributing free canned goods laced with cocaine. The "winged cartwheels" of the title are silver dollars overstamped with a wing emblem, used as identification among the professor's henchmen.

Bill's melodramatic, secret-service antics can be discounted on the strength of the aviation materials appearing in at least the first three volumes of his adventures. Once again, the aircraft are real. Bill flies a Loening Amphibian, encounters Boeing PB-1 and Naval Aviation Factory PN-10 amphibians, and owns a Ryan M-1, while another character owns a Buhl-Verville CW-3 Airster, a three-place light plane whose folding wings allow it to be stored in an average garage. Even Baron von Hiemskirk's flying submarine has a hint of actuality; the British aeronautical journal, *Flying,* in 1920 featured a proposal for a "tessaurian," a craft allegedly capable of operating in the air as readily as atop or beneath the sea.[38]

The flying lore is equally reliable, for Sainsbury continues his borrowings from Barrett Studley's manuals. Bill frequently gives long disquisitions on flying techniques: the mechanics of a stall, the dynamics of a take-off, or the stunt maneuver called a wing-over, "a climbing turn followed by a diving turn, the two aggregating 180 degrees." In each instance, the language is taken with little change from Studley's book, and it comes as no surprise when, after one such lecture, Bill's father observes that his son "talks like a textbook."[39]

Sainsbury's books differ, however, from the Lindbergh-based books in one respect. Although both Billy Smith and Bill Bolton are knowledgeable, dedicated pilots, their feelings toward aviation are practical and professional. Flight is the practical means that enables them to carry out their more adventure some activities and, while they have the highest regard for flying skills and aircraft technology, they can hardly be called enthusiasts. That quality is reserved for twelve-year-old Charlie Evans, introduced in *Bill Bolton and the Flying Fish.* Charlie is the air-minded youngster toward whom the series books are directed:

> From the time that he was a little tad of a fellow, Charlie had been crazy to fly. At home, his bedroom was decorated with pictures of famous flyers and their planes. He fairly ate up airplane stories and his book shelves were crowded with literature on flying, although he found some of the volumes too technical.

> Now that he had a chance to witness a take-of at first hand, he wasn't going to miss a single detail if he could help it.[40]

He is the quintessential youth of the Golden Age, and, when Bill gives him some elementary flying lessons, his joy is complete.

Recognizing a potential market when they saw it, the Stratemeyer Syndicate re-entered the field with two air adventure series: the "Slim Tyler Air Stories," by "Richard H. Stone" (1930–1932; six titles) and the "Randy Starr" series by "Eugene Martin" (1931–32; three titles). The series are notable for two reasons. The "Slim Tyler" books (Slim's name acknowledges the legacy of Charles Lindbergh) were the last aviation series created by Edward Stratemeyer himself, while the "Randy Starr" titles were the syndicate's last venture into dedicated aviation fiction. The Stratemeyer daughters continued to support the "Ted Scott" books, dividing creation of the outlines for later volumes between Edna C. Squier and Howard Garis, but quickly put an end to the two most recent flying series when sales did not live up to expectations.[41]

The "Slim Tyler" stories base their appeal on a combination of excitement and modernity. Advertised as stories of air adventure "so realistically written and so up to the minute in all their implications as to win ready admiration from all readers," the books involve endurance flights, distance records, airborne exploration, and commercial transport as they unfold, with Slim the continuing central figure. Stratemeyer, seeing the success of the "Ted Scott" books, turned to John W. Duffield for the new series, relying upon him to give it the contemporaneity and authenticity he sought.[42] *Sky Riders of the Atlantic or Slim Tyler's First Trip in the Clouds* (1930) sets the scene. After running away from his foster home because he is unfairly implicated in the burning of a lumberyard, eighteen-year-old, air-minded Slim finds work at a small airfield. He catches the attention of Dave Boyd, a world-famous aviator, when he returns two thousand dollars that Boyd has lost. Boyd in return finances flying lessons for Slim and the series is under way.

Slim and his chum Jerry Marbury enter an endurance contest to test in-flight refueling in the second volume, *Lost Over Greenland or Slim Tyler's Search for Dave Boyd* (1930), but, with reporter friend Dick Mylert, drop out to travel to Greenland where Boyd's airplane has disappeared. They rescue Boyd and his companions, and return to find that Dick's newspaper may sponsor a new contest to make up for the one they forfeited. *An Air Cargo of Gold or Slim Tyler, Special Bank Messenger* (1930) opens with Slim proving the practicality of blind flying. He next wins an endurance contest, setting a new record, and makes a cross-country flight with a substantial shipment of gold to help a business acquaintance close a deal. He flies a second rescue mission in *Adrift Over Hudson Bay or Slim Tyler in the Land of Ice* (1931), rescuing a group of explorers who are seeking a great-circle route from North America to Liverpool. *An Airplane Mystery or Slim Tyler on the Trail* (1931) follows Slim, Dick, and a new companion, expert pilot Lee Roth, on a nonstop flight from New York to Mexico, where they break up a drug-smuggling ring. In the final volume, *Secret Sky Express or Slim Tyler Saving a Fortune* (1932), Slim and Lee join an undercover airline network that shuttles financiers, securities, and cash from coast to coast to bolster the nation's shaky financial condition.

The books have a greater-than-usual emphasis on hairbreadth adventure and cops-and-robbers goings-on, but unfailingly uphold the modernity and the distinctiveness of aviation. As he does in the "Ted Scott" books, John W. Duffield, the principal writer, draws extensively on current events. Slim's interest in endurance records and in-flight refueling (1930) comes close on the heels of the record-setting flight of the army airplane, *Question Mark*. Refueled in mid-air using gasoline pumped from a support plane through a connecting hose, the *Question Mark* stayed in the air for 150 hours, 40 minutes, and 15 seconds, landing on 7 January 1929 after experiencing engine problems. Slim duplicates the feat, receiving fuel via a hose dropped to him and food and water lowered by rope.[43]

Slim uses tetraethyl lead as a gasoline additive to boost engine power in *An Air Cargo of Gold,* and, in the same volume, successfully takes off and lands using instruments only, a matter of weeks after Jimmy Doolittle does the same. The book opens with Slim's giving an authoritative description of the instruments he will use, including an artificial horizon, a directional gyroscope, a barometric altimeter, and a radio beacon. These, he says, will enable him to "take a tremendous step . . . for the safety of all airmen," and he readily sets aside any thoughts of his own safety for the sake of his contribution to flying. Slim—and Duffield—know whereof they speak. Slim describes the instruments and importance of the achievement in the language of a 9 October 1929 article in *Aviation,* communicating a notable advance in aviation to American youth and apprising them of its significance.[44]

Along with their technological up-to-dateness, the "Slim Tyler" books also convey a sense of the distinctiveness of the aviator and the flying life. Readers learn that "the one absorbing passion of Slim Tyler's life was aviation," which becomes "a passionate craving to be an airman, a craving at his heart that refused to be stilled." When he drops out of the endurance contest, he is heartbroken, for a victory "would have been the opening wedge of a great flying career." And, when he and Jerry win a subsequent contest, they refuse to exploit the associated publicity: "They were proud of their profession and would not belittle it. 'We are airmen, and nothing can make us forget it,' declared Slim Tyler. 'We're not actors or movie heroes or advertising men and don't want to be. Flying is good enough for us.'"[45] Patriotic, honorable, and superbly competent, Slim personifies the special appeal of the Golden Age professional flier and explicitly conveys his attributes to his young readers.

The same qualities recur in the "Randy Starr" books. Student pilot Randy Starr befriends the wealthy flier Raymond Bricknell and, with Bricknell's backing, embarks on a series of flying ventures. *Randy Starr After an Air Prize or The Sky Flyers Down the States* (1931) relates Randy's preparation for, and victory in, the Maine-to-Miami race sponsored by the Offenheim Foundation.

Randy Starr Above Stormy Seas (1931), written, like the preceding volume, by Roger Garis, takes Randy and his mechanic sidekick, Tubby Benson, to Cuba, where they weather mechanical problems and a hurricane, and their return with a cargo of gold artifacts. The final volume, *Randy Starr Leading the Air Circus or The Sky Flyers in a Daring Stunt* (1932), written by Howard Garis, finds Randy and Tubby employed as aeronautics instructors as Ryder College, where they mount an air circus to publicize the college's new aviation program. Many of the maneuvers featured in the latter event are reported in the language of Barrett Studley's *How to Fly: The Pilot and His Problems* (1929), a sequel to his *Practical Flight Training,* providing still more accurate flight lore for the series' young readers.[46]

The books once again emphasize the modernity of flight and show the effects of new government regulations. As a student pilot, Randy is well-informed about the latest Department of Commerce regulations for pilots and airfields, notes the government-stipulated beacons at the airfield, and eagerly awaits the time when he can satisfy government certification requirements for his license. His father, nonplussed by Randy's passion for flight, at last accepts it philosophically. To Randy's mother he muses, "Things are different than they were when you and I were young, Mother. There weren't so many autos then, or radios or airplanes, The young men are bound to be different from us, and the girls, too." Randy wins his license at last and eagerly joins "that intrepid band of young men who are making history in a new way," an up-and-coming citizen of the emerging flying culture.[47]

Although he is repeatedly described as a "born flier" or a "natural" flier, Randy understands that prowess in flying does not come without effort. He familiarizes himself with the workings of the radio beam, masters the complex instruments needed for an over-water flight, and readily takes on academic studies to make himself a better pilot. He and Tubby attend classes at Ryder College "on literature, history, economics, and mathematics, this last science playing no small part in flying work," because they recognize "that they were adding to their own education" and becoming better equipped to understand the place of aviation in the larger social and intellectual context.[48] Flying, the books affirm, requires more than just mechanical skill, if the aviator is properly to take his place in the evolving world.

A third class of books, new to the aviation series genre, focuses upon the growing involvement of aircraft in various daily occupations. These are jobs that, prior to the coming of aviation, had been carried out effectively enough, but, with the incorporation of airplanes, become even more effective and more far-ranging in their scope. Exciting adventures and hairbreadth escapes continue to play a part in the action, but the stories in general are object lessons in the growing uses of aviation. Although at times far-fetched, as in Ambrose Newcomb's "Sky Detective" series (1930–1931; six titles), which postulates an air-borne branch of the federal Secret Service, the books more often mirror uses of the airplane becoming evident in reality.

The Newcomb stories feature Jack Ralston, a former barnstormer and airmail pilot, and his sidekick Perk Perkiser, an expert marksman and one-time Canadian Mountie, whose countrified dialect adds comic relief, as they travel through the American South and West at the behest of their superiors in Washington. *The Sky Detectives or How Jack Ralston Got His Man* (1930) relates their patrolling of the lighted airways of the nation; *Eagles of the Sky or With Jack Ralston Along the Air Lanes* (1930) has them thwarting rum-runners along the coast of the Gulf of Mexico. They undertake a search for a lost airmail pilot across Arizona in *Wings Over the Rockies or Jack Ralston's New Cloud Chaser* (1930), travel to Canada in *The Sky Pilot's Great Chase or Jack Ralston's Dead Stick Landing* (1930) to break up a smuggling ring, and, in *Trackers of the Fog Pack or Jack Ralston Flying Blind* (1931), capture a gang of counterfeiters working out of the California mountains. Their final adventure, *Flying the Coast Skyways or Jack Ralston's Swift Patrol* (1931), places them in Georgia and South Carolina, where they track down a gang of sophisticated drug and jewel smugglers.

For all the melodrama of the events they relate, the books give a vividly realized picture of the state of American aviation in the early 1930s. Aircraft of the times—Stinson Detroiters, Lockheed Vegas, Pitcairn Mailwings, and Curtiss Kingbirds, among others—appear in profusion, and *Flying the Coast Skyways* includes a lengthy description of the operations of Eastern Air Transport and Southern Air Fast Express out of Candler Field in Atlanta. Current events figure, as well. Jack and Perk talk of a parachute for aircraft as a safety feature, reflecting publicity given Roscoe Turner's demonstration of such a device in April 1929. The September 1929 crash of TAT's *City of San Francisco* is mentioned twice, and Perk shakes his head in dismay over the press's tendency to link Lindbergh with any notable event in aviation, whether or not he was present.[49]

Although Jack and Perk make their living as federal agents, they think of themselves as airmen, and their stories regularly include some testimonial to the wonders of flight. The two friends happily while away idle hours watching the activities of an airport, for "so bred in the bone had their love for their profession grown to be that everything connected with flying drew them as the Polar star does the magnetic needle of a compass." Even the hardened Perk responds to the joys of the air, thinking "What air pilot who has tasted of the joys of such hours could ever dream of forsaking his vocation, so long as Fortune allowed him . . . the faculty for guiding an onrushing ship through the realms of unlimited space." Even still more pointedly, the narrator intervenes to remark that flying's appeal extends even to women: "In these modern days a multitude of daring girls and young women were becoming air minded and filled with the ambition to become pilots. The fascination of such a life appealed to them with irresistible force."[50] Detective work with the Secret Service has its thrilling moments, but, for sustained exhilaration and uplift, nothing will compete with the air.

A more realistic picture of the melding of aviation with daily work comes in three series dealing with air-borne journalists. These works, Lewis E. Theiss's

"Air Mail" series (1927–1932; six titles), Keith Russell's "Young Birdmen" books (1929–1930; three titles), and Graham Dean's "Tim Murphy" stories (1931–1934; four titles), all involve protagonists who are at once aviators and working newsmen. Journalism pays their bills, aviation gives them its own satisfactions, and the ability to fly to a news scene on a moment's notice gives them prominence in both professions. The stories reflect various newspapers' well-publicized use of aircraft in their news-gathering activities. As early as 1920, the *Baltimore Evening Sun* acquired a Canadian-built training plane to ferry reporters and photographers to breaking news sites. Other papers bought or chartered aircraft to cover special events, and in the early 1930s the *Detroit News* made use of an autogiro, a Lockheed Vega, and a Lockheed Orion specially fitted with an automatic pilot, a writing desk, and built-in cameras operable from either the cockpit or the cabin.[51]

Lewis E. Theiss's "Air Mail" books (more properly called the "Jimmy Donnelly" series) are the most realistic of the lot. Theiss, a professor of journalism at Bucknell University, worked for the *New York Sun* and *Good Housekeeping* magazine before turning to writing for boys. Early books dealt with wireless, Scouting, and dirigibles; he turned to stories of heavier-than-air craft in 1927, introducing the aspiring airmail pilot, Jimmy Donnelly. His books are carefully researched, frequently drawing upon interviews with individuals working in the field of his particular topic, and he regularly includes a foreword citing the real-life models for his characters and calling attention to the authenticity of the events he relates.[52]

The airmail as such figures only in the first book, *Piloting the U.S. Air Mail; Flying for Uncle Sam* (1927), which relates Jimmy Donnelly's dream of becoming a pilot with the mail service and his work helping to install the beacon system across Pennsylvania. He wins appointment to the mail service just before it is replaced by the contract carriers, and is forced to find some other work. In *The Search for the Lost Mail Plane* (1928), he persuades the *New York Morning Press* to sponsor his search for a downed pilot; his vivid report of the hunt wins him a job as cub reporter and air mechanic. *Trailing the Air Mail Bandit* (1929) deals with Jimmy's apprentice days at the *Morning Press,* where he works part-time in the newsroom and part-time at the airfield tending to the paper's airplane. His success in covering the varied events of *The Flying Reporter* (1930), including a hospital fire in Ohio, a flood in New Hampshire, and a cross-state prison riot, proves his worth, and he becomes a full-time reporter covering aviation events.

The final two volumes take Jimmy away from the *Morning Press,* but into new endeavors. In *The Pursuit of the Flying Smugglers* (1931), he leaves the paper to pilot Wall Street financier Worthington Chase between his rural estate and his downtown office, hoping to earn enough money to finance his new dream of becoming an aircraft designer. After several months he leaves Chase's employ, joins the Coast Guard, and, in *Wings of the Coast Guard; Aloft with the Flying Service of Uncle Sam's Life Savers* (1932), thwarts an effort to smuggle in illegal Chinese and successfully represents the Coast Guard in a series of air races.

Keith Russell's "Young Birdmen" books are more melodramatic, but give an equally plausible picture of the possibilities of air-borne journalism. *The Young Birdmen on the Wing, or The Rescue at Greenly Island* (1929) retells the 1928 rescue of James Fitzmaurice, Hermann Koehl, and Baron von Huenefeld after their trans-Atlantic ship, the *Bremen,* was forced down on Greenly Island. Jerry MacRae, an air-struck cub reporter for the *New York Star,* and Peter O'Brien, the equally air-struck son of the *Star*'s publisher, accompany the professional pilot Danersk in a "Lord" tri-motor to seek the missing fliers. Danersk, who appears in all three volumes, closely resembles the Norwegian-born airman, Bernt Balchen, who participated in Richard E. Byrd's Arctic and Antarctic expeditions, and flew the Ford tri-motor sent to rescue the crew of the *Bremen.*[53]

When the boys return, the senior O'Brien decides to start an aviation page in the *Star,* and taps Jerry to write it. *The Young Birdmen Across the Continent or The Coast-to-Coast Flight of the Night Mail* (1930) follows Jerry and Peter on a cross-country flight in the super-amphibian *Night Mail,* the latest creation of the Russian designer, Keronsky, in a *Star*-sponsored attempt to promote air travel. In the final volume, *The Young Birdmen Up the Amazon or Secrets of the Tropic Jungle* (1930), Jerry and Peter cover the South American expedition of an anthropologist with the American Museum of Natural History for the *Star,* and bring back not only news of unknown ruins like those at Machu Picchu but also a scoop describing a revolution in the Latin-American state of "Palamba."

Graham M. Dean's "Tim Murphy" books continue the exciting blend of journalism and flight. Dean, a professional journalist and editor, was also a flying enthusiast and a member of the Civil Air Patrol, and he drew upon both interests to invigorate his stories. The front-cover blurb for the first volume minces no words in making the linkage: "The skyways unfold great tales of romance and daring. Boys naturally love the exciting tales and experiences of newspaper men and when they are joined with the thrill of aviation . . . , one can be sure every boy will enjoy reading this book."[54] What the stories may lack in plausibility they make up for with aviation lore, and the mix is a potent one.

Daring Wings (1931) introduces Tim Murphy, flying reporter for the *Atkinson News.* His work is varied but exciting, as he covers the mysterious Sky Hawk's attacks on airmail ships with an engine-stopping electric beam, flies food and serum to flood victims, meets with Mexican rebels, and takes part in a national good-will flying tour. The excitement continues in *The Sky Trail* (1932), as he photographs a refinery fire from the air, uses aerial bombs to break up a flood-causing ice dam, and, commissioned as a special deputy in the state police, rounds up members of the Sky Hawk gang. *The Circle 4 Patrol* (1933) relates his coverage of an armed standoff between dairy farmers, the state veterinarian, and the National Guard (the farmers are resisting tuberculin testing for their cattle), and a later trip to Wyoming to report on an elaborate cattle-rustling scheme. His last venture, *The Treasure Hunt of the S-18* (1934), gives a good picture of the burgeoning transcontinental air service, and allows him to scoop his rivals with a story about the recovery of gold from a sunken submarine.

The stories of air-borne journalism, while differing considerably in the amount of melodrama that figures in them, nonetheless have common characteristics. They show, throughout, reporters and photographers at work. "Getting the story" is essential to their unfolding, and the use of aircraft only simplifies the task. All three series show young men flying great distances to bring back first-hand accounts of newsworthy events, and all three readily acknowledge that the airplane makes their success possible. All three, moreover, give a sense of the airplane's utility as a news-gathering—and news-*making*—device. Not only does it transport reporters to news-making events, but, as in Jerry MacRae's cross-country air tour and expedition to the Amazon, it also *creates* the news. The airplane has become an object of public engagement in its own right.

All of the books also incorporate, and romanticize, the latest developments in aircraft and aeronautical technology. Theiss dwells at length on the practical details and possibilities of the lighted airway, yet has Jimmy Donnelly find in the beacons "a suggestion of romance." Jimmy uses the radio beam to find his way to an airfield, later persuades Worthington Chase to buy an amphibian Loening Commuter because of its sturdiness and reliability, and flies Chase to the up-to-date "commuter terminal" on New York's East River. The career of Keith Russell's Russian designer, Keronsky, parallels that of Igor Sikorsky, and his vision of the aircraft of the future echoes several public statements made by Sikorsky. The twin-hulled seaplane that takes Jerry and Peter to the Amazon is a clone of the American-made version of the Savoia-Marchetti S-55, an Italian design much publicized during the late 1920s and early 1930s, even to its engine horsepower and passenger capacity.[55] Tim Murphy encounters an experimental helicopter resembling the Johnson

Helicopter-Airplane of 1925–1930, and, in *Circle 4 Patrol,* learns the comforts of modern commercial flying in a "60-B" airliner that has all of the attributes of a United Airlines Boeing 247, including an attractive stewardess who distributes fruit and chewing gum.[56]

Finally, all three series share a faith in the future of aviation, and the benefits it will bring to those who participate in it, and to the nation at large. When the lighted airway is complete, his supervisor tells Jimmy Donnelly, "America will wake up to the possibilities of flying. And when this nation does wake up, there's the big chance." Jimmy himself loves "airplanes as another lad might love horses or dogs," and, when he is "flying to get the news . . . , [feels] like a crusader of old, like a knight errant." A mechanic tells Jerry MacRae that "A fellow that can't fly nowadays is pretty near as badly off as a fellow who can't drive a car," while Peter O'Brien's father tells Jerry that "Aviation is going to play a greater and greater part in American life and affairs. . . . The public must be fully acquainted with the . . . possibilities." Danersk, as the boys get to know him, emerges as "a representative of a new type of human being which aviation had developed—a man who could not be measured and gauged by the old standards set up for humanity before the flying age." An articulate spokesman for the next stage of commercial aviation, he is "his own self only when flying," another testimonial to the liberating qualities of flight.[57] For individual and nation alike, aviation is the hope of the future; it remains only for the upcoming generation represented by America's youth to capitalize upon it.

Another innovation of the Golden Age aviation series is the subclass of stories dealing with flying professionals. These are stories of individuals who are full-time, dedicated aviators, who make their living entirely as professional pilots. The protagonists are little concerned with speed, distance, or endurance records. They look instead upon aviation as a business, with its own set of mercantile rules and requirements. They accept the reality of obtaining commercial licenses from the Department of Commerce, they respect the schedules posted for their flights, and they understand that their interests are inseparable from the interests of their employers. These persons are, however, *professional* pilots in a second sense. Flying, for them, is their vocation, and they approach it with the care, skill, and dedication of any professional. Their approach to flying is driven by a genuine sense of calling, and a belief that they are serving a higher goal through flying permeates their thinking. They freely acknowledge that flying pays their salaries, but see themselves as more than employees. They are a chosen few, persons who have been called to advance the interests of their employers *and* aviation as they go about their work.

The stories of professional flying, not surprisingly, are the most realistic of the series in their presentation of flight and flight-related activities. Crashes, forced landings, and the occasional clash with criminals still occur, to be sure, but, more clearly than in any other group of Golden Age stories, the hardware, technology, and attributes of established commercial flying carry the brunt of the story. As they tell of flying mail for contract carriers, establishing fixed-base charter services or small regional carriers, or the operating of an international major carrier, the books carry the message that flying has arrived. It has applications for many realms of daily life, and it is steadily becoming an integrated part of American personal and business activity.

Philip Lee Wright's "Air Pilot" series (1930–1931; three titles) examines flying for a contract mail carrier. *The East Bound Air Mail or Fighting Fog, Storm and Hard Luck* (1930) introduces pilots George Selkirk and his comic sidekick, Hack Custer, who fly for Western Air Express. They and their occasional passengers weather fog, damaged landing gear, and a tornado, and look ahead to the coming of new multi-engined craft for the company. *An Air Express Holdup or How Pilot George Selkirk Carried Through* (1930) continues their adventures as they ferry a valuable parcel from Los Angeles to Salt Lake City and fend off hijackers. In the final volume, *The Mail Pilot's Hunch or A Crash in Death Valley* (1931), the two, now flying a Fokker tri-motor, learn that their sole passenger is a noted criminal. Mechanical problems force them down in Death Valley, but they are saved by a search plane and their passenger is turned over to authorities.

Internal evidence within the "Air Pilot" series suggests that "Wright" may well be a pseudonym for Ambrose Newcomb, for the books are strikingly similar to Newcomb's "Sky Detective" stories. "Wright," like "Langley," is a common pen-name for an aviation series-writer. George Selkirk and Hack Custer, moreover, are indistinguishable from Jack Ralston and Perk Perkiser. Hack is a former cowboy rather than Mountie, but otherwise plays the same role, even speaking in a similar countrified dialect. George and Hack refer to many of the same events (notably the TAT crash in 1929 and the testing of a parachute to lower a disabled craft) that Jack and Perk remark upon, and, like them, refer to passengers as "sandbags" or "kiwis."[58] Their adventures, however, are more flight-related than mystery-related, and they speak throughout for the future of flying.

Whoever "Wright" may be, he never fails to give a picture of the operations of a contract mail carrier. George's arrival at the terminal precisely on schedule stirs no comment, for "punctuality and George Selkirk were held synonymous terms at that coast terminus." He and Hack follow closely the inauguration of TAT's transcontinental air-and-rail service, determined to do their part "to prove that aviation is already just as safe a means for traveling as by limited express trains." They take pride in being part of a progressive enterprise, and their final adventure makes reference to aviation's becoming "such an established institution that in Los Angeles alone there were some seven air transport companies operating twenty-seven planes leaving every day . . . , showing to what gigantic proportions the new business had attained in the brief period of its existence."[59]

Two further series deal with small-scale flying operations: Percy Keese Fitzhugh's "Mark Gilmore" stories (1930–31; three titles) and Harris Patton's "Young Eagles" books (1932; three titles). Fitzhugh was a well-established boys' author who produced more than one hundred books in the course of a forty-year career; his best-known works, the "Tom Slade" series, he wrote for Franklin K. Mathiews and the Boy Scouts of America.[60] In the "Mark Gilmore" books he turns to flying, with the initial book combining it with Scouting. *Mark Gilmore, Scout of the Air* (1930) introduces fifteen-year-old Mark, who is about to be sent to military school because of his apparent truancy. He helps a lost airplane land during a storm, accompanies it to Camp Leatherstocking in the Adirondacks, and stays on to learn Scouting and flying. His flying lessons complete, he in *Mark Gilmore's Lucky Landing* (1931) takes up work in Greeley, Kentucky, teaching flying for East Coast Airlines. He becomes involved with moonshiners and a long-standing feud between two families, and finally returns to work with the parent company. In *Mark Gilmore, Speed Flyer* (1931), he changes jobs, going to Colorado to fly for Inter-Mountain Airways. He flies the route safely and on time, and Inter-Mountain Airways wins a lucrative mail-and-passenger contract that ensures its continued operation.

Patton's "Young Eagles" books relate the development of a fixed-base operation and its eventual merger with a larger airline. Nebraskans Dick Davis and Bert Bowman first appear in *Young Eagles* (1932), winning their commercial licenses and setting up as Newton Airways, a small-town service flying for hire, with a second-hand Curtiss Robin. A local millionaire charters their airplane to search for his missing son, and their reward funds a new aircraft and business in earnest. *Wings of the North* (1932) follows their buying a "Jupiter" cabin model (an airplane reminiscent of the Lockheed Vega) and their reluctant leasing of their airfield to Red Arrow Airlines as a midwestern operations base. In *Flying Down* (1932), now Red Arrow pilots, they foil a hijacking effort by two sacked Red Arrow fliers and a sinister Mexican, and retrieve a half-million dollars in securities.

Both series, whether by Fitzhugh or Patton, give an extended picture of small-scale enterprises. These are operations that make their way giving rides, teaching flying, and taking on charter service. Dick Davis and Bert Bowman proudly offer "pleasure or commercial flying by transport pilots" to their Nebraska townsfolk, and are professionally impressed when Red Arrow transforms their grass strip into a fully modern field with weather, navigation, and communication instruments. Such a life is for Mark Gilmore an exhausting task, as "from early morning until nearly sundown he used up a considerable amount of gas and oil, lung-power and energy, in endeavoring to convince his rustic onlookers that it behooved every man, and even woman, to become air-minded."[61] The books give a plausible sense of a small operator's motivation, as well as the rewards and shortcomings of such an enterprise, and handily demonstrate how small operations worked as necessary parts of the developing national air network.

The most substantial professional series, Lewis E. Theiss's "Mail Pilot" stories (1934–1937; five titles), looks to the operations of a major international carrier, Pan American Airways, or PanAm. Headed by Juan Trippe and drawing on the aerial expertise of Charles Lindbergh in developing routes and hardware, PanAm had by 1930 become the dominant American carrier flying between the United States and the Caribbean and on into South America. Its success was due as much to marketing as to maintenance, though it became legendary for the care with which its ships were serviced. In a shrewd ploy bearing out Roscoe Turner's views on uniforms, Trippe outfitted his crews in naval-style uniforms, referred to the pilots as "captains," and in general ran operations with military-style precision and punctuality. The line used the most up-to-date airplanes and prided itself on its weather and communications systems, all of which contributed to its safety record.[62]

Theiss's books follow the apprenticeship of air-struck Eagle Scout Joe "Ginger" Hale. *Flying the U.S. Mail to South America: How Pan American Airships Carry On in Sun and Storm Above the Rolling Caribbean* (1932) introduces Ginger and traces his earnest progress through PanAm ranks until he wins appointment as a flight mechanic and radio operator. *The Mail Pilot of the Caribbean, the Adventures of Ginger Hale Above the Southern Seas* (1934) finds Ginger, now serving as copilot, on the Havana-Merida run. He rescues a party of stranded explorers, avoids a hurricane using the PanAm radio guidance system, and becomes at last a full junior pilot with the prospect of earning senior status.

In *The Flying Explorer: How a Mail Pilot Penetrated the Basin of the Amazon* (1935) Ginger is detached to fly a scientific expedition into Brazil, surviving jungle adventures and winning the praise of his superiors. A senior pilot at last, he flies (via United Airlines) in *From Coast to Coast With the U.S. Air Mail* (1938) to oversee the departure of PanAm's China Clipper, allowing Theiss to compare over-water and over-land flying. The final volume, *Flood Mappers Aloft: How Ginger Hale and the Scouts of the Bald Eagle Patrol Surveyed the Watershed of the Susquehanna* (1937), finds him recuperating from malaria acquired during the Brazil expedition. Back home in Pennsylvania, he helps a small-field operator and the local Scout troop fly an aerial photographic survey of the area flooded by the Susquehanna River in 1936.

Whatever the particular concerns of the book at hand, Theiss emphasizes the professionalism and dedication of Pan American management and crew. As Ginger moves from runway work to the dispatch office, and thence to the maintenance shops, he repeatedly witnesses the care that goes into every part of the operation. He later learns that the company wants to prepare its pilots as "actual commanders . . . , qualified to represent the company in any port of the world, and . . . capable of meeting government officials and outstanding citizens of the highest rank on a footing of equality." When he returns from the Brazil expedition, his superiors' praise for his contributions to the company awakens him to "a new view of his own services and his own part in the success of the expedition. Far from being merely the conductor of a conveyance, the main agent of transportation . . . , in his hands he held, or might hold, the very existence of every member of the expedition."[63] He has learned what professionalism entails, and he willingly accepts the responsibility.

Like the stories of air-supported work, the stories of professionalism emphasize contemporaneity. Aviation-related current events appear throughout, attesting to the authors' efforts to find their materials in the latest reports. Philip Lee Wright in a single volume makes reference to Lindbergh's marriage, the inauguration of TAT transcontinental service, the endurance record of the *Question Mark,* and, explicitly citing a February 1929 *Aero Digest* article, the record number of hours flown by a commercial pilot for Western Air Express. Harris Patton relates in detail the procedures, theoretical as well as practical, of a commercial pilot's licensing examination, while Lewis Theiss with the Ginger Hale stories explicitly states his intention to celebrate "a flying organization that is typically American, the Pan American Airways."[64] Here, for their young readers, is the current state of commercial aviation and all that it entails.

Paralleling the books' modernity is their picture of contemporary aircraft. George Selkirk and Hack Custer cross paths with a Lockheed Vega and are awed by its speed. After they join Red Arrow Airways, Dick Davis and Bert Bowman fly a modern Boeing "60-B" mail and passenger ship—a fictional craft, but identical in its specifications to the Boeing 40-B. The 40-B, a single-engined biplane, could carry 1200 pounds of mail in addition to two passengers. Theiss utilizes still other modern aircraft throughout the Ginger Hale books. Consolidated Commodores, twin-engined flying boats carrying twenty-two passengers, fly the principal routes around the Caribbean and South America. Ginger flies "a trim little sesquiplane" (most likely a Sikorsky S-38) on the route between Havana and Merida, and anticipates seeing the departure of the four-engined, Martin-built "China Clipper," which started service in January 1935.[65]

Theiss's fullest homage to the modern airplane, however, occurs in *From Coast to Coast With the U.S. Air Mail.* Having flown from Miami to Newark in a single-engined Northrop, Ginger boards the transcontinental United flight and strikes out for San Francisco. To his delight, he's flying in a Boeing 247, a "beautiful, low wing, all metal monoplane" representing six-and-a-half tons of aeronautical achievement with which "no bird alive could compete." For more than thirty consecutive pages, readers share his wonder as he explores the ship, reveling in its interior decor, marveling over its electronic navigational instruments, and remembering the remarkable record that the design achieved in the MacRobertson Race to Australia. With unutterable joy, he discovers that he's flying in the very ship—registration number NC 13369—that made the race, "and had subsequently become the flagship of the United fleet."[66] Roscoe Turner and Ginger Hale, Pan American Airways and United Airlines, all come together in a loving hymn to the modern commercial airplane.

The love that Theiss extends to the 247 recurs in the other series as a more general love of aviation and its possibilities. Even the regimentation imposed by licensing requirements and the unvarying routine inherent in airline flying (a hoary joke among commercial pilots describes the latter as "hours of boredom punctuated by moments of stark terror") cannot dampen the enthusiasm that flying stirs in the heart, nor lessen the benefits that will accrue from flying. The pilots themselves, one and all, feel the excitement. George Selkirk says he can "feel the blood tingle" in his veins every time he stops to think that he belongs "to that up-to-date profession of air pilots." Sidekick Hack agrees that "the folk who stick as *kiwis* on the ground c'n never understand [that] it's a bully life." "Wright" goes on to praise as "the belted knights of old" the growing band of air pilots who choose to take "part in the miraculous drama of aviation," suggestively shifting the accolade of flying knighthood from the military pilot to the commercial flier.[67]

Mark Gilmore waxes romantic over the mountains and clouds he sees on a night flight, thinking of his airplane as "his first and only love," while Lewis Theiss, speaking in his own voice, affirms that flying achievements, whether individual or corporate, are imbued with the most modern form of romance:

> To find romance, even in America in this year 1934, one has only to open one's eyes and look. It is everywhere. Nowhere is it more conspicuous than in the skies. . . . If [PanAm's accomplishments] be not romance, and it be not a matter for pride in every

> American heart, where shall we find romance and where shall we discover anything to make us proud?[68]

Even when it is fully assimilated into an international, corporate operation, flight retains its magic and its power to elevate the human soul.

As this passage implies, flight also exalts the national soul, and the benefits that accrue to the nation are at least as great as those experienced by the individual. "The time's comin' right soon," says Hack, "when it'll be safer to be up in a plane than walkin' along Main Street." Mark Gilmore agrees to help introduce aviation into the mountains of Kentucky, because "flying will be a salvation to [the mountaineers]. It will bring them into immediate contact with the whole world." Ginger Hale, speaking for himself to a supervisor but echoing the mystique of the series books, articulates an idealistic vision of all that aviation can offer:

> Think what flying can do for people. It speeds up the mails, it carries food and supplies and money and people and other helpful things from country to country . . . ; and that draws nations together and builds up business and good will and international friendships and helps to do away with war. . . . I should think you would see and feel all the magnificent possibilities in flying.[69]

The gains to come to civilization will be spiritual as well as commercial, humane as well as practical. Flying, the books make clear, is a means to a better world—the dominant motif of the Golden Age. It was a view lasting until well into the early days of the Second World War.

NOTES TO CHAPTER SIX

1 Robert Dane, "Midnight Suns of the Air Mail," *Aero Digest,* 7 (July, 1925): 359–60; F. Robert van der Linden, *Airlines & Air Mail: The Post Office and the Birth of the Commercial Aviation Industry* (Lexington: University Press of Kentucky, 2002), 12–18.

2 James P. Wines, "The 48 Hr. Coast to Coast Air-Rail Service of Transcontinental Air Transport," *Aviation,* 27 (6 July 1929): 26–29; R.E.G. Davies, *Airlines of the United States Since 1914* (Washington, DC: Smithsonian Institution Press, 1998), 56–108.

3 Horace R. Byers, "The Guggenheim Airway Meteorological Service," *Aviation,* 25 (15 September 1928): 866–867, 886–889; Fred E. Weick, "The New N.A.C.A. Low Drag Cowling," *Aviation,* 25 (17 November 1928): 1556–1557, 1586–1590; Frederick R. Neely, "Cowling of Air-Cooled Radial Engines Develops Enormous Increase in Speed," *Aeronautic Review,* 6 (November 1928): 172, 182; Gerard F. Vultee, "20 Miles Faster," *Western Flying,* 5 (March 1929): 38–39, 140.

4 Daniel Guggenheim Fund for the Promotion of Aeronautics, *Equipment Used in Experiments to Solve the Problem of Fog Flying* (New York: Daniel Guggenheim Fund for the Promotion of Aeronautics, 1930).

5 Herbert Hoover, Jr., "Blind Flying and Radio," *Aero Digest,* 17 (July, August 1930): 59–61, 44–45.

6 Roger E. Bilstein, *Flight in America: From the Wrights to the Astronauts.* Rev. ed. (Baltimore: Johns Hopkins University Press, 1994), 88; F. Robert van der Linden, *The Boeing 247: The First Modern Airliner* (Seattle: University of Washington Press, 1991), 46.

7 Terry Gwynne-Jones, *Farther and Faster: Aviation's Adventuring Years, 1909–1939* (Washington, DC: Smithsonian Institution Press, 1991), 140–151, 158–162. See also a more skeptical opinion, C.M. Keys, "Value of Racing Planes," *Aero Digest,* 7 (October 1925): 535–536, 568–570.

8 Associated Press, "World's Greatest Aviator in Battle to Save a Life," *Washington Post,* 25 April 1928: 1; "Lindbergh On Way to Seek Lost Plane," *New York Times,* 7 September 1929, 1:1 2; Fletcher Pratt, "'Lindy' Charts the Atlantic Skies," *Universal Model Airplane News,* 10 (March 1934): 6–8, 36–39; A. Scott Berg, *Lindbergh* (New York: G.P. Putnam's Sons, 1998), 226–232, 284–290.

9 Bilstein, *Flight in America,* 76, 84. A reliable biography of Earhart is Doris L. Rich, *Amelia Earhart: A Biography* (Washington, DC: Smithsonian Institution Press, 1989).

10 Richard Sanders Allen, *Revolution in the Sky: The Lockheeds of Aviation's Golden Age.* Rev. ed. (Atglen, PA: Schiffer Aviation History, 1993), 76–78, 3–85; Gwynne-Jones, *Farther and Faster,* 247–251, 15; Bilstein, *Flight in America,* 84; A.K. [Alexander Klemin]. "Wiley Post's Altitude Suit," *Scientific American,* 151 (October 1934): 215–216. See also Stanley R. Moher and Bobby H. Johnson, *Wiley Post, his Winnie Mae, and the World's First Pressure Suit.* Smithsonian annals of flight, No. 8 (Washington, DC: Smithsonian Institution Press, 1971).

11 George Smedal, "Jimmy Doolittle—Air Wizard," *Popular Aviation,* 8 (May 1931): 23–24, 58; Gwynne-Jones, *Farther and Faster,* 304, 166–67. Doolittle's own account of his life appears in James H. Doolittle and Carroll V. Glines, *I Could Never Be So Lucky Again: An Autobiography of James H. "Jimmy" Doolittle* (Atglen, PA: Schiffer Publishing, 1995).

12 Creighton Merrell, "Transcontinental Speed," *Southern Flight,* 7 (February 1937): 10–12; van der Linden, *The Boeing 247,* 102–114; Carroll V. Glines, *Roscoe Turner: Aviation's Master Showman* (Washington, DC: Smithsonian Institution Press, 1995), 264–266.

13 Glines, *Roscoe Turner,* 114–115, 22–23, 103–104, 124–127, 139–140.

14 Glines, *Roscoe Turner,* 219, 22; "A Commercial Aviator's Uniform," *Aerial Age Weekly,* 13 (20 June 1921): 344; Beirne Lay, Jr., "Good Judgment," *Sportsman Pilot,* 16 (15 October 1936): 19, 37–39. Lay also comments on Turner's cautious approach to hazardous flying. Another comment on the importance of a professional image in aviation is Donald Kehoe, "Dressing Up Aviation," *Aviation,* 25 (10 November 1928): 1485, 1510–1514. "Kehoe" is a misprint for "Keyhoe."

15 The transition from wood-and-fabric to all-metal construction is traced in Eric Schatzberg, *Wings of Wood, Wings of Metal: Culture and Technical Choice in American Airplane Materials, 1914—1945* (Princeton: Princeton University Press, 1999).

16 Allen, *Revolution in the Sky,* 242–245; Wayne Biddle, *Barons of the Sky: From Early Flight to Strategic Warfare, the Story of the American Aerospace Industry* (New York: Simon & Schuster, 1991), 150–151.

17 Allen, *Revolution in the Sky,* 35, 225.

18 Richard Sanders Allen, *The Northrop Story, 1929–1939* (Atglen, PA: Schiffer Aviation History, 1993), 13–14, 28; Biddle, *Barons of the Sky,* 178.

19 Sanders, *The Northrop Story,* 36–46, 50–57.

20 van der Linden, *The Boeing 247,* 25–26, 63–69.

21 "Boeing's New Model 247 Transport," *Aviation,* 32 (April 1932): 124–26; "New Boeing Commercial Transport Surpasses Expectations in Test Flight," *U.S. Air Services,* 18 (April 1933): 12–15; R.B.R., "Boeing's hand from the new deal in air transport," *Sportsman Pilot,* 9 (April 1933): 34–39; "6,000 Times Across America in One Year," United Airlines promotional brochure, Document file F1U-560075–11, "United Airlines (USA)," National Air & Space Museum Library, Smithsonian Institutuion, Washington, DC.

22 van der Linden, *The Boeing 247,* 88.

23 Biddle, *Barons of the Sky,* 129–137; Douglas J. Ingells, *The Plane that Changed the World: a Biography of the DC-3* (Fallbrook, CA: Aero Publishers, 1966), 28–46; Donald W. Douglas, "The Douglas DC-1 Airliner," *Aero Digest,* 23 (October 1933): 45–46; Donald W. Douglas, "Transcontinental & Western Air Accepts the Douglas 'Airliner,'" *U.S. Air Services,* 18 (October 1933): 28–30; "Air-Brakes for Douglas DC-1," *Popular Aviation,* 14 (March 1934): 161.

24 Ingells, *The Plane the Changed the World,* 72, 85–89; Gwynne-Jones, *Farther and Faster,* 251–255; Max Karant, "Air-Sleepers On American Line," *Popular Aviation,* 18 (January 1936): 25–26, 72; "Douglas DST Sleeplane," *Aero Digest,* 28 (February 1936): 52–53; "More About the Douglas Sleeper," *Aviation,* 35 (February 1936): 35–36; Kurt Rand, "The D Ships," *Popular Aviation,* 26 (April 1940): 28–30, 72.

25 Frances Carol Locher, ed., "Crump, (James) Irving," *Current Authors,* Vol. 73–76 (Detroit: Gale Research, 1978), 143.

26 Irving Crump, *The Cloud Patrol* (New York: Grosset & Dunlap, 1929), 18–19; Irving Crump, *The Pilot of the Cloud Patrol* (New York: Grosset & Dunlap, 1929), 7–8, 24–25; Irving Crump, *Craig of the Cloud Patrol* (New York: Grosset & Dunlap, 1931), 55; Weick, "The New N.A.C.A. Low Drag Cowling," 1556–1557, 1586–1590; Gerard F. Vultee, "The New N.A.C.A. Cowling and its application to the Lockheed 'Air Express,'" *Aero Digest,* 14 (March 1929): 43–44, 222–223.

27 Crump, *Pilot of the Cloud Patrol,* 22, 7–8.

28 Crump, *Cloud Patrol,* 110, 125; Crump, *Craig of the Cloud Patrol,* 74.

29 Van Powell [A. VanBuren Powell], *The Mystery Crash* (Akron: Saalfield Publishing Co., 1932), 45–46, 64–66; Van Powell, [A. VanBuren Powell], *The Vanishing Air Liner* (Akron: Saalfield Publishing Co., 1932), 155–56; Roswell H. Ward, "The Airplane Diesel in 1940," *Scientific American,* 142 (January 1930): 36–38.

30 Van Powell [A. VanBuren Powell], *The Ghost of Mystery Airport* (Akron: Saalfield Publishing Co., 1932), 30, 100–01, 57, 20; Otto H. Lunde, "The Handley-Page Automatic Slot," *Aviation,* 24 (27 February 1928): 506–08; "Slots and Flaps Take the Lead," *Western Flying,* 7 (January 1930): 54–55, 134; Alexander Klemin, "Handley Page Slot and other Devices to Increase Wing Lift," *Aeronautics,* 6 (March 1930): 41–42, 54–55. For ship-to-shore airmail experiments, see C.H. Gale, "Ship to Shore Airmail Service," *Aviation,* 28 (31 May 1930): 1084–1087

31 Powell, *Vanishing Air Liner,* 7–8.

32 Van Powell [A. VanBuren Powell, *The Haunted Hangar* (Akron: Saalfield Publishing Co., 1932), 194–195, 105; Powell, *Vanishing Air Liner,* 228–229; "'Dusting' Pilots," *Aviation,* 24 (23 January 1928): 189; Powell, *Mystery Crash,* 189.

33 Cupples & Leon advertisement, Noel Sainsbury, Jr., *Billy Smith Mystery Ace or Airplane Discoveries in South America* (New York: Cupples & Leon, 1932), unpaged; "Sainsbury, Noel Everingham, Jr.," *Who Was Who in America,* Vol. VII: 1977–1981 (Chicago: Marquis Who's Who, 1981): 498.

34 The same eye-opening discovery recurs in Chapters 6 and 7 of Robert A. Heinlein's *Tunnel in the Sky* (1955). Heinlein read "Tom Swift" and other series as a youth, was a frequent contributor to *Boy's Life,* and kept up his familiarity with the series mode throughout his writing career. As a retired naval officer, he could well have known Sainsbury's work. See H. Bruce Franklin, *Robert A. Heinlein: America as Science Fiction* (New York: Oxford University Press, 1980), 10–12, 73–74.

35 "Fokker Universal," *Aero Digest,* 18 (April 1931): 98; Henry S. Cocklin, "Development of Navy Patrol Planes," *Aero Digest,* 6 (May 1925); 242–244, 280.

36 Noel Sainsbury, Jr., *Billy Smith Trail Eater Ace or Into the Wilds of Northern Alaska by Airplane* (New York: Cupples & Leon, 1933), 15, 110; W. L. LePage, "The Development of the Amphibious Airplane," *Aviation,* 22 (25 April 1927): 831–832.

37 Sainsbury, *Billy Smith Mystery Ace,* 27; Noel Sainsbury, Jr., *Billy Smith Secret Service Ace or Airplane Adventures in Arabia* (New York: Cupples & Leon, 1932), 121; Lieutenant Barrett Studley, *Practical Flight Training* (New York: Macmillan Co., 1928), 164–165, 416; Lieutenant Barrett Studley, "Foreword," *How to Fly: The Pilot and His Problems* (New York: Macmillan Co., 1929), unpaged.

38 Lieutenant Noel Sainsbury, Jr., *Bill Bolton and Hidden Danger* (Chicago: Goldsmith Publishing Co., 1933), 189; Lieutenant Noel Sainsbury, Jr., *Bill Bolton Flying Midshipman* (Chicago: Goldsmith Publishing Co., 1933), 245; "The Buhl-Verville Airster," *Aero Digest,* 8 (March 1926): 130–131; "The Flying Submarine or Submersible Seaplane," *Flying,* 9 (June 1920): 331.

39 Sainsbury, *Bill Bolton Flying Midshipman,* 19, 55; Lieutenant Noel Sainsbury, Jr., *Bill Bolton and the Flying Fish* (Chicago: Goldsmith Publishing Co., 1933), 79–80, 82–83; Sainsbury, *Bill Bolton and Hidden Danger,* 182–183; Studley, *Practical Flight Training,* 172, 155, 159, 266.

40 Sainsbury, *Bill Bolton and the Flying Fish,* 79.

41 Books (By Series) of the Stratemeyer Syndicate 1936, Stratemeyer Syndicate Records, MSS. & Archives Division, N.Y.P.L., Boxes 18–19, Reel 11.

42 Cupples & Leon Advertisement, Sainsbury, *Billy Smith Exploring Ace,* unpaged; Slim Tyler Outlines, Stratemeyer Syndicate Records, MSS. & Archives Section, N.Y.P.L., Box 307

43 "Air Corps Fokker Exceeds All Sustained Flight Marks," *Aviation,* 26 (12 January 1929): 108–109; Charles F. McReynolds, "The Refueling Flight of the 'Question Mark,'" *Aviation,* 26 (19 January 1929): 158–162; Richard H. Stone [John W. Duffield], *Lost Over Greenland or Slim Tyler's Search for Dave Boyd* (New York: Cupples & Leon, 1930), 5–6.

44 Richard H. Stone, *An Air Cargo of Gold or Slim Tyler, Special Bank Messenger* (New York: Cupples & Leon, 1930), 9; "Simulated Landings, Take-Offs In Fog Made by Lieut. Doolittle," *Aviation,* 27 (5 October 1929): 718, 724.

45 Richard H. Stone [John W. Duffield], *Sky Riders of the Atlantic or Slim Tyler's First Trip in the Clouds* (New York: Cupples & Leon, 1930), 30–31; Stone, *Lost Over Greenland,* 23; Stone, *Air Cargo of Gold,* 114.

46 Randy Starr Manuscript Releases, Stratemeyer Syndicate Records, MSS. & Archives Division, N.Y.P.L., Box 66; Eugene Martin [Howard R. Garis], *Randy Starr Leading the Air Circus, or The Sky Flyers in a Daring Stunt* (Akron: Saalfield Publishing Co., 1932), 132–133; Studley, *How to Fly,* 198–199, 129–130.

47 Eugene Martin [Roger Garis], *Randy Starr After an Air Prize, or The Sky Flyers in a Dash Down the States* (Akron: Saalfield Publishing Co., 1931), 49, 32, 128.

48 Martin, *Randy Starr After an Air Prize,* 188; Eugene Martin [Roger Garis], *Randy Starr Above Stormy Seas, or The Sky Flyers on a Perilous Journey* (Akron: Saalfield Publishing Co., 1931), 56; Martin, *Randy Starr Leading the Air Circus,* 148.

49 Ambrose Newcomb, *Flying the Coast Skyways or Jack Ralston's Swift Patrol* (Chicago: Goldsmith Publishing Co., 1931), 21, 58–59. See Davies, *Airlines of the United States,* 118–120, for Southern Air Fast Express. Ambrose Newcomb, *The Sky Detectives or How Jack Ralston Got His Man* (New York: Goldsmith Publishing Co., 1930), 200, 69; Glines, *Roscoe Turner,* 107–109; S.R. Winters, "A Plane-Size Parachute," *Popular Aviation,* 3 (October 1928): 24–25; F.D. Van Luven, "Successful Tests of Plane Parachute," *Southern Aviation,* 2 (October 1930): 43; Ambrose Newcomb, *Wings Over the Rockies or Jack Ralston's New Cloud Chaser* (Chicago: Goldsmith Publishing Co., 1930), 78, 26–27.

50 Ambrose Newcomb, *The Sky Pilot's Great Chase or Jack Ralston's Dead Stick Landing* (Chicago: Goldsmith Publishing Co., 1930), 58; Newcomb, *Sky Detectives,* 201; Newcomb, *Wings Over the Rockies,* 118.

51 "Airplane Purchased by *Baltimore Sun,*" *U.S. Air Services,* 4 (October 1920): 16; James V. Piersol, "Adapting the Airplane to the Newspaper," *Aero Digest,* 18 (January 1931): 35–39, 122; James V. Piersol, "The 'Early Bird'—A Flying Editorial Room," *National Aeronautics,* 13 (January 1935): 7–9.

52 David K. Vaughan, "The Educating Story-Teller: Lewis Theiss and the Jimmy Donnelly Air Mail Books," *Dime Novel Roundup,* 61 (June 1992): 42–49.

53 "Ferry Boat Brings Balchen into City," *New York World,* 29 April 1928, 2.

54 "Dean, Graham M.," *Who Was Who in America,* Vol. VI: 1974–1976 (Chicago: Marquis Who's Who, 1976), 107; Martha E. Ward and Dorothy A. Marquardt, "Dean, Graham M.," *Authors of Books for Young People.* Second ed. (Metuchen, NJ: Scarecrow Press, 1971), 152; Graham M. Dean, *Daring Wings* (Chicago: Goldsmith Publishing Co., 1931), front cover text.

55 Lewis E. Theiss, *Piloting the U.S. Air Mail: Flying for Uncle Sam* (Boston: W.A. Wilde Co., 1927), 139–153; Lewis E. Theiss, *The Flying Reporter.* 1930 (Chicago: Wilcox & Follett Co., 1945), 35–36; Lewis E. Theiss, *The Pursuit of the Flying Smugglers* (Boston: W.A. Wilde Co., 1931), 45–65, 122–123; "The Keystone-Loening '*Commuter,*'" *Aviation,* 29 (5 July 1930): 12–16; Keith Russell, *The Young Birdmen Across the Continent or The Coast-to-Coast Flight of The Night Mail* (New York: Sears Publishing Co., 1930), 15–16; "Sikorsky Predicts 100-Ton Air Liners," *New York Times,* 13 October 1929: 24; Charles J.V. Murphy, "A Shirt Flapping in the Breeze Became an Airplane in the Sky," *American Magazine,* 107 (May 1929): 29, 112–118; Igor I. Sikorsky, "Airplanes of the Future," *Aero Digest,* 15 (December 1929): 54–55; Keith Russell, *The Young Birdmen Up the Amazon or Secrets of the Tropic Jungle* (New York: Sears Publishing Co., 1930), 43–44, 163–164; M.L. Hoffman, "The American-Built Savoia-Marchetti S-55," *Air Transportation,* 11 (8 March 1930): 38.

56 Graham M. Dean, *The Sky Trail* (Chicago: Goldsmith Publishing Co., 1932), 234; "Helicopter Plane Passes Successful Tests," *Popular Mechanics,* 52 (February 1930): 233; "Report of the Johnson Helicopter Airplane," Document File CJ-337000–01, "Johnson, Jess C.," National Air & Space Museum; Graham M. Dean, *Circle 4 Patrol* (Chicago: Goldsmith Publishing Co., 1933), 23–31

57 Theiss, *Piloting the U.S. Air Mail,* 39; Lewis E. Theiss, *Trailing the Air Mail Bandit.* Rev. ed. 1929 (Repr. Chicago: Wilcox & Follett, 1946), 16–17, 19; Keith Russell, *The Young Birdmen on the Wing, or The Rescue at Greenly Island* (New York: J.J. Sears, 1929), 47–48, 247; Russell, *Young Birdmen Across the Continent,* 9, 15–16.

58 Philip Lee Wright, *The East Bound Air Mail or Fighting Fog, Storm and Hard Luck* (New York: Barse & Co., 1930), 18; Philip Lee Wright, *The Mail Pilot's Hunch or a Crash in Death Valley* (New York: Grosset & Dunlap, 1931), 30–31.

59 Wright, *East Bound Air Mail,* 5, 42; Wright, *Mail Pilot's Hunch,* 56.

60 John T. Dizer, "The Unknown Percy Keese Fitzhugh," *Dime Novel Roundup.* 62 (October 1993): 86–94.

61 Harris Patton, *Young Eagles* (Chicago: Goldsmith Publishing Co., 1932), 61, 68–69; Percy Keese Fitzhugh, *Mark Gilmore's Lucky Landing* (New York: Grosset & Dunlap, 1931), 52. It is tempting to link Fitzhugh's "Mark Gilmore" to Roscoe Turner's Gilmore; both began their public lives in 1930.

62 Davies, *Airlines of the United States,* 210–39; James P. Wines, "Operation of the Pan American Airways System," *Aviation,* 26 (27 April 1929): 1422–1429; "Communications on an international airline," *Aviation,* 31 (November 1932): 435–437. An instructive overview of Pan American's history is Marilyn Bender and Selig Altschul, *The Chosen Instrument: Pan Am, Juan Trippe: The Rise and Fall of an American Entrepreneur* (New York: Simon & Schuster, 1982).

63 Lewis Edwin Theiss, *Flying the U.S. Mail to South America: How Pan American Airlines Carry On in Sun and Storm Above the Rolling Caribbean* (Boston: W.A. Wilde, 1933), 205–208, 247–251; Lewis E. Theiss, *The Mail Pilot of the Caribbean, The Adventures of Ginger Hale Above the Southern Seas* (Boston: W.A. Wilde Co, 1934), 276–277; Lewis E. Theiss, *The Flying Explorer: How a Mail Pilot Penetrated the Basin of the Amazon* (Boston: W.A. Wilde Co., 1935), 208.

64 Wright, *East Bound Air Mail,* 13, 16, 41–42; "Pilot Kelly Flies 115,760 Miles in 1928," *Aero Digest,* 14 (February 1929): 132; Patton, *Young Eagles,* 11, 15–16; Theiss, *Mail Pilot of the Caribbean,* 3.

65 Philip Lee Wright, *An Air Express Holdup or How Pilot George Selkirk Carried Through* (New York: Grosset & Dunlap, 1930), 40; Harris Patton, *Riding Down* (Chicago: Goldsmith Publishing Co., 1932), 15–16; "The Boeing Mail Plane," *Aviation,* 23 (4 July 1927): 18–19; Peter M. Bowers, *Boeing Aircraft Since 1916* (New York: Funk & Wagnalls, 1968), 108–117; Theiss, *Flying the U.S. Air Mail,* 209–210; Leslie E. Neville, "Consolidated '*Commodore*' Flying Boat," *Aviation,* 28 (11 January 1930): 49–55; Theiss, *Mail Pilot of the Caribbean,* 39; Leslie E. Neville, "The Sikorsky S-38," *Aviation,* 25 (28 July 1928): 328–348; "The Americas and the Orient Linked by Air," *Aero Digest,* 27 (December 1935): 24–27, 72.

66 Lewis E. Theiss, *From Coast to Coast With the U.S. Air Mail* (Boston: W.A. Wilde Co, 1936), 80–118.

67 Dave English, *Slipping the Surly Bonds: Great Quotations on Flight* (New York: McGraw-Hill, 1998), 122; Wright, *Mail Pilot's Hunch,* 31, 41; Wright, *East Bound Air Mail,* 175–176.

68 Percy Keese Fitzhugh, *Mark Gilmore, Speed Flyer* (New York: Grosset & Dunlap, 1931), 190–191; Theiss,"Foreword," *Mail Pilot of the Caribbean,* 3.

69 Wright, *Mail Pilot's Hunch,* 30–31; Fitzhugh, *Mark Gilmore's Lucky Landing,* 17; Theiss, *Flying the U.S. Air Mail,* 122–123.

Chapter Seven

World War Two and Modern Aviation, 1939–1945

For all the national shock created by the Japanese attack on Pearl Harbor on 7 December 1941, the Second World War came as little surprise to most United States citizens. That the American military base at Pearl Harbor was the site of the attack *was* a surprise; that such an attack could eventually occur, somewhere, at some time, however, was almost a foregone conclusion. The international situation, in Asia as much as in Europe, had been deteriorating since at least 1935, when Adolph Hitler's National Socialist regime in Germany disavowed the disarmament rules imposed by the Versailles Treaty and unveiled its newly equipped air force, the Luftwaffe. The European nations responded with a frenzy of rearmament, while the United States strove to maintain a position of studied neutrality, and war seemed increasingly certain.

That certainty was especially apparent in the technical aviation press *and* in works directed toward young persons. With the same writers often publishing in both venues (as Robert McLarren did with *Model Airplane News* and *Aviation,* or Robert Sidney Bowen did by writing series fiction while working as an editor for *Aviation*), up-to-date information concerning developments in military aircraft was as readily available to air enthusiasts young and old as was information concerning civil aircraft, creating a climate in which the military applications of the airplane were increasingly taken for granted as world events evolved. McLarren's April 1939 article on the Curtiss-Wright CW-21 in *Model Airplane News,* warning against "a sudden, unannounced assault by enemy air raiders," assured young readers that the fighter was "an American interceptor which far surpasses anything of a like design the world has to offer," and the following month he spoke of the Lockheed XP-38 as boosting "this nation's . . .

pride in possessing the world's swiftest and most terrible fighting plane." His 1940 report on the twin-engined Grumman XF5F-1 bluntly called it "the fastest fighting plane in the entire world."[1] Young and old, the aviation world was ready for war—in spirit if not in materiel.

The initial phases of World War II occurred in Europe. By 1939 German territorial expansion had absorbed the Rhineland, Austria, and Czechoslovakia without overt hostilities. The September invasion of Poland, however, gave the world its first glimpse of *Blitzkrieg* tactics—a massive, coordinated attack by armed aircraft and mechanized ground forces. In response, France and Great Britain declared war against Germany, but took no immediate armed action. From September 1939 until May 1940, the period of the so-called "Phony War," the three great armies faced each other, with only occasional skirmishes and naval engagements breaking the peace. Then, on 10 May, German forces struck Belgium, Holland, and France with an overwhelming combination of ground and air forces, inexorably pushing French and British troops westward until they were stopped by the English Channel. The German army had control of the continent, and only the 26 May—4 June evacuation of Allied forces at Dunkirk by a ragtag fleet of private, commercial, and military ships prevented a total slaughter.[2]

With the continent secure, the German military began preparations for the invasion of Great Britain. The first stage of the invasion plan began with an all-out aerial assault on the British Isles, a series of night bombing raids in July 1940, building to the full-scale "Blitz" of late 1940 and early 1941. What the Germans had not counted on, however, was the persistence and strength of the Royal Air Force (RAF). Countering the German air attacks with Hawker Hurricane and Supermarine Spitfire fighters, the RAF proved a deadly adversary, and the following months of conflict, the "Battle of Britain," gave the world its first vision of large-scale aerial warfare. By the end of September, the British were the clear winners. The Luftwaffe had lost more than 1700 aircraft to the RAF's 1000, the invasion of Great Britain was postponed indefinitely, and, although bombing of London and other cities continued, the main force of the German military was diverted to other targets.[3]

The United States, for all its proclaimed neutrality, was not blind to events. As early as 1938, President Franklin D. Roosevelt had called for the annual production of 50,000 airplanes and the training of an equivalent number of pilots. Prominent figures in aviation, recognizing the inferiority of American military aviation in comparison with the forces of Germany and Great Britain, spoke out for new development and production priorities. New aircraft were on the drawing boards or in the early stages of flight development, and, through a congressionally authorized emendation of the existing Neutrality Act, American weapons, ships, and aircraft were being channeled to the British. This arrangement, the "Lend-Lease" agreement, provided the British with badly needed hardware, while the necessity of ferrying aircraft across the Atlantic gave American pilots valuable experience in long-distance flying.[4]

Rearmament did not come without opposition. A sizable anti-war faction developed in the United States during the late 1930s, with its most prominent member none other than Charles A. Lindbergh. At the request of the army air corps, Lindbergh had toured a number of German air factories and airports during 1937. His prominence gained him extraordinary access to first-line aircraft that had been denied other observers, and what he saw convinced him of Germany's technological superiority in the air. He summed up his findings and his conclusions in an outspoken document that was circulated throughout military, diplomatic, and congressional circles. He visited Germany again in 1938, spending a week visiting factories and other aviation sites, and for his contributions to aviation was decorated by Hermann Goering, head of the Luftwaffe, with the Service Cross of the German Eagle. The award was to come back to haunt him. By 1939 he was actively engaged in examining the state of American military aviation, visiting numerous factories and airfields and meeting with Dr. Robert Goddard, whose early experimentation with liquid-fueled rockets he had encouraged the Guggenheim Foundation to support.[5]

For all his commitment to the advancing of American aviation, Lindbergh grew increasingly opposed to American involvement in a European war. He began to write and speak against such an involvement, and, in September 1939, made a nationally aired radio broadcast stating his opposition. He continued his public opposition to American involvement as the Battle of Britain raged, calling instead for strengthened national defenses, testified before Congress against the Lend-Lease bill, and, in mid-1941, allied himself with the America First movement (along with, among other notable Americans, Eddie Rickenbacker, the World War I ace and president of Eastern Air Lines). Public criticism of his views grew more and more vocal. His acceptance of the German medal and his praise of German air superiority made many paint him as pro-Nazi, and, when President Roosevelt himself implied he was somehow unpatriotic, Lindbergh resigned his commission as colonel in the army air corps reserve. He went on to make distinguished and unpublicized contributions to high-altitude research and tactical combat training, but, in the eyes of an increasing number of Americans, the hero of 1927 was no more.[6]

American opposition to the war, Lindbergh's and others, ended abruptly in December 1941, with the attack on Pearl Harbor. Drawn into the fighting whether it intended or not, the United States declared war on Japan, and, in turn, was declared war upon by Germany. What had begun as essentially limited conflicts in Europe and Asia was now a truly global war involving all the principal industrialized nations. The United States, finally in the thick of it, had to develop weapons, tactics, and strategies to oppose those of the Germans and the Japanese. The war was to become a war of distances, with combat theaters extending from China-Burma-India across the Pacific to the Mediterranean and Europe, and the United States had to cope with them. It was, in addition, a war calling for new tactics needed to confront the combined air-and-ground strikes of the Germans and the aircraft-carrier-based warfare developed by the Japanese to overcome vast distances of open sea.

More than anything else, it was a war of the air, as one of the principal model magazines spelled out to its young readers. "The airplane has no Maginot or Siegfried Lines threatening its passage," an April 1940 article in *Model Airplane News* began. "The skies have become 'the third battlefield,' where the Allies and the Reich may fight at will and only the fitness of the weapon and the man behind it decide the outcome." In the opening phases of the war, both the Japanese and the German forces had demonstrated the devastating possibilities of air power, and the aviation press quickly began publishing silhouettes of Axis and Allied planes to familiarize the public with the types and to aid in speedy identification. If the United States and its allies were to prevail, air superiority was to be a necessity.[7]

When war finally came to the United States, the aviation series books rose to the occasion. Between 1936 and 1946, six series, comprising forty-six titles, emerged. All featured stalwart young Americans, in late adolescence or of college age, who threw themselves into the Allied cause with fervor and determination. All of these young heroes were adept at flying (they learned their skills through either civilian training programs or military flight school), so they immediately gravitated to the aerial wings of the military services, army and navy, British and American, where they could put their skills to best use, and served with dramatic distinction in all theaters of the war.[8] Since the earliest titles appeared before the outbreak of actual hostilities, the books provided a picture of the trajectory of the war, from the early period of American rearmament to the emergence of new world dilemmas with the coming of peace. As a body, they kept their young readers as well informed of aviation technology, foreign and domestic, as security restrictions would allow, gave a glimpse of the implications of a truly global war, proudly proclaimed the superiority of American aircraft and pilots, and preached the doctrines of air progress and air supremacy with the passionate zeal of the true believer.

Reports of the European *Blitzkrieg,* and, later, the Battle of Britain and subsequent Blitz, quickly familiarized Americans with the principal German aircraft, while, after Pearl Harbor, details of various Japanese aircraft slowly became public. Discussions and analyses of Axis aircraft, especially after captured airplanes became available for examination, permeated the aviation and model-making press, speaking to the quality and merits of the craft (in the process vindicating Lindbergh's early estimate) to both young and old. Popular estimates of the nature of Axis fliers were often grossly slanted, demeaning and racist; the Japanese came in for particular scorn, with one otherwise responsible aviation periodical eventually creating a fictional pilot named "Asaka Manura" to typify Japanese aviators. The aircraft themselves, however, became objects of fascination for youths and adults alike.[9]

A relatively small number of individual Axis designs dominated the technical and popular coverage of the air war. Three were fighters: the Japanese Mitsubishi A6M (the "Zero"), the German Messerschmitt Bf 109, and the Messerschmitt Me 163 *Komet*. The A6M was the surprise of the war. Early estimates of Japanese air strength played down any particular distinction. A September 1941 article in *Aviation* described Japan as "weak in aircraft numbers and quality, [with] her air force of low offensive strength," while *Western Flying*,

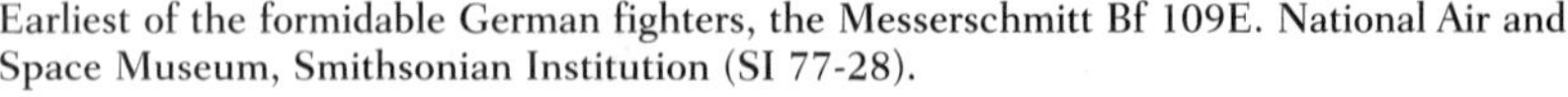
Earliest of the formidable German fighters, the Messerschmitt Bf 109E. National Air and Space Museum, Smithsonian Institution (SI 77-28).

The Mitsubishi A6M3 "Zero," the surprise of the early days of the Pacific War. National Air and Space Museum, Smithsonian Institution (SI 88-6596).

A glimpse of the future: the rocket-powered Messerschmitt Me-163 "Komet." National Air and Space Museum, Smithsonian Institution (SI 89-21535).

in the same month, said bluntly that "Japan can never compete with our own American forces." Events proved otherwise. When the A6M appeared on the scene, its all-metal construction, speed, and maneuverability in dogfights made it a formidable combatant and, for the time, the most advanced carrier-based fighter airplane in the air.[10]

The Germans likewise contributed two superlative aircraft. Few aircraft after the Wright Flier could genuinely be called "revolutionary," but the Messerschmitt Bf 109 came close. An all-metal, single-engined monoplane that first flew in 1935, it was the first truly modern fighter aircraft. An early version set a world speed record for military aircraft in 1937, while later ones dominated air combat during the Spanish Civil War and challenged British forces during the Battle of Britain. By war's end more Bf 109s had been produced than any other German fighter, and the distinctive square-tipped wings of the early versions were familiar to modelers and plane-spotters everywhere. Even more dramatic was the Me 163 *Komet,* a tailless, bat-like craft sporting swept-back wings that entered service in the last year of the European war. Powered by a chemically-fueled rocket engine and capable of speeds approaching 600 M.P.H., the *Komet* was designed as a response to Allied high-altitude bombing raids. Its rapid rate of climb, its maneuverability, and its speed let it dash through bomber formations with near-impunity; on one occasion, a single Me 163 shot down three B-17 bombers. The Allies were hard-pressed to develop defensive tactics against it, and only its limited production kept it from becoming a major threat to the bombing forces.[11]

The three prominently featured Axis bombers were all German: the Junkers Ju 87 *Stuka,* the Heinkel 111, and the Fieseler Fi 103—the V-1 "buzzbomb." The single-engined, two-seated Ju 87, with its angular lines, fixed landing gear, and inverted gull wings, was the most notorious and widely publicized bomber of the war years. It was formidable as a dive-bomber, and its impact as a psychological weapon was heightened when it was equipped with a siren that was sounded during its dive. The howl of the descending *Stukas* added to their menace and soon was a fixture of dive-bomber portrayals in films of the time. The Heinkel 111, which originated as a high-speed passenger design, was a twin-engined, all-metal craft with distinctive elliptical wings and a streamlined fuselage fronted with a paneled transparent enclosure for pilot and bombardier. Although quickly outclassed by Allied fighters, it continued as a principal German bomber throughout most of the war. The Fieseler Fi 103 won its own notoriety in the last years of the war as an ancestor of the modern cruise missile—an unpiloted, gyro-guided flying bomb, carrying a one-ton warhead and powered by a pulsejet engine derived from the same French designs used by "The Airship Boys" of three decades earlier. It entered service a month after the Normandy invasion in 1944, flying a straight-line course from its launch ramp until its fuel was exhausted or a preset timer sent it into a dive. A potent weapon against the civilian population, V-1s destroyed twenty-three-thousand buildings and killed more than five thousand citizens before the last launch in March 1945.[12]

The coverage of Allied aircraft appearing in the aviation press was equally divided between fighter and bomber aircraft, with advances being detailed as closely as wartime security permitted. The series books, however, were another matter entirely, for they were dominated by fighters. Bombers, when they appeared, were used mainly as transports, and generally were limited to American designs, often with Lend-Lease British markings—the Boeing B-17 "Flying Fortress" and the Consolidated B-24 "Liberator," both four-engined heavy bombers, and the twin-engined North American B-25 "Mitchell" medium bomber, which leapt into prominence as the airplane figuring in the Doolittle raid on Tokyo in April 1942. Fighters, however, with their single pilot, dramatic performance, and stylized, easily romanticized pilot-against-pilot combat, were ready-made for the series-book heroes, and the books became, almost without exception, stories of fighter missions in various theaters of the war.

The most familiar of the British fighters were the Hawker "Hurricane" and the Supermarine "Spitfire." The backbone of the RAF during the Battle of

Britain, the Hurricane was a single-engined, single-seat monoplane combining fabric and metal construction. It was lethal against Heinkel He 111 bombers and more than held its own against the faster Messerschmitt Bf 109, proving itself a sturdy, reliable, and versatile aircraft that reflected the latest in British fighter design for its time. Despite the Hurricane's prominence, the fighter inseparably associated with the Battle of Britain is the Supermarine Spitfire. A descendant of the record-setting Supermarine craft of the 1920s Schneider Trophy races, the Spitfire surpassed the Bf 109 in speed and maneuverability, and fought with distinction in every British theater of war. Its high performance and singular beauty made it a legendary craft in its own time, and its aura endures, even a half-century and more after the war.[13]

The best American fighters were still on the drawing boards or in the early stages of development in the early stages of the war, but, by war's end, had become the dominant aircraft in the skies. The early books reflect this situation, with their heroes flying Curtiss P-40 "Warhawks" and tubby Grumman F4F "Wildcats." A design that first flew in 1938, the P-40 was close to obsolescence

First of the "Iron Works" fighter dynasty, the Grumman F4F-3 "Wildcat," the principal American carrier-based fighter of the early war era. National Air and Space Museum, Smithsonian Institution (SI 76-2321).

when war broke out, but soldiered on; for all its shortcomings in speed and maneuverability, it was a reliable and durable warplane in the Pacific and Middle Eastern theaters. The P-40's prominence in popular accounts of the war stems in great part from its service with the American Volunteer Group (AVG), the "Flying Tigers," in China. Assembled by General Claire Chennault as an adjunct to Chinese forces, the AVG operated only from December 1941 until July 1942, but its shark-toothed P-40B aircraft (later replaced by more advanced P-40Es) quickly attained mythic status in the folklore of the early war. The P-40's naval counterpart was the Grumman F4F "Wildcat," a low-winged, single-engine, all-metal monoplane equipped with a radial, air-cooled engine and designed for carrier-based operation. Although slower and less maneuverable than its principal adversary, the Japanese Zero, the Wildcat's sturdiness and heavier armament made it a formidable warplane, and contributed to the Grumman corporation's becoming known as "The Iron Works."[14]

The most visually striking of the American fighters was the single-seated Lockheed P-38 "Lightning." The first twin-engined fighter accepted by the army air corps and the first American fighter to boast a turbo-supercharged engine, the P-38 first flew in 1939. It was effective in the North African campaigns and dominated combat in the Pacific, where its long range and twin-engined

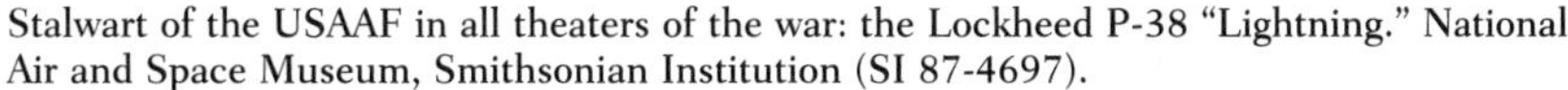
Stalwart of the USAAF in all theaters of the war: the Lockheed P-38 "Lightning." National Air and Space Museum, Smithsonian Institution (SI 87-4697).

reliability proved notable assets. (Charles Lindbergh, flying a P-38 as an "observer" in 1944, shot down at least one Japanese aircraft.) Perhaps more to the point, the P-38's dramatic and unusual lines, with a cockpit nacelle suspended between twin booms, made it a favorite of the films and comic strips, and it soon came to be thought of as an emblem of American air might.[15]

The final two aircraft prominent in the series books share the distinction of being, each for its own type, the best airplanes of the war. The Republic P-47 "Thunderbolt" first flew in 1941, the largest and heaviest single-seat fighter of the war, designed for long-range, high-altitude flight as a bomber escort. Its radial, air-cooled engine was turbosupercharged and the ship was equipped with a formidable set of six (sometimes eight) .50-caliber machine guns that, according to Lieut.-General Henry H. Arnold, head of the USAAF, had "an impact equal to the force of a five-ton truck hitting a brick wall at 60 miles per hour!" The P-47 performed superbly in its bomber-escort role, and subsequent models proved to be equally effective as fighter-bombers used for ground-attack purposes, and as high-speed defenders against the V-1.[16]

Sharing its laurels was the North American P-51 "Mustang," an aircraft that entered American service almost as an afterthought. The earliest version, which first flew in 1940, was built at the request of the British, entered service with the RAF in 1942, and came into its own when the British suggested mating the P-51 airframe with the Merlin engine. The resulting P-51B was a fast, agile, long-range aircraft that excelled in a variety of applications; its square-tipped wings and tail gave it a passing resemblance to the Bf 109, but its performance surpassed that of any German ship. The Mustang was revered as "probably the best all-round single-seat piston-engined fighter to be employed by any of the combatants," and remained in service until the 1950s, going against North Korean jets in the early days of the Korean War.[17]

The great range of development evident in the warplanes of the Axis and Allied forces produced, not surprisingly, widespread discussion and criticism. Japan and, to a lesser extent, Germany caught the world by surprise with the

A Messerschmitt "lookalike" and a premier American fighter: the North American P-51 "Mustang." National Air and Space Museum, Smithsonian Institution (SI 78-18403).

sophistication of their aircraft, while the clear inferiority of many extant American and British designs clashed dramatically with the publicity these craft had received during development. There were spots of excellence, even superiority, among the Allied aircraft, but Americans were nonetheless dismayed by their overall undistinguished performance. The aviation press rushed to counter the criticism. Eddie Rickenbacker, who had stood with Lindbergh in the anti-war movement, argued in *U.S. Air Services* of October 1942 that "American Fighting Planes are Superior to Those of the Enemy." In the same month, *Aviation,* the nation's oldest and most respected air journal, published two substantial articles detailing "The Truth About Our Fighter Planes" and "The Truth About Our Bombers." None of the three pieces minced words about design shortcomings, but went on to stress the virtues of the various craft. These essays, like others of the time, were published primarily to raise public morale, but served to fuel interest in flight technology and prepare the way for coverage of developments to come.[18]

Tactics, technology, and strategy evolved as the war progressed and the American aircraft industry built its production capabilities. For the Allies, long-range bombers and carrier fighters changed the complexion of the war in the Pacific, while high-altitude, long-range fighters capable of escorting bombers to and from the target made the strategic bombing of European sites feasible. These were, however, principally advances in conventional aircraft technology. Although American research into jet propulsion and, to a lesser degree, rocket propulsion, had been under way since Frank Whittle's invention of the turbo-jet engine in the mid-1930s, the United States introduced no warplanes so radical as the Me 163. Instead, they pushed conventional designs to new heights of capability, continuing the evolutionary process so associated with aviation in the earlier series. The workings of that evolution and the techno-tactical cross-fertilization brought about by British use of American craft became central issues in the series books of the war era.

The earliest of the war-era series, Blaine and Dupont Miller's "Bob Wakefield Series" (1936–1940; three titles), takes up the story of American aviation *in medias res* in the mid-1930s. Harold Blaine Miller, whose wife collaborated in writing the stories, was an Annapolis graduate and a career naval officer. Prior to the war, he wrote extensively, publishing articles on military flying for the aviation press, historical articles for the model-making press, and flying adventure fiction for *Boy's Life.* He instructed at the Pensacola, Florida, Naval Air Station, and flew Curtiss F9C "Sparrowhawks" attached to the airships *Akron* and *Macon.* These tiny biplanes were carried within the slow-moving dirigibles as on-board defenders, and were launched and retrieved with a trapeze-like device suspended beneath the airship. During the war, Miller served as a staff officer in the navy's training and public relations divisions, rising to the rank of rear admiral. After his retirement in 1945, he joined Trans World Airlines as a vice president, and later moved to Pan American World Airways as director of public relations.[19]

The "Bob Wakefield" stories parallel much of Miller's career. The opening volume, *Bob Wakefield, Naval Aviator* (1936) introduces Ensign Bob Wakefield, a naval academy graduate on the brink of washing out of naval flight school at Pensacola. Given a second chance when he saves the life of a classmate, he successfully completes his training and embarks on a series of assignments: carrier duty, flying Sparrowhawks from the airship *Miami,* and observation flying from the cruiser *Denver.* He participates in maneuvers in Panama and Cuba, uncovers a subversive plot in Cuba, and is promoted to Lieutenant (jg) to continue his career. The second book, *Bob Wakefield, Naval Inspector* (1937), takes him to the Albatross aircraft factory in California, where he investigates a plot to sabotage the supersecret X-339 airplane. He foils the plot, gains new respect for modern aircraft design and construction, and, substituting for the Albatross test pilot, proves the excellence of the X-339.

The final volume, *Bob Wakefield's Flight Log* (1940), is a collection of eleven loosely connected short stories that follow Bob from posting to posting, first to the Aleutians, then to the Pacific, flying observation craft from the *Denver.* He airlifts a Santa Claus to an isolated Alaskan village so the townspeople can have their Christmas celebration, diverts a lava flow in Hawaii by bombing it from the air, and flies protective cover for the inaugural flight of the Pacific Airways flying boat service between Hawaii and New Zealand. The service is threatened by a mysterious fighter plane from an unspecified Pacific nation, but Bob successfully shoots down the warplane and the flying boat reaches its destination.

The Wakefield stories evoke the evolutionary changes taking place in aviation in the years leading up to World War II. The books, Miller says in the introduction to the first volume, "closely parallel the progress of aviation, and . . . point out the adventures which lie just around the corner for any youth who is so fortunate as to live in this age." Those adventures, however, come at a price. The discipline of carrier-based flying and the tactics of the time, for example, make pilots "robots," who are "personalities no longer.

They were part of their planes, as integral as the engines." The pilots themselves are no longer free agents, thanks to changes in modern tactics. "We don't think in terms of individual pilots any more," Bob tells a friend. "Now it is all formation work. The pilot who loses his squadron today is apt to find himself in trouble."[20] The free-spirited dogfighter of World War I seems to be no more.

Miller's familiarity with current civil and naval aircraft gives authority to the craft he builds into his stories. Bob initially flies a single-seat biplane fighter with retractable landing gear, an aircraft with "speed . . . in its very outline, sturdiness . . . inherent in its stocky struts." The craft echoes the design of the Grumman F3F-2, the basic carrier fighter of the late 1930s and the last biplane fighter of the American military. He then does a stint flying the Curtiss F9C Sparrowhawk, a "trim fighting plane with its strange hook apparatus on the top. A stout little plane especially designed for the thrilling work of hooking on the navy's big airship, the *U.S.S. Miami.*" Later still, he flies out of San Diego in a Boeing 247 airliner, marveling at its stability and ease of control, then transfers to a Douglas DST sleeper plane that astonishes him with its fighter-like speed and internal comfort.[21]

Advances taking place in aviation technology also enter into the stories. Most of *Bob Wakefield, Naval Inspector* is given over to relating the design, construction, and testing of the high-speed Albatross X-339, an all-metal, high-altitude monoplane that, except for its extensible wings to adjust to high- and low-speed flight, resembles contemporaneous designs for the next generation of naval fighters. As he learns of the calculations that go into an airplane's design, the specific questions a designer must consider, the ways in which metal construction provides structural strength and reduced weight, and the endless testing that goes into each component of the craft, Bob finds himself awed by the complexity of the task. He

> began to perceive a new phase of aviation. . . . Before, the actual flying of an airplane had seemed to him the ultimate in joyful accomplishment. But now . . . , he realized that he was on

> the threshold of mental adventures—essays into the field of stress analysis, bending moments, and shearing stresses. . . . This preliminary creative work could be as fascinating as the more active work he had hitherto known.

Everything about the X-339 reflects the best of current aeronautical design thinking, even its seemingly fanciful extensible wings. The Makhonine Variable Area Monoplane, which could adjust its wingspan in flight, initially flew in 1931. It was described in *Flight* in 1932 and included in *Jane's All the World's Aircraft* during the 1930s. Emphasizing the technical side of aircraft design as he does, Miller gives readers a sense of the drama that can accompany the engineering methods and developments that support and complement the wonder of flight.[22]

For all their technical modernity, however, the Bob Wakefield stories also extol the joys and potentials of flight as overtly as do the earlier series. Flying alone at night in pursuit of the *Miami,* Bob listens to radio reports from other craft and musical broadcasts to the public, savors his isolation in the midst of so much, and thinks to himself: "What a world this was! What a world to be young and alive and flying!" He is conscious of the continuity of his profession, as well; as he departs San Diego, he reflects on its place in aviation history, as the site of Glenn Curtiss's first seaplane flights and the starting-off point for Lindbergh and the *Spirit of St. Louis.* And, at the Albatross plant, looking at the X-339 prototypes, he feels an instant identification with his airplane that is as real as any attachment to a living thing: "Life had been built into each of the machines by masters of design; life which could be awakened by the careful touch of a skilled pilot."[23] A military flier he may be, but he is also a person deeply attached to the hardware and history of flight, and the relationship of man and machine is increasingly complementary.

When that complementary relationship is shared by all, Miller suggests, the world will be a better place, unified and elevated by the marvels of flight. American aircraft and technology already dominate the aeronautical scene.

"There's scarcely a country in the world that doesn't see American aircraft soaring aloft daily," an engineer tells Bob. "What's more, they are pulled through the air by American engines." But this is only the start, for the next generation of young Americans will bring to their society an understanding, an acceptance, and an application of aviation unequaled in the history of the world. "All of the boys and many girls of today are air-minded," his friend continues. "Their generation will fly an airplane as instinctively as they drive an automobile. . . . The youngsters of today are building models based on sound engineering. They understand the theory of flight. It is only a step to the actual flying of a plane for them."[24]

The social revolution that follows will benefit both the United States and the larger world. In the thirty-four years since the Wrights' first flight, aircraft, Bob muses, had already become "a peaceful Armada which would reduce the size of the world until it was hardly more than a miniature map." He reinforces this view with his thoughts on the successful arrival of the Hawaii-New Zealand ship: "The world was shrinking! Mail would move more swiftly. . . . Orders would be received and goods sent in response. . . . Closer international relations would follow the short cuts made possible by the air route."[25] Despite the reality of war in Europe and its likelihood in the Pacific, despite his professional knowledge of air tactics and strategy, Miller clings to the vision of a world linked politically, commercially, and culturally by the airplane, and passes it along to his readers.

As the war began to accelerate, first involving England, then expanding into the Pacific, writers scrambled to build it into their series, seeking to dramatize the new warfare and to stir American patriotism. The United States' initial neutrality posed some difficulty, for the aviation press reflected a greater awareness of war's likely coming than did the popular press. As American involvement grew and as Lend-Lease shipments intensified, though, writers quickly found ways to extend their stories to use the adventure of the changing scene. One such writer was Theodore B.F. Copp, who, as "Ted Copp", produced the "Steve Knight Flying Stories" (1941–1942; three titles). Copp, a journalist and publicist for the Metropolitan Life Insurance Company of New York, also wrote adventure fiction for a range of pulp magazines and plays for presentation by amateur theatrical groups.[26]

The Knight stories open with *The Mystery of Devil's Hand* (1941), when Steve, frustrated by his inability to qualify for naval air training, agrees to pilot a charter flight to Honduras. He is shot down by an unmarked fighter plane on his return flight, joins forces with Pedro Hennessey and the gypsy Venga Savricas, and uncovers a German spy ring attempting to upset the American Good Neighbor Policy in Latin America. Praised by the U.S. government for his work, he wins admission to flight school and a chance to join the "bridge of bombers" crossing the Atlantic. *The Bridge of Bombers* (1941) picks up soon afterward, with Steve helping to ferry B-24 bombers to England. When he's accused of espionage, he joins forces with a wealthy Canadian, Raoul Haye Chambert, only to discover that Chambert, a German spy with a private air force, is planning attacks on domestic flights. Steve alerts the authorities and, though Chambert escapes, they destroy his secret base and Steve learns that the espionage accusation was a ruse to mask his undercover work.

The final volume, *The Phantom Fleet* (1942), takes place in the Pacific, where Steve is enjoying a leave on Hawaii. During a solo joy ride in an unarmed Waco Model E light plane, he is forced down by Japanese aircraft and learns of the attack on Pearl Harbor. Pedro Hennessey and Venga Savricas rescue him, and the three set out to scout for further enemy ships. They discover a Japanese carrier task force lurking in an uncharted island chain, sink several mini-submarines, and return to Honolulu to alert the military. Army B-17 Flying Fortresses sink one of the aircraft carriers and disable several other ships, echoing Capt. Colin P. Kelly's highly publicized 10 December 1941 attack on a Japanese cruiser with a B-17, while Steve and his friends, back in Honolulu, look ahead to the coming war.[27]

The Steve Knight stories in many ways make a convenient transition to the stories of overt war. Steve recognizes the threat to America of the European war, and wants to join the military. He remains, though, a civilian pilot in spirit, and responds to his airplanes as a civilian might, his response to flying a purely ecstatic one. Totally unaware that he will soon be under attack, Steve finds only bliss as he takes off in his light plane: "Up, up, up went the Waco. Steve felt peaceful and relaxed. This was the life—a steady wind, perfect visibility, and a grand ship. The 400-horse-power Pratt and Whitney motor kicked over with a gentle, powerful hum that was like a lullaby to the young American flier."[28] Flying is a joy; while military considerations will soon intrude, until they do the joy of flight is still present.

New times bring new requirements, though, and Steve makes the adjustment with ease, quietly dramatizing the progressive nature of the aviator. He comes to understand that wartime flying in advanced aircraft requires "training and knowledge, and a well-grounded understanding of aerodynamics," while the complex instrument panel of the B-24, that once "meant absolutely nothing to him," has become a window into another world, where "each dial, each control was a friend ready to do its part to make the trip a success." He is at ease with multi-engined flight and an automated gyropilot, and finds nothing unusual about cruising at 10,000 feet as part of a twelve-craft flight headed non-stop for England. Yet he retains a sense of flying's history, musing that he is leaving from the same location where "Alcock and Brown had taken off for their epoch-making flight that ended in an Irish peat bog. And here he was, Steve Knight, following the trail they blazed."[29] Circumstances change and techniques develop, but flying remains a coherent, linear enterprise with the present dependent upon the past and the flier the beneficiary of it all.

Copp gives the books an air of authenticity by incorporating actual aircraft. Steve's Waco E is a modern private plane, introduced in 1940 and sporting impressive speed and a 23,000 feet service ceiling. The B-17s and B-24s that figure in the stories are staples of the Lend-Lease reinforcement of

England, and quickly come to the fore as the United States moves deeper into the war. Chambert's private air force includes Ju-87 *Stukas* and Messerschmitt Bf 109s, and when Steve sees one of the latter in flight, Copp reveals his assumptions about readers' familiarity with combat craft by remarking that "There was no mistaking the lines of his plane, its square wing tips. The average twelve-year-old would recognize it as a 'Schmitt.'" Throughout *The Phantom Fleet,* Steve and his friends fly a twin-engined Grumman G-21A amphibian. Copp exaggerates its performance for patriotic propaganda purposes ("This Grumman, as a matter of fact most American planes, can outclimb anything the Japs ever made."), but otherwise makes plausible use of a craft that was in wide service, civil as well as military.[30]

The Steve Knight books, all in all, prepare the way for the series to come. They reflect Americans' initial ambivalence toward the war, and the national unification of purpose that occurred after Pearl Harbor. They employ generally accurate descriptions of up-to-date aircraft, acquainting readers with the ships' traits and performance and reinforcing the sense that this knowledge is something that an up-to-date citizen must have. They maintain the regard of earlier series for the airplane as a creation, even creature, in its own right; on take-off, Steve's lumbering B-24 becomes "an animate object and not a dead weight hurtling through space and subject to the law of gravity."[31] And, even as war nears, they retain the liberating, exalting sensation that flight imparts. It is a difficult mix to manage, but Copp succeeds. So, too, do the authors following him, even as they incorporate ever more military matters.

Rutherford G. Montgomery, writing as "Al Avery," took a somewhat different approach to the war. Montgomery, who had served as a sergeant with the Army Air Service during World War I, was a former teacher and free-lance writer. He specialized in adventure fiction, Westerns, and nature writing, doing several animal stories in conjunction with Walt Disney Studios. He maintained an interest in flying throughout his career, writing and editing free-standing books on aviation, and producing the Cold-War-era "Kent

Barstow" series in the late 1950s and early 1960s. He is, however, best-known for the "Yankee Flier Series" (1941–1946; nine titles), which spans the Second World War from the earliest days of the Blitz through post-war concerns about resurgent Nazism and the nuclear threat.[32]

Colorado-born Stan Wilson, the "Yankee Flier" of the series title and a youthful test pilot for the Hendee Aircraft Corporation, passes himself off as a Canadian so as to enlist in the RAF during the time of American neutrality. Teamed with the taciturn Britisher March Allison and the volatile Irishman Bill O'Malley (a ready source of comic relief), Stan in *A Yankee Flier With the R.A.F.* (1941) flies first Spitfires, then the more advanced Hendee "Hawk," uncovers a German spy, and becomes an integral part of an RAF squadron. When he, Allison, and O'Malley go to Singapore on recreational leave in *A Yankee Flier in the Far East* (1942), the three volunteer to join a Flying Tiger detachment in the defense of Rangoon. They uncover another German spy, rescue a prisoner of the Japanese, and learn of the attack on Pearl Harbor.

Subsequent volumes take Stan and his comrades to a variety of combat zones. *A Yankee Flier in the South Pacific* (1943) has them flying Lockheed P-38s among the small islands of the region and defeating Japanese invasion efforts. *A Yankee Flier in North Africa* (1943) takes the three to the North African theater, where they fly P-38s and Curtiss P-40s in reconnaissance and ground-support missions, while *A Yankee Flier in Italy* (1944) includes them in the invasion of Sicily and the surrender of Italy. The group divides in *A Yankee Flier Over Berlin* (1944); Stan and O'Malley join the American 8th Air Force and fly bomber escort missions in Republic P-47s, while Allison transfers to the British Bomber Command.

The three reunite for the last days of the war. In England to train pilots for the Allied invasion of Europe in *A Yankee Flier in Normandy* (1945), they also fly supplies to the French resistance forces, find themselves in the midst of D-Day combat, and lend air support to a paratroop battalion. In *A Yankee Flier On a Rescue Mission* (1945), flying North American P-51 Mustangs, Stan and

O'Malley liberate Allison and American POWs from a German prison camp, while, as newly discharged civilians in *A Yankee Flier Under Secret Orders* (1946), the team takes part in an undercover FBI mission to ferret out a team of Nazi terrorists in South America who are rushing to develop an atomic bomb.

Like the heroes of Miller's and Copp's stories, Stan and his friends must learn new tactics. After their early days of relative independence over the English Channel and with the Flying Tigers, they confront the new combat roles for air power: "The day of free lancing is over. The Germans have taught us that we must have close co-operation between ground and air units. . . . Our Flying Fortresses have about ended the days of supremacy for the dogfighting fighter pilot." The B-17s, with their heavy armament, nominally depend upon the power of massed guns rather than fighter escort. Flying in a carefully structured formation, "their cross fire was deadly from every angle. They were more deadly in a pack than any fighter plane formation." The trio now must become accustomed to flying with disposable auxiliary fuel tanks on high-altitude bomber escort flights, and they need to learn the skills of low-altitude flying for ground-support attack and strafing.[33]

More than any of the preceding characters, though, they must also learn to deal with the new, high-performance aircraft that mark the aerial war. The Hendee Hawk is capable of high-speed aerobatic maneuvers at 20,000 feet and requires supplementary oxygen for its pilot. New engine designs require new attention to temperature and revolutions if a ship is to complete its mission. High-altitude flying requires heated flight suits as well as oxygen if the pilots are to function, while the speed of ships like the P-38 and the DeHavilland "Mosquito" demands new flight skills. Both of the latter aircraft are subject to compressibility problems caused by the inability of air to cross the wing smoothly as the ship builds speed, and can be shaken to pieces if the phenomenon is not recognized in time. Their speed, moreover, makes the pilot particularly susceptible to *g*-forces, as Stan discovers when he almost blacks out in recovering from a dive.[34]

The Republic P-47 "Thunderbolt," model for the "Hendee Hawk" of "Al Avery's" *A Yankee Flier with the RAF* (1941. National Air and Space Museum, Smithsonian Institution (SI73-11312).

Throughout the series, "Avery" focuses upon the evolving capabilities of the airplanes he describes, introducing the latest warships as they are reported in the press and describing them in as much detail as wartime censorship allowed. Although Stan flies Republic P-47s later in the series, the Hendee Hawk of the first volume is recognizably patterned after the real-life aircraft, possessing the same radial, air-cooled engine, the same armament, and the same performance. Reports of the development of the P-47 were in circulation as early as 1940 and 1941, and "Avery" drew heavily upon them for his description of the Hawk. Curtiss P-40s and Lockheed P-38s figure in the middle books of the series, with "Avery's" remarks on compressibility coming from a *Life* magazine account of the P-38. As he dives in his Mosquito (a high-speed, Merlin-powered aircraft of lightweight plywood construction), Stan reflects that "only the Lockheed Lightning could fly a dive fast enough to bank up air like snow." *Life* published a lengthy account of the P-38 and its capabilities in mid-1943, remarking in passing that the craft encountered compressibility problems when "air piles up ahead of the wing like snow in front of a snowplow."[35]

"Avery" reserves his greatest admiration, however, for the North American P-51. Stan and his friends first encounter the P-51 in *A Yankee Flier Over Berlin,* and are impressed by its load-carrying capabilities and remarkable speed at low altitudes. When they get their hands on the latest version (probably the agile P-51D, introduced into the European theater in mid-1944), though, they become total converts to the craft. Allison muses that it "looks like the Messerschmitt 109, except for the rounding wing and that hump on the body." O'Malley, "devouring the Mustang with his eyes," is smitten by its in-line engine and clean lines, seeing it as "sleek as a dancer in spite of its size." Stan, for his part, calling it "the answer to a Spit pilot's dream," delights in the "speed to burn" that makes it "as quick as a cat in the air." The Mustang is close to the ultimate flying machine for its time, and the three young pilots readily recognize its worth.[36]

The "Yankee Flier" books, for all their emphasis on modern technological marvels, are notable for two other qualities. First, they continue the model of the irreverent, devil-may-care young pilot that dates back to at least the World War I stories. Stan Wilson could easily be a kinsman of Rex Lee. His "blue eyes . . . [gleam] with a great zest for living," and possess a penetrating look that comes from watching "the limitless spaces a flier sees," while Stan himself rarely encounters "a moment so danger-filled that [he] could not laugh at himself." The pilots of the Flying Tigers are painted as "easy-going, loose on discipline, [and] deadly in the air . . . lone wolves of the air, prowling in threes or in pairs or alone," and Stan and his friends fit right in. Indeed, the three maintain their panache throughout the series, flying as independently as a Rex Lee as often as they participate in group missions, until even a general shouts in frustration, "Will you fellows never learn that you fly them and we do the planning?"[37]

Behind their irreverent independence is a regard for the airplane that also attests to the characters' ancestry. As with the earlier series characters, Stan, O'Malley, and Allison look upon the airplane as far more than just a high-tech machine or an effective weapon. Stan considers a motor "a living thing and he hated to see one abused." The comic O'Malley bonds romantically with his Mustang on first sight, calling it "a beautiful colleen." Even after war's end, when Stan finds himself flying an obsolescent C-87 freighter, a cargo version of the B-24 Liberator, he responds to all that the elderly craft has to offer: "Stan grinned. It was good to hear and to feel the big radials up ahead of you, to know that those four giants were hurling you into the sky and into adventure." Modern aircraft may compel changes in tactics and skill, "Avery" implies, but they retain their emotional and sensual appeal, and continue to evoke wonder, admiration, and regard in all who work with them.[38]

The second trait distinguishing the "Yankee Flier" books is their awareness of world events, and their readiness to build these events into the stories. United States support to England through Lend-Lease figures extensively in the opening volumes. Stan early on spots an American aeronautical engineer with whom he has worked, and "reflected bitterly that he should have known the British Isles would be swarming with American experts and engineers, now that a great effort was being made to help the besieged English nation." The Pearl Harbor attack and Franklin D. Roosevelt's call for fifty thousand and more aircraft per year emerge in the second volume and Stan, like the Americans in the Flying Tigers who "wanted to fly under their own flag," considers the possibility of transferring to the American air forces. Finally, when the war ends, "Avery" takes up the question of nuclear warfare. He introduces the possibility of renegade Nazis using atomic bombs to terrorize American cities, making the series the only one to mention the nuclear threat, and gives to Stan a telling comment: "It's modern war. . . . The war we just got out of is now ancient history." The war has ended, but the rules have changed. New times bring new perils, and young readers must be aware of the state of the changing world if they are to be effective citizens of the future.[39]

Far more problematic for the thoughtful reader are two series by Robert Sidney Bowen, the "Dave Dawson Series" (1941–1946; fifteen titles), tracing the war from its onset in Europe to close to its ending in the Pacific, and the "Red Randall Series" (1944–1946; eight titles), dealing exclusively with the Pacific War. Bowen came to his work well-prepared. A combat flier in World War I, he became a well-established aviation journalist; he served as an editor for *Aviation* magazine, and wrote or edited a number of books seeking to familiarize the public with elements of aviation. In one of these, *Flying from the Ground Up* (1931), much of which had been published serially in the popular magazine, *Flying Aces,* he explicitly states his determination to support flight and its potential for the larger society. He wants to stimulate the developing "air-mindedness" of the public, he says, for "Every new convert to aviation is another worker for the advancement of modern aviation." He preached this doctrine in all of his flight-related books, and, with the twenty-three volumes of the combined "Dawson" and "Randall" series, was the most prolific series author of the war years.[40]

Whereas the "Yankee Flier" books, for all their intense action, have moments of reflection on the larger issues of the war, Bowen's books are unrelentingly bellicose. He flings down the gauntlet in *Dave Dawson at Dunkirk* (1941), when seventeen-year-old Dave, traveling with his diplomat father in France, is left behind in the aftermath of the German invasion. Dave wastes no time in bemoaning his plight:

> Impulsively he clenched his two fists and wished very much he was up there in a swift, deadly pursuit or fighter plane. . . . Today there had been born in him a blazing desire to do what he could to spare Europe, and perhaps the whole world, from the bullets and bombs and the tyranny of the Nazi legions.[41]

Teaming up with Freddy Farmer, a British ambulance driver (not quite the stereotypical silly-ass Englishman, and a superb flier comparable to Dave himself), he works his way to the coast, assists in the evacuation at Dunkirk, and with Freddy is received at Buckingham Palace.

Dave Dawson With the R.A.F. (1941) finds Dave and Freddy parachuting into Belgium to seek out German invasion plans. Although captured by German forces, they winkle out the information and fly home in a stolen Messerschmitt. The next books take the pair to Libya (1941), where they fly Blackburn "Skua" dive-bombers from a carrier of the Fleet Air Arm, and to *Dave Dawson on Convoy Patrol* (1941), as they join the elite Emergency Command piloting Consolidated PBY "Catalina" flying boats in anti-submarine service. Both are promoted for *Dave Dawson, Flight Lieutenant* (1941), and make reconnaissance missions in Spitfire Mark V aircraft to gain photographs of a new Nazi weapon, a remote-controlled glider bomb. Their next two missions take them to Singapore (1942), still with the British Navy, where they assist a Flying Tigers group and learn of Pearl Harbor, and into the United States Army Air Force (1942), assisting American airmen in defending the Panama Canal.

Returning to the European theater in *Dave Dawson with the Commandos* (1942), Dave and Freddy penetrate occupied France and kidnap high-ranking officers of the Luftwaffe and the Wehrmacht. From here they go on to *Dave Dawson on the Russian Front* (1943), flying North American B-25 Mitchell bombers and nonplussed to discover that Senior Lieutenant Nasha Petrovski of Soviet Intelligence is a blooded fighter despite being a woman. *Dave Dawson With the Flying Tigers* (1943) returns them to the Pacific and a secret mission to Chinese leader Chiang Kai-Shek. They salvage an Allied invasion of the Solomon Islands in *Dave Dawson on Guadalcanal* (1943) when they discover a hidden Japanese task force in time to prevent its attacking the Allied forces, then move on to *Dave Dawson at Casablanca* (1944) to explore air routes for a super-secret meeting between Franklin D. Roosevelt and British Prime Minister Winston Churchill.

Their final adventures are divided between Europe and the Pacific. *Dave Dawson With the Eighth Air Force* (1944), picking up immediately after the

Casablanca mission, traces their efforts to stymie a German plan to use captured Allied aircraft as explosives-laden flying bombs, while *Dave Dawson at Truk* (1946) takes them back to the island-hopping of the late war.[42] There they elude capture by Japanese spies, talk their way aboard the American task force headed for the island of Truk, and, although nominally observers, take on Japanese fighters to distract them from the invading force. A final volume, *Dave Dawson Over Berlin,* was announced for 1946 and appears in some listings of the series, but was never published.

The problematic nature of the "Dawson" series appears in its stereotypical and propagandistic portrayal of the Germans and Japanese. The Germans throughout the series are emotionless, calculating, and often cruel, their thinking mechanistic and regimented. Comparing the Spitfire Mark V with the German craft opposing it, Dave takes comfort in reflecting that "The Royal Air Force will always be better tomorrow than it is today, but the Luftwaffe gets just so good, and there it stops. There just isn't that something in the Nazi aeronautical make-up that drives a man on to improve upon his best efforts!"[43] The British and Americans, in contrast, with their regard for individualism and their unwavering belief in progress, are more versatile and more humane in their conduct of the war.

The Japanese, for their part, are equally cruel but little more than simple-minded imitators of superior American technology. Dave thinks of the Nakajima 96 fighter as "a Land of the Rising Sun copy of the American Boeing F4B" (a carrier-borne biplane fighter already obsolete in American service, and therefore indicative of Japanese poor judgment in copying it), while a Kawanishi long-range flying boat is an antiquated design "copied from the type of flying boat that the French had used before the war on the mail and passenger run between Dakar and Brazil." Still, the Japanese character (as Bowen represents it) works in Dave's favor when he steals a Karigane Mark II fighter. "As the Jap-copied American aircraft engine caught on the first time over, he blessed the odd simplicity of Jap instrument panels and engine gadgets."[44] Bowen's racial bias is clear throughout. The Japanese can neither develop original aircraft nor deal with complex designs, and superior American technology and the more capable American mind will inevitably triumph over imitation.

Perhaps because of his condescending attitudes toward the Axis forces, Bowen is a strident voice for the moral rightness of the Allied cause. Any and all measures are appropriate if the Axis are to be defeated, and paramount among these measures is the achievement of air superiority. In 1941, even before the United States entered the war, he gives to Freddy Farmer an impassioned speech in support of the air: "This war has proved that the side that has control of the air is the side that comes out on top. So, if the Nazis are able to maintain control of the air over Occupied Europe, all the invasion troops in the world wouldn't [be] of much use to us."[45] The war is a war for the survival of free nations over evil ones, and superiority in the air is the only tactic that will make that survival certain. Here, as explicitly as anywhere else in all the war series, is the aerial warrior's manifesto.

His national stereotyping notwithstanding, Bowen does give an up-to-date account of the aircraft that all the combatants fly, introducing a host of types throughout the books. The principal German fighters cited are the twin-engined Messerschmitt Me 110, much respected by the Allies as a night-fighter, and the Messerschmitt Bf 109. German bombers include Heinkel He 111s and Junkers Ju 88s. Against the Germans the British fly Spitfires of increasingly advanced design, Hurricanes, and a range of carrier-based craft, including Blackburn Skua dive-bombers and Fairey "Swordfish" seaplanes. The Japanese rely upon Karigane Mark II and Mitsubishi A6M fighters. As an aviation journalist, Bowen knew his sources, but seems to have turned to the most readily available ones; all of the characteristics he gives the craft can be found in the annual editions of *Jane's All the World's Aircraft* embracing the war years.

American hardware, of course, is inevitably superior to anything the Axis has to offer. Once Dave and Freddy begin flying American-made craft, they marvel at their merits and power. As with the other aircraft cited, details of the ships mentioned are readily found in volumes of *Jane's*. Bowen, however, goes beyond a simple listing of technical data, personifying the aircraft at every opportunity. A Vultee fighter, "as though it were something human, and desperately eager to get into the air . . . , streaked forward and picked up more and more speed with every revolution of its steel-bladed prop." A "giant" B-17 warms Dave's heart with its "four Wright 'Cyclone' engines thundering out their synchronized song of power." A Douglas SBD "Dauntless" dive-bomber, "the latest thing in long range scout-bombing planes [and] sleek, yet powerfully built," offers Dave and Freddy "the what it takes, in case we bump into Zeroes and such;" and North American P-51 Mustangs for Dave are the "best things ever to have wings."[46] Personality melds with technology in the aircraft of the Bowen books, making the craft personifications of national virtues at least as valuable as their technological merits.

Despite his chauvinistic zeal and admiration for technological mastery, Bowen like his forebears speaks to the subtle, emotional appeal that the airplane exerts for those who work with it. Dave considers flying for the RAF "like living a wonderful dream, and it was doubly wonderful because it was true." When he crashes a German training plane in the opening volume, his sorrow is real, despite its being an enemy craft, and he couches his regret in the language of an earlier time, using an image first seen in "The Flying Machine Boys" books of three decades past: "I guess a plane to me is something like what his horse is to a cowpuncher. It's . . . it's almost something human." The image reoccurs when Dave decides to burn a crashed Skua. Recalling seeing a man weeping as he shot a crippled horse, he murmurs to his disabled ship: "Sort of like that horse, old girl. . . . We've got to put you out of the way—yeah, sort of out of your misery, I guess you could call it. The desert, and the Nazis, would only do you harm." Still later, in the series, as Dave and Freddy reflect upon their current aircraft, Bowen gives full statement to the bond of man and machine. The ship, they feel, is:

> Made of metal, and plastics, and wood, and fabric, to be sure. But to its pilot, it was something human and full of understanding. Something that couldn't be put into words, because there are no words in any language that can adequately describe the feeling a pilot holds in his heart for his plane.[47]

The man-machine bonding between the flier and his craft is profoundly intense, ranking with the most deep-seated emotions.

By linking the airplane with the cowboy's horse, Bowen suggests one possible reason for the peculiar attachment that aircraft hold for Americans. The myth of the American West is an evocative one, and at its heart is the figure of the cowboy, a solitary, armed individual driven by integrity and his inherent sense of good and evil. Dependent upon, and given mobility by, his horse, he roams the West in the name of justice. He resorts to violence when he must, but always he is driven by his sense of propriety and the fitness of things. Dave and Freddy are dedicated fighters for their countries' cause, empowered by the airplane just as the cowboy's crusade for justice is enabled by his horse. The airplanes, moreover, are military craft designed as weapons, but retain an innate, mystical quality that transcends their deadly purpose. Western heroes of the air, Dave and Freddy take the American quest for justice to the global theater, armed with American-made aircraft as the cowboy was armed with his American-made Colt six-shooter. Just as the union of man, weapon, and horse made possible the expression and fulfillment of American principles in the nineteenth century, the union of man and airplane enables and extends those principles in the twentieth century—for the world as much as for a region.[48]

Around the time of the Allied invasion of Normandy (6 June 1944), Bowen shifted his attention more fully to the Pacific war. He wrote two further volumes of the "Dawson" series set in Europe and Africa, then sent Dave and Freddy to the Pacific and began a new series set wholly in the Pacific theater. These relate the exploits of eighteen-year-old Robert ("Red") Randall, the son of an army air corps officer stationed in Hawaii, as he experiences the Pearl

Harbor attack, enlists in the air force, and sets out to take up the war against evil. His companion throughout the eight volumes of the series is Jimmy Joyce, whose naval officer father is killed when the battleship U.S.S. *Arizona* goes down during the Japanese attack. Jimmy, in a notable break with series-book tradition, is far from a comic character; as capable a flier as Red, he, like Red, ardently supports and vehemently speaks for the American cause.

Red Randall at Pearl Harbor (1944), intended for "any boy who thrills to flying and adventure, heroism and swift tense action," introduces Red and immediately plunges him into difficulties.[49] He is waylaid by Japanese spies, rescues Jimmy Joyce (whose unarmed light plane has been shot down by enemy fighters), uncovers tactical information crucial to U.S. military intelligence, and prepares to enlist in the military. *Red Randall On Active Duty* (1944) finds Red and Jimmy, now second lieutenants in the army air force, in Australia. They volunteer for a secret mission in aid of General Douglas MacArthur, escape from Japanese captors, and sink two destroyers before recuperating from their wounds (all minor) in Mindanao. The boys receive Distinguished Flying Crosses in *Red Randall Over Tokyo* (1944) for their work with MacArthur, then are sent by B-17 and submarine on a secret intelligence mission to China. They arrive on the day of James Doolittle's raid on Tokyo (18 April 1942), infiltrate Japan, retrieve critical information from a dying American agent, and, in a stolen Japanese airplane, fly over the still-burning Tokyo as they make their way back to China.

The next books put Red and Jimmy at the scene of two major conflicts of the Pacific war, the Battle of Midway and that of New Guinea. In *Red Randall at Midway* (1944), the two, newly promoted to army captains, join an Allied task force in search of an immense Japanese fleet. Flying for the first time from an aircraft carrier, they sink a submarine carrying the Japanese regional supreme commander (possibly suggested by the assassination of Japanese admiral Yamamoto Isoruku by a flight of American P-38s on 18 April 1943), and survive swarms of Zeros to return vital information to the Allied command.

In *Red Randall on New Guinea* (1944), advertised as emphasizing Red's "indomitable fighting spirit and spectacular flying skill," they fly air cover for Seven Mile Field on Port Moresby and join with a troop of Australian commandos to destroy a secret Japanese airfield.[50]

The two volumes of 1945 take Red and Jimmy to still more varied locales. *Red Randall in the Aleutians* details their patrol flying using Consolidated PBY amphibians, and their destruction of a Japanese shore emplacement. *Red Randall in Burma* teams them with British forces seeking to rescue a unit trapped in Burma. Flying Hurricane fighter-bombers, they escort an RAF "Dakota" (the British designation for the Douglas DC-3) into the region, recover the stranded men, and themselves fly the Dakota back to safety. The series' final volume, *Red Randall's One-Man War* (1946), is one of frenzied activity, even for the "Randall" series. Red and Jimmy fly into Japanese-held Luzon to rescue a guerrilla officer who has information vital to the impending invasion of the Philippines. Jimmy flies the officer back to their carrier, while Red, staying behind, mounts an attack on a Japanese prison camp, liberates 150 POWs, and learns that the invasion has been successful.

The "Randall" books give Bowen a free hand to vent his disdain for the Japanese, who come in for even greater stereotyping than in the "Dawson" series. A Japanese spy in the initial book has "lips twisted back over a row of buck teeth" and is described by an army officer as "a son of a son of Satan to boot!" Later in the same volume, he and his ilk are called "devil savages," who "should be killed and removed from the face of the earth. Just as you would uproot and destroy an ugly vine that was choking the life from a beautiful tree." Later in the series, in *Red Randall On New Guinea,* Bowen meditates on the joys of peace-time flying, then remarks that "that had been long ago—before that December Sunday in Nineteen Forty-one when the savages of Nippon had screamed 'Banzai!" and set forth to make the greatest mistake ever made by any nation in history." There is no doubt as to where Bowen—and, by extension, Red and Jimmy—stand in their view of the war.[51]

As in the "Dawson" books, Bowen accurately represents the aircraft of both sides. The Japanese fly Nakajima 19 land-based bombers, Mitsubishi Karigane Mark II carrier-based fighters, Showa Sho 98 fighter-bombers, a Kawanishi flying boat described in the same language that appears in the "Dawson" stories, and, of course, the Mitsubishi A6M Zero fighter. American forces use a variety of carrier-based craft, including Grumman F4F Wildcat fighters, Grumman TBF "Avenger" torpedo bombers, and Douglas SBD Dauntless dive-bombers. Land-based airplanes include B-17 Flying Fortresses, Curtiss P-40s, Consolidated PBY Catalinas, and Lockheed P-38 Lightnings. Although the Japanese aircraft can be deadly in combat ("high up . . . , their Zero can do plenty against a Kittyhawk [an early model P-40] or an Airacobra [the Bell P-39]") they are frequently out-classed by the American ships. "A ten-year-old kid could have told [a Japanese pilot] that no bomber ever made could out-dive a P-40." Grumman Wildcats, though slower than the Zero, are "sturdy" and "hard-flying," and the Consolidated PBY "is one of the best long-range patrol flying boats in the world, [but] it possesses neither the speed nor the maneuverability that is an absolute must against fighter aircraft."[52]

Bowen also continues his personification of the aircraft, insisting that they are more than just creations of metal and plastic. When Red steals a Japanese fighter, he mumbles to it, "Up, up, old girl . . . ! You may be Jap-made, but you're a whole lot of airplane just the same." The airplane, apparently able to understand English, responds: "As though it were a thing alive, with ears that could hear and a brain that could understand, the Jap Mitsubishi climbed upward through the smoke and the darkness." The American craft, however, have even greater merits. Thus, for example, the Wright engine of a Douglas SBD sings "a song of power that was sweet music to Red Randall's ears," and, when a heavily loaded Douglas DC-3 drags itself once more off the ground, Bowen proclaims that "A stouthearted airplane and a stouthearted pilot had won through again." American or alien, these machines have lives and personalities all their own.[53]

Although his passion for the war and his contempt for the Japanese dominate Bowen's work throughout the "Randall" books, he cannot shake off his own commitment to the consistent, inherent nature of the aviation series. Even in the midst of war, the essential patterns of the flying books endures. Red, like his series forebears, "is just a red-blooded American boy, full of pep and ginger and ready and eager to tackle any kind of a job that even had the faintest hint of excitement and adventure." It is young men—fliers all—like him who will shape the outcome of the war; their competence in the air is making American air power distinctive and dominant.[54] The machines themselves, battered and camouflaged, still manage to evoke the wonder and ecstasy of flight. When Bowen writes of a war-weary DC-3 parked on a makeshift jungle airstrip, its scars cannot hide the magic of its past:

> She had once been a man-made bird of gleaming beauty. . . . From her rounded nose to her tail rudder she had been the last word in commercial air travel and the pride of the fleet. She had carried ambassadors, visiting potentates, movie stars and all kinds of celebrities in her luxuriously appointed passenger cabin. She had held the record from Los Angeles to New York. She had been something to see in the air. She had been something to ride in.[55]

The golden days of flight, with all their light and color, have been replaced by the duties of war, but the qualities that made them still reside in the aircraft. By implication, they will return again, once the war is won by air power.

Bowen speaks of the postwar world in only one other spot in either of his series. Late in *Dave Dawson with the Eighth Air Force,* Freddy and Dave are thinking of the possibility of peace, and the changes they may find. There will be, Freddy maintains, many things "that most of us never dreamed of before the start of the war." Among these he lists radar, "the Nazi rocket gun. And our own jet-propulsion plane for another. And that's saying nothing at all about the miracles in medicine that have come out of this war so far."[56] Here Bowen makes an effort to project a view of the future, but seems unable to look beyond the aircraft and the times that he has known. It is a progressive and hopeful vision, but oddly lacking in the optimistic fervor so often found in other evocations of flight. For him, the true merits of flight reside in the aircraft and practices of the recent past, and any brilliance the future may hold is unclear.

An alternative vision of the brilliance that peacetime aviation may bring comes in the final volume of Canfield Cook's "Lucky Terrell Flying Stories" (1942–1946; eight titles). Whereas "Al Avery's" *A Yankee Flier Under Secret Orders,* the last of the "Yankee Flier" books, deals with a peacetime world fraught with counterespionage and the nuclear threat, Cook's *The Flying Jet* (1946) looks to a resurgence of commercial aviation in the postwar world. This revival will be stimulated and supported by the advances in speed, comfort, and efficiency that will emerge when war-developed technology is converted to civilian purposes. The author, Canadian-born Haswell Canfield Cook, was well-qualified to speak to the issue. Cook served with the Royal Flying Corps during World War I, reaching the rank of captain by war's end. His interest in flying continued, and he established himself as a lecturer and documentary film-maker specializing in aviation topics. His goal in both endeavors was to try "to develop a consciousness as to the implications of air power and a pride in our achievements in aviation," while making the case to the public that aviation "will prove a permanent boon, closely knitting the world of the future," and that "the sky is literally the limit when Aviation is chosen as a Career."[57]

The early volumes of the "Lucky Terrell" series follow the aviation series' established formula. Robert "Lucky" Terrell, an American youth flying with the Royal Canadian Air Force, is transferred to an RAF Spitfire squadron in England. *Spitfire Pilot* (1942) talks of his problems adjusting to the social rigors of British life and establishes him as an outstanding combat pilot. *Sky Attack* (1942) follows him, with his English chums Eric Prentiss and Don White and the Scots navigator Sandy McTavish, to Bomber Command, where they begin flying the new, high-performance Stratohawk fighter-bomber. After conducting a bombing raid on Berlin and being forced down in the Soviet Union, the team returns to England and is transferred to the Far East theater. *Secret Mission* (1943) opens with Terrell a newly promoted Flight Lieutenant en route to Asia with a squadron of Stratohawks. He and his friends foil a sabotage attempt, capture a Japanese submarine, and at last reach China.

The next three volumes take up Terrell's activities in Asia. In *Lost Squadron* (1943), Terrell, now a squadron commander, is forced down by bad weather and captured by the Japanese. He escapes, bringing with him an American missionary and a senior Japanese officer hostile to the Japanese war aims, aids the Chinese forces, and makes his way back to his base. Modernizing and securing the base occupies much of *Springboard to Tokyo* (1943), but the squadron fends off Japanese attacks, sinks an aircraft carrier, and, at book's end, is preparing to attack the Japanese homeland. A wing commander in *Wings Over Japan* (1944), Terrell leads his squadron in a succession of air attacks on a secret Japanese shipyard where giant battleships are under construction, while American B-24s, also flying from the site, begin to raid Tokyo.

Terrell returns to Europe in *The Flying Jet* (1945), flying the mysterious Señor X from Canada to England. There he learns that Señor X is a rocket expert slipping into Germany to learn details of V-1 and V-2 construction, and is introduced to the Stratojet, an upgraded Stratohawk combining propeller-driven flight with jet propulsion. He retrieves Señor X, downs several V-1s, and marks the rocket plant for incoming Allied bombers. When he is discharged from the RAF at war's end, Terrell returns to the United States. He crosses paths with Victor Bordon, a well-known aircraft designer, in *The Flying Wing* (1946), and wins a job as test pilot with Bordon's Meadowvale Aircraft Company. In Bordon's revolutionary jet-powered flying wing, he breaks the sound barrier, sets a transcontinental speed record, and prepares the way for commercial air service using the Wing.

Unlike the books of his contemporaries, Cook's stories hark back to Andy Lane and Ted Scott, focusing less upon combat sequences and the exaltation of flight and more upon the nature and implications of aeronautical progress. Although "all sense of strangeness disappeared" when Terrell takes off in a Spitfire, and he is "happy and completely relaxed" when he at last gets back to "his beloved Stratohawk," the books convey remarkably little of the emotional side of flying.[58] The shift is an important one. Rather than speaking to the individual benefits that may come from aircraft and aviation, Cook is more concerned with the technological and social implications that flight will bring. He recognizes, as few others among the wartime writers do, that aerial warfare and aerial military developments are changing the nature of all aviation. The postwar world may indeed be one that is improved by the airplane, but it will undergo profound changes in the process. Exciting and exalting the act of flying is likely to continue to be, but it will, of necessity, have to be conducted in a different manner, with different strictures, in a different kind of aircraft.

Cook dwells upon technological developments throughout the books. He introduces a pressurized cabin for high-altitude flying in 1942, while both fighter and bomber pilots alike were still using insulated flight suits and oxygen masks for their protection, and, in 1943, an air-borne electronic detection system that is "far superior to human ability." The twin-engined Stratohawk, though a fictional design, is equipped with high-efficiency, counter-rotating, variable-pitch propellers in its 1943 iteration, building upon the aviation press's announcement of such devices in early 1943. The counter-rotating propeller, two sets of blades on the same axis, but rotating in opposite directions, increases aircraft performance through a more efficient use of engine power. The Stratohawk's jet-powered counterpart, the Stratojet, provides a superior officer an opportunity to lecture Terrell about the advantages of jet propulsion at high speeds and high altitudes. The lecture is wholly up-to-date, for Cook uses information and language from 1944 issues of *Air Force* magazine and *Southern Flight* to support his case.[59]

The advancing technology of flight is even more apparent in the airplanes Cook introduces. Most are actual craft, accurately portrayed. Terrell early on learns that the Messerschmitt Bf 109 is a deadly antagonist. His commander takes the group minutely over a captured example "to prove to you that Fritz isn't using poor materials in his airplanes," and Cook gives the demonstration authority using details from a *Popular Aviation* account that spell out the 109's efficacy. Four-engined Douglas C-54s come in for special comment because of their tricycle landing gear, and Terrell admires "the clean lines of [a] super-fast, high-altitude Mustang" and its four-hundred-plus M.P.H. top speed. He later encounters rocket-powered Me 163s, "batlike aircraft" with a "stubby fuselage behind the V-shaped wings [and] no tail assembly," has a realistically-described encounter with a V-1 flying bomb, and hears that the V-2 is a "rocket bomb that can be fired from points deep inside Germany at ranges that may even include America."[60] Cook documents, in the space of seven books, the shift from propeller-driven aircraft to jet- and rocket-powered ones, making his series a telling chronicle of technical progress in aviation.

The McDonnell XP-67 "Bat" (1945), like the "Stratohawk" of Canfield Cook's *Sky Attack* (1942), is reminiscent of the "Manta" mockup of 1942. Image D4e-3420 ™ & © Boeing. Used under license.

For all his emphasis on actual aircraft throughout the books, the two imaginary machines Cook describes reflect the most advanced technology—often, in several instances, still in the experimental stages when Cook writes. The Stratohawk, a sleek, all-black craft that "looks like a cross between a Martin Maryland and a Lockheed Lightning," draws upon fiction as much as fact for its specifications. Much of the craft derives from the futuristic "Manta" aircraft, a design much-publicized in the 1941–42 era. This design, all-black like the Stratohawk and equipped with a Davis high-performance wing and counter-rotating propellers, never flew, but shared many details with the Stratohawk and pointed the way to the McDonnell XP-67, which combined propeller and jet power much as does the Stratojet.[61]

The Stratohawk also shares at least a Darwinian kinship with a fictional airplane, the Bill Barnes "Charger" of the late 1930s. Barnes was the multi-talented hero of "George L. Eaton's" series of pulp flying-adventure tales published in *Air Trails* magazine, a periodical reaching both adult and youthful readers. "Eaton" introduced his twin-engined fighter-bomber in October 1938, in "The Charger Goes to Sydney," a story that an "Editor's Note" proclaimed as "Combining the unquestioned progress of the next few years, or even months, of aeronautical drafting and design . . . , [this story will] give you a prophetic glimpse into the future of aerial transport and adventure." The Charger's internal layout and much of its equipment anticipate those of the Stratohawk, and the later craft may well be Cook's homage to a pulp-fiction forebear.[62]

The other fictional craft, Vernon Bordon's Flying Wing, has its origins in the "lifting fuselage" designs of Vincent J. Burnelli. Burnelli, beginning in the mid-1920s, launched a crusade for a radical new design that would do away with the tubular fuselage and tail structure of a conventional air liner or bomber. He proposed housing passengers and cargo within a massively enlarged wing structure, mounting engines and control surfaces in nacelles and booms ahead of and behind the wing. Although technically not a true "flying

Cutaway view of the Burnelli UB-14 (1936), one of several Burnelli designs prefiguring "Victor Bordon's" flying wing in Canfield Cook's *The Flying Wing* (1946). Burnelli Corporation, via National Air and Space Museum, Smithsonian Institution (SI 90-3174).

wing" (a design wholly eliminating fuselage and tail surfaces, as in the Northrop XB-35 or the modern B-2 stealth bomber), the design, Burnelli maintained, would eliminate the drag of a conventional fuselage, would provide additional lifting power from the airfoil-shaped central compartment, and, through its denser construction, would provide both greater space and greater protection for passengers. Burnelli's designs, which flew in several versions but neither threatened speed records nor attained production status, were seen by many as the next generation of aircraft; one design proposed to incorporate jet power, but only propeller-driven craft ever flew. Bordon's ship (the "Bordon"/"Burnelli" echo would not be lost on Cook's aviation-savvy readers) possesses the same structural attributes, and adds jet propulsion to supplement the counter-rotating propellers. Bordon plans to offer it to the military as a bomber as well as to the airlines as a commercial craft, for its technological superiority would give both enterprises a significant advantage.[63]

Fictional though these aircraft are, Cook uses them to look to the future in ways that no other author does. He anticipates by almost two years the jet-powered Northrop YB-49 Flying Wing and the breaking of the sound barrier by the rocket-powered Bell XS-1.[64] He anticipates the possibility of large-capacity, jet-powered commercial aircraft; at the end of *The Flying Wing,* airline owners are lining up to buy Bordon ships for their lines, just as later owners lined up for the Boeing 707. He anticipates supersonic commercial transports two decades in advance of the Concorde, and acknowledges the impact that these craft will have upon the industry. He understands that aviation progress is steadily pushing the envelope of technology and the human body, and he recognizes the consequences to aviation in general.

Cook's world of high-performance aircraft, real or fictional, moreover, is no place for the amateur. It requires well-trained, highly capable professionals who have the knowledge, the skills, and the endurance to master these craft. It is a world that, as Blaine Miller hinted at in the 1930s, but did not elaborate upon, increasingly requires the skills of trained engineers and designers, who grasp the requirements of high-speed, high-altitude flight and understand the materials and systems needed to make it possible. New speeds and new temperatures require new metals; new metals require new techniques for dealing with them. Research and development costs and manufacturing complexity will mount, until only large, well-funded corporations will be able to introduce new aircraft. The day of the backyard designer-builder is waning fast, and Cook gives a glimpse of the times that will replace it.

The aviation series of the World War II era constitute a capsule history of American military aviation between 1939 and 1945. As the technology and tactics of the air war evolve, so, too, do the books. Early volumes have their young aviators flying open cockpit biplanes and employing carefully choreographed formation tactics rather than individual sorties. The final volumes show all-metal aircraft construction, once unusual enough to warrant special comment, as a commonplace. Fighters and bombers are capable of sustained action at altitudes that, a decade earlier, were accessible only by specially equipped test aircraft. The series protagonists encounter—and at times fly—jet-propelled aircraft, and employ a range of mixed new tactics in both aerial and ground-support combat. Rocket propulsion begins to be mentioned as the next step beyond jet propulsion, and the German A-4 rocket (popularly called the "V-2") prefigures the era of the ballistic missile.[65]

The fliers themselves, however, remain direct descendants of Russ Farrell, Andy Lane, and Ted Scott. Their duty may be to thwart the Axis, but their outlook is grounded in the persistent American belief in flight. Al Williams's "Incredible Age," a brief essay widely syndicated in the popular and aviation press during the late spring of 1941, attests to that belief. Williams, an oil-company executive and ex-military flier who was one of the most prominent American spokespersons for aviation during the 1930s and 1940s, acknowledged the grim aerial war going on in Europe, but then spoke for the flying community:

> Not only do we love to fly, but apparently we love the vision we see of an entire world which will fly some day. We didn't plan it, but knowing and believing that some day flying will be commonplace and regarded as necessity, rather than emergency convenience, we have been carrying bright crusading banners. . . .
>
> Quit aviation? Forever give up the indescribable joys of dancing around the heavens? Why, we can't! This flying business is natural for us. It is our life, our breath—our blood. It is 'life' to us—as it will be soon to millions of others. The luxury of today is the routine necessity of tomorrow.[66]

Williams could as easily have been speaking for the protagonists of the wartime flying series. They begin as civilian fliers, reveling in the joys of flight. When war comes, they accept its realities; they focus on their military mission, and their staunch belief in the rightness of the American cause never wavers. Yet, behind their military determination, their overt patriotism, and their combat skills, their inherent devotion to flying and the airplane is as unflinching as that of Ted Scott, Andy Lane, and Rex Lee. The young fliers, without exception, admire the technology that makes the airplane possible and continues to power it to new heights. They look upon the airplane, even a fighting plane, as an organism that quickly forges a spiritual bond with those fortunate enough to work with it. It becomes the object of their deep-seated affection and the mere act of flying remains an exalting one. Warfare, though grimly necessary for the moment, is only one more stimulus for advancing flying's potential, and the aeronautical progress they see about them is a harbinger of the world to come. Warriors they may be, but the young pilots remain, without exception or hesitation, believers in the mystique of flight.

NOTES TO CHAPTER SEVEN

1 Robert McLarren, "A Motor with Wings," *Model Airplane News* 20 (April 1939): 11; Robert McLarren, "The Bomber Catcher," *Model Airplane News,* 20 (May 1939): 28; Robert McLarren, "Skyrocket with Wings," *Model Airplane News,* 23 (August 1940): 58. Fewer than three dozen CW-21s were built, all sold as export, and the XF5F-1 never went past the flying prototype stage. The P-38, on the other hand, went into production and built a distinguished record in all theaters of the war.

2 Walter J. Boyne, *Clash of Wings: World War II in the Air* (New York: Simon & Schuster, 1994), 25–30, 35–48, 55–65.

3 Boyne, *Clash of Wings,* 72–85.

4 Al Williams, "A National Air Policy," *Southern Flight,* 11 (March 1939): 8–14; T.N. Sandifer, "American Military Airplanes Will Meet Every Test," *U.S. Air Services,* 26 (January 1941): 16–17, 34; C.B. Allen, "Along the Air Frontier," *Western Flying,* 21 (June 1941): 21; DeWitt Wendell, "Transatlantic Bridge," *Flying and Popular Aviation,* 28 (May 1941): 18–19, 68–72; Capt. V. Edward Smith, "North Atlantic Ferry," *Aviation,* 40 (May 1941): 30–31, 132–136.

5 A. Scott Berg, *Lindbergh* (New York: G.P. Putnam's Sons, 1998), 355–368, 37–78, 387–389.

6 Berg, *Lindbergh,* 394–398, 408–424. See also Lauren D. Lyman, "Lindbergh: 'Tech Rep,'" *Air Trails Pictorial,* 34 (June 1950): 26–27, 64–66.

7 Erwin J. Bulban and Alice J. Molbeck, "Germany's Air Force Wages War," *Model Airplane News,* 22 (April 1940): 6–7, 56–59; "America At War," *Aviation,* 41 (February 1942): 78–79, 305; "War in the Air," *Western Flying,* 22 (January 1942): 31–32, 60.

8 The Civilian Pilot Training Program of 1939–1946 is examined fully in Dominick A. Pisano, *To Fill the Skies With Pilots* (Washington, DC: Smithsonian Institution Press, 2001).

9 Robert McLarren, "War Wings Over Europe," *Model Airplane News,* 22 (January 1940): 8–10, 30–36; DeWitt Wendell, "An Analysis of Captured Nazi Warplanes," *Flying and Popular Aviation,* 28 (March 1941): 14–15, 64–68; Ernest Bruce, "No Ersatz," *Aviation,* 40 (June 1941): 44–45, 142–144; Larry McRoberts, "Air Fighters of the 'Setting' Sun," *Model Airplane News,* 26 (February 1942): 4, 58–64; George Stromme, "Nippon Teikoku Kugan," *Western Flying,* 24 (June, July 1944): 46–47, 112–120; 50–51, 94–102. Hal Higdon, "Combat Comics," *Air & Space/Smithsonian,* 8 (December 1993): 58–63, discusses how the wartime comic strips helped to encourage aeronautical knowledge and racial stereotyping.

10 Lucien Zacharoff, "Japanese Air Power," *Aviation,* 40 (September 1941): 48–49, 146–150; Lynn C. Thomas, "The Japanese Air Force," *Western Flying,* 21 (September 1941): 22–23; William Green, *Famous Fighters of the Second World War.* 1957 (Garden City: Doubleday & Co., 1969): 50–56; Rex Sydney, "The Zero," *Flying,* 31 (November 1942): 25–26, 90–92.

11 Boyne, *Clash of Eagles,* 31–32; Green, *Famous Fighters,* 5–16, 124–128; "Messerschmitt Menace," *Aviation,* 40 (October 1941): 50–51; "Know Your Enemy," *Air Force,* 28 (January 1945): 14–15; Maj. Oliver Stewart, "Fighter Progress in Britain," *Flying,* 36 (February 1945): 48, 136–138; Roy Healy, "How Nazis' Walter Engine Powered Manned Rocket-Craft," *Aviation,* 45 (January 1946): 77–80.

12 Boyne, *Clash of Eagles,* 34–35, 32–33; William Green, *Famous Bombers of the Second World War.* 1959 (Garden City: Doubleday & Co., 1967), 5–16, 37–46; Cpl. Francis J. Benton, "Those Who Were Buzzbombed Will Never Forget," *U.S. Air Services,* 30 (July 1945): 14–15, 56; Chester S. Ricker, "Design and Construction of Nazi V-1 Flying Bomb," *Aviation,* 43 (November 1944): 190–191, 289–293.

13 Green, *Famous Fighters,* 17–24, 25–36; William Winter, "The 'Spitter,'" *Flying,* 31 (July 1942): 30–32, 64–69, 104.

14 Green, *Famous Fighters,* 43–49; Robert McLarren, "392 Per—in the Curtiss XP-40," *Model Airplane News,* 20 (February 1939): 9, 53–54; Russ Johnston, "Japs are Their Specialty," *Flying,* 31 (August 1942): 22–24, 86–88; William Green, *Famous Fighters of the Second World War, Second Series.* 1962 (Garden City: Doubleday & Co., 1969), 36–48; "Wildcat Warrior," *Model Airplane News,* 26 (June 1942): 22–24, 86–88.

15 Green, *Famous Fighters,* 71–77; Berg, *Lindbergh,* 453; "The Fork-Tailed Devil," *Flying,* 37 (August 1945): 26–28, 124–126.

16 Green, *Famous Fighters,* 84–90; "The Thunderbolt," *Model Airplane News,* 27 (December 1942): 21, 58–61; William S. Friedman, "The Thunderbolt," *Popular Science,* 141 (December 1942): 108–113, 226–228; Peter Masefield, "First Analysis of the Thunderbolt," *Flying,* 33 (August 1943): 47–48, 188–190.

17 Green, *Famous Fighters,* 91–98; Robert McLarren, "The Flying 'Mustang,'" *Model Airplane News,* 25 (September 1941): 21, 54–58; "The Mustang," *Model Airplane News,* 30 (May 1944): 25, 48–50; Ray Wagner, *Mustang Designer: Edgar Schmued and the P-51* (Washington, DC: Smithsonian Institution Press, 1990).

18 Capt. E.V. (Eddie) Rickenbacker, "American Fighting Planes are Superior to Those of the Enemy," *U.S. Air Services,* 27 (October 1942): 13–16; "The Truth About Our Fighter Planes," *Aviation,* 41 (October 1942): 93–95, 334–368; "The Truth About Our Bombers," *Aviation,* 41 (October 1942): 96–97, 328–329.

19 Document File CM-410000–01, "Miller, Harold Blaine," National Air and Space Museum Library. Smithsonian Institution: Washington, D.C.

20 Blaine and Dupont Miller, *Bob Wakefield, Naval Aviator* (New York: Dodd, Mead, 1939), Foreword, 44, 207; "War in the Air," *Popular Science,* 135 (December 1939): 84–87.

21 Miller, *Bob Wakefield, Naval Aviator,* 30, 65; Gordon Swanborough and Peter M. Bowers, *United States Navy Aircraft Since 1911* (New York: Funk & Wagnalls, 1968), 196–200; Blaine and Dupont Miller, *Bob Wakefield, Naval Inspector* (New York: Dodd, Mead, 1937), 28–29, 32–37; Lieutenant H.B. Miller, "Navy Skyhooks," *U.S. Naval Institute Proceedings,* 61 (February 1935): 234–241.

22 Miller, *Bob Wakefield, Naval Inspector,* 72; "The Makhonine Way," *Flight,* 24 (13 May 1932): 417–18; Robert Arentz, "Retractable Wing," *Popular Aviation,* 25 (December 1939), 53, 83. Howard Hughes's H-1 Racer, which set a world speed record of 352 M.P.H. in 1935, had two sets of interchangeable wings: one short for speed runs, the other longer for long-distance flights. See Preston Lerner, "Silver Bullet," *Air & Space/Smithsonian,* 18 (April/May 2003): 40–49.

23 Miller, *Bob Wakefield, Naval Aviator,* 107–08; Miller, *Bob Wakefield, Naval Inspector,* 24–25, 10.

24 Miller, *Bob Wakefield, Naval Inspector,* 110, 145.

25 Ibid., 111; Blaine and Dupont Miller, *Bob Wakefield's Flight Log* (New York: Dodd, Mead, 1940), 163–64.

26 "Theodore B. Copp, Fiction Writer, 42," *New York Times,* 3 January 1945, 17.

27 Boyne, *Clash of Eagles,* 116–117.

28 Ted Copp, *The Phantom Fleet* (New York: Grosset & Dunlap, 1942), 10–11.

29 Ted Copp, *The Bridge of Bombers* (New York: Grosset & Dunlap, 1941), 13, 17. John Alcock and Arthur Whitten-Brown, flying a Vickers Vimy long-range bomber, made the first non-stop Atlantic crossing in June 1919, flying from Newfoundland to Ireland. See Terry Gwynn-Jones, *Farther and Faster: Aviation's Adventuring Years, 1909–1939* (Washington, DC: Smithsonian Institution Press, 1991), 86–88.

30 Copp, *Bridge of Bombers,* 148, 197; Copp, *Phantom Fleet,* 6, 69; C.G. Grey and Leonard Bridgman, eds., *Jane's All the World's Aircraft, 1940* (London: Sampson Low, Marston & Co., 1941), 241c; René J. Francillon, *Grumman Aircraft since 1929* (Annapolis: Naval Institute Press, 1989), 95–112. The Grumman G-21 "Goose," a twin-engined amphibian, was hardly a high-performance aircraft; climbing at 1100 feet per minute, it was outclassed by even its single-engined stablemate, the Grumman J2F observation plane.

31 Copp, *Bridge of Bombers,* 75.

32 Claire D. Kinsman and Mary Ann Tennenhouse, eds., "Montgomery, Rutherford George," *Contemporary Authors 9–12.* First revision. (Detroit: Gale Research, 1974), 641. See also David K. Vaughan, "Rutherford G. Montgomery's Kent Barstow Series," *Dime Novel Round-up,* 70 (August 2001): 115–122.

33 Al Avery [Rutherford G. Montgomery]. *A Yankee Flier in North Africa* (New York: Grosset & Dunlap, 1943), 174; Al Avery [Rutherford G. Montgomery], *A Yankee Flier in the South Pacific* (New York: Grosset & Dunlap, 1943), 202; Comdr. A. F. Bonnalie, U.S.N.R., "How Our Bombers are Protected," *U.S. Air Services,* 29 (April 1944): 12–14, 38.

34 Al Avery [Rutherford G. Montgomery], *A Yankee Flier with the R.A.F.* (New York: Grosset & Dunlap, 1941), 4; Al Avery [Rutherford G. Montgomery], *A Yankee Flier in the Far East* (New York: Grosset & Dunlap, 1943), 163; Al Avery [Rutherford G. Montgomery], *A Yankee Flier Over Berlin* (New York: Grosset & Dunlap, 1944), 10; Al Avery [Rutherford G. Montgomery], *A Yankee Flier in Italy* (New York: Grosset & Dunlap, 1941), 135–136. For a discussion of compressibility, see Costas Ernest Pappas, "Compressibility Calls a Challenge," *Aviation,* 43 (December 1944): 171–175, 433.

35 Avery, *A Yankee Flier in the R.A.F.,* 3–4; "U.S. Building Plane to Pursue Bombers in Substratosphere," *New York Times,* 8 January 1941, 1; Avery, *A Yankee Flier in Italy,* 136; William P. Gray, "P-38," *Life,* 15 (16 August 1943): 51–56, 58.

36 Avery, *A Yankee Flier Over Berlin,* 67; Al Avery [Rutherford G. Montgomery], *A Yankee Flier on a Rescue Mission* (New York: Grosset & Dunlap, 1945), 3–4.

37 Avery, *A Yankee Flier with the R.A.F.,* 24; Avery, *A Yankee Flier on a Rescue Mission,* 4; Al Avery [Rutherford G. Montgomery], *A Yankee Flier Under Secret Orders* (New York: Grosset & Dunlap, 1946), 28.

38 Avery, *A Yankee Flier with the R.A.F.,* 24; Avery, *A Yankee Flier on a Rescue Mission,* 4; Avery, *A Yankee Flier Under Secret Orders,* 28.

39 Avery, *A Yankee Flier with the R.A.F.*, 92; Avery, *A Yankee Flier in the Far East*, 100–101, 127; Avery, *A Yankee Flier Under Secret Orders*, 12–13.

40 R. Sidney Bowen, Jr., *Flying from the Ground Up* (New York: McGraw-Hill, 1931), vi; M. Paul Holsinger, "For Freedom and the American Way," *Newsboy*, 32 (March-April 1994): 9–16.

41 R. Sidney Bowen, *Dave Dawson at Dunkirk* (New York: Crown Publishers, 1941), 50, 72.

42 The German plan for guided bombs outlined in *Dave Dawson With the Eighth Air Force* echoes "Project 'Perilous,'" an American experiment along the same lines in 1944. Crewless B-17s, crammed with explosives and designated BQ-7s, were to be guided by radio into high-risk targets. See Green, *Famous Bombers*, 35.

43 R. Sidney Bowen, *Dave Dawson, Flight Lieutenant* (New York: Crown Publishers, 1941), 16.

44 R. Sidney Bowen, *Dave Dawson at Singapore* (New York: Crown Publishers, 1942), 195; R. Sidney Bowen, *Dave Dawson on Guadalcanal* (New York: Crown Publishers, 1943), 81; R. Sidney Bowen, *Dave Dawson with the Flying Tigers* (New York: Crown Publishers, 1943), 188.

45 Bowen, *Dave Dawson, Flight Lieutenant*, 109.

46 R. Sidney Bowen, *Dave Dawson with the Air Corps* (New York: Crown Publishers, 1942), 160; Bowen, *Dave Dawson on Guadalcanal*, 76; R. Sidney Bowen, *Dave Dawson with the Eighth Air Force* (New York: Crown Publishers, 1944), 131.

47 Bowen, *Dave Dawson at Dunkirk*, 146; R. Sidney Bowen, *Dave Dawson with the R.A.F.* (New York: Crown Publishers, 1941), 11; R. Sidney Bowen, *Dave Dawson in Libya* (New York: Crown Publishers, 1941), 109–10; R. Sidney Bowen, *Dave Dawson at Casablanca* (New York: Crown Publishers, 1944), 176.

48 Scholarship dealing with the American West is immense. Owen Wister's seminal novel, *The Virginian* (1902), is a necessary starting point, while Richard Slotkin's *Gunfighter Nation: the Myth of the Frontier in Twentieth-Century America* (New York: Atheneum, 1992) is but one of many valuable overviews examining the power of the Western myth.

49 R. Sidney Bowen, *Red Randall at Pearl Harbor* (New York: Grosset & Dunlap, 1944), back jacket.

50 R. Sidney Bowen, *Red Randall on New Guinea* (New York: Grosset & Dunlap, 1944), jacket copy. For the Yamamoto mission, see Boyne, *Clash of Eagles*, 237–239.

51 Bowen, *Red Randall at Pearl Harbor*, 15, 33, 129; Bowen, *Red Randall on New Guinea*, 1–2.

52 Bowen, *Red Randall on New Guinea*, 4; R. Sidney Bowen, *Red Randall On Active Duty* (Grosset & Dunlap, 1944), 22; R. Sidney Bowen, *Red Randall at Midway* (New York: Grosset & Dunlap, 1944), 38, 83, 201; "The Cat," *Model Airplane News*, 30 (April 1944): 17, 48–50.

53 Bowen, *Red Randall on Active Duty*, 183; Bowen, *Red Randall at Midway*, 91; R. Sidney Bowen, *Red Randall in Burma* (New York: Grosset & Dunlap, 1945), 196.

54 Bowen, *Red Randall at Pearl Harbor*, 64.

55 Bowen, *Red Randall on New Guinea*, 1.

56 Bowen, *Dave Dawson With the Eighth Air Force*, 218. The jet aircraft of which Freddy speaks is the twin-jet Gloster "Meteor," which went into service with the RAF in 1944. See Owen Thetford, *Aircraft of the Royal Air Force since 1918* (New York: Funk & Wagnalls, 1968), 248–251.

57 Document file CC-543500–01, "Cook, Haswell Canfield," National Air and Space Museum Library. Smithsonian Institution: Washington, DC.

58 Canfield Cook, *Sky Attack* (New York: Grosset & Dunlap, 1942), 13; Canfield Cook, *The Flying Jet* (New York: Grosset & Dunlap, 1945), 54, 20.

59 Cook, *Sky Attack*, 90; Canfield Cook, *Secret Mission* (New York: Grosset & Dunlap, 1943), 42–43; Canfield Cook, *Lost Squadron* (New York: Grosset & Dunlap, 1943), 65; "Contra-Rotating Propellers," *Aero Digest*, 42 (February 1943): 228–229; Cook, *Flying Jet*, 48–49; Capt. Ezra Kotcher, "Our Jet Propelled Fighter," *Air Force*, 27 (March 1944): 6–8, 64; "Bell's Twin-Jet Fighter," *Southern Flight*, 22 (October 1944): 27, 79. The first wholly pressurized

bomber of the war to enter service was the American B-29 Superfortress, which does not appear in any of the wartime series. See Herb Powell, "Boeing B-29 'Superfortress,'" *Aviation,* 43 (July 1944): 110–111, 278–285.

60 Canfield Cook, *Spitfire Pilot* (New York: Grosset & Dunlap, 1942): 121–122; "The Messerschmitt Me-109," *Popular Aviation,* 26 (March 1940): 27; Canfield Cook, *Springboard to Tokyo* (New York: Grosset & Dunlap, 1943), 126–127; Canfield Cook, *Wings Over Japan* (New York: Grosset & Dunlap, 1944), 168–169; Cook, *Flying Jet,* 52, 100–107; Kenneth R. Porter, "Jet Bomb," *Flying,* 35 (September 1944): 24–25, 128–130.

61 Cook, *Sky Attack,* 79; Cook, *Lost Squadron,* 2; "Manta Mock-Up," *Aviation,* 41 (February 1942): 11; "Manta Fighter Has Contra-Rotating Props," *Popular Science,* 140 (June 1942): 62–64; Edward Churchill, "Manta," *Flying,* 31 (November 1942): 54, 100–103. For the XP-67, see "McDonnell XP-67," *Model Airplane News,* 32 (June 1945): 22–23, 56–59.

62 "Editor's Note," George L. Eaton, "The Charger Goes to Sydney," *Air Trails,* 11 (October 1938), 37–45, 50–56, 88. The Charger itself is illustrated and detailed in Frank Tinsley, "The Barnes Charger," *Air Trails,* 11 (October 1938): 46–49, 88. Tinsley, a commercial artist, illustrated the Barnes stories. Many of the Barnes stories were written by Charles Spain Verral; however, since "Eaton" was a house name for *Air Trails,* other authors may well have contributed to the series as well.

63 Canfield Cook, *The Flying Wing* (New York: Grosset & Dunlap, 1946), 39–42, 53; Robert McLarren, "Flying Wing of Destruction," *Model Airplane News,* 21 (December 1939): 14; Frederick Graham, "Will Tomorrow's Planes Look Like This?" *Saturday Evening Post,* 29 January 1944, 36, 39; "Burnelli and the Flying Wing Design," *Air World,* March, 1945, 34–37, 65; Devon Francis, "Putting Plane's Fuselage to Work," *Popular Science,* 147 (November 1945): 65–70.

64 Robert McLarren, "Bell XS-1 Makes Supersonic Flight," *Aviation Week,* 47 (22 December 1947): 9–10; "Flying Wing Jet Bomber Completed," *Aviation Week,* 47 (13 October 1947): 14; Rus Walton, "Jack Northrop and his Wonderful Wing," *Flying,* 42 (February 1948): 19–21, 56–58.

65 An authoritative account of German rocket development is Michael J. Neufeld, *The Rocket and the Reich: Peenemünde and the Coming of the Ballistic Missile Era* (New York: Free Press, 1995).

66 Al Williams, "Incredible Age," *U.S. Air Services,* 26 (May 1941): 25.

Chapter Eight

Aftermath: A-Bombs, Rockets, and Space Flight, 1945–1950

Readers of a certain age would recognize the scene in an instant. A yellow Piper Cub circles the field, heads into the wind, and makes a smooth, three-point landing on the grass strip. Two boys, both in their late teens, clamber from the airplane, unload several sacks of groceries, and, laughing and arguing amiably, disappear with their load into the rambling, homey house some distance from the field.

It's a moment instantly familiar to any fan of Rex Lee, Ted Scott, or Andy Lane, introducing a story full of promise for flying adventures to come. As *this* tale progresses, however, differences begin to emerge, and the entire episode foreshadows the fading away of the aviation series and the diminishing of their dreams. The time is 1947, not 1927 or 1937. The place is Spindrift Island, a cloistered scientific community off the coast of New Jersey. The boys are Rick Brant, son of the leader of the Spindrift enclave, and Don Scott, known as "Scotty," an orphaned ex-Marine who lied about his age and saw combat in World War II. The book is "John Blaine's" *The Rocket's Shadow,* and it introduces a series billed as the "Rick Brant Electronic Adventures."

Despite his flying skills and his attachment to his light plane, Rick's heart is not in aviation; he is closer to Tom Swift than he is to Ted Scott. He's an inveterate tinkerer, raised in a milieu of scientific research and experimentation, who regularly produces some gadget that helps to save the day—e.g., a miniature radio transceiver, an ultra-intense silent dog whistle, or an infra-red ciné camera for motion pictures in the dark—but is generally tangential to the larger story. He draws freely on the expertise of the scientists at the Spindrift compound, especially that of his father, engineer and nuclear physicist Hartson Brant, mathematician Julius Weiss, and electronics wizard Hobart Zircon. Unlike Tom, however, he has no yen to be an industrialist. He moves instead in the new world of pure science and grant- or government-sponsored research, the only world he really has ever known. As their adventures progress, Rick and Scotty become the leading edge of a dramatic shift in the series-book genre. They prefigure characters who turn their backs upon the innovation and individualism of aviation *per se* and stride into the updated world of corporate- or governmentally-supported electronics, rocketry, nucleonics, and, eventually, interplanetary travel. The pure aviation series, as a genre, is ended, overcome and overwhelmed by the events of the war years and after.

The changing technological world that would confront aeronautical enthusiasts and series-book authors was apparent even before war's end, as signs of things to come crept into the technical and popular aviation press. Writing in *Aviation* in February, 1945, Major General Kenneth B. Wolfe announced that "We Must Retain Technological Supremacy" in aeronautical development in the post-war years. Only with an on-going program of research and development funded by congressional appropriations and supported by a vibrant aviation industry could the United States continue its role as the premier aeronautical country in the world. Five months later, following the surrender of German forces in Europe, Roy Healy, an officer of the American Rocket Society, published in the same journal a two-part article arguing that "Aeronautical Supremacy Demands Jet and Rocket Research." The war-born collaborative research efforts of the military, government agencies, and the aeronautical industry must be continued and encouraged in peacetime, exploring jet and rocket applications for scientific and peaceful purposes as well as military ones.[1]

The journal's most comprehensive statement, for the time, came in September 1945, with its publication of Herb Powell's "The Atomic Frame of

Reference—Or Else." Powell, an associate editor, clearly understood the implications of the atomic bomb. It required, he argued, an immediate reshaping of conventional military and political thought; it made imperative an enormous expansion of scientific research; and it pointed out the necessity for a new cooperation of science and industry. Each of these changes would have its effect upon the world of aviation, and every member of that world will have to adapt, for matters would never again be as they were before the coming of nuclear power.[2]

A scant year later, the popular aviation press was well along with its own adjustment to technological change. In "Air Trails and New Frontiers," the newly appointed editor of *Air Trails Pictorial* spoke of rocket-powered ships for high speed, high altitude, and lunar research; of the potential of nucleonics to expedite research at the sub-molecular level; and of electronic researches that could lead as easily to death rays as to superior means of detection or communication. The editor, John W. Campbell, Jr., was himself science-trained, a well-established writer of science fiction, and since 1937 editor of *Astounding Science Fiction,* the leading American science fiction magazine, a position he continued to hold. *Air Trails,* he wrote in conclusion, would continue its balance of general aviation and model-related articles, but would add to them articles dealing with the newer topics. "Each of us must live and make our living in that new, ever-changing world. . . . The progress of the world is not something we are free to accept or reject; it happens inescapably."[3] Campbell's vision of a progressive world continued that of the aviation series, but the world he postulated was one dramatically different from the one in which aviation was the driving force of progress.

Two of the areas of research that Campbell sketched out were already resonating throughout the aviation press. One was the realm of transonic and supersonic flight. Fliers had long been talking of the "sonic barrier;" the compressibility problems experienced by the P-38 and P-47 during high-speed dives in the last years of the war, it developed, were caused in great part by the ships' approaching the speed of sound. Now, however, with workable jet and rocket engines at hand and the availability of German scientists' researches into swept-wing design, speeds that only months before had been unattainable were within reach. *Air Trails Pictorial* published a lengthy consideration of "Beyond the Speed of Sound" in December 1945, and followed it in September 1946 with an equally lengthy "1,000 Miles an Hour," talking of Mach cones, airfoil shapes, and the effects of various degrees of sweepback. Almost simultaneously, *Model Airplane News* ran photographs of early American experiments with swept-back wings and British and American designs for jet-powered research vehicles.[4]

The dedicated research craft beginning to appear came in for their own share of attention. Articles began to call attention to the Bell XS-1, a rocket-powered craft undergoing glide tests in late 1946 prior to its attempt on the sound barrier in 1947, and the ship was featured on the cover of *Model*

The Bell XS-1, the rocket-powered aircraft that first exceeded the speed of sound (ca. 1946-1947). Courtesy of Bell Helicopter Textron via National Air and Space Museum, Smithsonian Institution (SI 87-6748).

Airplane News in March 1947. Two designs by Douglas Aircraft appeared in 1947: the jet-powered D-558 "Skystreak," a cylindrical, straight-winged ship, and the sleek D-558–2 "Skyrocket," which featured swept-back wings and both jet and rocket engines. Problems caused by the swept-back wing were discussed in magazines from *Aviation Week* (successor to *Aviation*) to *Air Trails Pictorial,* while other accounts focused upon the physiological problems of supersonic flight and the potential advantages of delta-wing design.[5] When news at last broke that the XS-1 had exceeded the speed of sound in October 1947, readers were already prepared to accept the advance.

Campbell's other research realm, high-altitude investigation, had its own advocates. Studies that in the past had been carried out by atmosphere-dependent, propeller-driven aircraft or specialized balloons now had access to rockets, and flight to the very limits of the atmosphere, if not beyond, was possible. The aviation press, of course, was no stranger to rocketry. Early stories had traced the experiments of the German *Verein für Raumschiffahrt* (*VfR,* or Society for Space Travel), a first outlet for the talents of the young Wernher von Braun, and of the American Rocket Society. Robert H. Goddard's development of the liquid-fueled rocket did not go unnoticed, and his later experiments outside Roswell, New Mexico, were supported by the Guggenheim Fund on the recommendation of Charles Lindbergh. Combat reports dealing with the Messerschmitt Me 163 were commonplace in the last months of the war, while accounts of V-2 attacks on England and Belgium established the practicality of the rocket and its emergence as a long-range weapon.

Following the war, as American scientists began experimenting with captured V-2 rockets and working their way through the records of German rocket research, the coverage changed. Factual articles on rocketry throughout the aviation press began to incorporate reflections on space flight, blurring the line between science journalism and science fiction. In early 1946, *Aviation* published an article on "The Rocket's Future Influence on Transport

German "V-2" (A-4) rockets being readied for launch (1944-1945). National Air and Space Museum, Smithsonian Institution (SI 77-4218).

Designs," and headed a report on a press-attended demonstration of a V-2 with the question, "Can We Catch Up in Rocket Research?" Almost simultaneously, Willy Ley, a founder of the *VfR* and a well-regarded science popularizer, published a two-part essay, "V-2—and Beyond," in *Air Trails Pictorial,* relating the links between the *VfR* and German plans for a trans-Atlantic ballistic missile and speculating about the research and military potential of an orbital space station. *Flying* chipped in with "Uncle Sam 'Discovers' the Rocket," tut-tutting over America's pre-war indifference to rocket research, while *Aviation Week,* after first asking "What's Ahead for Rockets?," asked a second question, "How High Is Up?" in a report of the 51-mile altitude reached by an American-designed Viking rocket.[6]

Research quickly led to realization, and the effects of various discoveries began to be felt in the aeronautical and public arenas. Advocates for general aviation were not long in considering the possibilities of the jet engine. Major

Charles M. Fischer, writing in *Flying* in June 1945, talked of the joys of jet-powered flight, spoke of the need to make flying as accessible to John Citizen as the automobile had become, and affirmed his belief that the next generation of light planes would jet-powered.[7] Commercial designs were not far behind. Four years later, in mid-1949, England awed the aeronautical world with its introduction of the DeHavilland DH-106 "Comet," the world's first jet designed exclusively for passenger use.

A clean-lined design with four jet engines embedded in a modestly swept-back wing, the Comet promised to carry thirty-six passengers at a speed of 500 M.P.H. and an altitude of 40,000 feet, making possible a six-hour flight from London to New York. It did not enter service until 1952, but its appearance sent shock waves through the American commercial aircraft industry. Lockheed in early 1950 proposed a larger, longer-ranged design influenced by current developments in fighter design, but questioned the reliability of jet engines for commercial use. Six months later, Boeing released news that it was studying a swept-wing design similar to its B-47 bomber, but with a larger fuselage to make it comparable to the propeller-driven Stratocruiser (the civilian version of the military's C-97). Out of these studies came the Boeing 367–80, known to history as the Boeing 707. Faster and roomier than the Comet, the 707 like the DC-3 came to be flown by most of the world's major airlines.[8]

The most visible applications of jet flight and high-speed aircraft came from the military. As early as 1946, the United States Navy announced its first jet-powered fighter, the Ryan XFR-1 "Fireball," which used both a conventional piston engine and a turbojet engine. The conservatism of the design hinted at the navy's relatively slow progress toward jet flight. The service added the McDonnell FD-1 "Phantom," its first all-jet craft, the following year, to be sure, and pushed the testing of the North American XFJ-1 and the Chance Vought XF6U-1. Nevertheless, the navy's commitment to the aircraft carrier necessitated a wholesale revision of tactics and procedures to accommodate the higher speeds and performance characteristics of the jet craft, and jet acquisitions lagged. Although some naval jet aircraft were in active service by 1950 and saw combat in the Korean War (1950 and after), the navy was still devoting most of its aviation budget to propeller-driven, World War II-era craft such as the Chance Vought F4U-5 "Corsair" and the Grumman F8F-1 "Bearcat" as its first-line weapons. Its first potentially supersonic craft, the swept-wing, tailless Chance Vought F7U-1 "Cutlass," did not begin experimental flight tests until late 1948.[9]

The army air force, which became the free-standing United States Air Force in 1947, was flying jets at war's end, principally the Lockheed P-80 "Shooting Star." Though none saw combat service, their merits were obvious, and air force leaders began planning for a totally jet-powered armory by 1950.[10] By 1946, jet bombers as well as new jet fighters were being designed or flight-tested, and the service was thinking toward supersonic craft. Most of these designs incorporated the most recent developments of high-speed, high-altitude research: swept wings, pressurized cabins, and speeds and operating ceilings that five years earlier seemed impossible. Among them were airplanes that would change the nature of aerial warfare. One was the North American XP-86, a single-engined, swept-wing design that, as the F-86 "Sabre," would give the United States air superiority over Chinese MiG 15s in Korea. Another was the Boeing XB-47 "Stratojet," the first multi-engined, swept-wing bomber, with fighter-like performance that effectively ended the design of straight-winged bombing planes.[11]

By 1948, nearly forty jet designs were operational or being tested, compelling the military to rethink such matters as strategy, operations, and maintenance. The very act of flying a high-performance, jet-powered airplane called for major revisions in training. Conventional procedures, based on relatively slow speeds, ready access to ground features, and predictable aircraft response, were not adequate. Some writers argued higher speeds putting greater demands on the body and skills of the pilot meant that the day of the single-seat fighter was over (anticipating modern, two-seated warplanes such as the air force's McDonnell F-4 "Phantom" and the navy's Grumman F-14 "Tomcat"). Others detailed at length the differences between the flying characteristics of a jet craft and those of a propeller-driven one, while one predicted the outright end of piloted fighter craft and the replacement of fighters by unmanned, supersonic guided missiles. Even simple actions like "bailing out" of a disabled ship were affected by speed and altitude and ejection seats and pressurized escape capsules were under development. It was, then, not surprising that, in mid-1950, *Aviation Week* reported on a program to train military fliers as "pilot-scientists," allowing them to bring military experience to bear in the designing and flying of still newer aircraft. The back-yard builder and the self-taught flier of the Golden Age were becoming as obsolete as their aircraft.[12]

All of these considerations were based upon actual developments. Aviation enthusiasts could see jet aircraft in the air or read of them in the press, and the daunting consequences of jet development were apparent to all. Even more daunting was the speculative prospect of warfare and aircraft yet to come. A new phrase, "push-button warfare," entered the vocabulary as articles began to explore the likelihood of missiles armed with atomic warheads. As early as August 1946, *Air Trails Pictorial* asked, "Can the Atom Bomb be Stopped?," considering both delivery systems (rocket-powered missiles) and defense systems (radar-guided anti-missile missiles). *Flying* attempted to push the threat of missile warfare well into the future with a 1947 article, "The Push-Button War Fable," but, a year later, was asking, "Will Subs Launch the Atom Air War?" Debate and discussion of missile warfare continued, until *Aviation Week,* in a 1950 editorial entitled "Overselling the Missile," pointed out the woeful state of American missile development and called for the creation of a separate missile force, to stand on a par with the army, navy, and air force.[13]

Nuclear energy as a possible propulsion source also came under scrutiny. Willy Ley sketched out the potential of atomic-powered aircraft in 1946 for *Air*

Trails Pictorial. Luis W. Alvarez, who had won the Collier Trophy for his development of the ground-controlled approach and landing system, cautioned that "There is No Obvious or Simple Way in Which to Use Atomic Energy for Space Ships" in early 1947, but, in mid-1948, *Aviation Week* published a short article on a British design for a nuclear-powered, multi-stage rocket using liquid hydrogen as a propellant. Meanwhile, the air force itself provided funds for the NEPA—"Nuclear Energy for the Propulsion of Aircraft"—Project, and the project's chief engineer, Andrew Kalitinsky, published articles on atomic-powered aircraft in *Aero Digest, Western Flying,* and *Flying* between mid-1948 and early 1949. *Air Trails* re-entered the debate with William Winter's "Atom Powered Bombers" in May 1949, concluding that nuclear power, whether applied to a manned warplane or a ballistic missile, was inevitable.[14] Elements of what once had been considered science fiction, appearing in the aviation press, were forcing still further changes upon perceptions of the larger realm of flight.

Those changes inevitably extended to the possibility of space flight. Although at least one writer could still argue, in 1947, the impossibility of such flight because there was "nothing for [propulsive] forces to act against" in space, most persons looked to the rocket experiments at White Sands, New Mexico, as the first steps toward actual space exploration. (Robert Goddard demonstrated the error of the "nothing to push against" belief in 1919, but many otherwise responsible technicians continued to hold out.) F.R. Stout discussed rocket research at the Guggenheim Aeronautical Laboratory of the California Institute of Technology (GALCIT) in a *Flying* article titled "Airline to the Moon?" in 1946, while Willy Ley, again writing in *Air Trails Pictorial,* also debunked the "nothing to push against" fallacy and proposed a manned, liquid-fueled rocket derived from existing V-2 and aeronautical technology. The following year, John W. Campbell, Jr., having changed the title of *Air Trails Pictorial* to *Air Trails and Science Frontiers,* called for a nuclear-armed military base on the Moon, bolstering his argument with Capt. B.A. Northrop's article, "Fortress in the Sky."[15]

The more technical aviation press did not stint on considerations of space flight. *Western Flying* devoted a two-part article to "The Conquest of Interplanetary Space" in late 1947, considering problems posed by nuclear propulsion, the accelerations and *g*-forces involved, and the temperature and radiation hazards likely to be encountered. *Aviation Week* reported on research pointing toward the feasibility of a multi-stage rocket capable of escaping Earth's gravity. An engineer working with Project Hermes, a missile-research enterprise, described establishing a station in low Earth orbit and the research possibilities afforded by such a station in a 1949 article in *Flying,* and went on to touch upon military interest in satellite vehicles. Even commercial rocket flight was being considered, for, in 1950, *Western Flying* printed excerpts from an academic paper proposing specifications for a sub-orbital, 3,000-M.P.H. rocket vehicle appropriate for passenger service.[16] Whereas "flight" once meant propellers, reciprocating engines, wings, and parachutes, the term was quickly expanding to include jet and rocket power, transonic and supersonic speeds, and high-altitude flight extending even into the vacuum of space.

Notions of space flight quickly led to notions of alien life, and writers began seriously considering the possibility of interplanetary life—another subject that in the past had been limited solely to science fiction. Allied pilots in the last years of the European war had reported odd manifestations they called "foo fighters." These were floating silver balls or mysterious flickering lights that appeared suddenly and easily kept pace with the aircraft, whatever its speed. The apparitions were at the time attributed to one or another kind of German secret weapon; not until later did fliers begin to speculate they might be of alien origin. That speculation began in June 1947, after a private pilot flying over Washington state reported sighting a series of "saucer-like" objects. The following month, national news sources carried reports that the air force had recovered wreckage of a "flying disc" outside Roswell, New Mexico. While the latter artifacts proved to be remnants of a high-altitude balloon (at least according to military sources, skeptics continue to say), "flying saucers" and the possibility of alien visitation became part of the public discourse. Aviation was changing dramatically, and aviation fiction had to follow.[17]

Rockets, space travel, and other kinds of scientific speculation had long been a staple of science fiction publishing, a literary realm generally consigned to the pulp magazines and considered a notch or two lower on the literary totem pole than even the series books. Until the early 1940s, however, the genre, especially those examples directed toward younger readers, had limited itself to the celebration of the wonders of science *in toto*. Magazines like *Amazing Stories, Dynamic Science Stories,* and *Thrilling Wonder Stories* set the tone. "Science" had no limits to what it might accomplish. The "mad" (or, if not crazed, at least certifiably eccentric) scientist was a familiar figure and his inventions were testimonials to the power of machine-age technology. Space ships, time machines, bizarre alien beings, disintegrator ray guns, atmospheric vehicles coasting along propelled by *outré* power sources, and vehicles for "hyperspatial" travel were commonplaces.[18]

This was the milieu in which the first science-fiction series books operated. The earliest, "Roy Rockwood's" Stratemeyer-created "Great Marvel" series (1906–1935; nine titles. See Chapter I, above), established the pattern for the next several decades: An elderly, eccentric scientist (a generalist, competent in all realms of science), his two young protégés, and assorted helpers enjoy adventures made possible by some form of scientific development. Initially limiting themselves to terrestrial derring-do, the "Great Marvel" books begin with an electrically-powered airship, a marvelous submarine, and a flying boat that penetrates the Earth's crust. Subsequent adventures move outward—by rocketship to Mars and the Moon, by volcanic eruption and an advanced airship to mysterious worlds in the Earth's orbit, and by electromagnetic spaceship to Venus and Saturn, meeting wonderful beings at every turning. While the scientific content of the books is minimal to the point of being fanciful, their attitude toward science and its potential is overwhelmingly positive. "Science," a generalized discipline complete unto itself, is the path to the future.

Howard Garis, the principal author of the "Great Marvel" stories, offered a marginally more realistic portrayal of the scientist and scientific advances in the "Rocket Riders" series (1933–1934; four titles), published under his own name and using rocketry as the central technological marvel. Three teenagers, Harry Donovan, Richard Westberry, and Albert Armitage, become friends with an exiled Russian inventor, Alex Sarnof, who has developed a controllable rocket engine powered by solid fuel. In the adventures detailed in the four books of the series, he and the boys take a rocket sled to Alaska, a rocket automobile to Arabia, a rocket boat to the Caribbean, and a rocket airplane (a conventional winged design propelled by rockets, not a dedicated rocketship) to Montana. They meet no aliens, their adventures are strictly limited to terrestrial locales, and an "editor's note" to the first volume proclaims the series' commitment to touting the coming practicality of rocket propulsion: "Recent experiments in rocket propulsion prove this means of power is past the stage of imaginative theory and that it will hold an important place in supplying future generations with their means of transportation."[19]

In most respects the "Rocket Riders" books are little more than extensions of the series of an earlier era (e.g., "The Motor Boys," or "The Railroad Boys") that used transportation as a vehicle for melodrama, and their factual scientific content is correspondingly limited. Sarnof does give the boys a reasonably accurate lecture on the theory of rocket propulsion, though he maintains that his vehicles are propelled by the rocket exhaust pushing against the resistance of the outside air.[20] Throughout the volumes, Garis also makes off-hand references to the well-publicized experiments being conducted in Germany by Fritz von Opel and Max Valier as well as the *VfR,* and the boys talk knowledgeably of high-speed wind-tunnel experiments being conducted by NACA at Langley Field.[21] Even so, the rocket engines themselves retain a certain degree of mystery while Sarnof's status as "a scientist" invests him with an aura of wonder that overshadows his eccentricities.

Far more fanciful is the "Adventures in the Unknown Series" (1933–1934; four titles) by Carl H. Claudy. Claudy, a science journalist working in the Washington, DC, area, had long been interested in aviation; he covered the Wrights' experimental work at Fort Myer, Maryland, in 1908; took some of the first photographs of the flights; and, in 1920 published his speculations on "Aircraft of the Future" in *Scientific American.*[22] In the four books of the "Adventures in the Unknown," though, he looks beyond simple flight to adventures of an elaborately science-fictional sort. His continuing characters, Alan Kane and Ted Dolliver, would be at home in any of the series. Alan is a serious, slightly-built intellectual of college age, while Ted, aged twenty-five, is irreverent, athletic, and muscular, with a cauliflower ear attesting to rounds in the boxing ring. The two become friends when Ted saves Alan from a gang of bullies, and, drawing upon their complementary talents, embark on a series of bizarre adventures that are far removed from those of the aviation series.

Each book features a different sort of scientific speculation, beginning with space travel. In *The Mystery Men of Mars* (1933), Alan and Ted travel to Mars in a gravity-bending sphere invented by the absurdly Germanic Isaac Luytens, the Aberdonian Professor of Physics and Higher Mathematics at an unnamed university. There they encounter insect-like Martians wholly devoid of humane or individualistic feelings, creatures for whom the good of the colony is the sole and ultimate goal. Safely returned from Mars, they travel next in time, in *A Thousand Years a Minute* (1933). Professor Ignatius Lazar, a distant kinsman, wills Alan his "tempomobile," and the two friends immediately test it. They travel to a prehistoric Virginia 966,460 years in the past, finding a jungle environment populated by dinosaurs, pterodactyls, and mammals large and small. Encountering a tribe of blood-worshipping Neanderthals, they make a hairsbreadth escape and return to 1933 and the security of their university community.

Their third adventure, *The Land of No Shadow* (1933) is still more speculative. Using Professor Kurt Arronson's electrically powered "gate," a device that "folds" space, Alan and Ted travel to a fourth-dimension world wholly lacking in color, where all normal terrestrial perceptions are reversed. There they are pursued by beings made up of invisible force and are on the brink of escape when an accident returns Ted to the present of 1932 [*sic*], destroys the "gate," and strands Alan in the alien dimension. Alan reappears in the final volume, *The Blue Grotto Terror* (1934), miraculously restored to this dimension and bearing a mysterious equation that, when solved, leads to the creation of an "X substance" that can convert matter to pure energy. Alan uses his newfound compound to dig a shaft twenty miles deep into the Earth, discovering a grotto containing normal air pressure and temperatures and populated by intangible blue entities. Alarmed by the power of the entities, Alan and Ted return to the surface, collapse the shaft, and destroy the equation so that its power cannot be launched into the world.

Claudy often speaks in his own voice, appearing as a frame narrator of the sort used by H. Rider Haggard and transcribing the adventures that Ted and Alan relate to him. The adventures themselves, for all their speculativeness, are presented as plausible extrapolations of current scientific thought. A testimonial in the opening volume by George F. Pierrot, Managing Editor of *American Boy Magazine* (where shorter versions of the stories had appeared), equates Claudy with Jules Verne in his ability to give credibility to even the most fanciful speculation: "Anyone who picks up a Carl Claudy book can be certain of excitement, adventure, the tang of mystery unsolved, and a stimulating plausibility that Mr. Claudy's wide scientific knowledge makes possible."[23]

The books remain, however, masterworks of semi-science (as opposed to pseudo-science), full of plausible-sounding explanations for the oddities Alan and Ted encounter. Luytens cites Einstein's theories of gravity and speed and derives from them a spaceship that "falls up" between lines of gravitational force. Lazar's "tempomobile," powered by a shimmering "chronostal," treats time like a river, moving with or against the current to move into the future or the past. Arronson explains his dimensional "gate" with the analogy of two-dimensional beings moving along the plane of a sheet of paper, unconscious of the paralleling world of the third dimension, and Alan's "X substance" has the qualities implied by Einstein's equation, $E = mc^2$. All three scientists carry out their experiments as individuals, in laboratories elaborately equipped with "Wheatstone bridges, galvanometers, high frequency tubes, gas containers, coils, wires, [and] all the impedimenta of a busy physicist investigating strange phenomena of nature." Theirs is a world of cutting-edge "science," in which they and they alone pursue the secrets of the universe, and those secrets can only be interpreted by persons schooled in "science's" arcane mysteries.[24]

Two series, both beginning in 1947, changed all that. The "Rick Brant Electronic Adventure" series (1947–1968; twenty-three titles) focused attention upon Earth-bound scientific developments paralleling those appearing in the technical and popular press, carried out by teams of well-funded researchers. The series, which in 1948 became the "Rick Brant Science-Adventure" series, was written by Harold L. Goodwin and Peter J. Harkins, collaborating as "John Blaine," and is solidly set in the post-war United States.[25] As such, it marks the transition from the independent scientific and technological research of the "Tom Swift" books to a scientific milieu more reflective of contemporary circumstances. Its emphasis is three-fold. First, it establishes the cooperative foundations of contemporary science, as the Spindrift workers collaborate to win grants supporting their efforts and, later, when Rick and Scotty ally themselves with various large, multi-talented research teams. Hartson Brant makes the point explicitly in *The Whispering Box Mystery* (1948), telling Rick that the success of the Spindrift community is due not to "the brilliance of any *one* of us, but because of the combined training of *all* of us."[26] The solitary scientist working independently in a privately funded laboratory has been supplanted by teams, institutes, and syndicates.

Second, it deals exclusively with problems and events set in a recognizable American present. No insect-like Martians or intangible entities appear in the stories, and supernatural effects, when they occur, always have a scientific basis. The "phantom shark" in the book of the same title (1949) proves to be a home-built submarine cobbled from a P-40 fuselage, while the eerie cries of *The Wailing Octopus* (1956) are generated by audible feedback from a new form of sonar. The experiments forming the background of the stories also have clearly stated implications for the present. Radar bounced off the Moon (*The Lost City* [1947]) may open the way to new means of communication; a maneuverable deep-sea submersible craft (*100 Fathoms Under* [1947]) makes underwater archeological explorations feasible; the discovery of an underground source for naturally occurring "heavy water" (*The Caves of Fear* [1951]) promises to speed the development of a hydrogen bomb.

Third, the series overtly reflects the changing civil, military, and governmental national contexts of the post-war era. The isolated Spindrift enclave resembles the sealed-off, mesa-top community of Los Alamos, New Mexico, that developed the atomic bomb. A disgruntled ex-Nazi, Manfred Wessel, tries to sabotage the Moon rocket project in *The Rocket's Shadow,* Rick and Scotty are recruited into JANIG (the super-secret Joint Army-Navy Intelligence Group) to carry out counter-espionage missions involving the Soviet Union and other Iron Curtain countries, and the sea-going expedition of *The Phantom Shark* is seeking out new fishing grounds to feed a hungry Asia. Rick's world is one in which the United States is subject to, and often at the mercy of, international movements, and world-wide consequences have to be considered as carefully as national ones.

For all of Rick's devotion to his Piper Cub, for all his flying skills, and for all his messing about in one laboratory or another, he is no longer the classic series-book hero, working to capitalize upon a single technology. He works in a changed—and changing—world, and his adventures reflect the change. His "inventions" are secondary in importance to the larger scientific projects on which "the team" is working, and those projects are the ones that must be protected from international spies. He responds to the exciting challenge of pure research, but he is conscious of the need for eventual practical applications of his work, if he is to continue to operate in his chosen field. The "Brant" stories, to be sure, inform their readers about current developments in modern science (e.g., the possibilities of microwaves, the coming of printed circuits and the transistor, the new science of cybernetics, etc.) as faithfully as the aviation series document those of flight, but they also point up the changing nature of science and the scientist. "The scientist" is no longer a generalist and no longer an independent experimenter; instead, scientific specialties are becoming more and more limited, and the technologies they require are becoming more and more complex. The stories illustrate just how dramatically the technological world changed during the World War II years, and they dramatize the conditions that make the old-style story of invention impossible.

If the "Rick Brant" stories illustrated the changes taking place in real-world science, the other emergent series of 1947 presented speculative science and alien societies with uncommon thoughtfulness and tough-minded plausibility. Although unnamed (its volumes are free-standing stories with no continuing characters), the series of juvenile novels written by Robert A. Heinlein and published by the Scribner firm (1947–1958; twelve titles) shaped post-war science fiction for adults and young persons alike, and documented the end of the classic series story. Heinlein, a Missouri-born 1929 Annapolis graduate who worked on high-altitude pressure-suit development during World War II, had turned to writing when health problems compelled him to retire from the navy in 1934. His first published story, "Life-Line," appeared in *Astounding Science Fiction* in 1939, and, by the time he gave up fiction-writing for the war effort in 1942, he had established himself as an authoritative and popular voice in American science fiction.[27]

When Heinlein resumed fiction-writing in 1946, he set himself two goals: to break into the higher-paying "slick" publications, and to educate the

American public about the realities of atomic warfare. He had little difficulty with the first goal, selling a story to *The Saturday Evening Post* as early as 1947, but was woefully unsuccessful with the second. Frustrated by his failure, he proposed a juvenile series, "The Young Atomic Engineers," to suit his "own propaganda purposes." The series seems to have been largely conventional in its original conception. The first volume was to introduce its young characters, and subsequent volumes, complete with dramatic subtitles (e.g., *The Young Atomic Engineers in the Asteroids, or The Mystery of the Broken Planet*), would take them to Mars, the Asteroids, and into business.[28] What developed instead was a cluster of books that stunningly documented the inadequacy of the classic series formula to cope with contemporary developments. In lieu of that formula, Heinlein offered a vision of a future in which the implications and advances of science, technological progress, and space travel permeated every level of society.

Heinlein's first book, *Rocket Ship Galileo* (1947), is a transitional text with unmistakable overtones of the classic series formula. It draws upon Heinlein's memories of his boyhood reading of "Tom Swift" and other series, and begins, as might any series book, with three college-bound teenagers, Ross Jenkins, Art Mueller, and Morrie Abrams, who make up the science-oriented Galileo Club. Its setting is shortly after the end of World War II, and the boys' backgrounds reflect the effects of the war: Ross's father is a retired electrical engineer, but knowledgeable in atomics; Art's father, a German scientist, died in a concentration camp because he would not hew to the Nazi line; and Morrie is explicitly portrayed as Jewish. In their well-equipped clubhouse they dabble in chemistry, electronics, and photography, and, together, are experimenting with liquid-fueled rockets along the lines of those pioneered by the *VfR*. All three are conscious of the possibilities of atomic energy, and they live in a time when domestic and trans-Atlantic service by chemically fueled rockets is an accepted fact.

It is the next development that marks the book's transitional role in the emerging series, for Heinlein falls back on a time-honored device. Art's uncle, nuclear scientist Donald Cargreaves, appears on the scene, and, impressed by the boys' scientific capabilities, invites them to help him build an atomic-powered rocket capable of flying to the Moon. The three accept, of course, and, after token opposition from their families, accompany Cargreaves to a New Mexico test site. There they effortlessly convert an obsolete freight rocket to atomic power (Cargreaves uses thorium for his fissionable source, and powdered zinc as the superheated propulsive mass) and successfully reach the Moon. But they are not the first. On the Moon, they discover a cell of renegade Nazis planning the nuclear bombardment of Earth. While they easily defeat the Nazi force and return to Earth in triumph, Cargreaves and the boys are the last vestiges of the traditional, do-it-yourself technological protagonists. Their story marks the end of the classic series tale, and the beginning of a new version of the genre.

Heinlein himself seems to have recognized the absurdity of trying to translate the workshop inventor into the nuclear age, for he never repeated the formula. He rejects the format of the continued-character series and, instead, develops a group of books that move, volume by volume, through the solar system and on to the stars. Though the later books continue many of the themes found in the aviation series, notably the importance of intelligence, learning, and general knowledge, the essential role of loyalty and integrity, and the power of individual courage, they present societies in which technological development has grown too immense for a single person, and in which the products of advanced science are apparent in every aspect of society.

The next volume, *Space Cadet* (1948) traces a youth's training for the Interplanetary Patrol, an elite, multi-national professional military force maintained by the United Nations to sustain world-wide peace with Earth-orbiting atomic weapons, and introduces its young protagonists to the matriarchal natives of Venus. *Red Planet* (1949) supposes a vast corporation ("the Company") that is a global agency for the colonization of Mars and considers what that colonization might involve, while *Farmer in the Sky* (1950) explores attempts to ease population pressures on an overcrowded Earth by developing colonies on Ganymede, a satellite of Jupiter. Each features a young protagonist working within an enormously complex system of global—and interplanetary—interdependence, and each assumes the existence of a society visibly shaped by the application of scientific discoveries.

Later books continue and expand Heinlein's vision of the future. *Tunnel in the Sky* (1956) postulates an Earth so overcrowded that high-school graduates, female as well as male, undergo life-or-death survival training to prepare them for settling on other planets. *Time for the Stars* (1956) candidly discusses the relativistic time changes wrought by near-faster-than-light travel and the need to seek out Earthlike planets in other star systems that are suitable for colonization. *Citizen of the Galaxy* (1957) assumes propulsion systems that make interstellar travel practical, then looks at some of the societies and agencies that might result: the far-traveling Traders, proud of their independence; the Patrol, a thinly stretched military force trying to maintain peace among many planets and many cultures; and the far-flung Rudbek military-industrial complex on Earth, which among its many products supplies advanced starships to the Traders, the Patrol, and the slave trade. The last book of the twelve, *Have Space Suit, Will Travel* (1958), takes its soda-jerk hero from Earth to the Moon, then to Pluto, and finally to the Lesser Magellanic Clouds, where he confronts a multi-world, multi-species council passing judgment on all the planets within its scope.

All twelve of Heinlein's books are unified by a handful of traits. The societies he describes are sketched with deceptive ease, giving them an air of total plausibility; given the technological advances he assumes, Heinlein seems to say, *this* is the kind of society that might evolve. The scientific elements are rigorously considered and consistently maintained; devices in the books are shown to be the result of lengthy research and development, and there is no evidence of the invention-on-demand so familiar from earlier series. The human characters are recognizable as well: Adults are engineers, teachers, merchants, physicians, tradespeople, or businesspersons, while the young protagonists (predominantly male but frequently with strong female characters in prominent supporting roles) are students and adolescents on the edge of adulthood. Aliens, when they appear, are logical products of their planetary environment as it was known in the 1940s and 1950s; their cultures and technologies are carefully worked out, and they are neither the bug-eyed monsters nor the world-saving super-intelligences of earlier pulp fiction. Heinlein's future societies are credibly shaped by technology, but are far removed from the simplistic and more hopeful future of the aviation series.

The Heinlein juveniles are set in what science fictionists call "the near future." This is an era obviously in the future, but not so far removed that daily life has been totally changed. Thus, the young characters may be more technically sophisticated than readers of the same age, better-schooled and more scientifically aware, but they are otherwise recognizable as American adolescents. They attend high school, college, or service academies. They earn pocket money doing chores or working part-time jobs in local businesses. They take part in conventional social events such as dances or Scouting, they date and socialize at local ice cream parlors, and they experience the jealousies and antagonisms of 1950s teenagers. Because the characters are so closely linked to their intended audience and, as a result, so easily identified with, their acceptance of the technically sophisticated world in which they live makes that world still more credible.

Far more incredible is the "distant future" world of the last two space series, the "Tom Corbett, Space Cadet" series by "Carey Rockwell" (1952–1956; eight titles) and the "Lucky Starr Adventures" (1952–1958; six titles) by "Paul French." Neither series makes more than a token effort to evoke current events and developments, and neither pauses to reflect more than briefly upon the implications of the future society it describes. Both present, instead, a distant future when the solar system, if not the galaxy, has been colonized, when a single government oversees the welfare of citizens of all the planets, and when that government is influenced, if not led, by the work of an elite coalition of scientists.

Tom Corbett's society, ironically, begins in Heinlein's. Television producers saw the dramatic possibilities of *Space Cadet,* bought video rights to the book, and, in 1950, launched the television series, *Tom Corbett, Space Cadet* (1950–1955). Heinlein early on disavowed any credit for the series (it had, he wrote, "the high moral standards of soap opera"), but its popularity made it one of the first television series to spin off licensed products.[29] "Tom Corbett" products of various sorts, from games to lunch boxes, quickly appeared on the market, and in 1952, their sales led to the first of the "Tom Corbett" books. These were written by the pseudonymous "Carey Rockwell," but made at least a small gesture toward technological authenticity; Willy Ley's name appeared on the title page as "Technical Adviser."

Apart from their invocation of Ley as an authority, the books are purest space opera. In the first, *Stand By for Mars* (1952), young Tom Corbett enters the Space Academy as a cadet in the Solar Guard, where he meets fellow cadets Astro, a Venusian who is a propulsion specialist, and Roger Manning, an electronics genius. After early friction (Roger, son of a space hero, is trying to make his way on his own merits, freed from his father's reputation), the three meld into a team, salvage a stranded space liner, and survive a gruelling trek across the Martian landscape. *Danger in Deep Space* (1953) takes them to Venusport, where they ready a spaceship for conversion to hyperdrive. They travel by hyperdrive to Tara, a planet of Alpha Centauri, thwart an effort to take over a copper-rich Moon of the planet, and bring the entire satellite back to the solar system using a series of controlled atomic explosions.

Later titles are, if anything, more melodramatic. In *On the Trail of the Space Pirates* (1953) the three foil attacks upon space liners laden with wealthy passengers. They travel thirteen light years to the planet Roald in *The Space Pioneers* (1953), screening applicants for colonization and putting down a revolt fomented by Roald's governor. There's yet another uprising in *The*

Revolt on Venus (1956), when a Venusian nationalist movement tries unsuccessfully to overthrow the colonial government of the Solar Alliance and establish its independence. *Treachery in Outer Space* (1954) tracks a space race to Titan, a uranium-rich satellite of Jupiter, while *Sabotage in Space* (1955) has Tom, Astro, and Roger helping to perfect a method of automated freight service through space. In the final volume, *The Robot Rocket* (1956), Roger is transferred to Mars Academy, while Tom, Astro, and their new companion, cadet T.J. Thistle, travel to a planet of Sirius to investigate the disappearance of a survey rocket.

The stories are set a precise four centuries in the future—2353 to 2356—and posit a society based upon highly advanced science and technology. Automated surface transports crisscross the American landscape, and rocket craft ply the atmosphere. At the heart of the society is cooperation. An officer at the Space Academy tells the cadets that "The unit is the backbone of the Academy. . . . Three men who could be taught to think, feel and act as one intelligent brain," and the Solar Alliance itself is "a unified society of billions of people who lived in peace with one another though sprawled throughout the universe."[30] The Solar Guard itself, founded in the twenty-second century, is the protector of the Alliance, striving through the Academy to assure that "the society we're building now will be in the hands of imaginative men trained for the job of leadership, and with an understanding of what the word *progress* means."[31] Social good outweighs individual good, and the efforts of the best and the brightest must be united to confirm that good.

The scientific aristocracy implicit in the "Tom Corbett" stories comes to the fore in the "Lucky Starr Adventure" books. Written by biochemist and science-fiction author Isaac Asimov using the name "Paul French," the books follow the exploits of young David "Lucky" Starr, the orphaned son of scientists Lawrence and Barbara Starr. David, a member of the Council of Science in an unspecified distant future, investigates various threats to the Galactic Union. Asimov contends in later editions of the books that he worked with the best available information concerning the characteristics of Mars, Venus, and other solar planets, but the books draw far more heavily upon science-fiction conventions than upon science fact. Indeed, there's an aura of the much later *Star Trek* about the tales. Force fields for protection, blast guns for combat, diamagnetic cushions and pseudo-grav fields to provide comfort in space, and proton micro-reactors to power hyper-atomic drives crop up frequently, and David encounters bizarre alien creatures that range from spectral beings on Mars to Venusian V-frogs that work as telepathic amplifiers.

David experiences a series of swashbuckling space adventures. Teaming with the loud-mouthed Martian farmer John "Bigman" Jones, he uncovers random poisonings in Martian foods being exported to Earth, space pirates operating in the asteroids, and sabotage threats to the domed underwater cities of Venus. In his personal spaceship, *The Shooting Starr,* he zips to Mercury to protect a light-manipulating project, to Jupiter to trouble-shoot a gravity-conversion project, and finally to Saturn to counter a Sirian effort to colonize the Saturnian satellites and provoke interstellar war with Earth. (As a 1954 reviewer remarked, he "scoots outrageously around the solar system . . . , with no particular regard for scientific plausibility."[32]) His status as a councilman opens doors for him wherever he goes, for the Council of Science wields enormous power throughout the solar system.

That council, Asimov reports, came about because, "when science really permeated all human society and culture, scientists could no longer restrict themselves to their laboratories." It was originally conceived as a body to advise the government on extra-terrestrial matters, for "only trained scientists could have sufficient information to make intelligent decisions." As colonization spread, however, the council evolved first into a counterespionage agency, then into a governmental power in its own right. "Into its own hands it was drawing more and more of the threads of government [so that] through its activities there might grow, someday, a great Empire of the Milky Way in which all men might live in peace and harmony."[33] Here, then, is the culmination of the movement that began so many years before, with airship and airplane experimentation in the early days of the twentieth century. The solitary workshop tinkerer and his wire-and-fabric flying machine have evolved into a corporate technocracy with hyper-atomic spaceships. Dreams of reshaping a national society through the agency of the air have become visions of an empire stretching throughout the Milky Way. "Science," which once could be mastered by a single (albeit eccentric) person, has grown so complex that a council is needed to oversee its consequences, and the council itself seems likely to be the next phase of government. The future that is likely to come about is a world of staggering complexity, far removed from that of "The Airship Boys" and "The Boy Aviators," and its complexities put an end to the clean simplicity of the aeronautical society.[34]

* * *

For forty years and more, the aviation series books fed the dream of flight in the minds and hearts of American boys. The adult world had no need of such works. Daily reports in newspapers, weekly and monthly reports in the technical and popular press, and articles and stories in pulp productions such as Hugo Gernsback's *Air Wonder Stories* of the 1920s and 1930s supplied all the information an adult aviation enthusiast might desire. If the young were to benefit from the newest and most dramatic form of progress, though, the information had to be shaped and interpreted to increase its appeal, and so the aviation series books (and later the model-making press) came into being. Drawing upon the factual reports of the more technical press, and paralleling the development of aviation in America, the series-book authors advanced an aviation-oriented vision of the future for their young readers.

Even in the earliest stages of the aviation series, authors strove to give aircraft and their capabilities some degree of authenticity. Though the earliest series trafficked more in melodrama than in technology, factual matter had its place. Authors who were themselves perhaps unversed in aviation detail turned to those who were, with the result that the stories freely mingled elements of the latest, most current aeronautical developments with more fantastic elements. These developments extended even to the theoretical, as the early writers' reliance upon the sometimes polemical writings of Victor Lougheed and Alphonse Berget led them into the debates over stability and instability, Langley versus Montgomery, tandem wings versus "stacked" biplane wings. Even in the first decade of the aviation books, readers were becoming aware of, and informed about, issues and ideas in aeronautics.

Those earliest books, like the "Boy Aviators" stories that Roger Bilstein cites in his *Flight in America,* are little more than adventure stories onto which airships and airplanes have been grafted. They make relatively little claim to plausibility or technical accuracy, yet lay the groundwork for developments to come. They reverently invoke the great names of early flying (e.g., the Wright Brothers, Glenn E. Curtiss, John J. Montgomery, Alberto Santos-Dumont, or Louis Blériot) and frequently allude to their achievements. Capturing the spirit of the "birdman era," they acquaint their readers with the vocabulary of flight, suggest at least some of the increasing accessibility and potential of flight as the airplane is perfected, and link flight to adventure, patriotism, and progress.[35]

The events of World War I, the ready availability of aircraft as military airplanes were sold off following the war, and the public acclaim following Charles Lindbergh's 1927 crossing of the Atlantic contribute to a larger, more sophisticated, and more realistic group of books. Tales of combat flying come to the fore during the war years, and extend their appeal well into the early 1930s. If the World War I books at times temper the romantic view of "the ace" with a sanitized but still realistic portrayal of combat's dangers, they stress the appeal of open-cockpit flying and the camaraderie of the air. Reports of the war provided new technical material for the series writers, and the romanticizing of "the ace" contributed to the evolving image of "the aviator" as a paragon of American integrity and manhood.

More generally, the stories take up the process of learning to fly, the publicity associated with the setting of records, and the steady development of aviation technology, civil as well as military. Increasingly, they call attention to the special qualities of "the aviator" and present aviation as a venue for individual growth in which a person can readily make a living and (quite often) attain public prominence. This was the message conveyed by the real-life Charles Lindbergh, who, as bachelor barnstormer and married explorer, made his presence felt in every aspect of American flight. His achievements, whether in day-to-day flying, commercial airline work, or world exploration, made him the model for several of the most memorable series heroes, and the books preached the merits of flight as passionately as Lindbergh himself.

As aviation technology develops, the books follow along, so that, by the time of World War II and the immediate post-war period, they offer stories of aeronautical assimilation. In these books, aviation, commercial and civil as well as military, is a fully developed, fully integrated, wholly practical part of American national life. The stories document how general aviation offers the freedom of flight to the ordinary citizen. They extol the importance of commercial aviation and its contributions to mail, freight, and business and recreational travel. Furthermore, they make a case for how military aviation has proven itself and contributes to the United States' stature as a significant world power. In all these realms, the books present the airplane as an inherent part of everyday life. It is a device to be reckoned with, and society itself is adjusting to the benefits and the hazards that aviation generates. The books, therefore, dramatize the trajectory of aviation history in America and convey that history to America's youth.

A second contribution of the books is their reliance upon common themes, elements, and attitudes as they bring the story of aviation to their young readers. One such common element is their presentation of the backgrounds of flight, for they set aviation in a broad historical context rarely found in other series types, technological or non-technological. They establish that ideas do not occur in a vacuum. They suggest the extent to which aviators of other countries (initially England and France, and, later, Germany) contribute to the development of flight, and they reveal the developing range of aviation's potential as a practical adjunct to all aspects of life.

Another common element is the message that aviation progress is incremental and accretive. As they talk of the course of aircraft development, the books establish how the inventions of one person and one era lead to those of another. Their readers quietly learn that technological progress depends upon many participants. The lone inventor in his workshop continues to recur as a staple of technological fiction, but in aviation he draws upon the work of many others before him. This vision of technology leads to yet another motif: In an increasingly mechanized society, familiarity with, and mastery of, technology is essential. If a person is to become an active, contributing citizen of the present, he must at the very least be aware of the technologies about him. Still more particularly, they suggest, the person adept at aviation technology is the one who will most readily shape the world. The airplane is the vehicle of the future, and all of society's functions will be based upon it.

From this suggestion follows a third common element: the sense that aviation is changing the world. Speed, endurance, and distance records publicize the growing capabilities of the airplane, and those capabilities convey another, more serious message. The airplane breaks down the barriers of distance, and the result can only be good. Harry F. Guggenheim, president of the Daniel Guggenheim Fund for the Promotion of Aeronautics, writing in *The Seven Skies* (1930), remarks: "The airplane gives to man a new freedom, eliminating the geographical barriers of river, sea, mountain and desert between him and his kind, and thus eliminating those prejudices and misunderstandings which have jeopardised human relations in the past."[36] Guggenheim's views derive from the accomplishments of the Guggenheim Fund in advancing such accomplishments as blind flying and a stall-proof, "safety" airplane, but the series books anticipate him. Well before he speaks to the adult world, the series books offer the same views to young readers.

The books' vision of flight as a shaping force in society leads to a still larger recurring motif. This is the belief that "aviation" and its practitioners make up a notable, distinctive sub-culture within American life. From the very beginning of the flying series, the books dwell upon the personal demands of the art. Flying has special requirements: physical and mental prowess, judgment and prudence, conscientiousness and precision. Only those willing to accept aviation's physical, emotional, and intellectual challenges will prosper. "The aviator" or "the pilot" recognizes that flying is not a vocation for the lazy, the careless, or the ignorant, and constantly seeks to improve his capabilities.

For all its special demands, however, aviation is a singularly democratic enterprise. Its heroes come from all walks of life, linked solely by their devotion to flight and their determination to master its needs. Whether the flier is formally or informally educated, theoretically or practically trained, there is a role for him in aviation. The extent of that role, moreover, is limited only by his own skills and application. The world of aviation is a microcosm, embracing the same range of abilities and morals that appears in the larger world. It occasionally has its weak and its corrupt to counter its more dominant capable and upright, but these failures are quickly weeded out, sometimes foiled by the unflappable integrity of the aviator hero, at other times destroyed by their flouting of the laws of the air. The flying world offers a unique opportunity for a person—*any* person—to prosper if only he has the will and the strength of character to persevere. In this respect, the democratic spirit of the series books is a characteristically American one, harking back at least to Benjamin Franklin. The spirit presents the United States as a society of self-made entrepreneurs, and instills in its young readers a sense of the opportunities to be found in American life. The series extend that opportunity to aviation and its related fields, and the lesson is an important one.

As their depiction of what flight can offer as well as what it demands develops, the books move to yet another level of realization. They present the airman's life as demanding but fulfilling, and they extend that fulfillment even to the aviator's character. The "purity of the air," which all pilots encounter, can, and will, change a person. The person who masters flying skills will necessarily be touched by the transformational qualities of flight, and will inevitably change for the better. Flying will give to mankind—and the American citizenry, in particular—the opportunity and the means to rise above itself, to become higher, greater, and finer than ordinary life permits. The individual who gives himself over to flight will become somehow larger than life, somehow more than human, a "birdman" in the largest and most evocative sense of the term.

These messages go to three generations of American youth, and the series books, by their sheer numbers and rampant popularity in their heyday, establish their importance as interpreters of technological history. For their young readers, they supply access to a world of facts, ideas, and values, and bring the added message that these elements are stimulating, even exciting. They offer a glimpse into the process of popularization, as complex processes are described and made attractive. They provide a conduit for information, as the latest developments in technology are passed along to avid young readers. They advance an interpretation of those developments, presenting technology as romantic and its mastery as desirable. And they constitute the manner in which one generation speaks to the next, conveying to the young an idealistic way of looking at the world and thinking of the future. They give faces and forms to successful practitioners of aviation, and they leave their readers with the resounding message that they, too, can be a part of this world.

The very technology the aviation series celebrated contributed to their demise. The later world of flight is far removed from, even foreign to, that of the series books, with jet engines, rocket planes, and nuclear-powered starships supplanting Whirlwind engines and magneto compasses. The young people who will populate it are also a far cry from those of the traditional world of flight. They are no longer fliers *as such;* their skills at the control panel are secondary to other interests and the socio-scientific commitments that dominate their lives, as flying itself once dominated the lives of Ted Scott and "Lucky" Terrell. They are a well-educated population, technologically sophisticated and socially concerned, their eyes turned to the planets and the stars and their motives as idealistic as ever, but they are, as a people, no longer a part of the purely aeronautical world.

Their lives are tellingly different from those of the flying heroes. They are proficient in science (echoing, perhaps, James Doolittle's doctorate in aeronautical engineering), and that science dominates their activities far more than flying once did. They are, increasingly, young persons in the military or involved in comparably large, organized, social undertakings—the protecting of global security, the colonization and terraforming of a planet, the creating of a galactic government—whereas once their individual mastery of flight enabled them to establish and proclaim the individual's role in maintaining social responsibility. And they are young persons caught up in the sweep of events. They are part of an immense socio-political construct, and, while they can at times affect its actions and the consequences, they are no longer able, as individuals, to control it. Theirs is a future unimaginable in the era of Ted Scott.

Yet the old ways die hard. The authoritative *Aviation Week* magazine (once the authoritative *Aviation* and to become, in 1958, the equally authoritative *Aviation Week & Space Technology*) evidences this in an in-house advertisement published in early 1950. The presentation features a full-page photograph of a starry-eyed boy looking upward; the accompanying text, on the facing page, is addressed to "The kid that once was you:"

> As you watch him, you know he is not with you at all. He is piloting a plane through wind and clouds to the stars. He is no longer Earth-bound—but a man with wings.

> You know what he is thinking, for, once you stood somewhere—in a window, at a school desk, on a hill—and had the same dream of glory.
>
> * * * *
>
> When you were a youngster, chances are your first love affair was with a wire-strutted Jenny, or later, with a Winnie Mae, or a Spirit of St. Louis. Today's youngsters are enchanted with a Buck Rogers world come true—sleek, streamlined rocket planes; planes without pilots; jet- propelled planes that fly faster than sound.
>
> All of these are a part of modern aviation. It is a world fantastic beyond belief.[37]

The context is that of 1950, but the voice is that of the series books.

As the advertisement links the wonders of flight to the developments of the future, it recreates the aura of the past. It speaks of flight and fliers in ways reminiscent of the series: "a man with wings" consumed by a "love affair" that leads to a "dream of glory." It speaks only generally of rockets and jet-propelled craft, but explicitly invokes "a wire-strutted Jenny," the *Winnie Mae,* and *The Spirit of St. Louis,* while the ghostly figures of Wiley Post and Charles Lindbergh hover in the background. It is addressed to the very persons who read the series books—the young readers who have heeded the call of flight, have grown to adulthood and, by their work, are shaping the world of flight to come. Techniques and technology may change, the text asserts, but the inherent appeal of flight continues to evoke a passionate, deep-seated, and wondering response. Just as their lives were changed by the early generations of flight, so, too, will today's young persons have their lives changed by the later generations. It is a hopeful dream, however unlikely the chances of its realization. The advent of television stole the audience of the series books, and aerospace technology outstripped the capabilities of the backyard builder and the individualistic hero. Advertising's appeal to the mystique notwithstanding, the era of the lone eagle of the air was ended.

Walt Whitman, writing in the national centennial year of 1876, proclaimed the locomotive as "Type of the modern—emblem of motion and power—pulse of the continent," a creation whose roar and whistle echoed across the American prairies and "To the free skies unpent and glad and strong." It is a strikingly apposite metaphor for its times, yet, in a bit more than a quarter of a century, it is supplanted by a corresponding sense of the airplane. Just as the railroad captured the imagination of the 19th century, the airplane captures that of the 20th. For the American nation, the airplane becomes a machine of singular, even supernal possibilities, a unique means to advance the nation's fortunes and potential. Harry F. Guggenheim comments in 1930 that aviation (and, in particular, Charles A. Lindbergh's trans-Atlantic flight) "was indeed an inspiration for those 'immortal longings,' for those 'thoughts which sweep the heavens and wander through eternity.'" He, like the series books that preceded and followed his remarks, expresses what Joseph J. Corn calls the "messianic thrust of the winged gospel," the vision of a progressive future made cleaner and purer by the influence of the air.[38]

Corn bases his conclusions upon an extensive range of public and popular sources, from government documents and newspapers to film and radio. As he does so, he remarks that "it was only in the United States that enthusiasm over the airplane gave rise to anything like the winged gospel," and goes on to note the conscious efforts of advocates of aviation to capture the interest of the young with comic strips, model-making clubs, contests, and other activities.[39] He makes no mention of the boys' aviation series books as aiding in that capture, but he could easily have added them to his chronicle. In book after book the series writers spelled out the history, the expectations, and the possibilities of flight, linking it with adventure, with commerce, and with romance, and communicating it to the young in the most positive and appealing of manners.

Building upon the dreams of youth and the larger social trends of their times, the aviation books constitute a body of work of uncommon historical import. Throughout their run they consistently project a sense of a progressive future, and their message is not lost upon the air-minded youngsters toward whom they are directed. The stories hold out the possibility of a flying society shaped by air-minded youth. Those youths will grow to maturity, prominence, and influence. When they are able at last to lead their society and their world, they will put into place the lessons they have learned from aviation. For almost half a century, the aviation series held out the golden dream of a better world to come. Progressive America will lead the way, but, through the agency of popularly accessible aviation as it spreads throughout the world, all mankind will ascend to a new and higher level of human capability. It is an admirable, worthy vision, and its tragedy is that the reality of world events and the accelerating course of technology worked to frustrate its realization.

NOTES TO CHAPTER EIGHT

1 Maj. Gen Kenneth B. Wolfe, "We Must Retain Technological Supremacy," *Aviation,* 44 (February 1945): 113–115; Roy Healy, "Aeronautical Supremacy Demands Jet and Rocket Research," *Aviation,* 44 (July 1945, August 1945): 152–154, 149–151.

2 Herb Powell, "The Atomic Frame of Reference—Or Else," *Aviation,* 44 (September 1945): 106–107, 244–252.

3 The Editor [John W. Campbell, Jr.], "Air Trails and New Frontiers," *Air Trails Pictorial,* 26 (September 1946): 22–23.

4 Andrew R. Boone, "Beyond the Speed of Sound," *Air Trails Pictorial,* 25 (December 1945): 26–28, 105–108; James L.H. Peck, "1,000 Miles an Hour," *Air Trails Pictorial,* 26 (September 1946): 24–27, 70–72; "Flash," *Model Airplane News,* 35 (August 1946): 2; "Flash," *Model Airplane News,* 35 (September 1948): 2.

5 "The XS-1," *Western Flying,* 27 (January 1947): 18–19; Robert McLarren, "Bell XS-1: Plane on the Cover," *Model Airplane News,* 36 (March 1947): 25, 83–86; Robert McLarren, "XS-1: Design and Development," *Aviation Week,* 49 (26 July 1948): 22–27; Edward H. Heinemann, "The Skystreak," *Western Flying,* 27 (March 1947): 18–19, 38; Robert McLarren, "Douglas Unveils Its New Research Plane," *Aviation Week,* 47 (17 November 1947): 12–13; Richard G. Naugle, "Sweepback—the Supersonic Shape," *Air Trails Pictorial,* 29 (February 1948): 32–34, 102; Robert McLarren, "Swept Wing Taxes Piloting Skill," *Aviation Week,* 48 (8 March 1948): 30; "Man Girds for Supersonic Role," *Aviation Week,* 49 (27 September 1948): 21–24; Robert McLarren, "How Delta-Wing Aids High-Speed Flight," *Aviation Week,* 51 (4 July 1949): 21–24.

6 Dr. Martin Summerfield, "The Rocket's Future Influence on Transport Designs," *Aviation,* 45 (January 1946): 73–76; E.J. Tangerman, "Can We Catch Up in Rocket Research?" *Aviation,* 45 (June 1946): 40–41, 148–150; Willy Ley, "V-2—and Beyond," *Air Trails Pictorial,* 25 (March 1946): 26–28, 109–114; Willy Ley, "V-2—and Beyond," *Air Trails Pictorial,* 25 (April 1946): 36–38, 108–110; Curtis Fuller, "Uncle Sam 'Discovers' the Rocket," *Flying,* 40 (March 1947): 28–29, 72–76; "What's Ahead for Rockets?" *Aviation Week,* 49 (5 July 1948): 23; "How High Is Up?" *Aviation Week,* 50 (6 June 1949): 14.

7 Maj. Charles M. Fischer, "Jet Lightplanes?" *Flying,* 36 (June 1945): 31, 120–21.

8 Robert McLarren, "British Jet Transport Makes First Flight," *Aviation Week,* 51 (8 August 1949): 12–13; "Lockheed's Proposals for Jet Transports," *Aviation Week,* 52 (9 January 1950): 13–15; "Boeing Testing," *Aviation Week,* 53 (24 July 1950): 16–17; Peter M. Bowers, *Boeing Aircraft Since 1916,* 2nd edn. (New York: Funk & Wagnalls, 1968), 348–351.

9 "Birth of the Fireball," *Western Flying,* 26 (February 1946): 34–35, 56; Vice-Adm. A.W. Radford, USN, "Navy Planes—Today and Beyond," *Aero Digest,* 54 (January 1947): 96, 205–206; "Shipboard Jets," *Western Flying,* 27 (July 1947): 26–28, 36; Lieut. Comdr. William H. Huff, USN, "Jets at Sea," *Flying,* 41 (July 1946): 46–47, 76–80; "Navy Orders 1,632 New Planes," *Aviation Week,* 48 (12 January 1948): 13–14; "Jet Plane Problems On Aircraft Carriers," *Western Flying,* 28 (May 1948): 9, 18; Robert Hotz, "Navy Unwraps Its Fastest Fighter," *Aviation Week,* 49 (29 November 1948): 12–13.

10 "Air Force Reveals New Orders For 1,150 Military Planes," *Aviation Week,* 48 (5 January 1948): 12–13.

11 "Supersonic Plane and Jet Bombers Revealed by Army Air Forces," *Aviation,* 45 (July 1946): 68–69; "New AAF Jet-Rocket Fighters Designed for Supersonic Speeds," *Aviation Week,* 47 (21 July 1947): 11–12; "Swept Wing XP-86 Readied for Flight," *Aviation Week,* 47 (6 October 1947): 14; "Boeing Stratojet Bomber Heralds Transonic Combat," *Aviation Week.* 47 (22 September 1947): 14–15; Robert McLarren, "Plane On the Cover: Boeing XB-47," *Model Airplane News,* 38 (January 1948): 15, 60–62; Capt. S.R. Rechenschieber, "The Mighty B-47," *Flying,* 45 (August 1949): 15–17, 62–64; The Staff of *Flying,* "Jets of the U.S. Air Forces," *Flying,* 43 (December 1948): 17–27, 71–72.

12 Malcolm Cagle, "Are Single-Seat Fighters Out?" *Flying,* 43 (August 1948): 32–33, 74–75; Harland Wilson, "Flying the Jet . . . ," *Flying,* 43 (December 1948): 28–29, 76–77; Frank Tinsley, "Last of the Fighters," *Air Trails,* 33 (January 1950): 23–25; "Bail Out Babies," *Western Flying,* 30 (May 1950): 12; "Pilot-Scientists," *Aviation Week,* 52 (20 March 1950): 36–37. Robert McLarren raised the question of whether pilots could endure the physical and mental demands of greater speeds in 1939, in his "The Bomber Catcher," an account of the Lockheed XP-38 published in *Model Airplane News* 20 (May 1939): 19, 28–30.

13 William Roger, "Push-Button Warfare," *Flying,* 38 (February 1946): 38–39, 106–110; James L.H. Peck, "Can the Atom Bomb be Stopped?" *Air Trails Pictorial,* 26 (August 1946): 24–27, 68–72; William Winter, "The Push-Button War Fable," *Flying,* 41 (October 1947): 47–49, 71–72; J. William Welsh, "Will Subs Launch the Atom Air War?" *Flying,* 43 (November 1948): 20–21, 50–52; Robert H. Wood, "Editorial: Overselling the Missile," *Aviation Week,* 53 (31 July 1950): 46.

14 Willy Ley, "Atomic Engines," *Air Trails Pictorial,* 25 (January 1946): 24–25, 72–74; Dr. Luis W. Alvarez, "There is No Obvious or Simple Way in Which to Use Atomic Energy for Space Ships," *U.S. Air Services,* 32 (January 1947): 9–10, 26; Andrew Kalitinsky, "Atomic Power for Aircraft," *Aero Digest,* 57 (August 1948): 58–59, 121–123; Andrew Kalitinsky, "Atomic Engines for Aircraft," *Western Flying,* 28 (October 1948): 11, 24–26; Andrew Kalitinsky, "Atomic Engines for Aircraft," *Flying,* 44 (January 1949): 22–23, 52–54; William Winter, "Atom Powered Bombers," *Air Trails,* 32 (May 1949): 21–23, 85–89.

15 Fred W. Kraft, "Rocketing to the Moon," *U.S. Air Services,* 32 (July 1947): 15–16; F.R. Stout, "Airline to the Moon?" *Flying,* 39 (November 1946): 27–29, 68–72; Willy Ley, "Outward Bound," *Air Trails Pictorial,* 27 (November 1946): 28–33, 80–99; The Editor [John W. Campbell, Jr.], "Born Gambler," *Air Trails and Science Frontiers,* 28 (May 1947): 20–21; Capt. B.A. Northrop, "Fortress in the Sky," *Air Trails and Science Frontiers,* 28 (May 1947): 22–27, 70–74.

16 Arthur V. St. Germain, "The Conquest of Interplanetary Space," *Western Flying.* 27 (October 1947, November 1947): 14–15; 20, 26; Robert McLarren, "'Escape'-Rocket Design Research Indicates Practical Solution Near," *Aviation Week,* 48 (1 March 1948): 23; R.P. Haviland, "Can We Build a Station in Space?" *Flying,* 44 (May 1949): 19–21, 68–70; [H.S. Tsien], "Considerations on the 3,000-Mile Rocket Liner," *Western Flying,* 30 (November 1950): 20–22, 26.

17 "Flash," *Model Airplane News,* 32 (March 1945): 6–7; Curtis Fuller, "The Flying Saucers—Fact or Fiction?" *Flying,* 47 (July 1950): 16–17, 59–61; Dennis Stacy, "When Pilots See UFOs," *Air & Space/Smithsonian,* 2 (December 1987/January 1988): 96–103. For a careful and dispassionate evaluation of the flying saucer phenomenon, see Curtis Peebles, *Watch the Skies! A Chronicle of the Flying Saucer Myth* (Washington, DC: Smithsonian Institution Press, 1994).

18 For backgrounds, see Paul A. Carter, *The Creation of Tomorrow: Fifty Years of Magazine Science Fiction* (New York: Columbia University Press, 1977), and Fred Erisman, "Stratemeyer Boys' Books and the Gernsback Milieu," *Extrapolation,* 41 (Fall 2000): 272–282.

19 Howard R. Garis, *Rocket Riders Across the Ice or, Racing Against Time* (New York: A.L. Burt, 1933), unpaged.

20 Garis, *Rocket Riders Across the Ice,* 66, 123.

21 Howard R. Garis, *Rocket Riders in Stormy Seas, or, Trailing the Treasure Divers* (New York: A.L. Burt, 1933), 23; Howard R. Garis, *Rocket Riders in the Air, or, A Chase in the Clouds* (New York: A.L. Burt, 1934), 67, 104–105.

22 C.H. Claudy, "Aircraft of the Future," *Scientific American,* 123 (20 November 1920): 520.

23 George F. Pierrot, ["Introductory Note"], Carl H. Claudy, *The Mystery Men of Mars* (New York: Grosset & Dunlap, 1933), unpaged. This note introduces the second and third volumes as well.

24 Claudy, *Mystery Men of Mars,* 16–17; Carl H. Claudy, *A Thousand Years a Minute* (New York: Grosset & Dunlap, 1933), 28–31; Carl H. Claudy, *The Land of No Shadow* (New York: Grosset & Dunlap, 1933), 37–42; Carl H. Claudy, *The Blue Grotto Terror* (New York: Grosset & Dunlap, 1934), 12.

25 Harry K. Hudson, *A Bibliography of Hard-Cover, Series Type Boys Books.* Revised edn. (Tampa, FL: Data Print, 1977), 181–182.

26 John Blaine [pseud. Harold L. Goodwin and Peter J. Harkins], *The Whispering Box Mystery* (New York: Grosset & Dunlap, 1948), 115.

27 H. Bruce Franklin, *Robert A. Heinlein: America as Science Fiction* (New York: Oxford University Press, 1980), 213.

28 Robert A. Heinlein, *Expanded Universe* (New York: Ace Books, 1980), 145; Robert A. Heinlein, *Grumbles from the Grave,* ed. Virginia Heinlein (New York: Ballantine Books, 1989), 41–43.

29 Heinlein, *Grumbles from the Grave,* 45. For a brief history of the "Tom Corbett" television program, see Frank Kuznik, "The Original Space Cadet," *Air & Space/Smithsonian,* 10 (April/May 1995): 68–75.

30 Carey Rockwell [pseud.], *Stand By for Mars!* (New York: Grosset & Dunlap, 1952), 40; Carey Rockwell [pseud.], *On the Trail of the Space Pirates* (New York: Grosset & Dunlap, 1953), 7.

31 Carey Rockwell [pseud.], *The Robot Rocket* (New York: Grosset & Dunlap, 1956), 30.

32 P. Schuyler Miller, "The Reference Library," *Astounding Science Fiction,* 54 (November 1954): 141–146.

33 Paul French [Isaac Asimov], *Lucky Starr and the Oceans of Venus.* 1954 (Greenwich, CT: Fawcett, 1978), 33–34.

34 Howard E. McCurdy, *Space and the American Imagination* (Washington, DC: Smithsonian Institution Press, 1997), is a thoughtful consideration of the growing public awareness of rocketry and space flight.

35 Roger A. Bilstein, *Flight in America: From the Wrights to the Astronauts.* Revised edn. (Baltimore: John Hopkins University Press, 1994), 19.

36 Harry F. Guggenheim, *The Seven Skies* (New York: G.P. Putnam's Sons, 1930), 12.

37 "The kid that once was you . . ." [*Aviation Week* advertisement], *Aviation Week,* 52 (6 March 1950): 26–27.

[38] Walt Whitman, "To a Locomotive in Winter, *The Best of Whitman*. Ed. Harold W. Blodgett. (New York: Ronald Press, 1953), 276–77; Guggenheim, *The Seven Skies,* 104; Joseph J. Corn, *The Winged Gospel: America's Romance with Aviation, 1900–1950* (New York: Oxford University Press, 1983), 34.

[39] Corn, *Winged Gospel,* 44.

Bibliography

I. Archival Sources

The Hess Collection of Dime Novels and Series Books, Children's Literature Research Collections, University of Minnesota, Minneapolis.

National Air and Space Museum Library and Archives, Smithsonian Institution, Washington, DC.

Stratemeyer Syndicate Records, Archives and Manuscripts Division, New York Public Library, Astor, Lenox, and Tilden Foundations.

II. Primary Sources (Series Books)

Adams, Eustace L. *Across the Top of the World*. New York: Grosset & Dunlap, 1931.

———. *Doomed Demons*. New York: Grosset & Dunlap, 1935.

———. *Fifteen Days in the Air*. New York: Grosset & Dunlap, 1928.

———. *The Flying Windmill*. New York: Grosset & Dunlap, 1930.

———. *The Mysterious Monoplane*. New York: Grosset & Dunlap, 1930.

———. *On the Wings of Flame*. New York: Grosset & Dunlap, 1929.

———. *Over the Polar Ice*. New York: Grosset & Dunlap, 1928.

———. *Pirates of the Air*. New York: Grosset & Dunlap, 1929.

———. *The Plane Without a Pilot*. New York: Grosset & Dunlap, 1930.

———. *Prisoners of the Clouds*. New York: Grosset & Dunlap, 1932.

———. *Racing Around the World*. New York: Grosset & Dunlap, 1928.

———. *The Runaway Airship*. New York: Grosset & Dunlap, 1928.

———. *War Wings*. New York: Grosset & Dunlap, 1937.

———. *Wings of Adventure*. New York: Grosset & Dunlap, 1931.

———. *Wings of the Navy*. New York: Grosset & Dunlap, 1936.

Appleton, Victor [Howard R. Garis]. *Tom Swift and His Sky Racer; or the Quickest Flight on Record*. New York: Grosset & Dunlap, 1911.

——— [Howard R. Garis]. *Tom Swift and His Wireless Message; or the Castaways of Earthquake Island*. New York: Grosset & Dunlap, 1911.

Arnold, Major Henry H. *Bill Bruce and the Pioneer Aviators*. New York: A.L. Burt, 1928.

———. *Bill Bruce Becomes an Ace*. New York: A.L. Burt, 1928.

———. *Bill Bruce in the Trans-Continental Race*. New York: A.L. Burt, 1928.

———. *Bill Bruce on Border Patrol*. New York: A.L. Burt, 1928.

———. *Bill Bruce on Forest Patrol*. New York: A.L. Burt, 1928.

———. *Bill Bruce, the Flying Cadet*. New York: A.L. Burt, 1928.

Avery, Al [Rutherford G. Montgomery]. *A Yankee Flier in Italy*. New York: Grosset & Dunlap, 1944.

——— [Rutherford G. Montgomery]. *A Yankee Flier in Normandy*. New York: Grosset & Dunlap, 1945.

——— [Rutherford G. Montgomery]. *A Yankee Flier in North Africa*. New York: Grosset & Dunlap, 1943.

——— [Rutherford G. Montgomery]. *A Yankee Flier in the Far East*. New York: Grosset & Dunlap, 1942.

——— [Rutherford G. Montgomery]. *A Yankee Flier in the South Pacific*. New York: Grosset & Dunlap, 1943.

——— [Rutherford G. Montgomery]. *A Yankee Flier on a Rescue Mission*. New York: Grosset & Dunlap, 1945.

——— [Rutherford G. Montgomery]. *A Yankee Flier Over Berlin*. New York: Grosset & Dunlap, 1944.

——— [Rutherford G. Montgomery]. *A Yankee Flier Under Secret Orders*. New York: Grosset & Dunlap, 1946.

——— [Rutherford G. Montgomery]. *A Yankee Flier with the R.A.F.* New York: Grosset & Dunlap, 1941.

Beach, Charles Amory [St. George Rathborne]. *Air Service Boys Flying for France, or the Young Heroes of the Lafayette Escadrille*. Akron, OH: Saalfield Publishing Co., 1919.

——— [St. George Rathborne]. *Air Service Boys Flying for Victory, or Bombing the Last German Stronghold*. Cleveland, OH: Goldsmith Publishing Co., 1920.

——— [Howard R. Garis]. *Air Service Boys in the Big Battle, or Silencing the Big Guns*. Cleveland, OH: World Syndicate Publishing Co., 1919.

——— [St. George Rathborne]. *Air Service Boys Over the Atlantic, or the Longest Flight on Record*. Cleveland, OH: Goldsmith Publishing Co., 1920.

——— [St. George Rathborne]. *Air Service Boys Over the Enemy's Lines, or the German Spy's Secret*. Cleveland, OH: World Syndicate Publishing Co., 1919.

——— [Howard R. Garis]. *Air Service Boys Over the Rhine, or Fighting Above the Clouds*. New York: George Sully & Co., 1919.

Blaine, John [Harold L. Goodwin; Peter J. Harkins]. *100 Fathoms Under*. New York: Grosset & Dunlap, 1947.

——— [Harold L. Goodwin; Peter J. Harkins]. *The Blue Ghost Mystery*. New York: Grosset & Dunlap, 1960.

——— [Harold L. Goodwin; Peter J. Harkins]. *The Caves of Fear*. New York: Grosset & Dunlap, 1951.

——— [Harold L. Goodwin; Peter J. Harkins]. *The Egyptian Cat Mystery*. New York: Grosset & Dunlap, 1961.

——— [Harold L. Goodwin; Peter J. Harkins]. *The Electronic Mind Reader*. New York: Grosset & Dunlap, 1957.

——— [Harold L. Goodwin; Peter J. Harkins]. *The Flaming Mountain*. New York: Grosset & Dunlap, 1962.

——— [Harold L. Goodwin; Peter J. Harkins]. *The Golden Skull*. New York: Grosset & Dunlap, 1954.

——— [Harold L. Goodwin; Peter J. Harkins]. *The Lost City*. New York: Grosset & Dunlap, 1947.

——— [Harold L. Goodwin; Peter J. Harkins]. *The Phantom Shark*. New York: Grosset & Dunlap, 1949.

——— [Harold L. Goodwin; Peter J. Harkins]. *The Pirates of Shan*. New York: Grosset & Dunlap, 1958.

——— [Harold L. Goodwin; Peter J. Harkins]. *The Rocket's Shadow*. New York: Grosset & Dunlap, 1947.

——— [Harold L. Goodwin; Peter J. Harkins]. *The Ruby Ray Mystery*. New York: Grosset & Dunlap, 1964.

——— [Harold L. Goodwin; Peter J. Harkins]. *The Scarlet Lake Mystery*. New York: Grosset & Dunlap, 1958.

——— [Harold L. Goodwin; Peter J. Harkins]. *Sea Gold*. Grosset & Dunlap. New York, 1947.

——— [Harold L. Goodwin; Peter J. Harkins]. *Smugglers' Reef*. New York: Grosset & Dunlap, 1950.

——— [Harold L. Goodwin; Peter J. Harkins]. *Stairway to Danger*. New York: Grosset & Dunlap, 1952.

——— [Harold L. Goodwin; Peter J. Harkins]. *The Veiled Raiders*. New York: Grosset & Dunlap, 1965.

——— [Harold L. Goodwin; Peter J. Harkins]. *The Wailing Octopus*. New York: Grosset & Dunlap, 1956.

——— [Harold L. Goodwin; Peter J. Harkins]. *The Whispering Box Mystery*. New York: Grosset & Dunlap, 1948.

Bowen, R. Sidney. *Dave Dawson at Casablanca*. Akron, OH: Saalfield Publishing Co., 1944.

———. *Dave Dawson at Dunkirk*. New York: Crown Publishers, 1941.

———. *Dave Dawson at Singapore*. New York: Crown Publishers, 1942.

———. *Dave Dawson at Truk*. New York: Crown Publishers, 1946.

———. *Dave Dawson in Libya*. Akron, OH: Saalfield Publishing Co., 1941.

———. *Dave Dawson on Convoy Patrol*. Akron, OH: Saalfield Publishing Co., 1941.

———. *Dave Dawson on Guadalcanal*. Akron, OH: Saalfield Publishing Co., 1943.

———. *Dave Dawson on the Russian Front*. Akron, OH: Saalfield Publishing Co., 1943.

———. *Dave Dawson with the Air Corps*. Akron, OH: Saalfield Publishing Co., 1942.

———. *Dave Dawson with the Commandos*. Akron, OH: Saalfield Publishing Co., 1942.

———. *Dave Dawson with the Eighth Air Force*. New York: Crown Publishers, 1944.

———. *Dave Dawson with the Flying Tigers*. Akron, OH: Saalfield Publishing Co., 1943.

———. *Dave Dawson with the Pacific Fleet*. Akron, OH: Saalfield Publishing Co., 1942.

———. *Dave Dawson with the R.A.F.* New York: Crown Publishers, 1941.

———. *Dave Dawson, Flight Lieutenant*. Akron, OH: Saalfield Publishing Co., 1941.

———. *Red Randall at Midway*. New York: Grosset & Dunlap, 1944.

———. *Red Randall at Pearl Harbor*. New York: Grosset & Dunlap, 1944.

———. *Red Randall in Burma*. New York: Grosset & Dunlap, 1945.

———. *Red Randall in the Aleutians*. New York: Grosset & Dunlap, 1945.

———. *Red Randall on Active Duty*. New York: Grosset & Dunlap, 1944.

———. *Red Randall on New Guinea*. New York: Grosset & Dunlap, 1944.

———. *Red Randall Over Tokyo*. New York: Grosset & Dunlap, 1944.

———. *Red Randall's One-Man War*. New York: Grosset & Dunlap, 1946.

Burtis, Thomson. *Daredevils of the Air*. New York: Grosset & Dunlap, 1932.

———. *Flying Blackbirds*. New York: Grosset & Dunlap, 1932.

———. *Four Aces*. New York: Grosset & Dunlap, 1932.

———. *Rex Lee on the Border Patrol*. New York: Grosset & Dunlap, 1928.

———. *Rex Lee Trailing Air Bandits*. New York: Grosset & Dunlap, 1931.

———. *Rex Lee, Ace of the Air Mail*. New York: Grosset & Dunlap, 1929.

———. *Rex Lee, Aerial Acrobat*. New York: Grosset & Dunlap, 1930.

———. *Rex Lee, Flying Detective*. New York: Grosset & Dunlap, 1932.

———. *Rex Lee, Gypsy Flyer*. New York: Grosset & Dunlap, 1928.

———. *Rex Lee, Night Flyer*. New York: Grosset & Dunlap, 1929.

———. *Rex Lee, Ranger of the Sky*. New York: Grosset & Dunlap, 1928.

———. *Rex Lee, Rough Rider of the Air*. New York: Grosset & Dunlap, 1930.

———. *Rex Lee, Sky Trailer*. New York: Grosset & Dunlap, 1929.

———. *Rex Lee's Mysterious Flight*. New York: Grosset & Dunlap, 1930.

———. *Russ Farrell Over Mexico*. Garden City: Doubleday, Doran, 1929.

———. *Russ Farrell, Airman*. Garden City: Doubleday, Page, 1924.

———. *Russ Farrell, Border Patrolman*. Garden City: Doubleday, Doran, 1927.

———. *Russ Farrell, Circus Flyer*. Garden City: Doubleday, Doran, 1927.

———. *Russ Farrell, Test Pilot*. Garden City: Doubleday, Doran, 1926.

———. *Wing for Wing*. New York: Grosset & Dunlap, 1932.

Claudy, Carl H. *The Blue Grotto Terror*. New York: Grosset & Dunlap, 1934.

———. *The Land of No Shadow*. New York: Grosset & Dunlap, 1933.

———. *The Mystery Men of Mars*. New York: Grosset & Dunlap, 1933.

———. *A Thousand Years a Minute*. New York: Grosset & Dunlap, 1933.

Cobb, Captain Frank. *An Aviator's Luck, or the Camp Knox Plot*. Akron, OH: Saalfield Publishing Co., 1927.

———. *Battling the Clouds, or for a Comrade's Honor*. Akron, OH: Saalfield Publishing Co., 1927.

———. *Dangerous Deeds, or the Flight in the Dirigible*. Akron, OH: Saalfield Publishing Co., 1927.

Cook, Canfield. *The Flying Jet*. New York: Grosset & Dunlap, 1945.

———. *The Flying Wing*. New York: Grosset & Dunlap, 1946.

———. *Lost Squadron*. New York: Grosset & Dunlap, 1943.

———. *Secret Mission*. New York: Grosset & Dunlap, 1943.

———. *Sky Attack*. New York: Grosset & Dunlap, 1942.

———. *Spitfire Pilot*. New York: Grosset & Dunlap, 1942.

———. *Springboard to Tokyo*. New York: Grosset & Dunlap, 1943.

———. *Wings Over Japan*. New York: Grosset & Dunlap, 1944.

Copp, Ted [Theodore B.F. Copp]. *The Bridge of Bombers*. New York: Grosset & Dunlap, 1941.

——— [Theodore B.F. Copp]. *The Mystery of Devil's Hand*. New York: Grosset & Dunlap, 1941.

——— [Theodore B.F. Copp]. *The Phantom Fleet*. New York: Grosset & Dunlap, 1942.

Crump, Irving. *The Cloud Patrol*. New York: Grosset & Dunlap, 1929.

———. *Craig of the Cloud Patrol*. New York: Grosset & Dunlap, 1931.

———. *The Pilot of the Cloud Patrol*. New York: Grosset & Dunlap, 1929.

Dean, Graham M. *Circle 4 Patrol*. Chicago: Goldsmith Publishing Co., 1933.

———. *Daring Wings*. Chicago: Goldsmith Publishing Co., 1931.

———. *The Sky Trail*. Chicago: Goldsmith Publishing Co., 1932.

———. *The Treasure Hunt of the S-18*. Chicago: Goldsmith Publishing Co., 1934.

Dixon, Franklin W. [John W. Duffield]. *Across the Pacific or Ted Scott's Hop to Australia*. New York: Grosset & Dunlap, 1928.

——— [John W. Duffield]. *Battling the Wind or Ted Scott Flying Around Cape Horn*. New York: Grosset & Dunlap, 1933.

——— [John W. Duffield]. *Brushing the Mountain Top or Aiding the Lost Traveler*. New York: Grosset & Dunlap, 1934.

——— [John W. Duffield]. *Castaways of the Stratosphere or Hunting the Vanished Balloonists*. New York: Grosset & Dunlap, 1935.

——— [John W. Duffield]. *Danger Trails of the Sky or Ted Scott's Great Mountain Climb*. New York: Grosset & Dunlap, 1931.

——— [John W. Duffield]. *First Stop Honolulu or Ted Scott Over the Pacific*. New York: Grosset & Dunlap, 1927.

——— [John W. Duffield]. *Flying Against Time or Ted Scott Breaking the Ocean to Ocean Record*. New York: Grosset & Dunlap, 1929.

——— [John W. Duffield]. *Flying to the Rescue or Ted Scott and the Big Dirigible*. New York: Grosset & Dunlap, 1930.

——— [John W. Duffield]. *Following the Sun Shadow or Ted Scott and the Great Eclipse*. New York: Grosset & Dunlap, 1932.

——— [John W. Duffield]. *Hunting the Sky Spies or Testing the Invisible Plane*. New York: Grosset & Dunlap, 1941.

——— [John W. Duffield]. *The Lone Eagle of the Border or Ted Scott and the Diamond Smugglers*. New York: Grosset & Dunlap, 1929.

——— [John W. Duffield]. *Lost at the South Pole or Ted Scott in Blizzard Land*. New York: Grosset & Dunlap, 1930.

——— [John W. Duffield]. *Over the Jungle Trails or Ted Scott and the Missing Explorers*. New York: Grosset & Dunlap, 1929.

——— [John W. Duffield]. *Over the Ocean to Paris or Ted Scott's Daring Long-Distance Flight*. New York: Grosset & Dunlap, 1927.

——— [John W. Duffield]. *Over the Rockies with the Air Mail or Ted Scott Lost in the Wilderness*. New York: Grosset & Dunlap, 1927.

——— [John W. Duffield]. *The Pursuit Patrol or Chasing the Platinum Pirates*. New York: Grosset & Dunlap, 1943.

——— [John W. Duffield]. *Rescued in the Clouds or Ted Scott, Hero of the Air*. New York: Grosset & Dunlap, 1927.

——— [John W. Duffield]. *The Search for the Lost Flyers or Ted Scott Over the West Indies*. New York: Grosset & Dunlap, 1928.

——— [John W. Duffield]. *South of the Rio Grande or Ted Scott on a Secret Mission*. New York: Grosset & Dunlap, 1928.

——— [John W. Duffield]. *Through the Air to Alaska or Ted Scott's Search in Nugget Valley*. New York: Grosset & Dunlap, 1930.

Fitzhugh, Percy Keese. *Mark Gilmore, Scout of the Air*. New York: Grosset & Dunlap, 1930.

———. *Mark Gilmore, Speed Flyer*. New York: Grosset & Dunlap, 1931.

———. *Mark Gilmore's Lucky Landing*. New York: Grosset & Dunlap, 1931.

French, Paul [Isaac Asimov]. *David Starr, Space Ranger*. 1952. Reprint, New York: New American Library, 1971.

——— [Isaac Asimov]. *Lucky Starr and the Big Sun of Mercury*. 1956. Reprint, New York: Fawcett Crest, 1978.

——— [Isaac Asimov]. *Lucky Starr and the Moons of Jupiter*. 1957. Reprint, New York: New American Library, 1972.

——— [Isaac Asimov]. *Lucky Starr and the Oceans of Venus*. 1954. Reprint, Greenwich, CT: Fawcett, 1978.

——— [Isaac Asimov]. *Lucky Starr and the Pirates of the Asteroids.* 1953. Reprint, New York: Ballantine Books, 1984.

——— [Isaac Asimov]. *Lucky Starr and the Rings of Saturn.* 1958. Reprint, New York: New American Library, 1972.

Garis, Howard R. *Rocket Riders Across the Ice, or Racing Against Time.* New York: A.L. Burt, 1933.

———. *Rocket Riders in Stormy Seas, or Trailing the Treasure Divers.* New York: A.L. Burt, 1933.

———. *Rocket Riders in the Air, or a Chase in the Clouds.* New York: A.L. Burt, 1934.

———. *Rocket Riders Over the Desert, or Seeking the Lost City.* New York: A.L. Burt, 1933.

Heinlein, Robert A. *Between Planets.* New York: Charles Scribner's Sons, 1951.

———. *Citizen of the Galaxy.* New York: Charles Scribner's Sons, 1957.

———. *Farmer in the Sky.* New York: Charles Scribner's Sons, 1950.

———. *Have Space Suit – Will Travel.* New York: Charles Scribner's Sons, 1958.

———. *Red Planet.* New York: Charles Scribner's Sons, 1949.

———. *Rocket Ship Galileo.* New York: Charles Scribner's Sons, 1947.

———. *The Rolling Stones.* New York: Charles Scribner's Sons, 1952.

———. *Space Cadet.* New York: Charles Scribner's Sons, 1948.

———. *The Star Beast.* New York: Charles Scribner's Sons, 1954.

———. *Starman Jones.* New York: Charles Scribner's Sons, 1953.

———. *Time for the Stars.* New York: Charles Scribner's Sons, 1956.

———. *Tunnel in the Sky.* New York: Charles Scribner's Sons, 1955.

Lamar, Ashton [H.L. Sayler]. *The Aeroplane Express or, the Boy Aeronaut's Grit.* Chicago: Reilly & Britton, 1910.

——— [H.L. Sayler]. *Battling the Bighorn or, the Aeroplane in the Rockies.* Chicago: Reilly & Britton, 1911.

——— [H.L. Sayler]. *The Boy Aeronauts' Club or, Flying for Fun.* Chicago: Reilly & Britton, 1910.

——— [H.L. Sayler]. *A Cruise in the Sky or, the Legend of the Great Pink Pearl.* Chicago: Reilly & Britton, 1911.

——— [H.L. Sayler]. *In the Clouds for Uncle Sam or, Morey Marshall of the Signal Corps.* Chicago: Reilly & Britton, 1910.

——— [H.L. Sayler]. *On the Edge of the Arctic or, an Aeroplane in Snowland.* Chicago: Reilly & Britton, 1913.

——— [Sayler, H.L.]. *The Stolen Aeroplane or, How Bud Wilson Made Good.* Chicago: Reilly & Britton, 1910.

Langley, John Prentice [St. George Rathborne]. *Air Voyagers of the Arctic or Sky Pilots' Dash Across the Pole.* New York: Barse & Co., 1929.

——— [St. George Rathborne]. *Bridging the Seven Seas or on the Air-Lane to Singapore.* New York: Barse & Co., 1930.

——— [St. George Rathborne]. *Chasing the Setting Sun or a Hop, Skip, and Jump to Australia.* New York: Barse & Co., 1930.

——— [St. George Rathborne]. *Desert Hawks on the Wing or Headed South, Algiers to Cape Town.* New York: Barse & Co., 1929.

——— [St. George Rathborne]. *Masters of the Air-Lanes or Round the World in Fourteen Days.* New York: Barse & Co., 1928.

——— [St. George Rathborne]. *Spanning the Pacific or a Non-Stop Hop to Japan*. New York: Barse & Co., 1927.

——— [St. George Rathborne]. *The Staircase of the Wind or Over the Himalayas to Calcutta*. New York: Barse & Co., 1931.

——— [St. George Rathborne]. *Trailblazers of the Skies or Across to Paris, and Back*. New York: Barse & Co., 1927.

——— [St. George Rathborne]. *The "Pathfinder's" Great Flight or Cloud Chasers Over Amazon Jungles*. New York: Barse & Co., 1928.

Langworthy, John Luther. *The Aeroplane Boys Among the Clouds or, Young Aviators in a Wreck*. Chicago: M.A. Donohue, 1912.

———. *The Aeroplane Boys' Flight or, a Hydroplane Roundup*. Chicago: M.A. Donohue, 1914.

———. *The Aeroplane Boys on the Wing, or Aeroplane Chums in the Tropics*. Chicago: M.A. Donohue, 1912.

———. *The Aeroplane Boys, or the Young Sky Pilot's First Air Voyage*. Chicago: M.A. Donohue, 1912.

———. *The Aeroplane Boys' Aeroplane Wonder or, Young Aviators on a Cattle Ranch*. Chicago: M.A. Donohue, 1914.

Lawton, Captain Wilbur [John Henry Goldfrap]. *The Boy Aviators in Africa or, an Aerial Ivory Trail*. New York: Hurst & Co., 1910.

——— [John Henry Goldfrap]. *The Boy Aviators in Nicaragua or, in League with the Insurgents*. New York: Hurst & Co., 1910.

——— [John Henry Goldfrap]. *The Boy Aviators in Record Flight or, the Rival Aeroplane*. New York: Hurst & Co., 1910.

——— [John Henry Goldfrap]. *The Boy Aviators on Secret Service or, Working with Wireless*. New York: Hurst & Co., 1910.

——— [John Henry Goldfrap]. *The Boy Aviators with the Air Raiders, a Story of the Great World War*. New York: Hurst & Co., 1915.

——— [John Henry Goldfrap]. *The Boy Aviators' Flight for a Fortune*. New York: Hurst & Co., 1912.

——— [John Henry Goldfrap]. *The Boy Aviators' Polar Dash or, Facing Death in the Antarctic*. New York: Hurst & Co., 1910.

——— [John Henry Goldfrap]. *The Boy Aviators' Treasure Quest or, the Golden Galleon*. New York: Hurst & Co., 1910.

Martin, Eugene [Roger Garis]. *Randy Starr Above Stormy Seas, or the Sky Flyers on a Perilous Journey*. Akron, OH: Saalfield Publishing Co., 1931.

——— [Roger Garis]. *Randy Starr After an Air Prize, or the Sky Flyers in a Dash Down the States*. Akron, OH: Saalfield Publishing Co., 1931.

——— [Howard R. Garis]. *Randy Starr Leading the Air Circus, or the Sky Flyers in a Daring Stunt*. Akron, OH: Saalfield Publishing Co., 1932.

Miller, Blaine and Dupont. *Bob Wakefield, Naval Aviator*. New York: Dodd, Mead, 1936.

———. *Bob Wakefield, Naval Inspector*. New York: Dodd, Mead, 1937.

———. *Bob Wakefield's Flight Log*. New York: Dodd, Mead, 1940.

Newcomb, Ambrose. *Eagles of the Sky or with Jack Ralston Along the Air Lanes*. Chicago: Goldsmith Publishing Co., 1930.

———. *Flying the Coast Skyways or Jack Ralston's Swift Patrol*. Chicago: Goldsmith Publishing, 1931.

———. *The Sky Detectives or How Jack Ralston Got His Man*. Chicago: Goldsmith Publishing, 1930.

———. *The Sky Pilot's Great Chase or Jack Ralston's Dead Stick Landing*. Chicago: Goldsmith Publishing Co., 1930.

———. *Trackers of the Fog Pack or Jack Ralston Flying Blind*. Chicago: Goldsmith Publishing Co., 1931.

———. *Wings Over the Rockies or Jack Ralston's New Cloud Chaser*. Chicago: Goldsmith Publishing Co., 1930.

Otis, James [James Otis Kaler]. *The Aeroplane at Silver Fox Farm*. New York: Thomas Y. Crowell, 1911.

——— [James Otis Kaler]. *Airship Cruising from Silver Fox Farm*. New York: Thomas Y. Crowell, 1913.

——— [James Otis Kaler]. *The Wireless Station at Silver Fox Farm*. New York: Thomas Y. Crowell, 1910.

Patton, Harris. *Riding Down*. Chicago: Goldsmith Publishing Co., 1932.

———. *Wings of the North*. Chicago: Goldsmith Publishing Co., 1932.

———. *Young Eagles*. Chicago: Goldsmith Publishing Co., 1932.

Porter, Horace [Horace Porter DeHart]. *Our Young Aeroplane Scouts at the Marne, or Harrying the Huns from Allied Battleplanes*. New York: A.L. Burt, 1919.

——— [Horace Porter DeHart]. *Our Young Aeroplane Scouts at Verdun, or Driving Armored Meteors Over Flaming Battle Fronts*. New York: A.L. Burt, 1917.

——— [Horace Porter DeHart]. *Our Young Aeroplane Scouts Fighting to the Finish, or Striking Hard Over the Sea for the Stars and Stripes*. 1918: A.L. Burt, 1918.

——— [Horace Porter DeHart]. *Our Young Aeroplane Scouts in at the Victory, or Speedy High Flyers Smashing the Hindenburg Line*. New York: A.L. Burt, 1919.

——— [Horace Porter DeHart]. *Our Young Aeroplane Scouts in England, or Twin Stars in the London Sky Patrol*. New York: A.L. Burt, 1916.

——— [Horace Porter DeHart]. *Our Young Aeroplane Scouts in France and Belgium, or Saving the Fortunes of the Trouvilles*. New York: A.L. Burt, 1915.

——— [Horace Porter Dehart]. *Our Young Aeroplane Scouts in Germany, or Winning the Iron Cross*. New York: A.L. Burt, 1915.

——— [Horace Porter DeHart]. *Our Young Aeroplane Scouts in Italy, or Flying with the War Eagles of the Alps*. New York: A.L. Burt, 1916.

——— [Horace Porter DeHart]. *Our Young Aeroplane Scouts in Russia, or Lost on the Frozen Steppes*. New York: A.L. Burt, 1915.

——— [Horace Porter Dehart]. *Our Young Aeroplane Scouts in the Balkans, or Wearing the Red Badge of Courage Among the Warring Legions*. New York: A.L. Burt, 1917.

——— [Horace Porter DeHart]. *Our Young Aeroplane Scouts in the War Zone, or Serving Uncle Sam in the Great Cause of the Allies*. New York: A.L. Burt, 1918.

——— [Horace Porter DeHart]. *Our Young Aeroplane Scouts in Turkey, or Bringing the Light to Yusef*. New York: A.L. Burt, 1915.

Powell, Van [A. VanBuren Powell]. *The Ghost of Mystery Airport*. Akron, OH: Saalfield Publishing Co., 1932.

——— [A. VanBuren Powell]. *The Haunted Hangar*. Akron, OH: Saalfield Publishing Co., 1932.

——— [A. VanBuren Powell]. *The Mystery Crash*. Akron, OH: Saalfield Publishing Co., 1932.

——— [A. VanBuren Powell]. *The Vanishing Air Liner*. Akron, OH: Saalfield Publishing Co., 1932.

Rockwell, Carey [pseud.]. *Danger in Deep Space*. New York: Grosset & Dunlap, 1953.

——— [pseud.]. *On the Trail of the Space Pirates*. New York: Grosset & Dunlap, 1953.

——— [pseud.]. *The Revolt on Venus*. New York: Grosset & Dunlap, 1954.

——— [pseud.]. *The Robot Rocket*. New York: Grosset & Dunlap, 1956.

——— [pseud.]. *Sabotage in Space*. New York: Grosset & Dunlap, 1955.

——— [pseud.]. *The Space Pioneers*. New York: Grosset & Dunlap, 1953.

——— [pseud.]. *Stand by for Mars!* New York: Grosset & Dunlap, 1952.

——— [pseud.]. *Treachery in Outer Space*. New York: Grosset & Dunlap, 1954.

Rockwood, Roy [Weldon J. Cobb]. *Dave Dashaway and His Giant Airship or, a Marvellous Trip Across the Atlantic*. New York: Cupples & Leon, 1913.

——— [Weldon J. Cobb]. *Dave Dashaway and His Hydroplane or, Daring Adventures Over the Great Lakes*. New York: Cupples & Leon, 1913.

——— [Weldon J. Cobb]. *Dave Dashaway Around the World or, a Young Yankee Aviator Among Many Nations*. New York: Cupples & Leon, 1913.

——— [Weldon J. Cobb]. *Dave Dashaway the Young Aviator or, in the Clouds for Fame and Fortune*. New York: Cupples & Leon, 1913.

——— [Weldon J. Cobb]. *Dave Dashaway, Air Champion or, Wizard Work in the Clouds*. New York: Cupples & Leon, 1915.

Russell, Keith. *The Young Birdmen Across the Continent, or the Coast-to-Coast Flight of the Night Mail*. New York: Sears Publishing Co., 1930.

———. *The Young Birdmen on the Wing, or the Rescue at Greenly Island*. New York: J.H. Sears, 1929.

———. *The Young Birdmen up the Amazon or Secrets of the Tropic Jungle*. New York: Sears Publishing Co., 1930.

Sainsbury, Lieutenant Noel, Jr. *Bill Bolton and Hidden Danger*. Chicago: Goldsmith Publishing Co., 1933.

———. *Bill Bolton and the Flying Fish*. Chicago: Goldsmith Publishing Co., 1933.

———. *Bill Bolton and the Winged Cartwheels*. Chicago: Goldsmith Publishing Co., 1933.

———. *Bill Bolton Flying Midshipman*. Chicago: Goldsmith Publishing Co., 1933.

Sainsbury, Noel, Jr. *Billy Smith Exploring Ace or by Airplane to New Guinea*. New York: Cupples & Leon, 1928.

———. *Billy Smith Mystery Ace or Airplane Discoveries in South America*. New York: Cupples & Leon, 1932.

———. *Billy Smith Secret Service Ace or Airplane Adventures in Arabia*. New York: Cupples & Leon, 1932.

———. *Billy Smith Shanghaied Ace or Malay Pirates and Solomon Island Cannibals*. New York: Cupples & Leon, 1934.

———. *Billy Smith Trail Eater Ace or Into the Wilds of Northern Alaska by Airplane*. New York: Cupples & Leon, 1933.

Sayler, H.L. *The Airship Boys Adrift or, Saved by an Aeroplane*. Chicago: Reilly & Britton, 1909.

———. *The Airship Boys as Detectives or, Secret Service in Cloudland*. Chicago: Reilly & Britton, 1913.

———. *The Airship Boys Due North or, By Balloon to the Pole*. Chicago: Reilly & Britton, 1910.

———. *The Airship Boys in Finance or, The Flight of the Flying Cow*. Chicago: Reilly & Britton, 1911.

———. *The Airship Boys in the Barren Lands or, The Secret of the White Eskimos*. Chicago: Reilly & Britton, 1910.

——— [Delysle F. Cass]. *The Airship Boys in the Great War or, The Rescue of Bob Russell*. Chicago: Reilly & Britton, 1915.

———. *The Airship Boys or, The Quest of the Aztec Treasure*. Chicago: Reilly & Britton, 1909.

———. *The Airship Boys' Ocean Flyer or, New York to London in Twelve Hours*. Chicago: Reilly & Britton, 1911.

Stone, Richard H. [pseud.]. *Adrift Over Hudson Bay or Slim Tyler in the Land of Ice*. New York: Cupples & Leon, 1931.

——— [pseud.]. *An Air Cargo of Gold or Slim Tyler, Special Bank Messenger*. New York: Cupples & Leon, 1930.

——— [pseud.]. *An Airplane Mystery or Slim Tyler on the Trail*. New York: Cupples & Leon, 1931.

——— [John W. Duffield]. *Lost Over Greenland or Slim Tyler's Search for Dave Boyd*. New York: Cupples & Leon, 1930.

——— [pseud.]. *Secret Sky Express or Slim Tyler Saving a Fortune*. New York: Cupples & Leon, 1932.

——— [John W. Duffield]. *Sky Riders of the Atlantic or Slim Tyler's First Trip in the Clouds*. New York: Cupples & Leon, 1930.

Stuart, Gordon [Henry Bedford-Jones]. *The Boy Scouts of the Air at Cape Peril*. Chicago: Reilly & Lee, 1921.

——— [H.L. Sayler]. *The Boy Scouts of the Air at Eagle Camp*. Chicago: Reilly & Britton, 1912.

——— [H.L. Sayler]. *The Boy Scouts of the Air at Greenwood School*. Chicago: Reilly & Britton, 1912.

——— [G.N. Madison]. *The Boy Scouts of the Air in Belgium*. Chicago: Reilly & Lee, 1915.

——— [H.L. Sayler]. *The Boy Scouts of the Air in Indian Land*. Chicago: Reilly & Britton, 1912.

——— [H.L. Sayler]. *The Boy Scouts of the Air in Northern Wilds*. Chicago: Reilly & Lee, 1912.

——— [Henry Bedford-Jones]. *The Boy Scouts of the Air in the Dismal Swamp*. Chicago: Reilly & Lee, 1920.

——— [G.N. Madison]. *The Boy Scouts of the Air in the Lone Star Patrol*. Chicago: Reilly & Lee, 1916.

——— [Henry Bedford-Jones]. *The Boy Scouts of the Air on Baldcrest*. Chicago: Reilly & Lee, 1922.

——— [H.L. Sayler]. *The Boy Scouts of the Air on Flathead Mountain*. Chicago: Reilly & Britton, 1913.

——— [G.N. Madison]. *The Boy Scouts of the Air on Lost Island*. Chicago: Reilly & Britton, 1917.

——— [G.N. Madison]. *The Boy Scouts of the Air on the French Front*. Chicago: Reilly & Lee, 1918.

——— [G.N. Madison]. *The Boy Scouts of the Air on the Great Lakes*. Chicago: Reilly & Britton, 1914.

——— [G.N. Madison]. *The Boy Scouts of the Air with Pershing*. Chicago: Reilly & Lee, 1919.

Theiss, Lewis E. *Flood Mappers Aloft: How Ginger Hale and the Scouts of the Bald Eagle Patrol Surveyed the Watershed of the Susquehanna*. Boston: W.A. Wilde, 1937.

———. *The Flying Explorer: How a Mail Pilot Penetrated the Basin of the Amazon*. Boston: W.A. Wilde, 1935.

———. *The Flying Reporter*. 1930. Reprint, Chicago: Wilcox & Follett, 1945.

———. *Flying the U.S. Mail to South America: How Pan American Airships Carry on in Sun and Storm Above the Rolling Caribbean*. Boston: W.A. Wilde, 1933.

———. *From Coast to Coast with the U.S. Air Mail*. Boston: W.A. Wilde, 1936.

———. *The Mail Pilot of the Caribbean: The Adventures of Ginger Hale Above the Southern Seas*. Boston: W.A. Wilde, 1934.

———. *Piloting the U.S. Air Mail; Flying for Uncle Sam*. Boston: W.A. Wilde, 1927.

———. *The Pursuit of the Flying Smugglers*. Boston: W.A. Wilde, 1931.

———. *The Search for the Lost Mail Plane*. Boston: W.A. Wilde, 1928.

———. *Trailing the Air Mail Bandit*. 1929. Reprint, Chicago: Wilcox & Follett, 1946.

———. *Wings of the Coast Guard: Aloft with the Flying Service of Uncle Sam's Life Savers*. Boston: W.A. Wilde, 1932.

Walton, Frank. *The Flying Machine Boys in Deadly Peril or, Lost in the Clouds*. New York: A.L. Burt, 1914.

———. *The Flying Machine Boys in Mexico or, the Secret of the Crater*. New York: A.L. Burt, 1913.

———. *The Flying Machine Boys in the Frozen North or, the Trail in the Snow*. New York: A.L. Burt, 1915.

———. *The Flying Machine Boys in the Wilds or, the Mystery of the Andes*. New York: A.L. Burt, 1913.

———. *The Flying Machine Boys on Duty or, the Clue Above the Clouds*. New York: A.L. Burt, 1913.

———. *The Flying Machine Boys on Secret Service or, the Capture in the Air*. New York: A.L. Burt, 1913.

Wright, Philip Lee. *An Air Express Holdup or How Pilot George Selkirk Carried Through*. New York: Grosset & Dunlap, 1930.

———. *The East Bound Air Mail or Fighting Fog, Storm and Hard Luck*. New York: Barse & Co., 1930.

———. *The Mail Pilot's Hunch or a Crash in Death Valley*. New York: Grosset & Dunlap, 1931.

Wyman, L.P., Ph.D. *The Hunniwell Boys and the Platinum Mystery*. New York: A.L. Burt, 1928.

———. *The Hunniwell Boys in the Air*. New York: A.L. Burt, 1928.

———. *The Hunniwell Boys in the Caribbean*. New York: A.L. Burt, 1930.

———. *The Hunniwell Boys in the Gobi Desert*. New York: A.L. Burt, 1930.

———. *The Hunniwell Boys in the Secret Service*. New York: A.L. Burt, 1928.

———. *The Hunniwell Boys' Longest Flight*. New York: A.L. Burt, 1928.

———. *The Hunniwell Boys' Non-Stop Flight Around the World*. New York: A.L. Burt, 1931.

———. *The Hunniwell Boys' Victory*. New York: A.L. Burt, 1928.

III. Historical and Critical Sources

A. Books

Allen, Richard Sanders. *The Northrop Story, 1929-1939*. Atglen, PA: Schiffer Aviation History, 1993.

———. *Revolution in the Sky: The Lockheeds of Aviation's Golden Age*. Revised edn. Atglen, PA: Schiffer Aviation History, 1993.

Arthur, Reginald Wright. *Contact! Careers of U.S. Naval Aviators*. Washington, DC: Naval Aviator Register, 1967.

Bender, Marilyn, and Selig Altschul. *The Chosen Instrument: Pan Am, Juan Trippe: The Rise and Fall of an American Entrepreneur*. New York: Simon & Schuster, 1982.

Berg, A. Scott. *Lindbergh*. New York: G.P. Putnam, 1998.

Berget, Alphonse. *The Conquest of the Air*. New York: G.P. Putnam's Sons, 1909.

Biddle, Wayne. *Barons of the Sky: From Early Flight to Strategic Warfare, the Story of the American Aerospace Industry*. New York: Simon & Schuster, 1991.

Billman, Carol A. *The Secret of the Stratemeyer Syndicate*. New York: Ungar Publishing Co., 1986.

Bilstein, Roger E. *Flight in America: From the Wrights to the Astronauts*. Rev. edn. Baltimore: Johns Hopkins University Press, 1994.

Blodgett, Harold W. *The Best of Whitman*. New York: Ronald Press, 1953.

Bowen, R. Sidney, Jr. *Flying from the Ground Up*. New York: McGraw-Hill, 1931.

Bowers, Peter M. *Boeing Aircraft Since 1916*. 2d ed. New York: Funk & Wagnalls, 1968.

Boyne, Walter J. *Clash of Wings: World War II in the Air*. New York: Simon & Schuster, 1994.

Brooks, Peter W. *Cierva Autogiros: The Development of Rotary-Wing Flight*. Washington, DC: Smithsonian Institution Press, 1988.

Carter, Paul A. *The Creation of Tomorrow: Fifty Years of Magazine Science Fiction*. New York: Columbia University Press, 1977.

Chanute, Octave. *Progress in Flying Machines*. New York: American Engineer and Railroad Journal, 1894.

Cooke, James J. *The U.S. Air Service in the Great War, 1917-1919*. Westport, CT: Greenwood Press, 1996.

Corn, Joseph J. *The Winged Gospel: America's Romance with Aviation, 1900-1950*. New York: Oxford University Press, 1983.

Cowan, Ruth Schwartz. *A Social History of American Technology*. New York: Oxford University Press, 1997.

Curtiss, Glenn, and Augustus Post. *The Curtiss Aviation Book*. New York: Frederick A. Stokes, 1912.

Daniel Guggenheim Fund for the Promotion of Aeronautics. *Equipment Used in Experiments to Solve the Problem of Fog Flying*. New York: Daniel Guggenheim Fund for the Promotion of Aeronautics, 1930.

Daso, Dik Alan. *Hap Arnold and the Evolution of American Air Power*. Washington, DC: Smithsonian Institution Press, 2000.

Davies, R.E.G. *Airlines of the United States Since 1914*. Washington, DC: Smithsonian Institution Press, 1998.

Davis, Richard G. *Hap: Henry H. Arnold, Military Aviator*. Washington, DC: Air Force History and Museums Program, 1997.

Doolittle, James H., and Carroll V. Glines. *I Could Never Be So Lucky Again: An Autobiography of James H. "Jimmy" Doolittle*. Atglen, PA: Schiffer Publishing, 1995.

Dunlap, George T. *The Fleeting Years: A Memoir*. New York: Privately printed, 1937.

English, Dave. *Slipping the Surly Bonds: Great Quotations on Flight*. New York: McGraw-Hill, 1998.

Francillon, Rene J. *Grumman Aircraft Since 1929*. Annapolis: Naval Institute Press, 1989.

———. *Lockheed Aircraft Since 1913*. Annapolis: Naval Institute Press, 1987.

Franklin, H. Bruce. *Robert A. Heinlein: America as Science Fiction*. New York: Oxford University Press, 1980.

Girls' Series Books: A Checklist of Hardback Books Published 1900-1975. Minneapolis: Children's Literature Research Collections, 1978.

Glines, Carroll V. *Roscoe Turner: Aviation's Master Showman*. Washington DC: Smithsonian Institution Press, 1995.

Green, William. *Famous Bombers of the Second World War*. 1959. Reprint, Garden City: Doubleday & Co., 1967.

———. *Famous Fighters of the Second World War*. 1957. Reprint, Garden City: Doubleday & Co., 1969.

———. *Famous Fighters of the Second World War, Second Series*. 1962. Reprint, Garden City: Doubleday & Co., 1969.

Grey, C.G., and Leonard Bridgman, Eds. *Jane's All the World's Aircraft, 1940*. London: Sampson Low, Marston & Co., 1941.

Guggenheim, Harry F. *The Seven Skies*. New York: G.P. Putnam's Sons, 1930.

Gunston, Bill, ed. *Aviation Year by Year*. New York: DK Publishing, 2001.

Gwynne-Jones, Terry. *Farther and Faster: Aviation's Adventuring Years, 1909-1939*. Washington, DC: Smithsonian Institution Press, 1991.

Hall, Norman S. *The Balloon Buster: Frank Luke of Arizona*. Garden City: Doubleday, Doran, 1928.

Hallion, Richard P. *Taking Flight: Inventing the Aerial Age from Antiquity Through the First World War*. New York: Oxford University Press, 2003.

Heinlein, Robert A. *Expanded Universe*. New York: Ace Books, 1980.

———. *Grumbles from the Grave*. Edited by Virginia Heinlein. New York: Ballantine Books, 1989.

Herrmann, David G. *The Arming of Europe and the Making of the First World War*. Princeton: Princeton University Press, 1996.

Hudson, Harry K. *A Bibliography of Hard-Cover, Series Type Boys Books*. Revised edn. Tampa, FL: Data Print, 1977.

Hudson, James J. *Hostile Skies: A Combat History of the American Air Service in World War I*. Syracuse: Syracuse University Press, 1968.

Ingells, Douglas J. *The Plane That Changed the World: A Biography of the DC-3*. Fallbrook, CA: Aero Publishers, 1966.

Johnson, Deidre. *Edward Stratemeyer and the Stratemeyer Syndicate*. TUSAS 627. New York: Twayne Publishers, 1993.

———. *Stratemeyer Pseudonyms and Series Books*. Westport, CT: Greenwood Press, 1982.

Kennett, Lee. *The First Air War 1914-1918*. New York: Free Press, 1991.

Kinsman, Claire D., and Mary Ann Tennenhouse, Eds. *Contemporary Authors 9-12*. First revision. Detroit: Gale Research, 1974.

Lanes, Selma G. *Down the Rabbit Hole*. New York: Atheneum, 1971.

Learn, William M. *Aerial Pioneers: The U.S. Air Mail Service, 1918-1927*. Washington, DC: Smithsonian Institution Press, 1985.

Lindbergh, Charles A. *The Spirit of St. Louis*. 1953. Reprint, St. Paul: Minnesota Historical Society Press, 1993.

———. *We*. 1927. Reprint, Guildford, CT: Lyons Press, 2002.

Lougheed, Victor. *Aeroplane Designing for Amateurs*. Chicago: Reilly & Britton, 1912.

———. *Vehicles of the Air*. 3d ed. Chicago: Reilly & Britton, 1911.

Luckett, Perry D. *Charles A. Lindbergh: A Bio-Bibliography*. Westport, CT: Greenwood Press, 1986.

Magoun, F. Alexander, and Eric Hodgins. *A History of Aircraft*. New York: Whittlesey House, 1931.

McCurdy, Howard E. *Space and the American Imagination*. Washington, DC: Smithsonian Institution Press, 1997.

McFarlane, Leslie. *Ghost of the Hardy Boys*. New York: Two Continents, 1967.

Mechling, Jay. *On My Honor: Boy Scouts and the Making of American Youth*. Chicago: University of Chicago Press, 2001.

Moher, Stanley R., and Bobby H. Johnson. *Wiley Post, His Winnie Mae, and the World's First Pressure Suit*. Smithsonian Annals of Flight, vol. 8. Washington DC: Smithsonian Institution Press, 1971.

Morrow, John H., Jr. *The Great War in the Air: Military Aviation from 1909 to 1921*. Washington, DC: Smithsonian Institution Press, 1993.

Mott, Frank Luther. *A History of American Magazines, 1850-1865*. Cambridge: Belknap Press of Harvard University Press, 1938.

———. *A History of American Magazines, 1865-1885*. 1938. Reprint, Cambridge: Belknap Press of Harvard University Press, 1957.

Murray, William D. *The History of the Boy Scouts of America*. New York: Boy Scouts of America, 1937.

Neufeld, Michael J. *The Rocket and the Reich: Peenemünde and the Coming of the Ballistic Missile Era*. New York: Free Press, 1995.

Nye, Russel B. *The Unembarrassed Muse: The Popular Arts in America*. New York: Dial Press, 1970.

Peebles, Curtis. *Watch the Skies! a Chronicle of the Flying Saucer Myth*. Washington DC: Smithsonian Institution Press, 1994.

Pisano, Dominick A. *To Fill the Skies with Pilots*. Washington DC: Smithsonian Institution Press, 2001.

Pisano, Dominick A., and F. Robert van der Linden. *Charles Lindbergh and The Spirit of St. Louis*. Washington, DC: Smithsonian National Air and Space Museum; New York: Harry N. Abrams, 2000.

Pursell, Carroll. *The Machine in America: A Social History of Technology*. Baltimore: Johns Hopkins University Press, 1995.

Rich, Doris L. *Amelia Earhart: A Biography*. Washington DC: Smithsonian Institution Press, 1989.

Roseberry, C.R. *Glenn Curtiss: Pioneer of Flight*. Syracuse: Syracuse University Press, 1991.

Ross, Walter S. *The Last Hero: Charles A. Lindbergh*. New York: Harper & Row, 1976.

Schatzberg, Eric. *Wings of Wood, Wings of Metal: Culture and Technical Choice in American Airplane Materials, 1914-1945*. Princeton: Princeton University Press, 1999.

Science Fiction, Fantasy, and Weird Fiction Magazines. Edited by Marshall B. Tymn and Mike Ashley. Westport, CT: Greenwood Press, 1985.

Slotkin, Richard. *Gunfighter Nation: The Myth of the Frontier in Twentieth-Century America*. New York: Atheneum, 1992.

Studley, Lieutenant Barrett. *Practical Flight Training*. New York: Macmillan Co., 1928.

Swanborough, Gordon, and Peter M. Bowers. *United States Navy Aircraft Since 1911*. New York: Funk & Wagnalls, 1968.

Sweetser, Arthur. *The American Air Service*. New York: D. Appleton, 1919.

Thetford, Owen. *Aircraft of the Royal Air Force Since 1918*. New York: Funk & Wagnalls, 1968.

Tichi, Cecelia. *Shifting Gears: Technology, Literature, Culture in Modernist America*. Chapel Hill: University of North Carolina Press, 1987.

van der Linden, F. Robert. *The Boeing 247: The First Modern Airliner*. Seattle: University of Washington Press, 1991.

———. *The Post Office and the Birth of the Commercial Aviation Industry*. Lexington: University Press of Kentucky, 2002.

Wagner, Ray. *Mustang Designer: Edgar Schmued and the P-51*. Washington DC: Smithsonian Institution Press, 1990.

Wohl, Robert. *A Passion for Wings: Aviation and the Western Imagination 1908-1918*. New Haven: Yale University Press, 1994.

Wooldridge, E.T. *Winged Wonders: The Story of the Flying Wings*. Washington, DC: Smithsonian Institution Press, 1985.

Young, Philip H. *Children's Fiction Series: A Bibliography, 1850-1950*. Jefferson, NC: McFarland Publishers, 1997.

B. Articles and other sources

"1,550-Mile Flight Made by Lindbergh." *New York Times*, 12 May 1927, 1.

"Adams, Eustace Lane." In *Who Was Who Among North American Authors, 1921-1939*, vol. I, 8. Detroit: Gale Research, 1976.

Aellen, Richard. "The Autogiro and Its Legacy." *Air & Space/Smithsonian*, December/January 1988-1989, 52-59.

"Aeronitis." *Aerial Age Weekly* 13 (30 May 1921): 282.

"Air Corps Fokker Exceeds All Sustained Flight Marks." *Aviation* 26 (12 January 1929): 108-109.

"Air Force Reveals New Orders for 1,150 Military Planes." *Aviation Week* 48 (5 January 1948): 12-13.

"Air-Brakes for Douglas DC-1." *Popular Aviation*, March 1934, 161.

"Airplane Purchased by Baltimore *Sun*." *U.S. Air Services* 4 (October 1920): 16.

Alexanderson, E.F.W. "Height of Airplane Above Ground by Radio Echo." *Science* 68 (14 December 1928): 597-598.

Allen, C.B. "Along the Air Frontier." *Western Flying* 21 (June 1941): 21.

"The 'Alula' Wing Demonstrated." *Flight*, 20 October 1921, 687.

Alvarez, Dr. Luis W. "There is No Obvious or Simple Way in Which to Use Atomic Energy for Space Ships." *U.S. Air Services* 32 (January 1947): 9-10, 26.

"America at War." *Aviation* 41 (February 1942): 78-79, 305.

"The Americas and the Orient Linked by Air." *Aero Digest* 27 (December 1935): 24-27, 72.

"Another JN-4D Reduction!" [Curtiss Eastern Aeroplane Corp. Advertisement]. *Aerial Age Weekly* 13 (22 August 1921): 577.

Arentz, Robert. "Retractable Wing." *Popular Aviation*, December 1939, 53, 83.

"Aristocracy of Achievement." *Aviation* 22 (20 June 1927): 1349.

Armstrong, E.R. "Seadromes and Ocean Flying." *Aviation* 23 (28 November 1927): 1288-1290.

"The Army Flight to Hawaii." *Aero Digest* 11 (July 1927): 16-18.

Arnold, Col. H.H. "Building American Aviation." *Scientific American* 117 (6 October 1917): 414, 429-430.

"An Articulated Monoplane." *Fly Magazine*, February 1912, 17.

Associated Press. "World's Greatest Aviator in Battle to Save a Life." *Washington Post*, 25 April 1928, 1.

"Automatic Stabilizing System of the Wright Brothers." *Scientific American Supplement* 71 (14 January 1911): 20-21.

"The Aviator – the Superman of Now." [Wright Flying Field advertisement]. *Flying*, November 1916, 403.

"The Aviator – the Superman of Now." [Wright Flying Field advertisement]. *Flying*, August 1916, 273.

"Aviators to Bomb Ex-German Warships in Tests." *Aerial Age Weekly* 13 (14 March 1921): 8.

"Bail Out Babies." *Western Flying* 30 (May 1950): 12.

Bannerman-Philips, Maj. H. "Russia's Giant War Flyers." *Scientific American* 111 (22 August 1914): 135, 138-139.

"Barling Bomber – Army's Super Airplane." *U.S. Air Service* 8 (August 1922): 15-19.

"Bell's Twin-Jet Fighter." *Southern Flight* 22 (October 1944): 27, 79.

Benton, Cpl. Francis J. "Those Who Were Buzzbombed Will Never Forget." *U.S. Air Services* 30 (July 1945): 14-15, 56.

Bilstein, Roger E. "The Airplane, the Wrights, and the American Public." In *The Wright Brothers: Heirs of Prometheus*, edited by Richard P. Hallion, 39-51. Washington, DC: Smithsonian Institution Press, 1978.

"Birth of the Fireball." *Western Flying* 26 (February 1946): 34-35.

Bleiler, E.F. "From the Newark Steam Man to Tom Swift." *Extrapolation* 30 (Summer 1989): 101-116.

"The Boeing Mail Plane." *Aviation* 23 (4 July 1927): 18-19.

"Boeing Stratojet Bomber Heralds Transonic Combat." *Aviation Week* 47 (22 September 1947): 14-15.

"Boeing Testing." *Aviation Week* 53 (24 July 1950): 156-157.

"Boeing's New Model 247 Transport." *Aviation* 32 (April 1932): 124-126.

Bonnalie, Comdr. A.F., U.S.N.R. "How Our Bombers Are Protected." *U.S. Air Services* 29 (April 1944): 12-14, 38.

Boone, Andrew R. "Beyond the Speed of Sound." *Air Trails Pictorial*, December 1945, 26-28, 105-108.

Brady, Tim. "World War I." In *The American Aviation Experience: A History*, edited by Tim Brady, 98-124. Carbondale: Southern Illinois University Press, 2000.

Bruce, Ernest. "No Ersatz." *Aviation* 40 (June 1941): 44-45, 142-144.

"The Buhl-Verville Airster." *Aero Digest* 8 (March 1926): 130-131.

Bulban, Erwin J., and Alice J. Molbeck. "Germany's Air Force Wages War." *Model Airplane News*, April 1940, 6-7, 56-59.

"Burnelli and the Flying Wing Design." *Air World*, March 1945, 34-37, 65.

Byers, Horace R. "The Guggenheim Airway Meteorological Service." *Aviation* 25 (15 September 1928): 866-867, 886-889.

Cagle, Malcolm. "Are Single-Seat Fighters Out?" *Flying*, August 1948, 32-33, 74-75.

Campbell-Wood, G.F. "The International Aviation Meet." *Aircraft* 1 (December 1910): 353-359.

Campbell-Wood, George F. "The Wright-Curtiss-Paulhan Conflict." *Aircraft* 1 (April 1910): 50-55.

"The Cat." *Model Airplane News*, April 1944, 17, 48-50.

Cautley, R.V. "Fuel and Oil Consumption Important Factors on Long Distance Flights." *Aviation* 22 (6 June 1927): 1214-1215, 1243.

Chanute, Octave. "Twenty-Four Uses for Flying Machines." *Fly* 2 (November 1909): 18.

Churchill, Edward. "Manta." *Flying*, November 1942, 54, 100-103.

Claudy, C.H. "Aircraft of the Future." *Scientific American* 123 (20 November 1920): 520.

Cocklin, Henry S. "Development of Navy Patrol Planes." *Aero Digest* 6 (May 1925): 242-244, 280.

Collins, Frederick L. "The Battle of Detroit: 1,000 Horses in the Sky." *Liberty*, 14 February 1942, 32-34.

"Colonel Lindbergh's Homecoming." *Aero Digest* 11 (June 1927): 31.

"A Commercial Aviator's Uniform." *Aerial Age Weekly* 13 (20 June 1921): 344.

"Communications on an International Airline." *Aviation* 31 (November 1932): 435-437.

"Contra-Rotating Propellers." *Aero Digest* 42 (February 1943): 228-229.

"Cook, Haswell Canfield." National Air and Space Museum: Document File, CC-543500-01.

"The Cornu Helicopter." *Scientific American Supplement* 65 (16 May 1908): 316-318.

Crouch, Tom D. "Local Hero: John Joseph Montgomery and the First Winged Flight in America." *Journal of the West* 36 (July 1997): 21-28.

"Crump, (James) Irving." In *Current Authors*, edited by Frances Carol Locher, 143. Detroit: Gale Research, 1978.

"Curtiss Tanager." *Aero Digest* 16 (February 1930): 120-121.

"Curtiss-Bleecker Helicopter." *Aero Digest* 17 (July 1930): 110-112.

"Curtiss's Experiments in Rising from the Water." *Scientific American Supplement* 71 (4 March 1911): 132-133.

Dane, Robert. "Midnight Suns of the Air Mail." *Aero Digest* 7 (July 1925): 359-360.

"Dayton Celebrates Aviation Day." *Air Service News Letter* 7 (20 June 1923): 1-2.

de Pue, Elva. "Why a Modernistic Clubhouse." *Sportsman Pilot*, March 1929, 10, 38-39, 44-45.

"Dean, Graham M." In *Who Was Who in America*, 107. Chicago: Marquis Who's Who, 1976.

"The DeBothezat Helicopter." *Air Service News Letter* 7 (5 March 1923): 1-2.

Dizer, John T. "The Unknown Percy Keese Fitzhugh." *Dime Novel Roundup* 62 (October 1993): 86-94.

"Douglas DST Sleeplane." *Aero Digest* 28 (February 1936): 52-53.

Douglas, Donald W. "The Douglas DC-1 Airliner." *Aero Digest* 23 (October 1933): 45-46.

———. "Transcontinental & Western Air Accepts the Douglas 'Airliner.'" *U.S. Air Services* 18 (October 1933): 28-30.

"Dr. Levi P. Wyman, Author, Educator." *New York Times*, 18 April 1950, 31.

"'Dusting' Pilots." *Aviation* 24 (23 January 1928): 189.

Eaton, George L. [pseud.]. "The Charger Goes to Sydney." *Air Trails*, October 1938, 37-45, 50-56, 88.

Editor, The [John W. Campbell, Jr.]. "Air Trails and New Frontiers." *Air Trails Pictorial*, September 1946, 22-23.

——— [John W. Campbell, Jr.]. "Born Gambler." *Air Trails and Science Frontiers*, May 1947, 20-21.

"Entrants in Post Plane Test May Go with Winner." *Washington Post*, 25 June 1928, 14.

Erisman, Fred. "Stratemeyer Boys' Books and the Gernsback Milieu." *Extrapolation* 41 (Fall 2000): 272-282.

Erskine, John. "Flight: Some Thoughts on the Solitary Voyage of a Certain Young Aviator." *Century Magazine*, September 1927, 513-518.

"Ferry Boat Brings Balchen Into City." *New York World*, 29 April 1928, 2.

"First Demonstration of the Alula Wing." *Aviation* 11 (5 December 1921): 662.

"First Flight of an American Aeroplane from the Water." *Scientific American* 104 (11 February 1911): 132.

Fischer, Maj. Charles M. "Jet Lightplanes?" *Flying*, June 1945, 31, 120-121.

"Flash." *Model Airplane News*, March 1945, 6-7.

"Flash." *Model Airplane News*, August 1946, 2.

"Flash." *Model Airplane News*, September 1946, 2.

"The Flying Submarine or Submersible Seaplane." *Flying* 9 (June 1920): 331.

"Flying Wing Jet Bomber Completed." *Aviation Week* 47 (13 October 1947): 14.

Flying, The Staff of. "Jets of the U.S. Air Forces." *Flying*, December 1948, 17-27, 71-72.

"Fokker Universal." *Aero Digest* 18 (April 1931): 98.

"The Fork-Tailed Devil." *Flying*, August 1945, 26-28, 124-126.

Fournier, Lucien. "Gyroscopic Balancing of Aeroplanes." *Scientific American Supplement* 67 (15 May 1909): 309-310.

Francis, Devon. "Putting Plane's Fuselage to Work." *Popular Science*, November 1945, 65-70.

Friedman, William S. "The Thunderbolt." *Popular Science*, December 1942, 108-113, 226-228.

Fuller, Curtis. "The Flying Saucers – Fact or Fiction?" *Flying*, July 1950, 16-17, 59-61.

———. "Uncle Sam 'Discovers' the Rocket." *Flying*, March 1947, 28-29, 72-76.

"Funeral Tonight for E. Stratemeyer." *New York Times*, 12 May 1930, 16.

Gale, C.H. "Ship to Shore Airmail Service." *Aviation*, 28 (31 May 1930): 1084-1087.

"Garis, Lilian C." In *Who Was Who in America*, vol. III, 313. Chicago: A.N. Marquis, 1963.

"The German Long-Range Gun." *Scientific American* 118 (6 April 1918): 309, 332-333.

Goldsborough, Bruce. "The Earth Inductor Compass." *Aero Digest* 10 (June 1927): 542, 544.

Gowen, William R. "The Real Tom Swift." *Newsboy* 33 (January-February 1995): 5.

Graham, Frederick. "Will Tomorrow's Planes Look Like This?" *Saturday Evening Post*, 29 January 1944, 36, 39.

Gray, William P. "P-38." *Life*, 16 August 1943, 51-56, 58.

Greer, John Fulton. "First Flight of an American Aeroplane from the Water." *Scientific American* 104 (11 February 1911): 132.

Haviland, R.P. "Can We Build a Station in Space?" *Flying*, May 1949, 19-21, 68-70.

Healy, Roy. "Aeronautical Supremacy Demands Jet and Rocket Research." *Aviation* 44 (July, August 1945): 152-154; 149-151.

———. "How Nazis' Walter Engine Powered Manned Rocket-Craft." *Aviation* 45 (January 1946): 77-80.

Heinemann, Edward H. "The Skystreak." *Western Flying* 27 (March 1947): 18-19, 38.

"Helicopter Plane Passes Successful Tests." *Popular Mechanics*, February 1930, 233.

Higdon, Hal. "Combat Comics." *Air & Space/Smithsonian*, December 1993, 58-63.

Hoffman, M.L. "The American-Built Savoia-Marchetti S-55." *Air Transportation* 11 (March 1930): 38.

Holsinger, M. Paul. "For Freedom and the American Way." *Newsboy* 32 (March-April 1994): 9-16.

Hoover, Herbert, Jr. "Blind Flying and Radio." *Aero Digest* 17 (July, August 1930): 59-61, 44-45.

Hotz, Robert. "Navy Unwraps Its Fastest Fighter." *Aviation Week* 49 (29 November 1948): 12-13.

Hovgaard, William. "An Airplane Station in the Midocean." *New York Times*, 3 July 1927, 8: 1.

"How High is up?" *Aviation Week* 50 (6 June 1949): 14.

Huff, Lieut. Comdr William H., USN. "Jets at Sea." *Flying*, July 1946, 46-47.

Huggins, Marion. "Gyropilot Goes Cross-Country." *Aero Digest* 17 (July 1930): 51-52, 208.

Humphreys, W.J. "Holes in the Air." *Popular Science Monthly*, July 1912, 50-60.

"The International Aviation Meet." *Scientific American* 103 (5 November 1910): 361-362, 370-371.

Jacobs, A.M. "Unusual Navigation Tests at McCook Field." *Air Service News Letter* 8 (18 June 1924): 1-2.

Jannus, Antony H. "Learning How to Fly: Hints from a Professional Aviator." *Scientific American* 104 (24 June 1911): 624, 632.

Jardine, Robert. "Technical Description of the Salt-Cooled Valve." *Aviation Engineering* 5 (July 1931): 31-32.

"Jet Plane Problems on Aircraft Carriers." *Western Flying* 28 (May 1948): 9, 18.

Johnson, Deidre. "From Abbott to Animorphs, from Godly Books to Goosebumps: The Nineteenth-Century Origins of Modern Series." In *Scorned Literature: Essays on the History and Criticism of Popular Mass-Produced Fiction in America*, edited by Lydia Cushman Schurman and Deidre Johnson, 147-165. Westport, CT: Greenwood Press, 2002.

Johnston, Russ. "Japs Are Their Specialty." *Flying*, August 1942, 22-24, 86-88.

"Juvenile Story Writer Dies." *New York Times*, 12 December 1912, 13.

K., A. [Alexander Klemin]. "Wiley Post's Altitude Suit." *Scientific American* 151 (October 1934): 215-216.

Kalitinsky, Andrew. "Atomic Engines for Aircraft." *Western Flying* 28 (October 1948): 11, 24-26.

———. "Atomic Engines for Aircraft." *Flying*, January 1949, 22-23, 52-54.

———. "Atomic Power for Aircraft." *Aero Digest* 57 (August 1948): 58-59, 121-123.

Karant, Max. "Air-Sleepers on American Line." *Popular Aviation*, January 1936, 25-26, 72.

Kehoe [sic], Donald. "Dressing up Aviation." *Aviation* 25 (10 November 1928): 1485, 1510-1514.

Keys, C.M. "Value of Racing Planes." *Aero Digest* 7 (October 1925): 535-536, 568-570.

"The Keystone-Loening '*Commuter*.'" *Aviation* 29 (5 July 1930): 12-16.

"The Kid That Once Was You..." [*Aviation Week* advertisement]. *Aviation Week* 52 (6 March 1950): 26-27.

Klemin, Alexander. "Handley Page Slot and Other Devices to Increase Wing Lift." *Aeronautics*, March 1930, 41-42, 54-55.

———. "A Successful Metal-Clad Airship." *Scientific American* 140 (November 1929): 436-437, 454.

"Know Your Enemy." *Air Force*, January 1945, 14-15.

Kotcher, Capt. Ezra. "Our Jet Propelled Fighter." *Air Force*, March 1944, 6-8, 64.

Kraft, Fred W. "Rocketing to the Moon." *U.S. Air Services* 32 (July 1947): 15-16.

Kuznik, Frank. "The Original Space Cadet." *Air & Space/Smithsonian*, April/May 1995, 68-75.

"The Large Demand for Aeroplanes." *Aerial Age Weekly* 11 (28 June 1920): 539-540.

[Lawrence, Josephine]. "The Newarker Whose Name is Best Known." *Newark Sunday Call*, 9 December 1917, 1.

Lay, Beirne, Jr. "Good Judgment." *Sportsman Pilot*, 15 October 1936, 19, 37-39.

LePage, W.L. "The Development of the Amphibious Airplane." *Aviation* 22 (25 April 1927): 831-832.

Lerner, Preston. "Silver Bullet." *Air & Space/Smithsonian*, April/May 2003, 40-49.

Lescarboura, Austin C. "With the American Airmen of Tomorrow." *Scientific American* 117 (6 October 1917): 242-243.

Ley, Willy. "Atomic Engines." *Air Trails Pictorial*, January 1946, 24-25, 72-74.

———. "Outward Bound." *Air Trails Pictorial*, November 1946, 28-33, 80-99.

———. "V-2 – and Beyond." *Air Trails Pictorial*, March, April 1946, 26-28, 109-114; 36-38, 108-110.

"Lindbergh." *Aviation* 22 (30 May 1927): 1119.

"Lindbergh Arrives After Record Hops." *New York Times*, 13 May 1927, 1, 3.

"Lindbergh on Way to Seek Lost Plane." *New York Times*, 7 September 1929, 1, 2.

"Lindbergh to Tell His Story to Youths." *New York Times*, 13 July 1927, 4.

"Lindbergh Will Tour in Cause of Aviation." *New York Times*, 29 June 1927, 4.

Lindbergh, Captain Charles A. "Behind Europe in Flying Matters, Lindbergh's View of Our Status." *New York Times*, 2 June 1927, 1, 2.

———. "He Has Made 7,190 Flights in Five Years." *New York Times*, 28 May 1927, 1.

———. "Lindbergh Says Flying Boats Will Come in 5 to 10 Years." *New York Times*, 9 June 1927, 1, 4.

———. "Lindbergh 'Ready for Anything;' 'Feels Good to Be Back,' He Says." *New York Times*, 11 June 1927, 1, 2.

———. "Memphis Makes Record." *New York Times*, 10 June 1927, 1, 2.

Lindbergh, Charles A. "How Air Transport in America Has Reached a Healthy Basis." *New York Times*, 16 September 1928, 152.

Lindbergh, Col. Charles A. "Air Corps Reservist Training Hours Deemed Too Few." *New York Times*, 13 January 1929, 142.

———. "Air Speed Limited Only by Power and Streamline." *New York Times*, 3 February 1929, 144.

———. "Aircraft for Private Owners and How to Choose One." *New York Times*, 25 November 1928, 10.

———. "Airplanes Are Now Linking up the Two American Continents." *New York Times*, 21 October 1928, 152.

———. "Blind Landing in Fog Still Presents Many Problems." *New York Times*, 20 January 1929, 12.

———. "Growing Industry of Aviation Offers a Fine Future to Youth." *New York Times*, 16 September 1928, 134.

———. "He Sees Air Mail as Unifying the People and the Nation." *New York Times*, 28 October 1928, 168.

———. "Instruments That Guide Pilots Through Darkness or Fog." *New York Times*, 30 September 1928, 151.

———. "Lindbergh Writes of Aviation's Advance." *New York Times*, 26 August 1928, 1.

———. "Main Needs That Must Be Met in Selecting Airport Sites." *New York Times*, 11 November 1928, 168.

———. "New Possibilities Opened by Question Mark's Flight." *New York Times*, 27 January 1929, 8.

———. "New Types and Speedier Planes Being Evolved in Air Progress." *New York Times*, 14 October 1928, 10.

———. "The New Year Brings Transport by Air-Rail to a Reality." *New York Times*, 6 January 1929, 142.

———. "The Second Article of His Series Tells What Makes Planes Fly." *New York Times*, 2 September 1928, 99.

———. "Specialized Aviation Leaves Ocean Flight to Seaplanes." *New York Times*, 10 February 1929, 146.

———. "The Third Article of His Series Discusses the Safety Quest." *New York Times*, 9 September 1928, 133.

———. "Ways to Help Aviation Meet Its Business Destiny." *New York Times*, 17 February 1929, 150.

Lindbergh, Col. Chas. A. "Differing Types of Planes Now Built to Serve Special Uses." *New York Times*, 18 November 1928, 12.

———. "Guggenheim Fund Does Work Others Might Neglect." *New York Times*, 23 December 1928, 12.

Lindbergh, Colonel Charles A. "Lindbergh Calls for Airways to Link Capitals of Continent." *New York Times*, 16 December 1927, 1, 3.

———. "Lindbergh Says His Mind is Ablaze with Noise and an Ocean of Faces." *New York Times*, 14 June 1927, 1, 3.

"Lockheed's Proposals for Jet Transports." *Aviation Week* 52 (9 January 1950): 13-15.

Loening, Grover Cleveland. "Automatic Stability of Aeroplanes: Comments on Some American Patents." *Scientific American* 104 (13 May 1911): 470-471, 488-489.

Lorin, Rene. *"La Propulsion a Grande Vitesse Des Vehicules Aeriens." L'Aerophile* 17 (15 October 1909): 463-65.

Ludlow, Israel. "The Aeroplane and the Motion Picture Camera." *Aeronautics* 10 (January 1912): 13-14.

Lunde, Otto H. "The Handley-Page Automatic Slot." *Aviation* 24 (27 February 1928): 506-508.

Lyman, Lauren D. "Lindbergh: 'Tech Rep.'" *Air Trails Pictorial*, June 1950, 26-27, 64-66.

Macready, First Lieutenant John A. "Exploring the Earth's Stratosphere." *National Geographic* 50 (December 1926): 755-776.

"Mail Pilot Files Entry for Paris Flight." *New York Times*, 1 March 1927, 16.

"The Makhonine Way." *Flight*, 13 May 1932, 417-418.

"Man Girds for Supersonic Role." *Aviation Week* 49 (27 September 1948): 21-24.

"Manta Fighter Has Contra-Rotating Props." *Popular Science*, June 1942, 62-64.

"Manta Mock-up." *Aviation* 41 (February 1942): 11.

Masefield, Peter. "First Analysis of the Thunderbolt." *Flying*, August 1943, 47-48, 188-190.

"Mass of Material to Construct an Airplane." *Scientific American* 118 (9 March 1918): 213.

Mathiews, Franklin K. "Blowing Out the Boy's Brains." *The Outlook*, 21 November 1914, 652-654.

"The Maurice Farman Biplane." *Scientific American Supplement* 71 (13 May 1911): 300-301.

"May Try Flight to Paris." *New York Times*, 6 February 1927, 16.

"McCook Field's Air Carnival for Army Relief Fund." *Air Service News Letter* 7 (29 September 1923): 11-13.

"McDonnell XP-67." *Model Airplane News*, June 1945, 22-23, 56-59.

McLarren, Robert. "392 Per – in the Curtiss XP-40." *Model Airplane News*, February 1939, 9, 53-54.

———. "Bell XS-1 Makes Supersonic Flight." *Aviation Week* 47 (22 December 1947): 9-10.

———. "Bell XS-1: Plane on the Cover." *Model Airplane News*, March 1947, 25, 83-86.

———. "The Bomber Catcher." *Model Airplane News*, May 1939, 19, 28, 30.

———. "British Jet Transport Makes First Flight." *Aviation Week* 51 (8 August 1949): 12-13.

———. "Douglas Unveils Its New Research Plane." *Aviation Week* 47 (17 November 1947): 12-13.

———. "Flying Wing of Destruction." *Model Airplane News*, December 1939, 14.

———. "The Flying 'Mustang'." *Model Airplane News*, September 1941, 25, 48-50.

———. "How Delta-Wing Aids High-Speed Flight." *Aviation Week* 51 (4 July 1949): 21-24.

———. "A Motor with Wings." *Model Airplane News*, April 1939, 11, 42-48.

———. "Plane on the Cover: Boeing XB-47." *Model Airplane News*, January 1948, 15, 60-62.

———. "Skyrocket with Wings." *Model Airplane News*, August 1940, 27, 57-58.

———. "Swept Wing Taxes Piloting Skill." *Aviation Week* 48 (8 March 1948): 30.

———. "War Wings Over Europe." *Model Airplane News*, January 1940, 8-10, 30-36.

———. "XS-1: Design and Development." *Aviation Week* 49 (26 July 1948): 22-27.

———. "'Escape'-Rocket Design Research Indicates Practical Solution Near." *Aviation Week* 48 (1 March 1948): 23.

McLaughlin, George F. "Ford's Latest Monoplane." *Aero Digest* 10 (February 1927): 95.

———. "The Ryan NY-P Monoplane." *Aero Digest* 10 (June 1927): 536-537.

McLean, F. "Wireless Signaling in Aeronautics." *Scientific American Supplement* 69 (15 January 1910): 34.

McReynolds, Charles F. "The Refueling Flight of the 'Question Mark'." *Aviation* 26 (19 January 1929): 158-162.

McRoberts, Larry. "Air Fighters of the 'Setting' Sun." *Model Airplane News*, February 1942, 4, 58-64.

Merrell, Creighton. "Transcontinental Speed." *Southern Flight* 7 (February 1937): 10-12.

"The Messerschmitt Me-109." *Popular Aviation*, March 1940, 27.

"Messerschmitt Menace." *Aviation* 40 (October 1941): 50-51.

"The Metropolitan Flying Field." *Scientific American* 135 (August 1926): 146.

Miles, Russell H. "How the New York to Paris Plane Was Built." *Aviation* 22 (20 June 1927): 1352-1353.

"Miller, Harold Blaine." National Air and Space Museum: Document File, CM-410000-01.

Miller, Lieut. H.B. "A Forgotten Pioneer." *Model Airplane News*, June 1936, 6-7, 42-44.

Miller, Lieutenant H.B. "Navy Skyhooks." *U.S. Naval Institute Proceedings* 61 (February 1935): 234-41.

Miller, P. Schuyler. "The Reference Library." *Astounding Science Fiction*, November 1954, 141-46.

Mock, Richard M. "Engine Exhaust Silencers." *Aviation* 24 (18 June 1928): 1762-1763, 1794-1798.

———. "The Junkers G-38." *Aviation* 28 (18 January 1930): 113-117.

Moise, Robeson S. "Balloons and Dirigibles." In *The American Aviation Experience: A History*, edited by Tim Brady, 307-334. Carbondale: Southern Illinois University Press, 2000.

Molson, Francis J. "American Technological Fiction for Youth: 1900-1940." In *Young Adult Science Fiction*, edited by C.W. Sullivan, III, 7-20. Westport, CT: Greenwood Press, 1999.

"The Montgomery Airplane." *Scientific American* 92 (20 May 1905): 404-406.

Montgomery, Prof. J.J. "Some Early Gliding Experiments in America." *Aeronautics* 4 (January 1909): 47-50.

Moran, C. "War on the Boll Weevil." *U.S. Air Service* 8 (December 1923): 54-55.

"More About the Douglas Sleeper." *Aviation* 35 (February 1936): 35-36.

Murphy, Charles J.V. "A Shirt Flapping in the Breeze Became an Airplane in the Sky." *American Magazine*, May 1929, 29, 112-118.

"The Mustang." *Model Airplane News*, May 1944, 25, 48-50.

National Advisory Council for Aeronautics. "Nomenclature for Aeronautics." *Aviation* 1 (1 November 1919): 215-216.

Naugle, Richard G. "Sweepback – the Supersonic Shape." *Air Trails Pictorial*, February 1948, 32-34, 102.

"Navy Orders 1,632 New Planes." *Aviation Week* 48 (12 January 1948): 13-14.

"Navy Sale of Seaplanes" [United States Navy advertisement]. *Aerial Age Weekly* 11 (19 April 1920): 175.

Neely, Frederick R. "Cowling of Air-Cooled Radial Engines Develops Enormous Increase in Speed." *Aeronautic Review* 6 (November 1928): 172, 182A.

Neville, Leslie E. "Consolidated '*Commodore*' Flying Boat." *Aviation* 28 (11 January 1930): 49-55.

———. "The Sikorsky S-38." *Aviation* 25 (28 July 1928): 328-348.

"New AAF Jet-Rocket Fighters Designed for Supersonic Speeds." *Aviation Week* 47 (21 July 1947): 11-12.

"New Boeing Commercial Transport Surpasses Expectations in Test Flight." *U.S. Air Services* 18 (April 1933): 12-15.

"New York-Paris Flight a Reality." *Aviation* 22 (30 May 1927): 1120-1122.

"The New York-Paris Flight Projects." *Aviation* 22 (25 April 1927): 823-825.

Northrop, Capt. B.A. "Fortress in the Sky." *Air Trails and Science Frontiers*, May 1947, 22-27, 70-74.

"Nungesser and Coli Missing in Atlantic Flight Attempt." *Aviation* 22 (16 May 1927): 1041-1042.

Ochoa, V.L. "Are the Wrights Pirates?" *Aircraft* 1 (April 1910): 5.

Orb, G. Anderson. "The Juvenile Aircraft Industry." *Scientific American* 143 (October 1930): 294-295.

Osborn, Robert R. "On the Atlantic Flight Preparations." *Aviation* 22 (23 May 1927): 1082-1084.

Oulahan, Richard V. "Soars Away at 105 Miles an Hour." *New York Times*, 14 December 1927, 3.

Our Staff Correspondent. "The James Gordon Bennett Aviation Contest of 1912: How Vedrines Won." *Scientific American* 107 (21 September 1912): 245, 251.

"Our Winged Postmen." *Scientific American* 118 (25 May 1918): 476-477, 490-492.

Owen, Russell. "Flight to Paris Lures Noted Pilots." *New York Times*, 20 March 1927, 5.

Pappas, Costas Ernest. "Compressibility Calls a Challenge." *Aviation* 43 (December 1944): 171-175, 433.

Peck, James L.H. "1,000 Miles an Hour." *Air Trails Pictorial*, September 1946, 24-27, 70-72.

———. "Can the Atom Bomb Be Stopped?" *Air Trails Pictorial*, August 1946, 24-27, 68-72.

Piersol, James V. "Adapting the Airplane to the Newspaper." *Aero Digest* 18 (January 1931): 35-39, 122.

———. "The 'Early Bird' – a Flying Editorial Room." *National Aeronautics* 13 (January 1935): 7-9.

"Pilot Kelly Flies 115,760 Miles in 1928." *Aero Digest* 14 (February 1929): 132.

"Pilot-Scientists." *Aviation Week* 52 (20 March 1950): 36-37.

"Popularizing Aviation." *Popular Aviation*, August 1927, unpaged.

Porter, Kenneth R. "Jet Bomb." *Flying*, September 1944, 24-25, 128-130.

"Post Office Department Issues Call for Proposals for Operation of Aerial Mail Routes." *Aerial Age Weekly* 11 (19 July 1920): 644, 648.

"Post Office Department Issues Specifications for 10 Mail Planes." *Aerial Age Weekly* 9 (28 April 1919): 330.

Powell, Herb. "The Atomic Frame of Reference – or Else." *Aviation* 44 (September 1945): 106-107, 244-252.

———. "Boeing B-29 "Superfortress"." *Aviation* 43 (July 1944): 110-111, 278-285.

Prager, Arthur. "Edward Stratemeyer and His Book Machine." *Saturday Review*, 10 July 1971, 15-17, 52-53.

Pratt, Fletcher. "'Lindy' Charts the Atlantic Skies." *Universal Model Airplane News*, March 1934, 6-8, 36-39.

"Queer Camouflage of German Aeroplanes." *Scientific American* 117 (11 August 1917): 95.

R., R.B. "Boeing's Hand from the New Deal in Air Transport." *Sportsman Pilot*, April 1933, 34-39.

Radford, Vice-Adm. A.W., USN. "Navy Planes – Today and Beyond." *Aero Digest* 54 (January 1947): 96, 205-206.

Rand, Kurt. "The D Ships." *Popular Aviation*, April 1940, 28-30, 72.

"Rathborne, St. George H." In *Who Was Who Among North American Authors, 1921-1939*, vol. 2, 1195. Detroit: Gale Research, 1976.

"'Ray for Lindy!" *Aero Digest* 10 (June 1927): 560.

Rechenschieber, Capt. S.R. "The Mighty B-47." *Flying*, August 1949, 15-17, 62-64.

"Report of the Johnson Helicopter Airplane." National Air and Space Museum: Document File, CJ-337000-01, "Johnson, Jess C."

Richardson, Captain Holden C. "Prophecy in Retrospect." *Southern Flight* 19 (February 1943): 28-29, 39-40, 44, 45.

Rickenbacker, Capt. E.V. (Eddie). "American Fighting Planes Are Superior to Those of the Enemy." *U.S. Air Services* 27 (October 1942): 13-16.

Ricker, Chester S. "Design and Construction of Nazi V-1 Flying Bomb." *Aviation* 43 (November 1944): 190-191, 289-293.

Roger, William. "Push-Button Warfare." *Flying*, February 1946, 38-39, 106-110.

"The Roland." *Aviation* 2 (15 February 1917): 98.

"Rules Governing the Competition for the Scientific American Flying Machine Trophy." *Scientific American* 96 (27 April 1907): 191.

"Russ Farrell, Flyer Up-to-Date." *American Boy*, October 1925, 26.

"Ryan NY-P a Development of the Ryan M – 2." *Aviation* 22 (20 June 1927): 1364-1368.

S., E.S., and R.W. B. "Stratemeyer, Edward." In *Dictionary of American Biography*, edited by Dumas Malone, vol. IX, 125. New York: Charles Scribner's Sons, 1964.

"Sainsbury, Noel Everingham, Jr." In *Who Was Who in America*, 498. Chicago: Marquis Who's Who, 1981.

Sanderval, de. "*Recherches sur le Vol Plane*." *L'Aeronaute* 19 (November 1886): 203-206.

Sandifer, T.N. "American Military Airplanes Will Meet Every Test." *U.S. Air Services* 26 (January 1941): 16-17, 34.

Santiago, Chiori. "House Trailers Have Come a Long Way, Baby." *Smithsonian*, June 1998, 76-85.

"Schiff Trophy Award." *Aero Digest* 14 (January 1929): 10.

Seldes, Gilbert. "Transatlantic." *New Republic*, 1 June 1927, 46-47.

"Shall America Take the Lead in Aeronautics?" *Scientific American* 98 (29 February 1908): 138.

"Shipboard Jets." *Western Flying* 27 (July 1947): 26-28, 36.

"Sikorsky Predicts 100-Ton Air Liners." *New York Times*, 13 October 1929, 24.

Sikorsky, Igor I. "Airplanes of the Future." *Aero Digest* 15 (October 1929): 54-55.

"Sikorsky's Stupendous Biplane." *Scientific American Supplement* 77 (7 February 1914): 91.

"Simulated Landings, Take-Offs in Fog Made by Lieut. Doolittle." *Aviation* 27 (5 October 1929): 718, 724.

"Slots and Flaps Take the Lead." *Western Flying* 7 (January 1930): 54-55, 134.

Smedal, George. "Jimmy Doolittle – Air Wizard." *Popular Aviation*, May 1931, 23-24, 58.

Smith, Capt. V. Edward. "North Atlantic Ferry." *Aviation* 40 (May 1941): 30-31, 132-136.

Soderbergh, Peter A. "Edward Stratemeyer and the Juvenile Ethic, 1894-1930." *International Review of History and Political Science* 11 (February 1974): 61-71.

———. "The Great Book War: Edward Stratemeyer and the Boy Scouts of America, 1910-1930." *New Jersey History* 91 (Winter 1973): 235-248.

"A Solution to Landing Planes of Every Description" [Gibbons Co. Advertisement]. *Aero Digest* 12 (April 1928): 536-537.

"The Spirit of Youth." *Aero Digest* 11 (November 1927): 518.

"St. G.H. Rathborne, Novelist, Dies at 83." *New York Times*, 18 December 1938, 48.

St. Germain, Arthur V. "The Conquest of Interplanetary Space." *Western Flying* 27 (October, November 1947): 14-15; 20-26.

Stacy, Dennis. "When Pilots See UFOs." *Air & Space/Smithsonian*, January 1988, 96-103.

Stewart, Maj. Oliver. "Fighter Progress in Britain." *Flying*, February 1945, 48, 136-138.

Stout, F.R. "Airline to the Moon?" *Flying*, November 1946, 27-29, 68-72.

Street, Douglas. "Howard R. Garis." In *American Writers for Children, 1900-1960*, edited by John Cech, 191-199. Detroit: Gale Research, 1983.

Stromme, George. "Nippon Teikoku Kugan." *Western Flying* 24 (June, July 1944): 46-47, 112-120; 50-51, 94-102.

Studley, Lieutenant Barrett. "Foreword." In *How to Fly: The Pilot and His Problems*, unpaged. New York: Macmillan Co., 1929.

"Successful Test of the Cornu Helicopter." *Scientific American* 98 (18 April 1908): 276.

Summerfield, Dr. Martin. "The Rocket's Future Influence on Transport Designs." *Aviation* 45 (January 1946): 73-76.

"Supersonic Plane and Jet Bombers Revealed by Army Air Forces." *Aviation* 45 (July 1946): 68-69.

Sweetman, Bill. "Ba-Da-Boom." *Air & Space/Smithsonian*, October/November 2003, 13.

"Swept Wing XP-86 Readied for Flight." *Aviation Week* 47 (6 October 1947): 14.

Sydney, Rex. "The Zero." *Flying*, November 1942, 25-26, 90-92.

Tangerman, E.J. "Can We Catch up in Rocket Research?" *Aviation* 45 (June 1946): 40-41, 148-150.

Tear, J.D. "Electromagnetic Compass Systems for Aircraft." *Science* 68 (14 December 1928): 597.

"Termination of the Rheims Aviation Meeting." *Scientific American* 101 (11 September 1909): 180-181.

"Theodore B. Copp, Fiction Writer, 42." *New York Times*, 3 January 1945, 17.

"The Thunderbolt." *Model Airplane News*, December 1942, 21, 58-61.

Tinsley, Frank. "The Barnes Charger." *Air Trails*, October 1938, 46-49, 88.

———. "Last of the Fighters." *Air Trails*, January 1950, 23-25.

Tomas, Lynn C. "The Japanese Air Force." *Western Flying* 21 (September 1941): 22-23.

"The Transatlantic Plane 'American Legion.'" *Aero Digest* 10 (May 1927): 428.

"The Transcontinental Air Race." *Scientific American* 121 (25 October 1919): 423, 434, 436.

Truslow, Neil A. "The Transparent Airplane." *Scientific American* 113 (18 December 1915): 539.

"The Truth About Our Bombers." *Aviation* 41 (October 1942): 96-97, 328-329.

"The Truth About Our Fighter Planes." *Aviation* 41 (October 1942): 93-95, 334-368.

[Tsien, H.S]. "Considerations on the 3,000-Mile Rocket Liner." *Western Flying* 30 (November 1950): 20-22, 26.

"Turning Somersaults with an Aeroplane." *Scientific American* 109 (27 September 1913): 240.

"U.S. Building Plane to Pursue Bombers in Substratosphere." *New York Times*, 8 January 1931, 1.

"United Airlines (USA)." National Air and Space Museum: Document file, F1U-560075-11.

"United States to Europe and Return." *Aviation* 22 (20 June 1927): 1354-1355, 1398.

"The Valves Used in Lindbergh's Plane." *Aero Digest* 11 (August 1927): 175.

Van Luven, F.D. "Successful Tests of Plane Parachute." *Southern Aviation* 2 (October 1930): 43.

Vaughan, David K. "The Educating Story-Teller: Lewis Theiss and the Jimmy Donnelly Air Mail Books." *Dime Novel Roundup* 61 (June 1992): 42-49.

———. "Eustace Adams' Andy Lane Series." *Dime Novel Roundup*, 57 (August, October 1988): 52-60, 68-73.

———. "Girl Fliers in a World of Guys: Three 1930s Girls' Juvenile Aviation Series." *Dime Novel Roundup* 68 (February 1999): 16-27.

———. "James Otis Kaler's Silver Fox Farm Series: Aviation Reaches the New England Coast." *Dime Novel Roundup*, 64 (June, August 1995): 59-66, 94-101.

———. "Hap Arnold's Bill Bruce Books: Promoting Air Service Awareness in America." *Air Power History* 40 (Winter 1993): 43-49.

———. "Pioneer of Aviation Series Books: Harry L. Sayler and the Airship Boys." *Dime Novel Roundup* 59 (March 1990): 74-79.

———. "Rutherford G. Montgomery's Kent Barstow Series." *Dime Novel Roundup* 70 (August 2001): 115-122.

———. "Thomson Burtis' Rex Lee Aviation Stories." *Dime Novel Roundup* 59 (February 1990): 2-7.

Vultee, Gerard F. "20 Miles Faster." *Western Flying* 5 (March 1929): 38-39, 140.

———. "The New N.A.C.A. Cowling and Its Application to the Lockheed 'Air Express.'" *Aero Digest* 14 (March 1929): 43-44, 222-223.

Walker, J. Bernard. "The Racing Aeroplane of the Future — a Study." *Scientific American* 103 (22 October 1910): 317-318.

———. "Velocity and Range of Guns." *Scientific American* 118 (20 April 1918): 360-361.

Walton, Rus. "Jack Northrop and His Wonderful Wing." *Flying*, February 1948, 19-21, 56-58.

"War in the Air." *Popular Science*, December 1939, 84-87.

"War in the Air." *Western Flying* 22 (January 1942): 31-32, 60.

Ward, John William. "The Meaning of Lindbergh's Flight." *American Quarterly* 10 (Spring 1958): 3-16.

Ward, Martha E., and Dorothy A. Marquardt. "Dean, Graham M." In *Authors of Books for Young People*. 2d ed., 152. Metuchen, NJ: Scarecrow Press, 1971.

Ward, Roswell H. "The Airplane Diesel in 1940." *Scientific American* 142 (January 1930): 36-38.

Watter, Dr. Michael. "Engineering Aspects of Lindbergh's Transatlantic Flight." *Aero Digest* 11 (October 1927): 396-397, 483-485.

Weatherby, Silas. "Modelin' Planes." *Universal Model Airplane News* 9 (September 1933): 8.

Weick, Fred E. "The New N.A.C.A. Low Drag Cowling." *Aviation* 25 (17 November 1928): 1556-1557, 1586-1590.

Welsh, J. William. "Will Subs Launch the Atom Air War?" *Flying*, November 1948, 20-21, 50-52.

Wendell, DeWitt. "An Analysis of Captured Nazi Warplanes." *Flying and Popular Aviation*, March 1941, 14-15, 64-68.

———. "Transatlantic Bridge." *Flying and Popular Aviation*, May 1941, 18-19, 68-72.

"What McCook Field is Doing." *Air Service News* 9 (August 1925): 4.

"What's Ahead for Rockets?" *Aviation Week* 49 (5 July 1948): 23.

White, Paul W. "Bridging the Ocean with Man-Made Islands." *American Magazine*, November 1929, 46-49, 165-170.

"Why the World Makes Lindbergh Its Hero." *Literary Digest*, 25 June 1927, 5-8.

"Wildcat Warrior." *Model Airplane News*, June 1942, 22-24, 86-88.

Williams, Al. "Incredible Age." *U.S. Air Services* 26 (May 1941): 25.

———. "A National Air Policy." *Southern Flight* 11 (March 1939): 8-14.

Wilson, Harland. "Flying the Jet...." *Flying*, December 1948, 28-29, 76-77.

Wilson, P.W. "Lindbergh Symbolizes the Genius of America." *New York Times*, 12 June 1927, 4.

Wines, James P. "The 48 Hr. Coast to Coast Air-Rail Service of Transcontinental Air Transport." *Aviation* 27 (6 July 1929): 26-29.

———. "Operation of the Pan American Airways System." *Aviation* 26 (27 April 1929): 1422-1429.

"Wings for You" [American Sky Cadets Advertisement]. *Model Airplane News*, February 1931, inside front cover.

"The Winning Flight of the 'June Bug' Aeroplane for the Scientific American Trophy." *Scientific American* 99 (18 July 1908): 45.

"Wins Schiff Trophy for Safe Flights." *New York Times*, 15 December 1928, 13.

Winter, William. "Atom Powered Bombers." *Air Trails*, May 1949, 21-23, 85-89.

———. "The Push-Button War Fable." *Flying*, October 1947, 47-49, 71-72.

———. "The 'Spitter.'" *Flying*, July 1942, 30-32, 64-69, 104.

Winters, S.R. "A Plane-Size Parachute." *Popular Aviation*, October 1928, 24-25.

"Wireless on Aeroplane." *Scientific American Supplement* 71 (20 May 1911): 307.

"Wireless Telegraphy and the Aeroplane." *Scientific American Supplement* 72 (9 September 1911): 176.

Wolfe, Maj. Gen. Kenneth B. "We Must Retain Technological Supremacy." *Aviation* 44 (February 1945): 113-115.

Wood, Robert H. "Editorial: Overselling the Missile." *Aviation Week* 53 (31 July 1950): 46.

[Woodhouse, Henry]. "What Next?" *Aerial Age Weekly* 9 (7 July 1919): 804.

Wragg, C.A. "The New Age." *Aerial Age Weekly* 14 (10 October 1921): 107-108.

"The Wright Aeroplane and Its Fabled Performances." *Scientific American* 94 (13 January 1906): 40.

"The Wright Aeroplane and Its Performances." *Scientific American* 94 (7 April 1906): 291-292.

"The Wright Aeroplane Infringement Suit." *Scientific American* 101 (28 August 1909): 138.

"The Wright and Voisin (Farman) Flying Machines Compared." *Scientific American* 100 (9 January 1909): 230-234.

"The Wright Whirlwind J-5C Engine." *Aero Digest* 10 (June 1927): 540.

Wright, Orville, and Wilbur Wright. "The Wright Brothers' Aeroplane." *Century Magazine* 76 (September 1908): 641-650.

"The XS-1." *Western Flying* 27 (January 1947): 18-19.

Young, Clarence M. Introduction to *American Airport Designs*. 1930, 5-6. Washington, DC: American Institute of Architects Press, 1990.

Zacharoff, Lucien. "Japanese Air Power." *Aviation* 40 (September 1941): 48-49, 146-150.

INDEX

Page numbers in italics refer to illustrations. Generally, series titles are in quotation marks, titles of individual books in italics.

DATE DUE

GAYLORD			PRINTED IN U.S.A.